Inquiries into
MEDIEVAL PHILOSOPHY

Contributions in
Philosophy

Inquiries into
MEDIEVAL
PHILOSOPHY

A Collection
in Honor of
Francis P. Clarke

James F. Ross, Editor

Contributions in Philosophy, Number 4

Greenwood Publishing Co.
Westport, Connecticut

Library of Congress Catalog Card Number: 74-105984
SBN: 8371-3311-4

Greenwood Publishing Co.
A Division of Greenwood Press, Inc.
51 Riverside Avenue, Westport, Connecticut 06880

Printed in the United States of America

Designed by Selma Ordewer

CONTENTS

DISPLAYING MORE
TRADITIONAL METHODS

PREFACE

THESE essays corporately illustrate the methods by which contemporary philosophers explicate and criticize medieval philosophy. Each of their varied emphases of technique and inquiry has its place in the examination of medieval philosophy and each, as the essays disclose, yields results of interest and significance to the development of philosophical inquiry in our time.

Historical studies by philosophers usually reflect the current methods of philosophy and the subject-interests prevailing within the rest of the philosophical community. So too with these papers, among which topics on logic, linguistics, and the philosophy of mind predominate. Although all the papers are directed toward the reconstruction or explication of philosophically significant ideas which can be found in or derived from the medieval writers, no two of them represent exactly the same way of undertaking the interpretation of a medieval writer. Yet they do fall loosely into three groups, and when examined as members of those groups, exhibit noticeable differences from the papers within the other groups. The groups are characterized as Analytic, Formalistic, and Traditional. The names for the groups are not intended to convey more than a hint as to the similarity of technique which justifies our grouping the papers we have placed under those rubrics.

The papers within the Analytic group obviously display the influence of recent analytic philosophical practices, much more so than do those in the third group. The essays of the second group are marked by the authors' explicit use of modern formal logic for the formulation and criticism of the claims of the medieval writers. The papers classified as "Traditional" are grouped together primarily because they differ from the others by emphasizing the historical context within which philosophical debate developed, the examination of principal and subsidiary texts, the reconstruction, in one case, of an incomplete text, and by the development of their arguments with the sort of scholarly apparatus which has characterized good historical scholarship in philosophy for a long time. No invidious comparison is justified by such groupings; in fact, the sort of work we find within the first two groups cannot be developed successfully without the kind of information supplied by investigations of the third sort. Furthermore, philosophical perceptiveness is not a function of a particular method. Nevertheless, the analytically and logically oriented inquiries into medieval philosophy are something new in this half of the century and have resulted in an evident enrichment of our results. It is because the approach is new, not because it is inherently better, that the papers from those groups predominate.

Most of the papers are reprinted from journals where they were scattered and relatively inaccessible; and when presented together, they offer an accurate and interesting picture of the kinds of interests and techniques of research presently applied to medieval philosophy. Beyond the inherent interest of the individual papers, there is a supervenient value in their capacity to represent the present state of scholarship in medieval philosophy.

The occasion for assembling this collection is the retirement of Dr. Francis P. Clarke from the faculty of philosophy of the University of Pennsylvania. The editor felt that Dr. Clarke's more than forty years' service in the teaching of philosophy, especially medieval philosophy, and his enormous learning should be memorialized by a collection of papers portraying the scope and achievement of contemporary medieval scholarship in philosophy.

Dr. Clarke was born in Coal City, Illinois, November 29, 1895. He received his A.B. from the University of Colorado in 1920 and his A.M. from the University of Nebraska in 1922. He became a Harrison Fellow at the University of Pennsylvania in that year and received his Ph.D. in 1928. Instructor from 1924 to 1931, Assistant Professor from 1931 to 1937, Associate Professor from 1937 to 1939, he was Professor of Philosophy from 1939 to 1966, after which he became Emeritus Professor of Philosophy. He served as Chairman of the Philosophy Department from 1938 to 1945 and again from 1947 to 1960. Despite the many years devoted to the development of a distinguished faculty and graduate program, Dr. Clarke continued his studies of medieval texts throughout his career and displayed great sensitivity to the development of new interests and new methods for the study of medieval philosophy. His was certainly one of the earliest American graduate programs to provide extensive training in the history of medieval logic, philosophy of science, and semantics. It seems especially appropriate that the collection of essays should reflect his interest in and his respect for medieval logic and semantics.

The editor is most grateful both to the authors and to the editors of the journals in which the papers first appeared for their gracious permissions to reprint. He also gratefully acknowledges the perceptive criticisms of Professor James J. Walsh, whose comments on the organization of the book and the first version of the introduction were most helpful, and the invaluable assistance of Jacqueline Smith and Susan McKee in preparing the manuscript.

JAMES F. ROSS

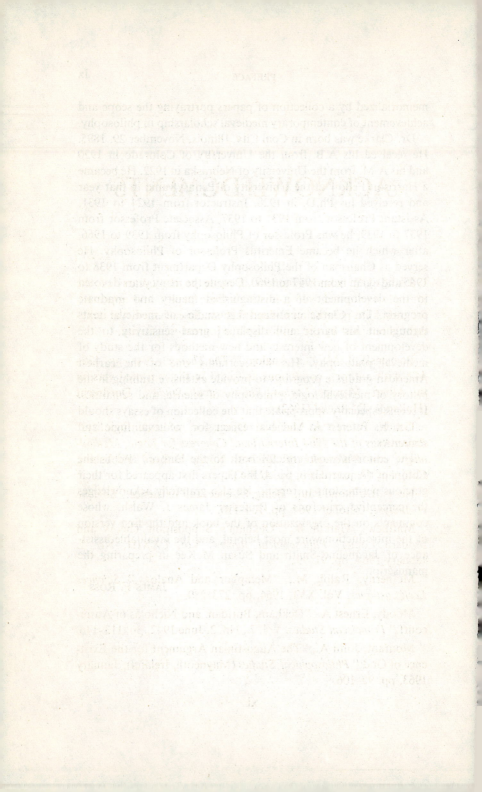

ACKNOWLEDGMENTS

GRATEFUL acknowledgment is made to the editors of the journals mentioned below, in which these papers first appeared, for their kind permission to reprint them. In each case, the copyright is retained by the author and/or journal mentioned.

Bochenski, I. M., "On Analogy," *The Thomist*, 1948, pp. 425–447, with author's corrections as found in the reprinted version in Albert Menne, *Logico—Philosophical Studies*, Dordrecht (Holland), D. Reidel (1962).

Geach, Peter, "A Medieval Discussion of Intentionality," *Proceedings of the 1964 International Congress for Logic, Methodology, and Philosophy of Science*, North Holland Publishing Company (Amsterdam), pp. 425–433.

Henry, Desmond Paul, "Being, Essence, and Existence," *Logique et Analyse*, October 1964, pp. 104–110.

Matthews, Gareth B., "Ockham's Supposition Theory and Modern Logic," *Philosophical Review*, Vol. LXXIII, No. 1, January 1964, pp. 91–99.

McInerny, Ralph M., "Metaphor and Analogy," *Sciences Ecclésiastiques*, Vol. XVI, 1964, pp. 273–289.

Moody, Ernest A., "Ockham, Buridan, and Nicholas of Autrecourt," *Franciscan Studies*, Vol. 7., No. 2, June 1947, pp. 113–146.

Mourant, John A., "The Augustinian Argument for the Existence of God," *Philosophical Studies* (Mayneoth, Ireland), January 1963, pp. 92–106.

Owens, Joseph, "Common Nature: A Point of Comparison Between Thomistic and Scotistic Metaphysics," *Medieval Studies*, XIX, 1957, pp. 1–14.

Potts, Timothy C., "Aquinas on Belief and Faith," September 1965, original in this volume.

Prior, A. N., "The Formalities of Omniscience," *Philosophy*, 1962, pp. 114–129.

Ross, James F., "Analogy as a Rule of Meaning for Religious Language," *International Philosophical Quarterly*, Vol. 1, No. 3, September 1961, pp. 468–502.

Weinberg, Julius R., "The Fifth Letter of Nicholas of Autrecourt to Bernard of Arezzo," *Journal of the History of Ideas*, Vol. 3, 1942, pp. 220–227.

Wolfson, Harry A., "The Twice-Revealed Averroes," specially revised version of paper originally printed in *Speculum*, Vol. XXXVI, No. 3, July 1961; originally delivered at the annual meeting of the Fellows of the Medieval Academy of America on 29 April 1960.

Wolter, Allan B., "Ockham and the Textbooks: On the Origin of Possibility," *Franziskanische Studien Vierteljahr-Schrift* Dietrich Coelde-Verlag (Munster, Westf.) 32, 1950, pp. 70–96.

DISPLAYING THE
ANALYTIC METHOD

1

AQUINAS ON BELIEF AND FAITH

Timothy C. Potts

THEOLOGIANS have devoted much attention to questions concerning faith, but for the most part they have been interested in specific issues such as whether a man can be saved by faith without good deeds rather than in giving a general account of the concept of faith and its relation to that of belief. Aquinas is an exception: the question on Faith (no. 14) in his *Disputed Questions on Truth* begins by asking "What is it to believe?" (article 1) and only then goes on to the question "What is faith?" (article 2). But subsequent theologians, influenced no doubt by the publicity provided by Luther for one of Aquinas' later questions, "Is 'unformed' faith a virtue?" (article 6), have tended to skip past the first two articles without much discussion. Perhaps, too, they have concentrated more on the lengthy treatise on faith in the *Summa theologiae* (2–2.1–16) as representing Aquinas' last and most mature thought on the subject; but that work was intended as a theological text-book, and though much of the material from the first two articles in the *Disputed Questions* is incorporated into the treatise in the *Summa*, the arrangement is different and the discussion greatly compressed.

Yet everything that is subsequently said about faith must depend on the general account which is given of the concept, and if we maintain as Aquinas does that faith is a species of belief, then we must also be clear what we understand by "belief." This alone is enough to justify independent consideration for the two articles in the *Disputed Questions*, and it may well be supposed

3

that their more leisurely and detailed pace, together with their wider coverage of objections, compensates for their earlier date. Accordingly, this paper is an examination of these two articles, with references to other texts only when necessary. I shall argue that Aquinas' account of belief rightly involves an element which has been ignored by philosophers since Descartes, but that the account as it stands is insufficient, and that this same inadequacy is carried over into the definition of faith.

The first article asks what belief is; its purpose is to provide a conceptual classification which will allow faith to be exhibited later as a species of belief, and the discussion is accordingly exclusively philosophical. As far as possible, it moves within an Aristotelian framework; but the modern reader is as surprised as one of the Greek commentators on Aristotle would no doubt have been, to discover that for Aquinas belief and *doxa* (*opinio*) occupy different, and indeed well-separated pigeon-holes. It is not evident that Latin usage either licenses or compels this distinction, and the suspicion must arise that either Aquinas was working backwards in view of what he wanted to say about faith, or he was moved to a more than merely reverential exposition of the definition from Augustine which he places at the head of his discussion: "to believe is to think out and assent."

He begins by stating the familiar Aristotelian distinction between the two intellectual activities of concept-formation and predication, and rightly goes on to say that the latter and not the former is involved in belief. He then follows Aristotle on to the softer ground of the passive intellect: for present purposes it is enough to note that predication is brought within the scope of Aristotle's doctrine of rational potentialities in *Metaphysics* 9 by treating affirmation and negation, two attitudes which we can adopt towards a given predication, as contraries. Thus for any predication, we can affirm either it or its negation to be true, and which of the two we affirm will depend upon the action of an appropriate agent upon intellect. Aquinas follows Aristotle in citing concepts as one such kind of agent; but he makes an important innovation by citing, with a reference to Anselm, will as another.

This analysis is now applied in order to classify doubt, opinion, knowledge and belief respectively. Presumably because affirmation implies some kind of outward expression, Aquinas uses "accept" instead of "affirm" to characterize these mental dispositions. Doubting whether *p* is to be expounded as not accepting that *p* and not accepting that not-*p*; it is a state which can arise either from lack of evidence for or against *p*, or alternatively when the evidence for seems to carry equal weight to the evidence against. Opinion, second, is the state where we accept that *p*, but not so firmly that we cease doubting whether not-*p*; or again, where we accept that *p* while continuing to fear that not-*p* may be true.

Knowledge and belief both fall within a third category, where we accept that *p* and do not accept that not-*p*; they differ only in what makes us accept the one and not the other. In the case of knowledge, concepts are the agent; in the case of belief, will. It is interesting to note how thoroughly Platonic Aquinas is in his account of knowledge, which he divides into two categories. The first, understanding premises whose truth is known as soon as their terms are known, is analytic *a priori* knowledge. The second, scientific knowledge, is the knowledge we have of deductive conclusions from premises which are either the analytic *a priori* truths from the first category or definitions of terms. Of course, to give a definition in the Aristotelian sense will usually involve empirical investigation: it isn't just a matter of giving a meaning to words, but rather of giving a classification based on the structure of the objects falling under the concepts concerned. It may also involve empirical research to discover which premises will together yield profitable deductions, i.e. to find what Aristotle called "the middle term."

But when all allowances have been made, most of what we should call knowledge lies outside either of Aquinas' categories. His second category is based on Aristotle's account of a science in the *Posterior Analytics*; but that was an account which from the first was plausible only for mathematics, and which, when combined with the thesis in *Metaphysics* 4 that First Philosophy has the task of justifying the axioms of the special sciences, renders the conclusions of such a science *a priori* too. There is no room here for the use of models as a vehicle of explanation, which is today so characteristic of the more advanced natural sciences, and common also in the social sciences. Nor can one see how on this account specific items of information, such as the thickness of the earth's crust, the number of planets in the solar system, or the events of history, could be possible objects of scientific knowledge. Aquinas, like Aristotle and Plato, restricts scientific knowledge to what is not merely true, but what is necessarily true, causally if not logically. This analysis is what lies behind their view that knowledge is of the universal rather than of the particular, the latter, if it is to be counted as knowledge at all, having to be derived from the universal by instantiation.

Belief, according to Aquinas, is like knowledge in that if I believe that *p*, then I accept that *p* and do not accept that not-*p*. But what lead me so to commit myself are not *a priori* considerations; rather, it is my wants which provide the impetus. Unfortunately Aquinas is not as clear about the way in which our wants are involved as we might wish, and it will be best to give a quotation, as there seems to be no parallel in the *Summa theologiae* to which we might appeal for elucidation:

> Sometimes the intellect cannot be bound to one limb of a contradiction either directly through the definition of terms, as with premisses, or yet in virtue of premisses, as in conclusions of proofs; it is, nevertheless, bound by will, which chooses to assent to one limb determinately and absolutely, because of something which is enough to change the will but not to change the intellect, since it seems good or suitable (*bonum vel conveniens*) to assent to this limb. This is the state of believing, as when someone believes what someone else says because it seems proper or useful (*decens vel utile*) [to do so]. It is in this way that we are prompted to believe [certain] sayings in so far as the reward of eternal life is promised to us if we believe them, and this reward changes the will so that it assents to what is said, even though the intellect is not changed by anything understood (*intellectum*).

The *general* characterization given here is extremely vague, merely that we assent because it seems "good or suitable" to do so. However, it is clear that the goodness or suitability must be other than the strength of the evidence for what is assented to, or will would not be involved; thus the goodness or suitability must arise somehow from the circumstances. For a clue to the kind of circumstances envisaged, we are driven to Aquinas' examples. The first is believing what someone else says because it is "proper or useful" to do so. Here again "proper" tells us little; at first sight it might seem to cover, e.g., cases in which we ask the advice of experts on some technical matter and believe what they say because we are in no position to form an independent judgment. But the ground of our belief there is our knowledge that the experts have studied the subject-matter of which we are ignorant, and that they therefore know about it; will does not seem to be involved at all, and these are either cases of knowledge at second-hand, or of justified opinion.

We therefore seem to be pushed back on to the more informative "useful," which suggests that we can be said to believe another person when we assent to what he says because we have an ulterior motive for doing so. Aquinas' final and most specific example fits this interpretation well, but it is unfortunate that it is precisely the case of religious belief, since the suspicion must remain that this may be a special case from whose features we are not intended to generalize. At any rate, Aquinas says that we believe the "articles of faith" because the reward of eternal life is promised to us if we believe them—a clear ulterior motive for assent.

If this case may be trusted as exemplifying Aquinas' general account of belief—and there is little else to go on in the text—his view seems to be that the will is involved in belief in the following way: I believe that *p* when I accept that *p as a means to some end* which I want to attain. This immediately rules out another possibility which might have suggested itself: that I want *p* to be the case (not knowing whether it is or not), and as a result accept that it is so. Such a situation is not *a priori* implausible: it is what we have in mind when we describe a certain person's belief as a wish-fulfilment or as a prejudice, to cite only two disreputable cases. But this is not what Aquinas intends: a second, slightly different position will follow from his account. If some state of affairs *p* is a necessary means to some other state of affairs *q*, and if I want *q* to be the case, then I must also want *p* to be the case. So if accepting that *r* is such a means to *q*, then in wanting *q* to be the case, I thereby want to accept that *r*. Hence for Aquinas it would seem that I can only believe what I want to accept, where the acceptance is not an end in itself, but a means to some further end.

So far, then, Aquinas is saying that *a* believes that *p* if and only if *a* accepts that *p* because he wishes that *q*, where accepting that *p* is a necessary means to *q*. But he does not specify whether the believer must *know* that accepting that *p* is a necessary means to *q*, or merely *believe* it, or perhaps only *be of the opinion* that it is. The final example seems to rule out knowledge as too strong a requirement and opinion as too weak; but if we have to invoke belief here as well, must it not be a kind of meta-belief which does not come within the scope of the original analysis?

In spite of this difficulty, to which I shall return later, and in spite of a widespread tendency among modern philosophers to make belief indistinguishable from opinion, Aquinas' view carries several advantages. Among what we should today call beliefs, some seem to be relatively easy to change, others exceedingly difficult. I may believe, as the result of reading a newspaper report and seeing an accompanying photograph, that political prisoners in Ghana are chained together and kept in squalid conditions. When the editor of the newspaper, discovering that the information on which the report was based was false and that the photograph was not taken in Ghana, publishes an apology, I abandon my belief without hesitation. But it is only with the greatest effort that I can be persuaded to modify, let alone abandon my religious, moral or political beliefs. It is not possible to draw a clear dividing line between beliefs which can be changed easily and those which can only be changed with difficulty on the basis of a distinction between the kinds of things believed. Some people hold very fixed beliefs on topics concerning which others will change their position very readily; thus no amount of statistics will convince some people that Negroes do not have a lower average intelligence than Europeans, or that colds cannot be caught by sitting in a draught.

Following the hint offered by Aquinas, the point seems to be that I am less likely to abandon a belief when I *care* whether it is true or not. If it makes no practical difference to me, and will not affect me in any way, then I will certainly abandon any belief when the evidence on which I based it is shewn to be false. Now by and large people's religious, moral and political beliefs are of great practical importance to them, so they do not abandon them lightly. Yet their position does not, I think, correspond exactly to Aquinas' analysis. Leaving aside religious beliefs for the moment, people do not normally think that merely holding certain moral or political beliefs will in itself lead to an end which they want; it is rather that they think that acting in accordance with such beliefs will bring about desired ends, e.g. happiness in the moral case and a better society in the political case. The notion of acting in accordance with a belief is, however, both difficult and obscure; it does not reduce without remainder to acting in accordance with a rule, since not all moral and political beliefs are rules.

In the case where what is believed is a rule, what would count as believing it is accepting it because one thought its acceptance a means to the desired end. Now the notion of accepting a rule involves some reference to action, but ἀκρασία prevents us from saying without qualification that a man who accepts a rule will always act in accordance with it, or even that he will do so for the most part. We cannot even say that he will always or for the most part *try* to act in accordance with it. So although there is *some* connexion between believing a rule and the attainment of a certain end, it is a complex one. In the case where what is believed is *not* a rule, as for instance that the Conservative Party is responsible for a bad economic state of the country, the connexion between the belief and some desired end is still more obscure. It might, for a given person, run somewhat as follows: I want the country to be economically healthy, and I believe that the Labour Party's policies will achieve this. But the country's economic position has deteriorated in the last twelve months, so if I believe that the Labour Party's policies have the opposite effect, the trouble must be due to the Conservatives.

I have taken this example because it illustrates a complication which arises where beliefs are concerned, namely, that we try as far as possible to avoid inconsistency in our beliefs, and even the weaker situation which Professor Williams has called "conflicting beliefs."[1] In the example the inconsistency to be avoided is believing that Labour policies will improve the economic situation and believing that they have in fact already worsened it. The same example also illustrates a second complication: if somebody asks: Why reject the suggestion that Labour policies will improve it? the answer—apart from the facts of the matter, which we may suppose to be presentable as evidence either way—must be that my belief about Labour policies coheres with my other political beliefs, and that by abandoning it I shall call them into question as well. Coherence of belief, in fact, is such a powerful factor that it will often operate successfully in the face of very strong evidence against a particular belief.

To return after this digression to religious belief, it is true that at least as far as Judaism and Christianity are concerned, the holding of certain beliefs is a necessary condition (in normal circumstances) of attaining eternal life, and hence a necessary means to that end. But these beliefs also fit into the pattern sketched above for the kinds of belief which are difficult to change: in Judaism and Christianity it is also a necessary condition for attaining eternal life that the believer shall act in accordance with his beliefs, and still more important, that the beliefs shall themselves be true. By contrast, the necessity of merely *holding* the beliefs is an exceptional feature. Aquinas' first example suggests to us that it is a general feature of belief; but if I believe what someone else says, I usually do so because I think he is telling the truth and knows what he is talking about. It is exceptional to believe a person because one thinks such belief will be useful, i.e. likely to lead to a desired end.

All these considerations suggest that Aquinas' scheme requires considerable modification. This conclusion is reinforced when we reconsider his account of opinion, the category into which all beliefs (in the modern sense) which can be easily changed must fit. His analysis of opinion, to begin with, is an impossible one. You will remember that he gives two formulations: the state where we accept that p, but not so firmly that we cease doubting whether not-p; or again, where we accept that p while continuing to fear that not-p may be true. Now doubting whether not-p will mean not accepting that not-p and not accepting that not-not-p, i.e., not accepting that p. So on this account holding the opinion that p will involve the inconsistency of accepting that p and not accepting that p. What has gone wrong here? Aquinas clearly intends doubt, on the one hand, and knowledge or belief, on the other, to be limiting cases, with everything in between called "opinion." In order to express this he really needs some such notion as "half-accepting," or perhaps so as to be able to vary the degree of acceptance, "partly-accepting"; for it is clear that the extent to which I accept that p must vary inversely with the extent to which I accept that not-p.

But does a man whom we are to suppose is not in a state of doubt, only partly accept that p when he says, e.g. "I *think* that p, but I may very well be wrong"? Surely not: he accepts that p, but admits that his present acceptance may be ill-founded and thus advises us of his preparedness to withdraw his acceptance if this is shewn to be so. If there is any use for a notion of part-acceptance which does not involve doubt, it must be acceptance of only part of what has been said or proposed; and this is acceptance, if limited in scope. The point about opinion, if we are to distinguish it *both* from doubt *and* from belief, is that people are indifferent about their opinions and will change them readily if conflicting evidence comes to hand (I am assuming that we are prepared to go at least so far with Aquinas that we do not insist on the equivalence of opinion and belief as in the English expressions "religious opinions" and "religious beliefs."). Aquinas' mistake here seems to be the result of his account of *doubt*: according to him, I am only in a state of doubt if *either* I have no evidence either way, *or* I have evidence of equal weight either way. But doubt is not so restricted: I may think p more probable than not-p, and still doubt that *p*. Thus the *whole* of the intermediate state ought to be included in the category of doubt, and opinion be included with belief and knowledge.

If this conclusion is accepted, a classification based on how far I am prepared to assert that *p*, or how far I accept that *p*, ceases to be much help. It removes from consideration various degrees of doubt, but leaves us to distinguish knowledge, belief and opinion. It is clear that knowledge must comprehend much more than the Platonists allow. I don't want to digress here into the very complicated question of how knowledge is to be analysed, but it must include more than just the *a priori*, and at least this can be said: "*a* knows that *p*" entails "*p*," whereas "*a* believes that *p*" and "*a* is of the opinion that *p*" do not.

Turning, then, to opinion and belief, I suggest that these together form one category and that they shade off one into the other. Always supposing that the conditions for knowledge (whatever they may be) are not involved, it seems that we must take account of four factors:

a) evidence for *p*, or for not-*p*.

b) consistency of *p* with my other opinions or beliefs.

c) coherence of *p* with any other opinions or beliefs.

d) relation of my wants to *p*: whether I want *p* to be the case, either for itself or as a means to an end; and whether I want to believe that *p* as a means to an end.

The situation is thus more complex than Aquinas would allow, and any change in one of the factors will influence my beliefs to the extent that the other factors are already weak. If we want to distinguish belief from opinion, we might say that we have a case of believing that *p* when *p* is closely related to my wants and coheres with my other opinions and beliefs, but a case of holding the opinion that *p* when these factors are more neutral and not-*p* is not inconsistent with my other opinions or beliefs.

In the last part of the article, Aquinas makes some potentially interesting remarks about the role of *thinking out* in knowledge and belief respectively. It seems clear that *cogitare* must be translated here as *think out* and not just as *think about*, because he refers to it as a *motus*, that is a *kinesis* or performance, whereas *thinking that p*, as an answer-schema to the question "What are you thinking about?" is an *actus secundus*, i.e. an *energeia* or activity.[2] If I am thinking that *p*, then I have thought that *p*; but if I am thinking out an argument which leads to a conclusion *p*, I have not yet thought it out. This translation also fits what he says about knowledge: that coming to know primary premisses does not involve thinking out (this is reiterated in objection 7), whereas scientific knowledge does. Aquinas was mistaken in supposing that analytic *a priori* truths are known immediately and infallibly, but this is certainly what he did think, and most other philosophers have likewise exaggerated the ease with which we arrive at such truths, although in fact considerable linguistic and logical analysis is often required before we are able to say that a given proposition is analytic *a priori*. Scientific knowledge, however, is for Aristotle the fruit of syllogizing, which is clearly a species of thinking out.

It may be remarked in this connexion that even in English it is correct to treat *think about* and *think out* as two separate verbs. In constructions containing a verb followed by prepositions of this kind, verb plus preposition behave as a single unit in transformations even though in some sentences they may be separated by other words; and when the verb is followed by a factive nominal (e.g. a 'that'-clause), the preposition is suppressed. We ought, therefore, to think of them as compound verbs just like those formed in Latin and Greek by means of prepositional suffixes; German is intermediate in this respect; in some constructions the suffix is attached to the verb root, while in others it appears separately at the end of the sentence. There is therefore no ambiguity in *think* here: *think about* and *think out* are two different verbs, just as *agitare* and *cogitare* (*co-agitare*) are in Latin.

Aquinas tells us that *thinking out* is also involved in belief, but whereas assent is the result of thinking out in the case of scientific knowledge, assent and thinking out are on a par in belief. Assent is the result of the want to whose fulfilment it is a means; but we cannot be satisfied with mere assent sustained only by our wants, and are driven to look further and think the matter out. Further, this explains why we can entertain doubts about our beliefs while yet holding firmly to them, but not do so in respect of our knowledge.

This part of Aquinas' account, which he owes to Augustine, is much more successful than the earlier part based on Aristotle. In fact, one might say of the whole article, as so often of Aquinas, that where he allows himself to be led by Aristotle he is led astray, and where he diverges from Aristotle he makes an interesting and useful contribution. The present distinction is of capital importance for elucidating the role of evidence in belief: we look for evidence, but although what we find may support our belief and make it reasonable, it is never conclusive—if it were, our state would be that of knowledge. The evidence thus provides some satisfaction for the mind, but always leaves open the possibility of further investigation; and if the evidence for *p* is not conclusive, then the evidence against not-*p* will not be conclusive either.

Newman has perhaps developed the description of this feature of belief more subtly than anyone else; but whereas he is thinking exclusively in *The Development of Christian Doctrine* of religious belief, on Aquinas' view the feature will be characteristic of all belief. I am indebted to Miss Iris Murdoch for an excellent illustration of Aquinas' view. A mother finds her daughter-in-law uncongenial; she describes the daughter-in-law's behaviour as jejune, her cooking as tasteless, her upbringing of her children as careless and casual—and so on. But being a sensible woman, she reflects that she does not want their relations to deteriorate to the point at which she will have to persuade her son to break up the marriage, or else herself break with both of them. So she tries to look at her daughter-in-law in a more favourable light, and as time passes she finds that she is redescribing the latter's behaviour: it is now delightfully spontaneous and unaffected, she is proficient at plain, wholesome cooking, and her children are being reared in an atmosphere free from unhealthy constraint.

Such remarkable changes in the attitudes of mothers-in-law are unfortunately rare; but the example is not an impossible one, and it illustrates how a person's beliefs about another's character and behaviour can be determined by his wants. In this case we may suppose that the daughter-in-law acted no differently throughout, so that the evidence on which the beliefs were based was the same for the first set and the second set. If the mother-in-law had been asked, after the event, to justify her change of beliefs, she would doubtless have done so by picking out the favourable features whereas earlier she would have noticed the bad ones. *She* would maintain that the evidence had changed; *we* should be inclined to say that she made two different selections from the same evidence, prompted by the reflection that the first set were not in accordance with her wants respecting her son.

This is a useful example, because it illustrates all the features, in a nonreligious context, to which Aquinas draws our attention. In this case holding the second set of beliefs is conducive to the end wanted, good relations with her son, and is thus the ground of her assent to them. On the other hand, she has also done much thinking out of the matter, and will defend her new beliefs as reasonable. Yet the evidence on which they are based is not conclusive; indeed we have previously seen her interpret it otherwise. We may also suspect that if, for instance, her son died suddenly, she might very well revise her opinion of her daughter-in-law yet again.

It is not difficult to find many such examples which support the main outlines of Aquinas' analysis as against those philosophers who have held that belief is an exclusively intellectual attitude. The blindness of people in love with each other to their faults of character is notorious, just as it is proverbial that they begin to discover them after marriage. But even in his account of the role of wants and evidence in belief, Aquinas' account requires a slight modification. He rightly says that assent and thinking out are on a par here; but when he goes on to insist that the ground of assent is our wants, and that the thinking out does not cause the assent, he is surely mistaken. There are limits to what most of us can believe, however much some beliefs might accord with our wants or be means to their realization; and conversely, in being prepared to argue for our beliefs as reasonable we are maintaining that they are based on evidence.

The correct account, I suggest, is that in the case of belief we accept that *p* as a result *both* of the evidence for *p and p*'s being in accordance with our wants (or accepting that *p* being so). The evidence is not conclusive, so alone would not lead us to assent; on the other hand, our wants would not secure our assent in the teeth of *all* the evidence. The role of wants is to fill the gap between what follows logically from the evidence and what we want to maintain. This is basically the position: but it requires modification to allow for three factors already mentioned: first, the need to maintain consistency of beliefs; second, coherence of beliefs; and third, the effect of our wants and these first two factors on how we select the evidence. In this scheme, the beliefs which are easily changed will be those in which there is little connexion with our wants. I do not, however, want to suggest that evidence varies inversely with wants in any belief.

We must now ask how all this can be applied to faith, and here we may consider Aquinas' second article, in which he asks what faith is, and defends the famous definition in the *Epistle to the Hebrews* (11:1): "What is faith? It is the substance of things to be hoped for, the proof of what is not evident."

The Greek reads "ἐλπιζομένων ὑπόστασις, πραγμάτων ἔλεγχος οὐ βλεπομένων." Aquinas says that although this reply to the question "What is faith?" is not cast in the canonical (Aristotelian) form of a definition, it contains all the elements necessary for a good definition and can easily be put into the required form. As a piece of Scriptural exegesis his discussion of the text is no longer of much interest; thus because St. Jerome translated ὑπόστασις by *substantia*, Aquinas devotes considerable ingenuity to bringing it within the scope of one use by Aristotle οα οὐσία, although as is obvious enough, he makes it clear that faith is not within Aristotle's *category* of substance. Again, he argues from the translation of ἔλεγχος as *argumentum* that the final phrase describes the actualization of faith, and thus shews faith itself to be a disposition.

Yet the article is not to be dismissed because of its deficiencies, in the light of modern knowledge, as exegesis; and even as exegesis it can be defended in part for taking each word of the text seriously and attempting to expound it systematically. What strikes us as so odd in the method, of course, is not Aquinas' meticulous attention to detail but his unwritten supposition that the author of the *Hebrews* can be treated almost as an Aristotelian commentator. Even so, if we look at the discussion not so much as exegesis but as Aquinas' own exposition of his view of faith, it offers us material which can still be taken seriously.

Aquinas' view is that faith is a species of belief, in the sense that the latter was expounded in article one. He therefore has to shew, first, that it is assent motivated by a want; and second, that it has an object to which the intellect can assent. In order to fulfil the first requirement, he distinguishes between natural wants, and, though he does not actually use the term, what might be called "supernatural wants." What he says about natural wants is thoroughly Platonic: our ultimate natural want is happiness, to be realized in contemplation of *a priori* truths on the one hand and in the exercise of practical wisdom ($\phi\rho\acute{o}\nu\eta\sigma\iota\varsigma$) on the other. But in addition to such an ultimate natural want, we are also given by God a corresponding ultimate supernatural want, namely for eternal life. It is this want, he says, which motivates our assent in faith.

There follows a curious paragraph based on Aristotle's account of final causes, and which refers implicitly to the paradigm in *Metaphysics* 7, 7–9 of the builder who has in his mind the form (or design) of a house, which he then proceeds to realize in bricks and mortar. All the actions which the builder takes in setting into motion and prosecuting the building operations can be described as being done for the sake of an end, in this case that there should be such a house. Now one feature of this example which Aristotle generalized for *all* final causality was the existence of the form of the end product in the agent from the beginning. It is presumably this doctrine which leads Aquinas to say that whenever we want something, there is an outline or sketch (*inchoatio*) or again a likeness, of something within us.

Now this doctrine is dubious, if not mistaken. The object of a want is properly not an object but a state of affairs, i.e. what would be described by a sentence. This can be seen from the grammar of the verb *want*; sentences containing *want* as their main verb are built up by a transformation from *two* sentences, the first of the form: "*a* wants that," where "that" is to be regarded as a demonstrative, the second a sentence which gives the object of the want. In certain cases the verb of the second sentence may be deleted by a further transformation; thus "Tom wanted that" and "Tom ate a slice of smoked salmon" will yield "Tom wanted to eat a slice of smoked salmon" and then by an optional deleting transformation "Tom wanted a slice of smoked salmon."

It is thus a grammatical mistake to parse the latter sentence as: subject, "Tom"; verb "wanted"; and object "some smoked salmon." The corresponding logical mistake is to treat wanting as a relation, analysing the sentence as: "for some x, x is a slice of smoked salmon and Tom wanted x."

I think that both Aristotle and Aquinas make just this mistake; Plato is explicit that wanting is a relation in *Republic* 6, and they follow him, as so often. On the other hand it is not difficult to modify the doctrine so as to make it acceptable. Setting aside the question whether we can have unconscious wants, which are not relevant to the present topic, any want must have some content; that is to say, it must be formulable in a way which describes the state of affairs bringing about which will count as the fulfilment of the want, the attainment of the goal. Wants are specified by describing their goals. Hence for a person to have a given want, he must already know what would count as its fulfilment, and in this sense there will be present in him an outline or sketch of the goal within us. But, returning to the distinction with which we began between the two mental activities of concept-formation and predication, the formulation of a want will involve predication (though not assertion or denial) and not merely the presence of a concept or intelligible form.

We are now in a position to apply this analysis to faith. Aquinas says that we have two ultimate wants: the first is happiness, i.e. to be happy, the second, eternal life. These descriptions are, however, in a sense empty; for we require to know what counts as being happy, or if you like, what will make us happy, and equally we need some account of what eternal life consists in. We need not delay over Aquinas' Platonic views about happiness; they are debatable, but not important here. As regards eternal life, however, he tells us, following St. John, that it consists in the knowledge of God. So our ultimate supernatural want is to know God; and I shall not pursue here the question whether this means merely knowledge *about* God, or personal acquaintance with God, or both; let us just assume the latter.

The point of calling this a *super*natural want is that God himself has to give us this desire. Aquinas says that we can neither think out nor want this goal unaided; but he does not make it clear whether two steps are involved or only one: is it merely a question of an intellectual enlightenment which tells us what eternal life consists in, upon which we naturally formulate a want of which it is the object, or must there also be a separate communication of the corresponding desire? It is difficult to make sense of the second suggestion, in view of this being an *ultimate* goal; one can see how a state of affairs already considered might come to be desired as a means to an end, but not how an end-in-itself could be not wanted and then wanted. So let us proceed on the supposition that all that has to be communicated to us is that eternal life consists in knowledge of God.

We now seem to be faced by a difficulty parallel to one which we encountered earlier apropos belief. Aquinas says that it is by faith that we have a sketch or outline of the knowledge of God within us. Yet this sketch or outline cannot itself be knowledge. We must have faith, i.e. believe supernaturally, both that there is such a thing as eternal life and that it consists in knowledge of God. So without faith we cannot formulate this ultimate supernatural want. How, then, can this want be the *cause* of our assent in faith? As with belief, it seems that we need a meta-faith in order to explain faith.

Let us now turn briefly to the content of faith. Aquinas has made it clear that predication is involved in belief, and thus that what we believe is the truth of certain descriptions of states of affairs. If faith is a species of belief, then, it too must be in the truth of certain predications. We may, however, expect that the range of these predications will be limited in some way. In article two he merely describes the content of faith in the words of the quotation from *Hebrews* as "what is not evident." But in articles eight and nine it is specified more exactly. In article eight he says that the First Truth (an Anselmian expression for God) is the *per se* object of faith. God, however, is an object and not a state of affairs, so this requires some modification, and he clarifies it by saying that "faith conjoins a man to the divine knowledge through assent," and earlier that if faith is to be a virtue, what we believe supernaturally must be true; so that lacking proof, it must have a guarantee of truth "because it is committed to the witness of someone in whom truth is infallibly discovered," i.e. God. From this it can be seen that the object of faith is *what God says*, under that description, and what God says, he knows to be the case.

There is, however, a further restriction imposed in article nine, where he argues that we cannot know and believe the same thing simultaneously. This, of course, follows from the original analysis of belief in article one. If we assent to some proposition because we have a proof of it, there is no gap for will to bridge; and although Aquinas envisages only necessary truths as objects of knowledge, we may interpret "proof" more liberally to include the proof of our senses, of experiment, etc. Since this conclusion is fully in accordance with our use of "know" and "believe," I need not discuss it further here. We need only notice that it leaves open the possibility that I *first* believe something, and only later come to *know* that it is the case. Hence there is no distinction *as such* between the objects of knowledge and of belief; Aquinas held that the object of knowledge is anything at all, i.e. there is no limitation of subject-matter, and the same will apply to belief. Of course we can believe what is not the case, although we can only know what is the case. But this is no principle for differentiating what one might call the material object of belief, since if any description of a state of affairs "p" is false, while I can believe that p but not know that p, I can always know that not-p.

Anything we *can* know, we can believe, providing only that we *don't* know it already; but is the argument above enough to establish the converse, providing that "anything" means "anything or its negation"? Aquinas says that we cannot know *in this life* some of the things which we believe supernaturally, because our *only* information about them derives from God's revelation.

But this does not affect the logical point: faith will be superseded by knowledge in the next life, so that it is clearly *logically* possible for a man to know what he believes supernaturally. Hence although there are differences between the formal objects of knowledge and belief, their material objects are co-terminous.

The material objects of faith, however, are a restricted class of propositions, namely those revealed by God. One difference between faith and belief—a formal difference—is that whereas I can falsely believe that *p*, I cannot falsely believe supernaturally that *p*. Believing supernaturally that *p*, like knowing that *p*, entails *p*. It is this restriction which explains the peculiarity. Believing supernaturally that *p* entails that God has revealed that *p*, and this in turn entails *p*. Hence this peculiarity is no objection to saying that faith is a species of belief.

It may be that some truths revealed by God can also be known in this life. Aquinas caters for this eventuality in article nine; no doubt he has the conclusions of natural theology in mind. Where this situation obtains, a man without a valid proof of such conclusions can believe them supernaturally, but if he then discovers a proof, his faith in them ceases and is superseded by knowledge. This part of the analysis seems quite correct, and I have no comment to make about it, except perhaps that there are fewer of us who are confident that we have valid proofs in this sphere than there used to be.

There are many further interesting questions about faith which must lie outside the scope of this paper. One central question of philosophical interest concerns the concept of *hope*: the author of *Hebrews* describes the objects of faith as "things to be hoped for," and Christians and Jews claim to be the sons of Abraham because through belief they are heirs to the promise God made to him. Perhaps the clue to resolving the apparent circularity which we have found in Aquinas' account of faith and of belief is to be found in their relation to hope: thus political beliefs, for instance, seem to be connected with people's hopes for a better world. But what Aquinas thought about hope would be matter for a paper in itself.

NOTES

1. B. A. O. Williams, "Ethical Consistency", in *Proceedings of the Aristotelian Society*, Supplementary Volume 39 (1965), 103–124.
2. This interpretation is confirmed by *Summa theologiae* 2-2.2.1.

2

A MEDIEVAL DISCUSSION OF INTENTIONALITY

Peter Geach

IN this paper I shall critically examine the way a fourteenth-century logician, Jean Buridan, dealt with certain puzzles about intentional verbs. The class of verbs I shall be considering will all of them be expressions that can be completed into propositions by adding two proper names; the class will include not only ordinary transitive verbs, but also phrases of the verb-preposition type like "look for" or "shoot at," and furthermore constructions like "hopes—will be a better man than his father" or "believes—to be a scoundrel," which turn into propositions as soon as we add mention of who hopes or believes this and about whom he does so. In modern grammar, the term "a verbal" rather than "a verb" is used for this wider class; following a suggestion of Professor Bar-Hillel, I adopt this term.

In either or both of the proper-name places that go with such a verbal, it is possible, without destroying the propositional structure (*salva congruitate*, as medieval logicians say), to substitute a phrase of some such form as "some A" or "every A" or "the (one and only) A"; the letter "A" here represents a simple or complex general term which is grammatically a noun or noun-phrase. The peculiarity of certain verbals that presently concern us comes out when such a phrase formed from a general term stands in object position, in a construction "b F'd an A" or the like. Consider for example the sentence "Geach looked for a detective story." This sentence is ambiguous: in ordinary conversation we might successfully resolve the ambiguity by asking the question "Was what Geach was looking for a particular detective story, or was it just *a* detective story?" It is an odd psychological fact that this question would convey the intended distinction of meanings; for logically the words of the question leave it wholly obscure what is intended. After all, nothing in this world or in any possible world could be "just *a* detective story" without being "a particular detective story"; and even if such an *individuum vagum* could somehow have being, Geach could not read it, so it certainly is not what he looked for.

A similar example in Buridan himself is "I owe you a horse." Here again one would quite naturally distinguish between owing a particular horse—the handing over of that very horse would be part of the bargain—and "just" owing *a* horse. Whatever we are to make of this distinction, it is clear that what the customer wants is a real live horse; not a possible horse, or an indefinite horse that is literally not all there. Buridan does have some very dubious passages in which he quantifies over *possibilia*, such as possible horses and possible men; he has, for example, a doctrine that when a general term "*A*" stands as subject to a modalized predicate, it is "ampliated" or stretched so that it relates to possible *A*s as well as actual *A*s. On this view, to use an example formally similar to Buridan's own, "Some man is necessarily damned" would be exponible as "Some actual or possible man is necessarily damned," which appears to draw the sting of the doctrine of reprobation. Anyhow, when it's a question of owing a horse Buridan will not bring in possible horses.

It may well appear equally out of place to bring into the picture such intentional entities as the senses of expressions; the sense of the term "horse" or "detective story" is assuredly not something whose possession would content a man when he is owed a horse or is looking for a detective story. All the same the sense, or as Buridan calls it the *ratio*, given us by an object expression really is somehow involved when the verbal is an intentional one; Buridan says the object expression *appellat suam rationem*, where we may perhaps render the verb *"appellat"* (perhaps the most obscurely and multifariously employed of all medieval semantic technicalities) by saying the expression "calls up" or "evokes" its own *ratio*. Buridan's main point is in any case clear: that the truth-value of a sentence whose verbal is an intentional one may be changed if we change the *ratio*, the sense, given in the object expression, even if this expression still relates to the same thing in the world. This point is clearly correct, as many of Buridan's examples show; thus, if a body is both white and sweet and I see it, I may truly say "I have discerned something white by my sense of sight," but not "I have discerned something sweet by my sense of sight."

Can't I, though, say I have discerned something sweet by my sense of sight, if the body I have discerned is in fact sweet? Well, it's better to say "There is something sweet that I have discerned by sight" if this is the case I have in mind. This means, according to Buridan, that the sweet thing is something which my sense of sight discerns under some *ratio* or other, not at all necessarily under the *ratio*: sweet—this *ratio* comes in only *sub disiunctione ad alias rationes*, as one possible alternative *ratio*.

Buridan here observes a tendency of Latin idiom, which comes out in much the same way in English: when a verbal is intentional, an object phrase is differently construed when it precedes the main verb that is a part of the whole of this verbal, and when it follows that verb. In general, taking "to *F*" as representative of an intentional verbal, we shall distinguish between the forms "b *F*'s an *A*" and "There is an *A* that b *F*'s." The latter form if construed in the spirit of Buridan will mean "There is some actual *A* of which it holds that b *F*'s it under some *ratio* or other"—possibly, though, under some other *ratio* than that of being an *A*. (In Buridan's Latin examples there are no words corresponding to "there is" and "that" in the form "There is an *A* that b *F*'s"; this difference between English and Latin idiom is obviously trivial.) Of course this distinction of word order is not *strictly* observed in ordinary English or Latin; we have to consider what is actually meant in the case under consideration. An instructive example, to which I shall presently return, is one I borrow with slight alteration from John Austin: "I saw a man born in Jerusalem" *versus* "I saw a man run over in Oxford." But we may very well decide for present purposes to stick to Buridan's convention of word order, as a way of marking the distinction he quite properly wishes to draw.

Buridan rightly regards the inference from "There is an A that b F'd" to "b F'd an A" as an invalid form; for if "There is an A that b F'd" is true, the general term represented by "A" need not give us the aspect of *ratio* under which such an A was the object of b's F'ing. Moreover, though Buridan himself does not consider (the Latin equivalent of) the verbal "was looking for," his machinery helps to clear up our puzzles about this verbal. We should use "There is a detective story Geach was looking for" for the case where one would say I was looking for "a particular" detective story, and reserve "Geach was looking for a detective story" rather for the case where I was "just" looking for *a* detective story. In the former case, if the book I was looking for was a book printed in Baskerville type, one might equally well say "There is a book printed in Baskerville type that Geach was looking for"; but one could not infer "Geach was looking for a book printed in Baskerville type," since the *ratio* under which I was looking for the book will have been the one expressed by "detective story," not the one expressed by "book printed in Baskerville type."

Buridan assumes that from "b F'd an A" we may infer "There is something that b F'd." In fact, as we shall presently see, he assumes more than this; and even this much is doubtful. But we may use this assumption to show how Buridan's theory looks in terms of modern quantification theory. The intentional verbal represented by "to F" would answer, not to a two-termed relation between a person and an object of his F'ing, but to a three-termed relation between a person, an object of F'ing, and a *ratio*; and the forms "b F's an A" and "There is an A that b F'd" would respectively come out as:

For some z, b F'd z under the *ratio: A*

For some z, and for some w, z is an A, and b F'd z under the *ratio w.*

It may be helpful to work out in this way the concrete example from John Austin that I mentioned just now. "I saw a man run over in Oxford" would come out as:

For some z, z is a man and I saw z in Oxford under the *ratio*: run over,

and "I saw a man born in Jerusalem" would come out as:

For some z, z is a man and z was born in Jerusalem and, for some w, I saw z under the *ratio w.*

Buridan's analysis, seen in this light, already raises one severe difficulty. The form with the term preceding the intentional verbal essentially involves quantifying over *rationes*. Now I am not at all impressed by rhetoric about mysterious entities, by questions in the peculiar (anti-) metaphysical tone of voice "But what *are* they?"; it is all right to quantify over entities if you can supply a sharp criterion of identity for them. The paradigm of this is Frege's sharp criterion of identity for numbers. But for *rationes* we can get out of Buridan no hint of such a criterion. He gives us many examples of *rationes* he takes to be patently different, like the *ratio*: white and the *ratio*: sweet; but we have not even one example of the same *ratio* differently expressed, from which we might divine a criterion of identity. This lacuna makes Buridan's account schematic at best.

A more serious defect is Buridan's acceptance of the inference from "b F'd an A" to "There is an A that b F'd." Notice that this would still be unacceptable even if we let pass the inference to "There is something that b F'd"; for this does follow from:

For some z, b F'd z under the *ratio*: A

but there is still no obvious necessity that what is F'd under the *ratio*: A should in fact be an A. And in concrete examples Buridan's pattern of inference, from the form "with the term after" to the form "with the term before," often seems patently invalid. He himself chooses examples that look all right, e.g. from "I see something white" to "There is something white I see," or from "I recognize somebody coming" to "There is somebody coming whom I recognize." But of course we may not pass from "James is looking for a universal solvent" to "There is a universal solvent James is looking for"; we may not even pass from "Geach is looking for a detective story" to "There is a detective story Geach is looking for," because, as we saw, the premise is compatible with my not having been looking for "a particular" detective story.

Even among the examples Buridan himself supplies, there are some that hardly favour his thesis. Suppose poor old Socrates is a competent astronomer immured in a dungeon where he cannot tell night from day. Then Buridan is willing to pass from the premise "Socrates knows some stars are above the horizon" to the conclusion "There are some stars Socrates knows are above the horizon." You naturally ask which stars Socrates knows are above the horizon; Buridan has a ready answer—the ones that are. To be sure, it is in a rather attenuated sense that the constellation Aries (say) is then known by Socrates to be above the horizon: namely, not in respect of the complex *ratio* expressed by "Aries is above the horizon," but only in respect of the one expressed by "Some stars are above the horizon." But at least Buridan can hardly be forced to pass from premises that would in this case be true to a conclusion that would in this case be false. Although in his view *one* true answer to the question "Which stars does Socrates know are above the horizon?" might be "There is the constellation Aries that Socrates knows is above the horizon," he can on his own principles disallow the inference from this to "Socrates knows that the constellation Aries is above the horizon"; this shift of the term, *from* before the main-verb part of the verbal—knows that—is above the horizon *to* after that verb, is just what Buridan disallows, as we saw. And Buridan's motive for wishing to pass to the conclusion "There are some stars that Socrates knows are above the horizon" is that even the abstract knowledge expressed in "Some stars are above the horizon"

ought in his eyes to latch on to some actual, and therefore definitely specifiable, stars.

This example is rather a cheat, though, because Buridan is
trading on a peculiarity of the verb "to know." What you know
is so; if Socrates knows some stars are above the horizon, then
some stars are above the horizon, and we may ask which ones are.
But suppose Socrates believes some lizards breathe fire—not
being so good a zoologist as an astronomer. May we pass to the
conclusion "There are some lizards that Socrates believes breathe
fire"? and if so, which lizards are these? Certainly not the ones
that do breathe fire, for Socrates' belief is false. Moreover, it may
be impossible to find any principle for picking out, from among
actual lizards, the ones Socrates believes to breathe fire. Buridan
often resorts, when faced by such an embarrassing choice, to a
parity-of-reasoning argument; what is true of some so-and-so,
if there is no reason to think it is true of one so-and-so rather than
another, must be true of each and every so-and-so. We should then
have to pass on from "There are some lizards that Socrates believes breathe fire," to the further conclusion "As regards each
lizard, Socrates believes that it breathes fire." From this, indeed,
we could on Buridan's principles not infer "Socrates believes that
each lizard breathes fire"; Socrates' belief would latch on to each
and every lizard, but only *via* the complex *ratio* expressed by
"Some lizards breathe fire." Still, in Buridan's own words,
videtur durum, it seems tough to swallow.

I now come to a similar puzzle of Buridan's own, in which his
own principles raise severe difficulties. A horse dealer, he supposes,
currently owns just three thoroughbreds, Brownie, Blackie, and
Fallow. The customer accepts the dealer's promise "I will give
you one of my thoroughbreds," but the dealer fails to deliver, and
denies that he owes the purchaser anything. "If I owe you any
horse," he argues, "I must owe you either Brownie or Blackie or
Fallow; they're the only horses I have, and you can't say I owe
you some other horse, let us say H.M. the King's charger. Now
what I said didn't relate specially to Blackie rather than Fallow, or
the other way round; what goes for one goes for the other; and
similarly for Brownie. So either I owe you both Brownie and

Blackie and Fallow, or I owe you not one of them. You'll surely not have the nerve to say I owe you all three, when I only said I'd let you have one; so I don't owe you even one. *Good* morning."

Part of the trouble Buridan has in saying what is wrong with the horse-coper's argument comes from his accepting the inference from "I owe you a horse" to "There is a horse I owe you"; and we have seen reason to doubt the validity of the rule by which Buridan has to allow this step. But even without this inferential move, Buridan can give the horse-coper a longer run for his (or rather his victim's) money. Even if in general we cannot validly pass from "b F's an *A*" to "There is an *A* that b F's," it seems plausible to accept this particular instance of a term-shifting inference: "I owe you something; *ergo*, there is something I owe you." And we can consistently accept it without accepting Buridan's invalid rule: many philosophers seem to think that any instance of an invalid form is an invalid argument, but this is a gross logical error. Let us then have our horse-coper arguing again, "If I owe you a horse, then I owe you something. And if I owe you something, then there is something I owe you. And this can only be a thoroughbred of mine; you aren't going to say that in virtue of what I said there's something else I owe you. Very well then: by your claim, there's one of my thoroughbreds I owe you. Please tell me which one it is."

Buridan has an ingenious way out of the difficulty. It can be said that *x* is owing by me to *y* if and only if by handing over *x* to *y* I should be quits with him (*essem quittus*). Now whichever thoroughbred (*bonus equus*) *x* may be, if the horse-coper hands over *x* to the purchaser then they are quits. Buridan concludes that, whichever thoroughbred *x* may be, the dealer owes *x* to the customer. This goes even for H.M. the King's charger; for if the horse-coper bought or were given this horse, he could be quits with his customer by handing it over, as he could not be if he had not handed over exactly what was owing.

We can now clear up the "parity of reasoning" argument about the three horses the dealer already has. It is true of Brownie, and it is true of Blackie, and it is also true of Fallow, that this is a horse the dealer owes his customer. So, considering just Brownie and

Blackie, we may in a sense say these are two horses the dealer owes. But Buridan rightly warns us to avoid confusing collective and distributive predication; it is not that there are two horses together which the dealer owes, but that of each one of the two it holds good that he is a horse the dealer owes. Moreover, by Buridan's general principle we may not pass from "There are two horses the dealer owes" to "The dealer owes two horses"; that would call up the *ratio*: two horses, which did not come into the dealer's original promise. Similarly, from "Brownie is a horse the dealer owes" we may not infer "The dealer owes Brownie"; this would be true only if the dealer's original promise had called up the *ratio* expressed by the name "Brownie," as *ex hypothesi* it did not.

It is very reluctantly that one finds fault with Buridan's brilliant way of securing obvious justice for the customer without bending the laws of logic. All the same, the inference from "I owe you something" to "There is something I owe you" cannot be let pass unchallenged. No doubt many an investor in the Post Office Savings Bank has inferred from "The Post Office owes me something" to "There is something the Post Office owes me"; his thought is "The Post Office has it all stacked up somewhere— *aes alienum*, other people's brass—and some of it's mine." The inference is invalid, and the conclusion is false; and the mistake is far from trivial—as those unscrupulous politicians were well aware who made use of this false impression in their highly successful propaganda to the effect "The Socialists were going to take *your* money out of the Savings Bank and pay it over to the unemployed"!

This difficulty is not confined to the present example; there are, I think, very many instances in which from "b F's an A" or "b F's something or other" we may by no means infer that there is an identifiable something-or-other which b is F'ing. On this point Buridan's theory stands in need of radical reconstruction. I think I can see in part how such a reconstruction would be possible; but there are difficulties that still remain.

Let us take the example "Geach was looking for a detective story." On our former analysis, which closely followed Buridan, this would come out as:

> For some *x*, Geach was looking for *x* under the *ratio*: detective story.

But this would have the unwelcome consequence that, even when I was "just" looking for *a* detective story, there was some identifiable *x*—not necessarily a detective story, to be sure—that I was looking for. We need rather a dyadic relation between Geach and a *ratio*: "Geach was-looking-for-something-under the *ratio*: detective story," where I have hyphenated the words of the verbal to show that logically it is just one indivisible relative term.

We may achieve considerable clarification if we expand this analysis to:

> Geach was looking for something under the *ratio* evoked (*appellata*) by the expression "detective story,"

and then treat "was looking . . . by" as a single relative term, which we may abbreviate to "was L'ing." We now have a verbal flanked by a name of a person and a quotation, rather than by a name of a person and a designation of a *ratio*. This dodge, suggested to me by Professor R. Montague, avoids our difficulties about quantifying over *rationes*; we may now analyse "There is a detective story Geach was looking for" as:

> For some *x*, *x* is a detective story, and, for some *w*, *w* is a description true just of *x*, and Geach was L'ing *w* (Geach was-looking-for-something-under-the-*ratio*-evoked-by the definite description *w*).

Here we quantify over forms of words, whose criterion of identity, if not completely clear, is a lot clearer than that of *rationes*.

A similar method suggests itself for dealing with problems of what may be called *intentional identity*. In a way parallel to the Buridan convention we may distinguish between "There is a poet whom both Smith and Brown admire" and "Smith and Brown both admire the same poet"; the latter would cover the case where both Smith and Brown are victims of the same literary fraud as to the existence of a poet, as well as the more normal case where they both admire (say) Wordsworth's poetry. Let us use the

expression "AP" as short for "admire as a poet someone conceived under the *ratio* evoked by"; then "There is a poet whom
both Smith and Brown admire" would come out as:

For some *x*, *x* is a poet and, for some *w*, *w* is a description
    true just of *x*, and both Smith and Brown AP *w*

whereas "Smith and Brown both admire the same poet," taken
as conveying only intentional identity, would come out in the
simpler form:

For some *w*, *w* is a definite description, and Smith and Brown
    both AP *w*.

Unfortunately, the line of solution we have been following
leads us into difficulties. Suppose we use "D'd" as short for the
verbal "dreamed of someone under the *ratio* expressed by."
Then in our present view we should have to paraphrase "There
is a red-head Harris dreamed of" as:

For some *x*, *x* is a red-head and, for some *w*, *w* is a description
    true just of *x*, and Harris D'd *w*.

Now suppose we take *w* to be the description "the fattest woman
in the world." The paraphrase would be true if Harris dreamed
of the fattest woman in the world and the fattest woman in the
world is in fact a red-head; but the proposition paraphrased
might then quite well be false, because in Harris's dream there
may have been no red-head, and the fattest woman he saw in his
dream may have been as bald as an egg. (I owe this counter-
example to my pupil Mr. David Bird.) Similar difficulties arise
for our account of intentional identity: for if c and d each worshipped something under the *ratio* expressed by "the deity of the
Sun," it does not follow that c and d both worshipped the same
deity—c might be an ancient Egyptian worshipping the ancestor
of Pharaoh, and d a Japanese worshipping the ancestress of the
Mikado.

I hope this paper shows why modern logicians still need to take
medieval logicians seriously. In great measure their problems are
ours; while for some of them, like the problems of *suppositio*,

modern logic provides adequate solutions, there are other problems, about modal and intentional contexts for example, that are still wide open; and the talent that was shown by medieval logicians in wrestling with their problems demands our deepest admiration.

3

ANALOGY AS A RULE OF MEANING FOR RELIGIOUS LANGUAGE

James F. Ross

IN this essay I am attempting to restate the analogy theory of St. Thomas Aquinas in terms of modern semantic analysis. I am restating it because its general outline is little known and because its vast significance for present-day philosophers concerned with problems of religious language is little understood.

In addition to its deserved philosophical interest, the theory has additional historical value as an example of a very common solution to the problem of informative theological language offered throughout the thirteenth century in Western philosophy. It is essentially a reply to the question: "Can you show that theological statements are meaningful?" A. N. Prior has remarked: "The real intellectual difficulty of the believer or would-be believer is not the problem of proof but the problem of meaning."[1] It is worth noting that the same question was hotly and subtly discussed by most of the medieval writers and the most common conclusion was that a theory of analogy was required. Most recent writers in philosophical theology have made some reference to the theory of analogy current in medieval times, and almost universally these writers have judged it hopeless. As will appear in the course of this paper, authors like Flew and MacKinnon,[2] Farrer,[3] and Mascall[4] have offered interpretations of the analogy doctrine considerably different from the one I shall propose. I consider their interpretations

35

as seriously deficient and misleading, and I shall endeavor to show implicitly[5] both how little they understood the complexity of the doctrine and how much more penetrating a language theory the analogy rules constitute than most modern writers have supposed.

St. Thomas Aquinas actually formulated four distinct but complementary analogy rules. In this essay I am concerned to analyze only the two most important of these, although the other two rules are stated in the list of definitions given below. This essay is divided into three main parts, the first two sections being summaries of the "exhibition analyses" by which the two rules in which we are interested are formulated. The third section is a brief sketch of how these rules were employed to solve the problems of informative discourse about God.

Before undertaking the analysis of analogy rules, I must make the following additional points of introduction:

1. The two rules of analogy herein discussed are concerned with the comparative meaning of two or more instances of the same term used as predicate in two or more statements of the form a) "X is T" and b) "Y is T."

2. As a result, we must distinguish between the *technical* sense of "analogy" which we shall use and at least one other ordinary language sense of "analogy."

When the word "analogous" occurs in ordinary language, there is usually a context of comparison: "Spanish is analogous to Portuguese"; "The navigator of a ship and the ruler of a state are analogous"; etc. *Things* are said to be analogous if they have common characteristics or similar relations. And the term "analogy" is often taken as a synonym of "similar" or "similarity."

We are not speaking of the analogy of things in this essay; we are speaking of the analogy of *terms*. And "being analogous" will signify a semantical property of a term in several of its instances. Which semantical property? The property of conforming in its employment to one of the analogy rules stated below. Hence, the analogy theory of St. Thomas is concerned with the similarity of *meaning* of instances of the same term—not directly with the similarity of things. Of course, Aquinas argues that similarity of meaning is connected with the similarity of the things signified by the terms in question; but that comes much later and is not part of the meaning-theory itself.

3. St. Thomas' analogy rules are the results of a language analysis and are designed to solve specific language problems. The first of these is this: Aquinas, for theological reasons, was committed to accepting the traditional Christian language about God which is found in the liturgy and in the traditional catechetical instruction given children and converts, as being accurate, informative and true. This was "ordinary language" and was to be accepted as being applicable to God. But Aquinas has undertaken to solve the following problem: How could he show that this language (all of the terms, expressions and employments of which are learned from human experience) can be applied, without such equivocation as would render invalid all argument, to God, an entity which is so different from the objects of experience as to be "inexperienceable" in any of the ways common to ordinary human experience? Although the analogy theory I am treating as a whole was actually formulated piecemeal as problems arose over the applicability of "experience" predicates to God, the object of the whole theory is to preserve the literal sense of ordinary beliefs about God.

The second specific language problem St. Thomas was trying to solve is as follows: He accepted the Aristotelian theory of the categories as a classification of predicates such that entities denoted by the predicates in a given category, say "substance," were all those things denoted by all the terms in that category used *univocally*. As a result, transcategorial statements cannot have univocal predicates. An example of a transcategorial statement is: "Both trees and numbers exist"—where "trees" belongs to the category of substance and "numbers" to quantity. Aquinas would remark that the whole statement given is elliptical for two statements in which the predicate "exists" occurs twice and is used analogously. Hence, the theory of analogy was required to justify the meaningfulness of transcategorial statements. And, since metaphysical statements were by their very generality transcategorial, the theory of analogy was required as a justification of the metaphysician's claim to be uttering meaningful discourse.

4. The following are the definitions employed in this study:[6]

DEFINITIONS

General Conditions:
1. (a) and (b) stand for sentences.
2. All definitions are for (a) and (b) in a language "l."

Def. I - 1: Verbal Symbol:
" 'S' is a verbal symbol":

if "S" is a recognizable pattern of marks or of sounds used for the purpose of expression and communication. (What is regarded as the same pattern in difficult instances is partly a matter of physical similarity, and partly a matter of conventional understanding.) Two marks or two sounds having the same recognizable pattern are two instances of the same symbol, not two different symbols.

Def. I - 2: Linguistic Expression:
" 'L' is a linguistic expression":

if "L" is a verbal symbol (S), and if S is associated with a fixed meaning either by convention or stipulation.

Def. I - 3: Same Expression:
" 'L' in sentence (a) and 'L' in sentence (b) are the same expression":

if "L" in (a) and "L" in (b) are instances of the same symbol, and if the two instances are not totally equivocal.

Def. I - 4: Word:
" 'W' is a word":

if "W" is a linguistic expression.

Def. I - 5: Same Word:
" 'W' in sentence (a) and 'W' in sentence (b) are the same word":

if "W" in (a) and (b) respectively is a linguistic expression, and if (*according to Def. I -* 1) "W" in (a) and "W" in (b) are numerical instances of the same verbal symbol. *Note:* "W" in (a) and "W" in (b) can be the same word without being the same expression.

Def. I - 6: Term:
" 'T' is a term":
if "T" is a word capable of naming or applying to a thing or things. *Note:* All terms are words, but not all words are terms.

Def. I - 7: Same Term:
" 'T' in (a) and 'T' in (b) are the same term":
if in each case "T" is a term and if "T" in (a) and in (b) is the same word. *Note:* Sometimes "T" in (a) and "T" in (b) will be the same word *and* the same expression (*Def. I - 3*), and sometimes the same word but *not* the same expression. When "T" in (a) and "T" in (b) are the same term, they are "instances of term 'T.' " This is a departure from the practice of C. I. Lewis in *Knowledge and Valuation*, but it conforms to the practice of the Scholastics whom I am explaining, and using Lewis' definitions would require two parallel sets of definitions which would constantly require correlation.

Def. I - 8: Same Term and Same Expression:
" 'T' in (a) and 'T' in (b) are the same term and the same expression":
if (1) "T" in (a) and "T" in (b) are the same word; and (2) if "T" in (a) and "T" in (b) are the same expression.

Def. I - 9: Same Meaning of Same Term:
" 'T' in (a) and 'T' in (b) have the same meaning":
if (1) "T" in (a) and "T" in (b) are instances of the term "T", i.e., are the same term; and (2) "T" in (a) and in (b) is used univocally (*Def. I - 12*).

Def. I - 10: Signification:
"Term 'T' signifies F":
if F is one of the properties which it is both necessary and sufficient for a thing to have in order to be denoted by "T."

Def. I - 11: Intention:
The intention of term "T" is the conjunction of all other terms each of which must be applicable to anything to which the term "T" is correctly applicable.

Def. I - 12: Univocity:

a) "Term 'T' is used univocally in (a) and (b)":

if "T" in (a) signifies the same property as "T" in (b).

b) "Term 'T' is used univocally in (a) and (b)".

if there is a one to one correspondence of the same terms in the intention of "T" in (a) and of "T" in (b).

Def. I - 13: Equivocity:

"Term 'T' is used equivocally in (a) and (b)":

if "T" in (a) and "T" in (b) are not univocal.

Def. I - 14: Total Equivocation:

"Term 'T' is totally equivocal in (a) and (b)":

if there is no property which is included both in the signification of "T" in (a) and in the signification of "T" in (b).

Def. I - 15: Partial Equivocation:

"Term 'T' is partially equivocal in (a) and (b)":

if "T" in (a) and "T" in (b) are used equivocally, but not totally equivocally.

Def. II - 1: Analogy of Inequality:

"Term 'T' is analogous by inequality in (a) and (b)":

if 1. "T" in (a) and "T" in (b) are instances of the same term.

2. "T" in (a) and "T" in (b) are univocal by *Def. I* - 12.

3. The property F, signified by "T" in (a) and (b) is either:

    1) not physically congruent, in the one case being a non-separable part of the subject, and in the other, all of the subject; or

    2) different in degree according to some standard; or

    3) possessed by the subject in (a) in a different mode (necessity, contingency, etc.) from the subject in (b).

Def. III - 1: Analogy of Attribution:

"Term 'T' is analogous by attribution in (a) and (b)":

if 1. "T" occurs as predicate in two or more indicative sentences: (a) "F is T" and (b) "G is T."

2. "T" in (a) signifies a property T of F.

3. "T" in (b) signifies a relation of G to F where G is either a

cause of F's having property T or is in some respect an effect or affected causally by F's having property T.

Def. IV - 1: Sameness of Res Significata:

"The *res significata* of 'T' is the same in (a) and (b)":

if 1. there are given at least two sentences (a) and (b) in which there is respectively a predicate term 'T.'

2. "T" in (a) and "T" in (b) are instances of the same term.

3. "T" signifies property T of X in (a) and T of Y in (b).

4. all the terms of the intention of "T" in (a) which specify the class of things to which property T belongs, occur in the intention of "T" in (b).

Def. IV - 2: Difference of Modus Significandi:

"The *modus significandi* of 'T' is different in (a) and (b)":

if 1, 2, 3, and 4 of *Def. IV -* 1 hold.

5. for any thing Z, having the property T implies that Z can perform either actions (A) 1, 2, 3, - n; or (B) 2, 3, 4, - n and not 1; or (C) 3, 4, - n and not 1 and 2; or....; or n....

6. the intention of "T" in sentence (a) and in (b) is determined by the intention of the subject term "X" or "Y" in such a way that only one of the alternative groups of actions is signified.

7. the terms of the intention of "T" in (a) which specify which of the alternates (A), (B) or (C) is performed, are not the same as the terms in the intention of "T" in (b) which, consequently, specify a different alternative.

Def. IV - 3: Similar:

"A is similar to B":

if 1. A and B are terms, things, properties, relations, or anything of any kind or kinds.

2. A and B are in some respect or respects identical.

3. A and B and the identical respect or respects are not numerically identical.

Def. IV - 4: Proportional Similarity:

"ATx and BTy are proportionally similar":

if 1. A and B are things, x and y are properties, actions, etc.

2. there is a term "T" which signifies the two instances of relation T.

3. ATx and BTy are proportions: i.e., A is related to x by T and B is related to y by T.

4. "T" when used in the statement "ATx is proportionally similar to BTy" is not univocal.

5. T in ATx and in BTy is not numerically identical.

6. T in ATx and T in BTy are similar.

Def. IV - 5: Analogy of Proper Proportionality:

"Term 'T' is used analogously by proper proportionality in (a) and (b)":

if 1. "T" occurs as predicate in two or more sentences of the form (a) "A is (or has) T," and (b) "B is (or has) T," where "B" and "A" denote individual things A and B.

2. "T" signifies a relation T which holds between x (where x is a property, action, event, relation, etc.) and A; and between y (property, action, relation, etc.) and B.

3. ATx and BTy are proportionally similar.

Def. IV - 6: Similarity of Relations:

"Relation R is similar to relation R¹":

if 1. both are relations.

2. they have common formal properties with respect to either a formal or merely linguistic set of axioms, the latter not being explicitly formulated in ordinary language.

Def. IV - 7: Analogy of Improper Proportionality:

"Term 'T' is analogous by improper proportionality in (a) and (b)":

if A) alternative 1:

1. "T" is used as a predicate in a sentence (a) of the form "F is T."

2. the denotation of "T" is a class of objects Z having as members individuals w, y, z, according to the ordinary rule for its employment.

3. F is not a member of Z.

4. between F and the members of Z there is a proportional similarity with respect to relations R and R^1 and the characteristic behavior or other properties of F and the members of Z.

5. "T" is used as a predicate of F to call attention to the similar relations of F and the elements of Z.

6. "T" is equivocal with respect to its occurrence in (a) and in sentences where it denotes members of Z.

B) alternative 2:

1. "T" is used as predicate in two indicative sentences of the form (a) "x is T" and (b) "y is T," where "x" and "y" denote x and y, individual things.

2. term "T" is used as predicate of "x" with respect to a language rule R which determines the intention of "T" and x has the property signified by "T."

3. "T" cannot be used as predicate of "y" because y does not have the property signified by "T."

4. in terms of R, sentence (b) is incorrect.

5. "T" is equivocal with respect to (a) and (b).

6. there is a similarity between a relation of x to its characteristics and the relation of y to its characteristics.

7. "T" is used of y to call attention to the similarity.

5. In the sections of this essay where I summarize two of the exhibition analyses by which Aquinas developed the language rules of Analogy of Attribution, *Def. III* - 1, and Proper Proportionality, *Def. IV* - 5, there is a basic presumption that the cases of ordinary language which are taken for examination are in fact cases of *informative* language. And the rules which result are supposed to be recipes by which St. Thomas can construct other parallel uses of language which will also be informative. These statements generated according to these rules will be applicable in arguments about God and in metaphysical contexts without further justification as to their meaningfulness, provided that St. Thomas' analysis of ordinary language has in fact produced the rules according to which the ordinary language employment of certain terms is rendered meaningful.

6. There is no direct argument for any philosophical point in

what follows. But I suggest that the analogy theory herein discussed does offer evidence for the following two claims:

a) If one regards talk of God as informative discourse (that is, the discourse of literal assertion) and employs the discourse of Christian tradition (the Creeds, etc.) one may appeal to an analogy theory something like that herein explained to account for the cognitive meaningfulness of such discourse.

b) If one wishes to maintain that there are any exclusive categories (in Aristotle's sense) of things in the world and at the same time supposes that there can be any universally true metaphysical statements, he presupposes a meaning-theory fundamentally similar to the proportionality theory of St. Thomas.

ANALOGY OF ATTRIBUTION

The first of the analogy rules is called the rule of "attribution." We are concerned here with sets of two statements of the form a) "F is T" and b) "G is T." We shall take two examples of such pairs of statements:
(1) a) Fido is healthy.
    b) Fido's bark is healthy.
(2) a) John is brilliant.
    b) John's work is brilliant.
The first of these pairs is roughly the example used by St. Thomas. The other is contributed to push his analysis a little further than he did in his own desultory discussions of attribution. It might be useful to keep in mind that I am following St. Thomas' line of thought up to *Def. III* - 1 and its corollaries.

In his analysis of attribution, St. Thomas wishes to discuss the cases where a term occurs as the predicate of two statements with different subjects, only *one* of which subjects, by the usual rules governing the employment of predicate terms to signify properties of the subject, could have the property signified by the predicate term.

It is easy to see what Aquinas means from his example.[7] Suppose we have two statements: (a) "The dog is healthy" and (b) "His bark is healthy." It is clear from conventional linguistic practice that both employments of the term are informative and proper in ordinary discourse. St. Thomas believed the property of "being healthy" to be compatible only with animals and plants as such, and he concludes rightly that at least part of what is signified by the term "healthy" in both these cases is numerically the same: the one state of affairs of the whole dog.[8] In other words, the term "healthy" in sentence (b) does not signify some property numerically *different* from what "healthy" signifies in sentence (a); it does not signify a numerically *different instance* of health. Presuming that the "bark" in (b) belongs to the dog in (a), then the health in (b) is one and the same as the health in (a).

He says that the predicates of some sentences signify properties which *inhere* in what is denoted by the grammatical subject, e.g., sentence (a); and the predicates in *other* sentences, like (b), do not signify properties all of which *inhere* in the subject of that sentence, but rather partially specify that the subject of that sentence is related to the subject of that other sentence in which the same predicate does signify a property *inherent* in the subject. (I am using "subject" to stand for "what is *denoted* by the grammatical subject.") The predicate term in (b) *partially* specifies the relation of the secondary subject of (b) to the primary subject because the predicate term in such a sentence usually only tells us which of the properties of the primary subject we should look to if we wish to figure out the relation of the secondary subject to the primary subject.[9] The other conditions which I shall cite for analogy of attribution will further specify the *kinds* of relations that may obtain between primary and secondary subjects. In any given use of ordinary language, reflection is expected to disclose the particular kind of relation which obtains. But when constructing philosophical instances of analogy of attribution, the philosopher will have to show the two subjects to be related in one or the other of the ways known from the forthcoming ordinary language exhibition to justify such uses of terms.

Before discussing the kinds of relations which are found to obtain in ordinary language instances, and before investigating the possibility and usefulness of philosophical constructions, it may be helpful to consider the following question. Given the sentences (a) and (b), above, and given that part of what is signified by "healthy" in (b) is numerically the same as that property signified by "healthy" in (a), and given further that there is only one health which is inherent in the dog, does sentence (b) say anything about the dog's *bark* or not? That is, sentences in general purport to say something about what the subject denotes (they do *not* say what the subject denotes, but only something about what the subject denotes). If "healthy" signifies a property of the dog, one might conclude that then the sentence (b) says nothing about the *bark*. However, Aquinas notes that if (b) is to function as sentences usually do, it will in fact say something about the dog's bark. St. Thomas' move was to say: "The sentence (b) says the dog's bark is related to the dog's health in a certain one of the specified kinds of ways in which a predicate of the 'dog' can be used of its 'bark' or of 'medicine'." This move is later found to be equivalent to saying: "Sentence (b) is a short-hand for the statement: 'The dog's bark is a sign that the dog is healthy.'" What is *said* is that the bark performs a signifying service with respect to the presence of an inhering property "health" in the dog. In summary, this analysis, so far, proposes that the statement (b) tells us *that* and *how* the subject either actually or potentially functions (i.e., is related) with respect to a certain property belonging to another subject. Most of the traditional Thomists, Cajetan and John of St. Thomas and many neo-Thomists, have expressly interpreted the "designation" of the analogous term with respect to the secondary subject (secondary analogate) to be merely "extrinsic," merely designating accidental (fortuitous, even though constant) relations.[10] However, these writers cautiously add that this does not *exclude* the "presence of the analogous property in the secondary analogates, although imperfectly." What they could mean by this is obscure and the fact that they place their emphasis on the extrinsic relations which they say are "designated" is the point I wish to emphasize. As far as I can see, what they are saying is exactly the analysis given above: that the sentence (b) tells us *that* and *how* the secondary subject either actually or potentially functions with respect to a certain property (signified by the predicate term) belonging to the primary subject in (a). For the authors mentioned, then, the initial conditions for an analogy of attribution are of two kinds: (1) The term is used at least once (in the two sentences under consideration) to signify a property inherent in a subject. (2) The term is used on other occasions of subjects which do not actually possess the property but are related in specified ways to the things which do have the property.

Many interpreters have claimed that the sentence containing the secondary use of an analogous term of this kind does not say anything about the nature or properties of its subject in itself, but only states facts about the relation of the subject to the primary subject with respect to the property signified by the analogous term. Contrary to this commonly accepted interpretation, I shall attempt to show that these secondary sentences *do* say something about the nature of the subject, even though it be very little and indirectly. A person who says "That's a healthy bark your dog's got" is saying something about the dog, to be sure, but he is also saying something about the bark.[11] And when I tell you "This food is healthful," I am not *only* telling you something about the *relation* of the food to your health; I am telling you something about the food, which is additional to its relation as cause of health. It is true that you would not know very much about the food if you did not know what properties food would have to have in order to be healthful. But if you did, it would be legitimate for you to conclude that this food has those properties (or at least that I believed it had these properties); and thus I would have told you something about the food.

Another example: When we say that a student's work is brilliant, we are not only saying something about the fact that this work is a sign of the brilliance of the student who wrote it, we are saying something about the work itself. Even though the term "brilliant" appears to be applied primarily to students who can and habitually do produce work of a given quality, saying "The work is brilliant" tells a person who has some information about the standards for being called "brilliant" and the kind of work brilliant people produce, something about the work produced.

However, this brings up a further problem. For the sake of an example, I assumed that the *primary* sense of "brilliant" was the instance of the term signifying the intellectual prowess and creativity of the student and that the secondary sense has its application to the work produced. Actually, in re-examining certain terms functioning analogously it is sometimes difficult to say which is the primary instance of the term, although it is clear that the two instances are different but related.

Aquinas, preparing for philosophical employment of analogy, offers a rule for deciding which instance is primary. He distinguishes between the order of things and the order of knowledge. In effect, he says that the use of the term which is supposed by the other uses of the same term is the primary one, the one which *must be known first* in order to use the term of the other cases.[12] Thus, it seems that to be correct in calling a student "brilliant" we must have evidence of the high quality of his work, and since the potentiality of producing high quality work is what is meant by "brilliant" when applied to the student, just the opposite of my previous assumption is the case: the primary sense of the term on Aquinas' rule is to signify "high quality work" although the more frequent use of the term may be to signify a person's capacity for producing such work.

Aquinas points out that the order of things may be different from the order of knowledge. There can be times when the order of things is neither the same as the order of knowledge nor as the order of applying the terms which follows it. Our example of "brilliant" is a case in point. As a matter of fact, the student must have certain powers before he can produce high quality work; this is a causal and logical priority. But we do not *know* his powers until he has produced some high quality work; this is a psychological priority. Hence, we *describe* his powers in terms of the quality of his work, although he works in terms of his powers.

It is this fact which Aquinas cites as part of one of the arguments to show that we can "name" God from His effects, because even though we *know* God from His effects, the properties of the effects are derived from the powers of God. St. Thomas says:

Sometimes, indeed, that which is prior in nature is secondary regarding knowledge, and then among the analogues there is not the same order both regarding the things and the order of the term: thus the power of healing which is in medicines is naturally prior to the health which is in the animal, as cause to effect; *but because we know that power through its effect, we also name it from its effect.* And thus it happens that "healthful" is prior in order of nature, but the animal is called "healthy" with priority in the order of naming.[13]

So far, the exposition of analogy of attribution has shown Aquinas to be exhibiting the following points about the function of certain words in ordinary language which are called "analogous by attribution":

1. The "analogy of attribution" is concerned with the comparative functions of two instances of the same term occurring as predicate in two sentences, one primary, the other secondary.

2. A term analogous in this way is used in at least one instance in a sentence as predicate where all the properties it signifies do not belong to the subject, but where it signifies a relation of that subject to another subject possessing the property normally signified by the term and related *via* that property.

3. These predicate terms always have a primary use where in some indicative sentence they signify a property inherent in the subject and have this property as their *definitive* property.

4. Irrespective of the fact that these secondary sentences do not signify a specific property of the entity denoted by the subject, they do give information about the properties of the subject.

5. The property signified by an analogous term in its primary and secondary occurrences is numerically one. That is, there is only one property of "health" which belongs to the dog, and the secondary sentence does *not* say it belongs to the bark.

The several other points so far made regarding (1) the kind of analysis Aquinas was doing, (2) the uses to which he would put the analysis, (3) the fact that the Thomists do not make much use of analogy of attribution in natural theology, and (4) the fact that there is a rule for deciding which of the terms, in doubtful cases, will be considered the primary one, are all points necessary in the exposition; however, they are not part of the special information necessary for the analysis which will be developed.

Let us consider the other properties of analogy of attribution.
6. "The primary analogate is put into the definition of the others with respect to the analogous name."[14] St. Thomas says:

> It is necessary in all cases where terms are used analogously of several things, that they are all used with respect to one; and thus, that one use must be contained in the definition of all. And since the notion which the term signifies is its definition, as is said in the *Fourth Book of the Metaphysics*, it is necessary that that term be used primarily of that which is supposed in the definition of the others, and secondarily of the others, in the order by which they approach more or less to the primary term: thus "healthy" which is used of "animal" is part of the definition of "healthy" which is used of "medicine," which is called healthy in as much as it causes health in the animal; and of the definition of "healthy" which is used of "urine," which is called "healthy" in as much as it is a sign of the health of the animal.[15]

Suppose we take "healthy" as used in the sentence (a) "My dog is healthy" to be defined as follows: "X is healthy" equals by definition: "X has a certain organic state characterized by properties a, b, c, ...n." We are not concerned that the assertion "X is healthy" is defeasible even though all the properties are present. By hypothesis, let us suppose it can be and is defined by a finite list of properties and degrees of properties. If we are going to define the term "healthy" in the following sentences, we shall have to appeal to the definitions already given of "healthy" in the sentence (a) above.

(b) "My dog's bark is healthy."

(c) "His pills and dog-food are healthy."

Sentence (b) can only mean something like this: "My dog's bark has those qualities which are signs to me that the dog is 'healthy,' that is, has the organic state characterized by a, b, c, ...n." Hence, I take it that Aquinas' point is clear: In all cases where a term is used as a predicate to attribute a relation to a subject with respect to a property possessed by a different subject, and where the term used normally signifies that property of the other subject, the

definition of the term in its primary sense is part of the definition
of the term in its secondary sense.[16]

Aquinas does not try to rule out the possibility that two different
people might disagree about which is the primary sense of the
analogous term, nor does he deny that they might even disagree
about when to use the term because of that. Suppose that someone
has been reared hearing the word "healthy" applied only when a
dog's or man's voice was loud and clear. The term "healthy" might
thus be associated with the meaning of "loud and clear voice."
When I say to him that the dog or man is healthy, he interprets
this to mean "capable of a loud and clear vocal utterance." Thus
his conception of the significance of both sentences (a) and (b) is
different from mine. Another person might learn that the term
"healthy" usually follows another set of rules which also reverse the
relative priority of the "senses" of the analogous term. But neither
event, his learning to apply the word by a different convention,
nor his reversing the convention, would be an exception to
the rule presupposed by Aquinas, which could be formulated
thus:

> In any case where a term is neither univocal nor totally equivocal
> but occurs in several instances as predicate of indicative sentences,
> the meaning it has in at least one instance (supposing that we have at
> hand at least one each of every kind of instance in which the word
> can be used according to the conventional rules for its employment)
> must be entirely included in the meaning it has in every other
> instance.

In fact, on the definitions given of univocity and total equivocity,
the rule is a tautology. Cajetan,[17] Pénido,[18] Aquinas,[19] and Aristotle[20] (at least as Cajetan interprets him) all seem to imply that
the secondary analogate can only be related to the primary analogate as efficient, final, material, or exemplary cause (which they
extend to equal: sign and symptom). When we say that a man is
charitable, Cajetan would say we are showing that he is disposi-
tionally (at least) the efficient cause of charitable acts; when we
say a given kind of action is charitable, we are saying that its

performance is usually a sign of a charitable act. It functions as a
sign because it is usually an effect of charity. Thus Aquinas' rule
for analogy of attribution contains a provision that the secondary
uses of the term will signify a causal relation of their subject to the
normal subject of the property. By this he means that the subject
of the secondary sentence must denote something which is either
cause or effect (in the wide, Aristotelian sense of the four causes)
of the property signified by the primary occurrence of the term,
as belonging to the primary subject.

7. Hence, this is the seventh characteristic: The secondary
analogate in its definition, in addition to the definitions of the
term in its primary instance, will also contain a phrase specifying
a causal relation to the signification of the primary term.

8. The eighth characteristic of this kind of analogy is that the
"term does not have one definite meaning common to all its
partial modes."[21] There is nothing about the term itself as it
occurs in various sentences which tells us that it is not being used
"denominatively," to signify its definitive property as inherent in
the subject; nor is there anything about the form of sentences
which tells us that the term is not being used to signify its definitive
property of the subject. When we formulate (1) "The dog is healthy"
and (2) "The bark is healthy," they are both of the same form: X is
F and Y is F. That the term "F" has not the same meaning in both
sentences is only known from the "logical rules of ordinary language."[22] Sometimes we are not sure whether a term indicates only
a property of its subject or a relation to a property of another
subject, as was shown by the example of "brilliant" when applied
to the student and his work. However, Cajetan's point is clear
enough. The term cannot possibly have exactly the same meaning
in all its instances if we include as part of its *meaning* in
some instances the *relationship* of the definitive property to the
subject.

Some Scotists have said that what is analogous is not the property term but the copula. "The dog *is* healthy" means: The dog
has the property "healthy"; "The bark *is* healthy" means: The
bark is related to the health of the dog. But Aquinas' supposition
seems to be recommended by its simplicity and by the fact that

relevant questions and answers about the dog's bark being healthy would indicate that in ordinary discourse the speaker realizes he doesn't mean by "healthy" exactly the same thing in both cases.

The analysis which St. Thomas suggests for the statement "Term 'T' is analogous by attribution in (a) and (b)" is as follows:

Def. III-1: Analogy of Attribution:

"Term 'T' is analogous by attribution in (a) and (b)":
if 1. "T" occurs as predicate in two or more indicative sentences: (a) "F is T" and (b) "G is T."

2. "T" in (a) signifies a property T of F.

3. "T" in (b) signifies a relation of G to F where G is either a cause of F's having property T or is in some respect an effect or affected causally by F's having property T.

The following propositions are implied by the definition and are corollaries:

1. There is only one (numerically) instance of the property T of "T" in (a) and it belongs to subject F.

2. The term "T" in sentence (b) cannot be defined unless the entire definition of the term "T" in sentence (a) is made part of its definition; and still the definition will not be complete, because part of the intention must be a specification of the causal relation of G to F.

3. The term "T" does not have the same intention in both of its instances in (a) and (b): i.e., the term "T" is not formally univocal, *Def. I*-12; nor is it totally equivocal.

Terms are said to be analogous by attribution not because they attribute a property to subjects which logically cannot have that property, but because the sentences in which they are used in their secondary meanings ascribe a causal relation of their subjects to the thing having that property, and at the same time imply that the subject of the secondary sentence has whatever properties, relations, and dispositions are necessary in order to be related in that way to the subject of the primary analogate (the term used in its primary sense).

ANALOGY OF PROPER PROPORTIONALITY

In looking at the language analysis by which this rule for Analogy of Proper Proportionality is generated, we are concerned with pairs of statements of the following forms:

1. a) "A is (or has) T."
   b) "B is (or has) T."

2. a) "ATx"
   b) "BTy"

And the supposition is that statements of the first form which fit the rule we are developing (*Def. IV*-5) are reducible in principle to statements of the second form. This supposition is not an integral part of the theory; and it seems to have independent justification. Examples of each form are:

1. a) Fido has knowledge of his dog house.
   b) Plato has knowledge of philosophy.
   or
   a) Fido is the cause of his barking.
   b) Plato is the cause of his actions.

2. a) Fido knows his dog house.
   b) Plato knows philosophy.
   or
   a) Fido caused the barking.
   b) Plato caused the murderous shot.

1. Let us take it as given, by inspection of the examples, that the *predicates* "knows" and "causes" *are not univocal in* (*a*) *and* (*b*) *of each set*. This is *the first characteristic* of the language rule. Later paragraphs will justify this presumption, if it should be in doubt here.

2. *The second characteristic* is that there are at least two instances of the property signified by "T."

On this condition rests the first and most important difference between Analogy of Proportionality and Attribution. In the latter case, there is numerically only one instance of the definitive property signified by both instances of the analogous term, whereas in this case there must be one instance of the property for each instance of the term as predicate of a sentence with a different subject.

A problem raised by this requirement can be phrased thus: if the term is equivocal, then the intention (or connotation) of the term must differ in its various instances; i.e., a sentence affirming and denying a term "T" of the same subject would be contradictory if the intention of the term was identical in each instance; and the term would not be equivocal by *Def. I*-13. If the intention of the term differs, then a criterion must be given of how far the intention of the term can vary in two instances of the term before a different property is signified. For if different properties are signified by a term in two of its instances, then the second condition of the analogy of proper proportionality is either unsatisfied or ambiguous. The second condition states, briefly, that the two things denoted by the term "T" must have the property signified by "T" and that the first condition must still be preserved: that the term is equivocal. On the assumption that "T" is equivocal, one might say, "Yes, the things denoted do have the property signified in each case, but the properties are not the same." And if "Term 'T' in its instances signifies the same property" equals by definition "Term 'T' in its instances has the same intention," then either the term is univocal or the second condition is unsatisfiable. Hence, we must demand some analysis from St. Thomas which will allow a term to be univocal in signification (*Def. I*-12-a) while being equivocal in not conforming to the rule for univocity in intention (*Def. I*-12-b).

St. Thomas claims to offer such an analysis; for he held the theory that the intention (*intentio*) of a term specifies not only the kind of property signified but the *way* the property is signified.[23] And hence, "signification" has two senses: the *res significata* and the *modus significandi*. It was part of his theory that the linguistic rules which govern the use of a term, and thereby determine its intention, make into elements of the intention of a term those terms which specify the *modus significandi* (which I shall explain shortly). To our objection that when we define a term we cite the terms characteristic of its intention and we never find a term indicating the mode of signification, Aquinas would reply that most of our predicates signify in the *same* mode of signification, and that for ordinary purposes it is not necessary to make such a distinction. Furthermore, it is only a logical technique for one to distinguish between what is signified and how it is signified, because in every actual instance of discourse about the world of experience the mode of signification corresponds to the *mode of existence* which the property has,[24] and, consequently, is implicit in the rule which governs the employment of a term. In the *Commentary on the First Book of Sentences*, Aquinas says:

Although every perfection which belongs to creatures is taken by exemplary causality from God, as from a principle having unified in itself all perfections, no creature can receive that perfection according to the same mode by which it is in God. So, the creature fails to be a perfect representation of the exemplar because of the different mode in which the perfections are received. And because of that (difference in the mode of receiving) there is a scale, as it were, among creatures according to which some creatures receive from God more and higher perfections and participate in His perfections more fully. And because of this there are two aspects of the terms to consider: the thing [*rem* which equals "what *kind* of thing"] signified and the mode of being signified. Therefore we must consider that when we, who know God only from creatures, employ a term, we always fall short of a representation of God with respect to the "mode of being signified": because the term signifies the divine perfections through the mode by which they are participated in by creatures.

If, however, we consider *what* is signified by the term, what the term is used to signify, we find that some terms are used primarily to signify the perfections exemplified in God alone, not being concerned with any mode in their signification; and that some terms are said to signify a perfection received according to a given mode of participation; for example, all knowing is an imitation of divine knowing, and all knowledge of divine knowledge. Therefore, the term "sense" is used to signify knowing through that mode by which knowledge is materially received through the power of the conjoined organ. But the term "knowledge" does not signify a particular mode of participating in its principal signification. Hence, it must be said that all those terms which are used to signify a perfection absolutely are properly used of God, and primarily are used of Him with respect to what is signified, even though not with respect to the mode of signification, such as "wisdom," "goodness," "essence," and others of this type.[25]

I have used this passage to illustrate two things: (1) that Aquinas understands a difference between what is signified (the kind of property signified) and what kinds of conditions are supposed as surrounding what is signified, even though both are signified simultaneously by any term given its use in a determinate context; and (2) that Aquinas has two different uses of the phrase "*modus significandi*" which function in entirely different ways. First, there is the sense in which "knowledge" as used of a man and of a dog is understood to be different, not in what is meant by "knowledge," but in what *kind* of knowledge is possible. Since "knowing" is a property which admits of degrees according to the ability of the person, and of kinds according to the nature of the thing which knows, in the two sentences (a) "Fido knows his dog house" and (b) "Plato knows philosophy," the term "knows" is different not as to *what* is signified but as to which *kind* of knowledge is signified. To avoid possible confusion, I point out that St. Thomas did not believe that sentence (a) is an anthropomorphic or metaphorical description of the dog's actions. He merely claimed that words like "knowing," "wise," "good" are vague with respect to classes of activity included in the signification of the term. He says the intention of "knows" is proportionally the same in sentence (a) and (b), but the mode in which the property is possessed makes entirely different the kinds of action which can be performed.

This allows the Thomist to construct a hierarchy of "powers" or "perfections" on the Neoplatonic assumption that (1) being a man is better than being an animal and an animal better than a plant, etc.; and (2) any other beings which know or will in a simpler (less complex), freer way and act more accurately to satisfy their desires are higher on the scale of perfection in beings. Those properties which belong to several levels of the hierarchy[26] and which are named by a single term are said to be named by an analogous term. Thus in Thomist terms the foundation of this kind of analogy is the unequal and different-in-kind participation of different natures in the same property according to differing modes of being determined by their natures.[27]

Divine knowing, human knowing, and animal knowing are all "knowing," but one is not the other; yet the term "knowing" (apart from any particular sentence) is neutral with respect to the three modes of knowing. An obvious objection is this: if the term "knowing" is neutral with respect to the three various modes, then why is the term not univocal? St. Thomas' answer is that terms are univocal or equivocal by comparison of their use in sentences, and "knowing" as used in a sentence with "dog" for a subject and in another sentence with "man" for a subject is not univocal, even though he would admit we may form a meta-language term "knowing" which is neutral with respect to all object-language senses of "know"; but then the meta-language sense of knowing will not be univocal with *any* object-language sense.

In considering this example, we must remember that St. Thomas' conception of knowing is considerably different from contemporary notions. He assumes (1) that the man is more than quantitatively different from the dog; he is *essentially* different; (2) the *possessio formae alterius ut alterius*, which constitutes knowing, is fundamentally known as a human activity involving abstraction and it is the mode of "abstraction" which is "cancelled out" as inapplicable when "knowing" is used in sentences about animals.

If, in attempting to criticize the Thomist claim that there is a foundation for the analogy of the term "knowing" in the unequal and disparate participations of things in the powers of knowing, we were to suggest that we could formulate three *different* concepts of knowing and terms for each, one for humans, animals, and God, St. Thomas would reply that the properties signified would have in common something which is the basis for an analogous term. (It is here that analogy becomes a theory about things, or at least supposes one.) For example, Aquinas could formulate a vague concept which would include the three concepts of knowing, as I said. To do this, let us accept Aquinas' technical and admittedly recondite partial definition of "knowing" as the *possessio formae alterius ut alterius*, "the possession of the form of another as belonging to another." For St. Thomas, however, this is not a

complete definition, for he wishes to add the phrase: "according to
one's natural mode of possession." So, "knowing" is "the possession
of the form of another as belonging to another according to one's
natural mode of possession." This concept is neutral with respect
to the concepts of knowing. But it is not on the same level as the
other three notions. It is a meta-language notion which includes
the other three and which signifies all three equally and alternatively. In the sentences (a) "Sense knowing is the possession of the
form of another as belonging to another according to one's natural
mode of possession" and "Divine knowing is the possession etc.,"
the phrase "possession of the form etc." serves as a univocal term.
It is a predicate in sentences about predicates of sentences used
earlier as examples; hence, it is a predicate in meta-language
sentences. But the fact that we can form a term in a meta-language
whose intention will include the intentions of terms occurring in
object-language statements and which are analogous, does not
make the analogous terms univocal. In fact, the only reason our
constructed term can include the intentions of the analogous terms
is that we *constructed* it to signify the intentions of the analogous
terms; and the only time it actually includes the intentions of the
other terms is when it occurs in a meta-language sentence.

From this discussion, it should be clear why St. Thomas could
say, "What is 'knowing' for a man is not what is 'knowing' for a
dog, although both are properly called 'knowing.' " [28] There are
some instances of terms used as predicates where they signify not
only what property is possessed but *what kind of possession* the
property is had by.

Moreover, the language rules which govern the employment of
terms like "knowing" make the intention of the term (which has a
section of its intention that, if imagined in C. I. Lewis' terms, *Def.
I*-12, is a conjunction of other terms) contain some *conjoined dis-
junctions* of terms. When a term like "knows" is used in a given sentence (b), a context is established which cancels out the inapplicable elements of the intention of "knows" in (a), thus making the
intention fixed in the sentence as a conjunction of terms. Aquinas
would say that the elements cancelled out are the inapplicable
modes of possession; i.e., from the intention of "knowing" in the

sentence "Fido knows his dog house" there are cancelled out of the intention any terms like "abstractly," "by deduction," "by induction," etc.[29]

The second sense of the phrase "*modus significandi*" refers to elements of the intention of a term which are derived from the *way we learn the term*.[30] For, Aquinas says, many people do not understand the difference between the way a dog knows and the way a human knows (in fact, it is almost impossible to specify), chiefly because we apply "knowing" to dogs, having recognized the similarity of their actions to ours. Hence, for these people, in the connotation of the term "knowing" there are elements which are appropriate only to humans; and most times, even when they are consciously ruled out when the term is used in sentences about animals, they are not replaced by anything definite.[31] That is, within the intention of the term applied to animals there is no term which specifies *how* the dog knows. This point is of considerable importance for Aquinas in his discussion of language about God. If the intentions of terms have as elements terms which express the mode by which the property signified by the term is possessed, and if all the modes of possession are determined by the nature of the thing which has the property, then the terms of our experience-language, if applied directly to God, would signify a way of having the property which is no more compatible with the nature of God than the elements of the intention of "knowing" which make it signify "knowing as humans know" would be compatible with the nature of the dog.

But if the sentence in which the term is used establishes for a person who understands the nature of the subject the context which "rules in" or "rules out" certain elements of the intention of a term, then some elements will not be common to the intention of the term "knows" in the sentences (a) "God knows" and (b) "A man knows." And St. Thomas' rule is: the nature of the thing denoted by the logical subject determines the modal elements of the intention of predicates which are applied to the subject.

This analysis has supplied the elements of Aquinas' answer to the problem proposed earlier: namely, if the analogous term signifies two different properties, it should be called "equivocal";

but Aquinas' second condition for analogy of proper proportionality is that the two things must have the property signified by the analogous term. Yet if the term signifies two instances of the same property, then there seems to be no reason why it should be called "equivocal," for it will be univocal on our definition of univocity *I*-12-a and not univocal on *Def. I*-12-b. However, in terms of *Def. I*-11: *Intention*, Aquinas would thus say that, in brief, the term is used univocally if it has the same intention in each instance, and the intention in two instances is the same if all elements of the intention in one instance are common to the intention of the term in the other. But he holds that the "mode of signification" is part of the intention of the term (wherever a mode of *possession* is relevant). Thus, if the "mode of signifying" is different, the intention of the term is different even though the property signified be the same; and hence the term is equivocal (*Def. I*-13). And, he would argue, there are cases where a term is univocal in signification but equivocal in intention, just because there are *modes* of signification.

Although I have indicated that St. Thomas does not believe it possible to separate, more than logically and artificially, the *res significata* from the *modus significandi*, the example of "knowing" is some help in understanding what he means. The *res significata* is what is common to all activities which we can call "knowing." But what we call "knowing" admits of kinds and of degrees. There is no instance of knowing which is not one kind or another, and both the kind, "sense" or "abstract," and the metaphysical mode, "finite" or "infinite," are part of the meaning of "knowing" in any synthetic statement in which it occurs. This is what is meant by *modus significandi*.

St. Thomas' two statements that the *modus significandi* differs and that the *res significata* is the same when some terms are applied to God can be defined as follows:

Def. IV - 1: Sameness of Res Significata:

"The *res significata* of 'T' is the same":

if 1. There are given at least two sentences (a) and (b) in which there is respectively a predicate term "T."

2. "T" in (a) and "T" in (b) are instances of the same term.

3. "T" signifies property T of X in (a) and T of Y in (b).

4. All the terms of the intention of "T" in (a) which specify the class of things to which property T belongs, occur in the intention of "T" in (b).

Def. IV - 2: Difference of Modus Significandi:
"The *modus significandi* of 'T' is different":
   if 1, 2, 3, and 4 of *Def. IV* - 1 hold.

5. For any thing Z, having the property T implies that Z can perform either actions (A) 1, 2, 3, - n; or (B) 2, 3, 4, - n and not 1; or (C) 3, 4, - n and not 1 and 2; or......; or n.....

6. The intention of "T" in sentence (a) and in (b) is determined by the intention of the subject term "X" or "Y" in such a way that only one of the alternative groups of actions is signified.

7. The terms of the intention of "T" in (a) which specify which of the alternates (A), (B), or (C) is performed, are not the same as the terms in the intention of "T" in (b) which, consequently, specify a different alternative.

Thus, St. Thomas could hold that a term which differs in *modus significandi* but is the same in *res significata* is equivocal, even though all things denoted by the term will have the same property signified. That there is at least one such term is evident from the example given: "knowing," provided we accept at least provisionally Aquinas' analysis of the nature of knowing.

One would be inclined to seek an easy formulation of the analogy of proper proportionality in terms of the points so far explained by saying that terms are analogous by proper proportionality if they differ in their respective instances in *modus significandi* but not with respect to *res significata*. However, this is *not* what Aquinas meant by analogy of proper proportionality. *This is merely the reason why certain terms cannot be used of God and creatures univocally and it is St. Thomas' explanation of how a term can in two instances signify the same property and yet be equivocal.* St. Thomas has merely explained how the first and second conditions of this analogy can be rendered compatible. He has yet to exhibit the other conditions of this analogy.

3. *The third characteristic* of terms analogous by proportionality is that there must be a proportional similarity between what is denoted by "T" in (a) and what is denoted by "T" in (b).

I shall briefly explain what Aquinas meant by *similarity*, secondly what he meant by *proportion*, and thirdly, what he meant by *proportional similarity*.

a) *Similarity*: Aquinas has four senses of "similarity"; since the explanation of these notions is not possible under the circumstances of this essay, let us, instead, take a very general definition of "similarity" as being sufficient for our purposes. "Two things are similar if they are in some respect or respects identical but never numerically identical." The "respect or respects" can be and must be specified, says Thomas, wherever a factual proposition "This A is similar to that B" is analyzed. This very general definition is what I have given as *Def. IV - 3*.

b) *Proportion*: For Aquinas the term "proportion" (not *proportionality*, now) is a synonym of "relation." And a proportion obtains between A and X where a *relation* obtains between A and X. *Note:* I stipulate that "property" is a one place predicate in object-language sentences; "relation" is a two or more place predicate.

c) *Proportionality*: When Aquinas says: "A proportionality holds between A and B," he means: There is a *similarity in the proportions* (or relations) of A and B. That is, a relation R obtains between A and some property, thing or event, K, and a relation R^1 obtains between B and some property, thing or event, Y, and R and R^1 are similar.

Hence, a proportional similarity obtains between any two things, A and B, which have similar relations to some property, event, or thing. So, Aquinas would say that a proportional similarity obtains between *Plato* and *Fido* because the relations signified by "knowing" which obtain between Fido and his dog house and Plato and his philosophy are similar (that is, in its two instances the relation signified by the term "knows" has some common properties or relations).

Since the term "knows" denotes both Fido and Plato, St. Thomas has formulated his third characteristic of the analogy as follows:

there must be a proportional similarity between what is denoted by "T" in (a) and "T" in (b).

4. Turning now to *Definitions IV - 4, Proportional Similarity*, and *IV - 5, Analogy of Proper Proportionality*, we observe that the latter is formulated in terms of the former. A term is analogous by proper proportionality if it signifies in both its instances relations of the respective subjects and if the subjects, in regard to these relations, are proportionally similar.

And the subjects are proportionally similar if there exist entities, relations, properties or events such that ATx and BTy are true or could be true, and term "T" used to refer to the two instances of T would not be univocal, and the relations T of ATx and BTy are similar.

5. *Similarity of Relations*. For the analogy of proportionality rule to be fully established, it must be possible to apply the definition of *proportional similarity* to things and to decide whether or not two things are *in fact* proportionally similar. But to do this, we need a criterion for *similarity of relations*. That is, it is a necessary condition of this analogy that the things denoted by the predicate be proportionally similar and it is a necessary condition of proportional similarity that the *relations* of the things be similar. Hence to apply the rule confidently in crucial cases we should need a criterion of similarity of relations.

Now, St. Thomas had not the slightest doubt that with regard to most ordinary language uses of terms like "knows," "exists," etc., in senses which fulfill this rule of analogy (like the two paradigm sentences: (a) "Plato knows philosophy" and (b) "Fido knows his dog house"), the reason the term was extended to its analogical use about dogs by human convention in the first place was that men had *recognized* the similarity in the relations. And later, in talking about God, Aquinas points out that if one can establish that God has certain relations to the world (from empirical premises) then it will follow from the general form of language that the relations are similar to relations of our experience.

Taking account of what Bochenski has proposed[32] and of what Aquinas seems to have had in mind, I suggest the following definition (*IV - 6*) of Similarity of Relations:

Def. IV - 6: Similarity of Relations:
"Relation R is similar to relation R¹":
if 1. Both are relations.
2. They have common formal properties with respect to either a formal or merely linguistic set of axioms, the latter not being explicitly formulated in ordinary language, or, they have a common property.

The difficulties with this criterion of similarity are obvious; Bochenski's proposed criterion says relations are similar if they have common formal properties, i.e., common syntactical and semantical properties. This is obviously not a thought which St. Thomas might have had. Furthermore, while this offers some hope for a more careful development of the analogy theory, it means that a great deal of analysis would have to be done to see if the relations attributed to God do have common properties with relations in the world of experience. Such a criterion supposes a more extensive formalized language than seems practicable. The second alternative, the proposal that the relations have common properties with respect to linguistic axioms which are presupposed by implicit language rules governing the employment of the analogous term, is very similar to St. Thomas' assumption that if the relations are sufficiently similar we will recognize that fact and use the same term to signify the two relations. I am not really sure what such language rules would be like.

This deficiency in the analogy theory is serious, because it is so difficult to imagine a set of rules under which the necessary conditions for analogy of proper proportionality (that the relations be similar) could be determined to have been fulfilled. Yet, it would be an *ad ignorantiam* error to argue that no such criterion is possible. However, let us go on to see how this theory is applied to language about God. For I think it will be found that the difficulty I have just mentioned is not so prominent when the rule is used in practice, although it is clear that a fully accurate and adequate analogy theory will have to contain a practicable criterion of similarity of relations.

APPLICATION OF THE ANALOGY RULES
TO LANGUAGE ABOUT GOD

1. Aquinas argues that he needs a theory of analogy for language about God because:

a) If the predicate terms in G-statements (statements with "God" or a synonym as the subject) are *totally equivocal* with respect to the occurrences of the same predicate terms in E-statements (with any object of ordinary, direct or indirect experience as subject), then all arguments with an E-statement in the premises and a G-statement as the conclusion will be invalid, committing the fallacy of equivocation; and all G-statements will be meaningless because none of human experience will count either as evidence for or as explications of those statements.

b) If the predicates of G-statements are *univocal* with respect to instances of the same predicates in E-statements, then God will be anthropomorphic, since all predicates we have are derived from experience and are primarily used of limited or finite things. And it was a basic thesis among the medievals that our descriptive categories of the world are of "the world-as-experienced," are homocentric. The term "finite" or "dependent" refers for Thomas to a mode of existence, and he holds that the context of all our language supposes that part of the meaning of the predicate terms is the *mode* of existence of the entity to which the property is attributed. I made this point earlier in distinguishing the *modus significandi* from the *res significata*. He insists that if you do not make such a distinction of kind from mode, you will not be describing the Christian God, the transcendent God. Furthermore, he also argues that if God is to have such properties as self-existence and omnipotence, He must be a significantly different[33] kind of thing from anything in our experience. So, the predicates attributed to Him cannot be univocal with any E-statement occurrences of the same terms.[34]

2. As a result, the terms in G-statements must be partially equivocal with respect to the same terms in E-statements. St. Thomas claims that he can show as a matter of empirical fact that if we use these analogy rules we can explain the way these

predicates in G-statements are related to ordinary E-sentence occurrences of the same terms; *and*, moreover, if we do explain the theological language this way, we shall (1) preserve the transcendence of God; (2) preserve the intelligibility of theological language; (3) make sense of the claim that human experience can furnish some evidence for the truth of the theological beliefs. For, God will be *at most* proportionally similar to the world. That is, God's *operations* will have properties in common with some operations, like causing, which are internal to the world. And we will *name*[35] God from his operations (in a way to be described). So, while all our natural knowledge of God's properties will be by inference from His operations, what we do attribute to God will not be grossly anthropomorphic and will not be arrived at by invalid arguments. How, in outline, this application of the analogy rules is carried out, I shall now describe.

1. Aquinas believes that he can show that between the world described in E-statements, the world of experience, and some entity not part of that world there obtain several relations: (1) "being moved by"; (2) "being efficiently caused by"; (3) "being conserved in existence by"; (4) "being excelled by"; (5) "being designed by" (each relation is established by one of the five existential arguments).[36]

2. A term which signifies these relations (let us take only one, for consideration, say, "being caused by") cannot be used in exactly the same way as it is used in a sentence like this: "My black eye was caused by John." For this latter is an E-statement and the fundamental assumption is that God won't have any properties or relations in the same way as any of His creatures. (This assumption is outside the purview of our analysis; let us take it as a supposition that all theologians would accept it.)

So, the argument is: God is at most proportionally similar to John (that is, is not *directly* similar) because the relation "being caused by" is similar (but not identical) in the statements of the form (a) wCg and (b) bCj.[37] And the term "being caused by" is analogous by proportionality because in its two occurrences it is used equivocally but not totally equivocally. The reason why we cannot replace *this* term ("being caused by") with a univocal term is that in (a) the "mode of signification" which is proper to "C" in (b) has been cancelled out; and because we don't know the characteristics of the *mode of possession* by which God has His properties, we can't fill in the part of the signification which is cancelled out.

So, the term "being caused by," while having all elements of its intention present which are necessary to distinguish "being caused by" from any other relation, *still* does not have present the positive elements (elements not made up of negations of finite modes) by which to distinguish the divine mode of being from the finite mode. And yet, even if these latter modal elements *were* present, the term would still be equivocal because the modal elements of "C" in (a) and "C" in (b) would be different.

3. All natural knowledge of God consists basically in showing that certain relationships with possible worlds actually obtain between things that exist and God.[38]

4. These relation terms, which are thus analogous by proper proportionality with instances of the same terms in statements about the world, are then transferred into *names* of the other relatum, "God." This transference of relation terms into names follows the rule of Analogy of Attribution, since you can call a person by the names of his actions, because he is the cause of his actions. Thus we call a man who smokes, a "smoker," and a man who judges, Judge, and a man who designs, a "designer." And transforming the name of an effect to become a name of the cause is an instance of analogy of attribution.[39] So, the entity X which has the relation "being mediate or immediate cause" of all other entities and events is called "First Cause."

5. Next, utilizing the fact that secondary employments of terms analogous by attribution still tell us something about the subject, St. Thomas proceeds to determine what properties God would have to have if He is the Cause, the Judge, the Conserver, etc. Thus He arrives at properties like: intelligence, free will, simplicity, etc. But *these* terms can all be turned into "relation predicates" and shown to be analogous by proportionality with respect to ordinary language occurrences of the same terms—occurrences which are psychologically prior.

6. Hence, all statements about God employ terms which are

analogous by proper proportionality with respect to psychologically prior instances of the same terms in ordinary experience-
describing statements. Thus analogy of proper proportionality
is the general form of language about God.

In a word, Aquinas supposes that there are two basic sets of
statements made in discussing the existence and nature of God.
(A) The statements which assert that some relation "R" obtains
between entities of a certain kind (the things of the world) and
some entity not a member of that kind. (B) The statements which
employ cognate forms of the relation term "R" as common nouns
or adjectives to either name or describe the entity. An example of
(A) is: "Every thing which has really distinct properties is causally
dependent upon some entity which does not have distinct properties; and there are some entities which have distinct properties."
An example of (B) is: "There exists a First Cause." It is immediately obvious that statements of set (B) logically presuppose both
the truth and meaningfulness of statements of set (A). How set
(B) is derived from (A) is described in the next section (7). The
relation terms that occur in sentences of set (A) are said to be
analogous by proper proportionality with ordinary language
occurrences of the same term, or suppose statements where terms
are employed in a manner according to that analogy rule.

7. Some statements about God employ terms which, in addition
to be being used analogously by proportionality with respect to
E-statements, are also used analogously by attribution with respect
to other and logically prior G-statements. That is, the statement
"The world is caused by God" is logically prior to "God is the
First Cause." The statements which attribute common names to
God employ predicates analogous by attribution with respect to
instances of the same predicates occurring in statements asserting
that certain relations obtain between the world and God. Thus,
to say "God is the artificer, the designer, the Judge," etc., is to
employ as a common name a term which by both logical and
psychological priority is employed in a statement which says
"The world is made, planned, and judged by God."

In summary, having ruled out univocal language about God,
Aquinas claims that his analogy rules offer a way of taking

ordinary language literally in orthodox claims about God. Furthermore, he claims that he cannot be accused of accepting an inadequate kind of language about God, for no other language is *possible* given the Christian assumption that God is transcendent and different in kind from all other things.

Perhaps the sense of the claim I made at the outset, but did not directly support, is now clearer: if one wishes to render philosophically plausible the claim of most orthodox Christians that their traditional descriptive statements about God are both literally meaningful and true, one must employ an analogy theory fundamentally similar to that of St. Thomas; and, I might add, the existence of such a theory as that of Aquinas, even with its substantial defects, renders quite plausible the belief of many Christians that their theological utterances are indeed literally meaningful. It seems that the whole question of whether or not explicit rules can be developed to give a criterion for the meaningfulness of religious statements must be re-opened and re-examined in the light of the substantial progress that can be made toward such rules with a properly understood and developed theory of analogy.

NOTES

1. This is the utterance of Logician in the conversation reported in "Can Religion Be Discussed?," *New Essays in Philosophical Theology*, ed. A. Flew and A. MacIntyre (New York: Macmillan, 1955), p. 3.

2. A. Flew and D. M. MacKinnon, "Creation," in *New Essays in Philosophical Theology*.

3. A. M. Farrer, *Finite and Infinite* (Westminster: Dacre Press, 1943), *passim*.

4. E. L. Mascall, *Existence and Analogy* (London: Longmans, 1949), *passim*. The chief problem is that Mascall follows Pénido, Cajetan, John of St. Thomas, Garrigou-Lagrange, and many other writers in interpreting the proportionality analogy on the model of a simple mathematical proportionality, with the result that analogy as a theory of *inference* (not employed by St. Thomas) is confused with analogy as a theory of *meaning*. This kind of

pseudo-mathematical talk, represented by formulas like "life of cabbage: essence of cabbage = life of elephant: essence of elephant"—even if one does not take the "=" literally—is inimical to the whole objective of St. Thomas, which was to make the meaningfulness of religious language obvious and clear from its very similarity to the way we talk in everyday life.

5. Lack of space will prevent an explicit critique of each of the above-mentioned interpretations.

6. It should be noted that the definitions beginning with Roman numeral I are derived in common from (and are not entirely attributed to either) St. Thomas and C. I. Lewis, *Knowledge and Valuation* (La Salle: Open Court, 1946).

The definitions beginning with Roman numerals II, III, and IV are derived from St. Thomas. Definitions II-1 and IV-7 are the two additional analogy rules which will not be explained in this essay.

It should also be remembered that the names given these four analogy rules were not coined by Aquinas but were applied by Thomas De Vio (Cardinal Cajetan) in his work *On the Analogy of Names*, trans. by Bushenski and Koren (Pittsburgh: Duquesne Univ. Press, 1953). It should be added that the interpretation of the analogy theory presented in this article coincides in the main with that put forward by Cajetan, not merely by election, but by selection, in that the writer thinks it appropriate both on exegetical grounds with regard to St. Thomas and on systematic grounds as part of the systematic equipment needed for a solution of the contemporary question of the meaningfulness of religious utterances.

7. *De Veritate*, q. 2, a. 11, c. This example occurs frequently in St. Thomas' passages on analogy. Some representative passages are: *De Veritate*, q. 1, a. 4, c. ad finem; *In IV Metaph.* lect. 1, n. 537; *Sum Theol.*, I, q. 16, a. 6; *C. Gent.*, I, 34; *I Sent.*, d. 19, q. 5, a. 2, ad 11.

8. Cf. *In IV Metaph.*, lect. 1, n. 539; *In XI Metaph.*, lect. 3, n. 2196; I, q. 16, a. 6, c.

9. Cf. *De Veritate*, q. 21, a. 4, ad. 12; *In XI Metaph.*, lect. 3, n. 2196; John of St. Thomas, *Logica* II, 13 (Reiser edition, Turin, 1930, p. 484).

10. In this connection one should consider: Hampus Lyttkens, *The Analogy between God and the World* (Uppsala Universitets Arsskrift, 1953); G. M. Manser, *Das Wesen des Thomismus*, 3 aufl. (Freiburg i, Schw.: Paulusverlag, 1949), p. 447; M. T.-L. Pénido, *Le rôle de l'analogie en théologie dogmatique* (Paris: Vrin, 1931), p. 34; K. Feckes, *Die Analogie in unserem Gotteserkennen* (Münster: Albertus-Magnus-Akademie zu Köln, Band II, Heft 3, 1928), p. 158. Also: J. Ramirez, "De Analogia secundum doctrinam aristotelico-thomisticam," *La Ciencia Tomista*, XXIV (1921), 243; A. Goergen, *Kardinal Cajetans Lehre von der Analogie* (München, 1938), pp. 68, 80; J. Maritain, *Degrees of Knowledge* (2d. ed.; New York: Scribner, 1959), p. 418; R. Garrigou-Lagrange, *God: His Existence and Nature* (St. Louis: Herder, 1936), II, 207; G. B. Phelan, *Saint Thomas and Analogy* (Milwaukee: Marquette

Univ. Press, 1948), p. 37; J. Le Rohellec, "De fundamento metaphysico analogiae," *Divus Thomas* XXIX (1926), 81–87.

11. Cf. I, q. 13, a. 2, ad 2; ad 3; I, q. 13, a. 6, c.; *De Potentia*, q. 7, a. 5.

12. See *C. Gent.*, I, 34. Many writers have accepted this rule as a means of distinguishing the analogates; see Goergen, *op. cit.*, p. 16; Manser, *op. cit.*. p. 450.

13. *C. Gent.*, I, 34. This argument is useful only if enough similarity has already been demonstrated between God and other things to justify a statement that a causal relation holds. It is this distinction which Hampus Lyttkens, *op. cit.*, p. 283, seizes upon to justify some statements about God. This position is similar to that of Sylvester of Ferrara. Even if there is such an analogy, it cannot be the basic one, for it supposes true statements about God.

14. Cajetan, *De. Nom. Anal.*, Ch. 2, par. 14.

15. I, q. 13, a. 6, c.

16. This point is made repeatedly and emphatically by St. Thomas. For example: I, q. 13, a. 10 corpus; I, q. 13, a. 6; III, q. 60, a. 1: "Omnia quae habent ordinem ad unum aliquid, licet diversimode, ab illo denominari possum . . . sic igitur sacramentum potest aliquid dici vel quia in se habet aliquam sanctitatem occultam, et secundum hoc sacramentum idem est quod sacrum secretum, vel quia habet aliquem ordinem ad hanc sanctitatem, vel causae, vel signi, vel secundum quamcumque aliam habitudinem." Also I, q. 15, a. 6: "Quando aliquid praedicatur univoce de multis, illud in quolibet eorum secundum propriam rationem invenitur . . . quando aliquid dicitur analogice de multis, illud invenitur secundum propriam rationem in uno eorum tantum a quo alia denominantur."

17. *De Nom. Anal.*, Ch. 2, par. 9.

18. Pénido, *op. cit.*, p. 33.

19. *De Principiis Naturae*, Ch. 6.

20. *In IV Metaph*, 2, 1003 a 34 ff.

21. Cajetan, *De. Nom. Anal.*, Ch. 2, par. 15. This is equivalent to the claim that the term is partially equivocal on our definitions.

22. This is not a phrase mentioned as one used by St. Thomas.

23. We are assuming that the sentences (a) and (b) are true, that the subjects are not numerically identical, and that the sentences say the subjects have a certain property. I am still using "subject" in the private sense stipulated in Part I, where it refers to *what is denoted by the grammatical subject*.

24. St. Thomas seems to assume this: *C. Gent.*, II, Ch. 98; I, q. 19, a. 4; q. 75, a. 5. I am using "element" to signify terms which make up the intention of another term.

25. I *Sent.*, d. 22, q. 1, a. 2 corpus.

26. The term "hierarchy" itself is analogous for St. Thomas in the statements about the hierarchy of things under God, I, q. 108, a. 1, c. He offers a definition in q. 108, a. 2, c. and *II Sent.* d. 9, q. 1, a. 1, where it is obvious that this term is itself used analogously by proper proportionality. This is further evidence

of the crucial nature of this language for St. Thomas' philosophy and theology.

27. Cf. I, q. 75, a. 5, ad 1; *C. Gent.*, III, Ch. 92.

28. The general assumption upon which this is based is stated by St. Thomas: *I Sent.*, d. 38, q. 1, a. 2: "Unumquodque autem est in aliquo per modum ipsius, et non per modum sui."

29. St. Thomas' analysis of meaning offers a clear sense of "contextual" meaning. That is: The contextual meaning of two instances of the same term is different if the difference in context is a sufficient condition for the claim that the two instances of the term differ in intention. "Contextual meaning" might be thus defined in terms of the effect of the context upon the intention of terms therein.

30. *De Potentia*, q. 9, a. 3, ad 1; I, q. 13, a. 8; *C. Gent.*, I, Ch. 30; *I Sent.*, d. 22, q. 1, a. 2.

31. This is, of course, an interpretation of St. Thomas. I am not assuming that present day philosophers would discuss various meanings of "knowing" in this way.

32. I. M. Bochenski, "On Analogy," *The Thomist*, XI (1948), 424–47. See also this volume, beginning on page 99.

33. I have said here "significantly different" because Aquinas is not committed to the absurd notion that God is entirely different from creatures. In fact, the analogy theory is designed to permit expression in language of the similarity between God and creatures while protecting our discourse from a claim that God is directly similar to creatures.

34. In effect, Aquinas admits both contemporary philosophical points: (a) if G-statement predicates are equivocal with respect to all E-statement occurrences of those predicates, then all G-statements are meaningless to us who have understanding only of the terms in our E-statement language; and (b) if the G-statement predicates are univocal with a representative set of instances of those predicates in E-statements, then our statements about God will be, in most cases, obviously false and in the remainder, misleading.

35. "Name" here is a verb which Aquinas used to cover both the description of God in terms of common nouns: "creator," "designer," etc. and to cover the process of attribution: "God is merciful," etc.

36. The application of the analogy theory will require the demonstration (logically prior) of the existence of a relation (say, "being caused by") between the objects of experience and some one entity not otherwise specified. The reason we choose to call the relationsip "being caused by" is that the kind of evidence at hand is exactly the kind of evidence present when we call the relationship between my black-eye and my antagonist one of "being caused by." It is true that the well-known difficulties against the traditional arguments for the existence of a First Cause, etc., may make the application of the analogy rules suspect. But, one can for the sake of the discussion either imagine that new evidence has been found that there exists an entity which is First Cause, or one can take it as a matter of religious faith that such a Creator exists. We

are now concerned with the sense of these statements ("A First Cause exists" or "A Creator exists") which will be analyzed by the application of the analogy rules.

37. Where "wCg" means "The World is caused by God" and "bCj" means "The black-eye is caused by John."

38. The term "God" is a shorthand for the definite description which would result from a combination of all the properties shown to be attributable to one unique being with some (psychologically prior) property such as "First Cause" or "Creator."

39. It may be argued that where morphological changes occur, such as from "smoke" to "smoker," there is no one term which is used according to the rule of analogy of attribution, and hence no linguistic analogy. Instead there is a case of a broader "conceptual" process called *denomination*, where the meaning of the one term is *derivative* from the meaning of the other. In every such case, however, a new term could be coined which would fulfill the functions of both the original and derivative terms and which would have its diverse functions related according to the rule of analogy of attribution.

Hence, while the analogy of attribution involved here is not actually linguistic (since there is no one term to fulfill the rules), it is highly probable that the conceptual operations which preceded the development of the differing terms were the same as those involved in any linguistic analogy of attribution. This is supported by the fact that in every case it is possible, by coining a new term, to construct such an analogy. Perhaps a more common case of naming a cause in terms of its effects is this: the sensed quality *red* has the same name as the property (physical dispositional) *red*; for the redness of things in their disposition to cause us to have the sensations called "red." Thus I would argue (cf. also *De Veritate*, q. 21, a. 4, ad 2) that wherever there is extrinsic denomination, there is analogy of attribution. This would, of course, render a large part of our knowledge of the world knowledge through analogy of attribution; but I think this is exactly what St. Thomas would have held.

4

METAPHOR AND ANALOGY

Ralph M. McInerny

THERE seems little reason to doubt that within the Thomist tradition it is assumed that a metaphor is one thing, an analogous term another, and that while metaphor is justifiable—certainly in poetry, but as well if for different reasons in Scripture—it is, generally speaking, something the philosopher should take pains to avoid, since it can vitiate arguments and obscure issues. St. Thomas himself often characterizes the metaphor as improper usage, thereby of course opposing it to proper usage. The question arises, however, when we consider the texts carefully, whether metaphor is opposed to the analogous name or whether proper and improper usage of the kind at issue are subtypes of something more commodious embracing them both; that is, it appears from a reading of some texts that St. Thomas does not so much oppose metaphor to analogy as that he contrasts the analogous usage which is metaphorical because improper to the analogous usage which is proper. Cajetan's division of analogy of proportionality into proper and improper responds to this suggestion of St. Thomas, and if the great commentator tends to regard metaphor as something less than a full-fledged analogy, well surely that does not mean that it is in no way an analogy.[1]

If it seems possible to say that the opposition between analogy and metaphor is not one between analogy and non-analogy but an opposition between modes of analogy, it seems equally possible to consider "metaphor" as a term common to the analogous term and the metaphor opposed to it; that is, as common to proper and improper usage. This can be based on the way in which Aristotle and St. Thomas speak of the extension of the name "nature" to signify any essence whatsoever; Aristotle used the dative, μεταφορᾷ; St. Thomas the phrase, *secundum quamdam metaphoram*,[2] yet I think no one would want to say we are speaking metaphorically, in the sense of improperly, when we talk of the nature of the triangle, for example.

These few remarks serve to indicate that the relative status of metaphor and analogy is somewhat problematic. The *aporia* can be tightened by recalling that Aristotle, in the *Poetics*, enumerates four species of metaphor only one of which is κατ' ἀναλογίαν.[3] Does this mean that only one species of metaphor is in play in the foregoing considerations? If that be true, any resolution of the questions which arise as to the opposition of metaphor to analogy as proper usage would not as such enlighten us on the nature of metaphor without qualification, i.e., the genus of which the metaphor based on analogy is a species.

Although we have introduced this discussion as if it were merely a matter of clarifying alternate classifications suggested by texts of Aquinas, it is obvious that such an effort, if seriously pursued, must inevitably go beyond the fairly superficial plane on which it presents itself. What we are finally after here is an answer to the question, "What, for Aquinas, is a metaphor?" and our way of broaching it serves to call attention to the fact that an answer to the question presumes that we can answer the equally or more difficult question, "What is analogy?" Our opening paragraphs prepare us, moreover, for the likelihood that the answer to the question about metaphor may well begin, "Metaphora dicitur multipliciter . . . ."

CAJETAN ON METAPHOR

Before turning to the texts of St. Thomas, we shall first of all say a few things about Cajetan's teaching on the nature of metaphor, and this without apology given Cajetan's generally admitted influence on this and related discussions. It is well known that in the *De nominum analogia*, Cajetan links metaphor with proportionality rather than with what he calls analogy of attribution. Having explained what is meant by proportionality, Cajetan writes, "Fit autem duobus modis analogia haec: scilicet metaphorice et proprie. *Metaphorice* quidem quando nomen illud commune absolute unam habet rationem formalem, quae in uno analogatorum salvatur, et per metaphoram de alio dicitur." [4] It is unfortunate that this cannot be considered a good definition because of the occurrence of *per metaphoram* in what purports to be an explication of metaphor. It should be noticed, moreover, that Cajetan's failure to define metaphor is not without its impact on his attempt to define proper proportionality: "*Proprie* vero fit, quando nomen illud commune in utroque analogatorum absque metaphoris dicitur." [5]

When we turn to the discussions of chapter seven of Cajetan's opusculum, we find further statements about metaphor of which the following is most important. "In analogia siquidem *secundum metaphoram*, oportet unum in alterius ratione poni, non indifferenter; sed proprie sumptum, in ratione sui metaphorice sumpti claudi necesse est; quoniam impossibile est intelligere quid sit aliquid secundum metaphoram nomen, nisi cognito illo, ad cuius metaphoram dicitur." [6] Now, as Cajetan points out in the following paragraph as well as in his commentary on the *Summa theologiae*,[7] in this the so-called analogy of improper proportionality and analogy of attribution are as one, since this is the third condition of Cajetan's analogy of attribution.[8]

If we ask why Cajetan has multiplied entities here rather than making what he calls attribution coalesce with his improper proportionality, the answer would seem to be the necessity for a proportionality in metaphor and its absence in attribution. The text on which Cajetan relies here is, of course, *Q. D. de veritate*, q. 2, a. 11, although it seems ambiguous on the question whether metaphor is a kind of analogy. Consider the phrase "Sed tamen hoc dupliciter contingit" which occurs after the description of analogy as implying no determinate relation between things sharing a common name. But the first member of the division is stated

thus: "quandoque enim illud nomen importat aliquid ex principali
significatione, in quo non potest attendi convenientia inter Deum
et creaturam, *etiam modo praedicto*; sicut est in omnibus quae
symbolice dicuntur de Deo, ut cum dicitur leo, vel sol, vel huius
modi, quia in horum definitione cadit materia, quae Deo attribui
non potest." To what does *etiam modo praedicto* refer? Does the
occurrence of *attribui* in the denial mean that it is Cajetan's
analogy of attribution which is being set aside? This seems unlikely,
even if we are willing to grant the accuracy of Cajetan's division of
analogy. What the text suggests is that a name is sometimes predicated of God on the basis of a proportionality which, because of
its principal signification, argues for no similarity between God
and creatures so named with respect to that principal signification.
Does this make metaphor a kind of analogous name? Does it mean
that for St. Thomas, unlike Aristotle, the metaphor is always
based on a proportionality? Whatever the answer to these questions, it must be said that the remarks of Cajetan we have con-
sulted are not very illuminating on the nature of metaphor. To
give the great commentator his due, we quote a definition he gives
in his commentary on the first question of the *Summa*. "In titulo,
uti metaphoris est uti locutionibus quae non verificantur de his de
quibus dicuntur, secundum propriam significationem, sed
secundum aliquam similitudinem ad propria significata: ut cum
dicitur quod 'Deus noster ignis consumens est,' utimus metaphora;
quia Deus non est vere ignis, sed se habet ad modum ignis con-
sumentis." [9]

This appeal to Cajetan serves as an oblique introduction to
some of the problems which await us when we turn to St. Thomas.
It will be noticed that if there is no formal connection between
metaphor and proportionality at least one member of Cajetan's
suggested division of analogy is gratuitous and unnecessary.
Moreover, what Cajetan calls analogy of attribution would then
be indistinguishable from metaphor and, since most discussions
of analogy in St. Thomas include examples which for Cajetan are
examples of analogy of attribution, the whole matter of a distinction between metaphor and analogy becomes considerably ob-
scured. But then the way Cajetan handles difficulties presented to

his division of analogy by Aquinas' discussions of analogy indicates that that division is not formal. Thus, when Cajetan asks us to notice that St. Thomas gives an example of so-called analogy of attribution in discussing names common to God and creature, he suggests that intrinsic and extrinsic denomination are really irrelevant when we want to know what an analogous name is.[10] But we have expatiated elsewhere on the deficiencies of Cajetan's treatment of analogy and need not repeat those criticisms here.[11] In short, our employment of Cajetan here is intended to intensify our problem rather than to commend the Cajetanian interpretation.

ANALOGY vs. METAPHOR

We are asking whether metaphor is a kind of analogous name or is to be distinguished from the analogous name. Some of our foregoing considerations give credence to the contention that metaphor is an analogous name. This is corroborated by St. Thomas' procedure in question thirteen of the *Prima Pars*, since in article three, when he asks if any name is said properly of God, the opposition brought into play is between usage *proprie* and *improprie* with the latter identified with metaphor.[12] Then, in article six, when he asks if names common to God and creature are first said of creatures, the distinction *proprie/improprie* seems to be a subdivision of analogous name. St. Thomas begins by saying that "in omnibus nominibus quae de pluribus analogice dicuntur, necesse est quod omnia dicuntur per respectum ad unum: et ideo illud unum oportet quod ponatur in definitione omnium. Et quia ratio quam significat nomen per prius dicitur de eo quod ponitur in definitione aliorum, et per posterius de aliis, secundum ordinem quo appropinquant ad illud primum vel magis vel minus." This is exemplified by the old reliable, "healthy." "Sic ergo omnia nomina quae metaphorice de Deo dicuntur per prius de creaturis dicuntur quam de Deo: quia dicta de Deo, nihil aliud significant quam similitudines ad tales creaturas."[13] St. Thomas notices the similarity of proportion (*similitudo proportionum*) implied in "smiling meadow" and in calling God a lion. When he goes on to talk of other names "quae non metaphorice dicuntur de Deo," the clear impression is that he is talking of other instances of analogous names than metaphors.

Are there texts where St. Thomas opposes metaphor and analogy? If we turn to the commentary on the *Metaphysics*, we find St. Thomas distinguishing "potency" into analogous and equivocal modes. "Potency" means a number of things. "Sed ista multiplicitas quantum ad quosdam modos est multiplicitas aequivocationis, sed quantum ad quosdam analogiae." [14] The equivocal modes of potency are exemplified by the way we speak of 3 to the third power and of the cube as the power of the line. "Et propter hoc per quamdam similitudinem dicitur potens in quadratum, sicut dicitur materia potens in rem." [15] Once more a proportionality, notice. That these equivocal modes are indeed metaphors is clear from the parallel passage in Book Delta in commenting on which St. Thomas begins, "Ostendit quomodo potentia sumatur metaphorice." [16] Why are these modes metaphorical and not analogical? "His ergo modis praetermissis, considerandum est de potentiis, quae reducuntur ad unam speciem, quia quaelibet earum est principium quoddam, et omnes potentiae sic dictae reducantur ad aliquod principium ex quo omnes aliae dicuntur." [17] In short, St. Thomas here opposes metaphor to analogous uses of a name because the latter and not the former involve a reduction to what is primarily denominated by the word in question whereas, should it need pointing out, in the text of the *Summa* we considered a moment ago, the metaphor was not distinguished from the extension *proprie* on this basis. Or is it the manner of the reference to what is principally signified by the name which distinguishes metaphor from analogy, usage *proprie* from *improprie*? Things named metaphorically are, after all, taken to be similar to what the name properly signifies.

An *aporia* has clearly emerged, therefore, and its resolution can only be had by determining what a metaphor is and what an analogous name is. Answers to these questions should enable us to understand the apparently conflicting statements of Aquinas. What we shall be looking for is some way of justifying the fairly common distinction of metaphor and analogy such that no appeal is made to Cajetan's division of analogy into attribution and proper proportionality.

RATIO PROPRIA NON INVENITUR NISI IN UNO

We have seen St. Thomas distinguish metaphor from the proper use of a term and clearly we can understand the meaning of *improprie* only if a meaning of *proprie* be established. Now metaphorical usage is distinguished from the variety of meanings of a term which refer to what is principally signified by the term in question. That is, in what at least sometimes St. Thomas calls a *multiplicitas analogiae*, it would seem that each meaning permits proper usage. This may seem surprising since St. Thomas distinguishes the univocal term from the analogous term by saying that, when things are named univocally, the *ratio propria* is found in each of the things so named, whereas when things are named analogically, *ratio propria non invenitur nisi in uno*.[18] How can a thing be named *proprie* by a term whose *ratio propria* it does not save? It is just this puzzle that seems to have led Cajetan to write his incredible commentary on the passage in which our phrase occurs; he there maintains, in direct opposition to the text before him that in truly analogous names the *ratio propria* is found in all things named. "Esse ergo nomen aliquod secundum propriam rationem in uno tantum, est conditio nominum quae sunt *ad unum* aut *ab uno*, etc et non nominum proportionaliter dictorum."[19] Cajetan thereby assigns the distinction in the text between univocals and analogates to a new role; now analogy in the strict sense, analogy of proper proportionality, is grouped with univocity and opposed to analogy of attribution. In order to separate analogy of proper proportionality from univocation, Cajetan says that while things named analogically in the full sense of the term all save the *ratio propria* of their common name, unlike things named univocally they do not do so *secundum eamdem rationem*. What prompts this prestidigitation is clear from the following remark. "Quoniam si analogum in uno tantum secundum propriam rationem salvatur; et ex qu. xiii constat omnia nomina communia Deo et aliis esse analoga, et consequenter veritatem analogice inveniri in intellectu divino et aliis intellectibus, sequitur quod in multis intellectibus non sunt multae veritates, sed omnes intellectus sunt veri una sola veritate, scilicet intellectus divini."[20] Cajetan may be taken to mean that unless the *ratio propria* of a word is saved by that of which the word is said or predicated, we will be speaking improperly and metaphorically and we see once more the affinity of metaphor to what Cajetan calls analogy of attribution. If Cajetan is mistaken here, and we will see that he is, the text does demand that we look for a way in which, when things are named analogically, the proper notion of the name is saved by only one of them and yet the others are named properly as opposed to improperly.

THE SIGNIFICATION OF NAMES[21]

Cajetan cannot accept St. Thomas' description of things named analogically as things which share a common name but the *ratio propria* is found in only one of them, the one from which the others are denominated. Cajetan has trouble here because he is thinking of the many places where St. Thomas says that in names analogically common to God and creature, the *res significata* is found in both. Now if the *ratio propria* of a name were the same as the *res significata*, St. Thomas would be in contradiction with himself; therefore, it is just that identification, apparently assumed by Cajetan, that must be questioned.

St. Thomas accepts the view of Aristotle that the spoken word signifies a thing through the mediation of an intellectual concept. In short, what is immediately signified by the name is the *conceptus* which is also called the *ratio nominis*. This view of signification is triadic: word, concept, thing. The triad may seem immediately threatened when we consider that there are words or names whose very signification indicates that they signify nothing "out there." For example, the meaning of the term, *genus*, is precisely a relation among concepts, among things as they are known. The *ratio* of such a name does not purport to have anything answering to it, as such, in things as they exist. When we think of the names of fictions, e.g., *centaur*, it is even more clear that not all words signify even mediately things out-there.[22] The difficulty is resolved, I think, by calling attention to the characteristic procedure of St. Thomas. *Word* or *name* are first of all described or defined in terms of a most obvious instance where the triad mentioned is easily verified. That this is the best known, the most familiar, seems suggested by the fact that we have problems about logical and fictional words, and others, because they do not seem to behave as words should. It may then seem necessary either to redefine *word* or to rule against calling *genus* and *centaur* names. St. Thomas does not honor the exhaustiveness of the implied division. He prefers to take an obvious instance, assign a definition on its basis, and consider other things to be called by the same name insofar as they approximate more or less to that normative case. Not all names fulfill perfectly the definition of *name*, but to the degree they do they deserve the appellation.

The question as to the meaning of the phrase *res significata* arises if we ask whether when "animal," "man" and "rational" and "substance" are all taken as names of Socrates, they thereby have the same *res significata*. The problem is less acute, of course, when we consider the thing as the recipient of several synonyms. Thus, if I call my coat clothing, apparel and, less likely, vestment, I am naming the same thing and the various names have the same meaning. When we speak of the *res significata*, do we mean the thing named or the meaning of the name? What has already been said about signification indicates that the *res significata* in the first sense is the meaning or concept. Does this suggest that Cajetan's identification of the *ratio propria nominis* and the *res significata* is well-founded?

The *res significata* is distinguished from the *modus significandi*; the two together make up the *ratio nominis*. What a name signifies must be distinguished first of all from its etymology. The latter is often what is meant by the phrase, *id a quo nomen imponitur*, and St. Thomas' standard example is *lapis*, whose etymology he takes to be *laedens pedem*. That is, the stone is denominated from the fact that we can trip over it, but what we are naming is not a menace to pedestrians, since we can trip on many things which are not called stones. Thus, the etymology is a description, a citing of various accidents, which enable us to indicate what we want to name. The etymology of *breakfast* is not what is named—we may break our fast with lunch or before breakfast. When the etymology is called the *id a quo nomen imponitur*, the meaning is said to be *id ad quod nomen imponitur ad significandum*. At other times, the phrase *id a quo nomen imponitur* refers not to the etymology of the term but rather to the denominating form. Whatever the etymology of *sanum*, its *id a quo* in the sense of what it principally signifies is *sanitas*. The *id a quo*, in the sense of the principal signification of the term, is opposed to *id cui nomen supponitur*; that is, to that for which the name supposes because it falls under the *res significata*. The denominating form is always signified in a given manner, according to a *modus significandi*. *Sanum* and *sanitas* have the same *res significata* but they signify it differently: concretely and abstractly, respectively. The concrete name signifies the form as "that which has health"; the abstract name as "that whereby healthy things are healthy." Every name involves a mode of signifying, a way in which the denominating form is meant. This is of crucial importance for analogous names.[23]

When St. Thomas wants to say how univocal, equivocal and analogous names are divided, he writes, "Aequivocum enim dividitur secundum res significatas, univocum vero dividitur secundum diversas differentias; sed analogum dividitur secundum diversos modos."[24] When a name is common to many things equivocally, it is imposed to signify from different denominating forms, different *res significatae*. We see here that the *res significata* cannot be that for which the word supposes, since then the univocal term would be equivocal.[25] Since the *res significatae* of the equivocal name differ, there is no need to go into a discussion of the modes of signifying those forms to establish the difference involved in *bark*'s meaning part of a tree and a canine noise. The univocal word is divided by differences; that is, by further denominating forms which determine the generic perfection thus revealed as material. When considered as named by the generic name, certain things are named univocally and the word has the same *res significata* as said of each. Specific names, imposed from more determinate forms, divide the generic perfection. The analogous name is one which is predicable of many things thanks to the same denominating form or *res significata*, but the ways that form is signified, the *modi significandi*, vary and give rise to an ordered diversity of signification insofar as the *res significata* signified in one way makes up the *ratio propria* of the term in question: its familiar, usual, normative, focal meaning.

We can do no better than appeal to the familiar example of *healthy* to illustrate these remarks about the analogous name. The denominating form, the *res significata*, of "healthy" in its analogous modes is always the same: health. It is the way health is signified that causes a variation in the meaning of "healthy": what has health, what signifies health, what causes health whether by restoring it when lost or preserving it when had. The *res significata*, then, remains the same while the modes and *rationes* change. But this is not all; the various *rationes* of the common name are said to be related *per prius et posterius* in such fashion that one *ratio*, one way of signifying the denominating form is taken to be regulative and constitutes a focal meaning. This meaning reveals its priority by the fact that it enters into the subsequent *rationes*. The same state of affairs is present in the case of the analogous term, *being*. *Esse* is that from which the word *being* is imposed to signify; it is what *ens* principally signifies. But the ways of signifying it vary, the meanings of the common term vary—it is an analogous term.

RATIO COMMUNIS AND RATIO PROPRIA[26]

We have suggested that the *ratio propria* of a term comprises the *res significata* and the usual, familiar mode of signifying it and that the *ratio propria* is discoverable by looking for that mode of signifying which enters into the other modes of signifying the same *res significata*. But we often find St. Thomas speaking of the *ratio communis* of the analogous name. How, we must ask, does such a common notion relate to the proper notion of the same name? Let us approach the problem by getting hold of a distinction of common and proper notions in things named univocally. It seems clear that things are considered to be named univocally with respect to a name signifying a common notion; if that name is generic, not all such things would be considered to be named by a word signifying a subalternate proper notion. That is, some things may be considered to be named univocally by *animal* which would not be named by *man*. We are calling what *animal* signifies a *ratio communis*, what *man* signifies a *ratio propria*. Since the proper notion is not a meaning of the generic term, this distinction between common and proper notions involves different names and not one name.[27] In the case of things named analogously, it is the same name whose *ratio communis* is apparently opposed to its *ratio propria*, and while the name does not change there seems to be suggested an appropriation, a shrinking, as it were, of the common notion.

Let us pose this question with reference to *sanum*. The *ratio propria* would seem to be "subject of the quality, health." Would the *ratio communis* then be, "related in some way to health"? In the case of *ens*, the proper notion is "id cui debet esse in se et non in alio" and the common notion *habens esse* in whatever mode. The common notion is a kind of blank check, almost a propositional function: "existence (x)." Scotus, noticing this, felt that *ens* could be univocally common to substance and accidents but the great difficulty with that suggestion is that it fails to take into account that we want the mode of signification to vary as we predicate the term. What permits us to speak of the *ratio communis* of the analogous name is the *res significata*; what prevents this common notion from giving rise to univocation is the fact that the things denominated from the form are not denominated in the same way; they are unequal with respect to what the name principally signifies.[28] As predicated, the analogous term must always involve some mode of signifying as well as the denominating form and, unless otherwise specified, this will constitute the *ratio propria*. The proper notion, again, will relate to the common notion as what states the usual or more obvious mode of the form in question. For this reason, Aristotle and St. Thomas hold that he who would study being as being must, since *being* is analogous, chiefly concern himself with the principal mode of being, substance.

PROPRIE, COMMUNITER, METAPHORICE

Earlier we saw St. Thomas making apparently conflicting remarks about metaphor. On the one hand, he speaks of the way in which the metaphorical use of a term involves reference to its proper meaning; on the other hand he contrasts metaphorical or equivocal modes to analogical community by saying that the latter and not the former involves reference to the proper meaning. We are now in a position to say quite formally what the reference to the proper notion entails: it is a reference on the part of something named by a given word to the most familiar mode of signifying the denominating form of the word. The question now arises: is this or is this not a difference between metaphor and analogy or, if you prefer, between the proper and improper use of a term? Consider the following remark: ". . . per prius dicitur nomen de illo in quo salvatur tota ratio nominis perfecte, quam de illo in quo salvatur secundum quid: de hoc enim dicitur quasi per similitudinem ad id in quo perfecte salvatur, quia omnia imperfecta sumuntur a perfectis." [29] St. Thomas seems clearly to be speaking of a metaphor here. "Et inde est quod hoc nomen *leo* per prius dicitur de animali in quo tota ratio leonis salvatur, quod proprie dicitur leo, quam de aliquo homine in quo invenitur aliquid de ratione leonis, ut puta audacia vel fortitudo . . . ." [30] We have already cited *Q. D. de ver.*, q. 7, a. 2, c., where St. Thomas said that metaphor is based on a similarity "in illo quod est de propria ratione eius cuius nomen transfertur."

That metaphorical usage involves such a reference to the *ratio propria*, one which is part and parcel of what he means by analogical signification, also seems implied by the adverbial scale Aquinas often employs in speaking of the range of the analogical term. This scale sometimes goes, *propriissime, proprie, communiter*; sometimes, *proprie, minus proprie, minime proprie*. [31] At least once, when he is speaking in this second fashion, St. Thomas suggests that metaphor is simply a trailing off into impropriety because of the remoteness of its reference to the *ratio propria* of the word. "Nam tripliciter invenitur motus in operationibus animae. In quibusdam enim invenitur motus proprie, in quibusdam minus proprie, in quibusdam vero minime proprie." [32] And then this rather startling remark: "Minimum autem de proprietate motus, *et nihil nisi metaphorice*, invenitur in intellectu." [33] The thing named metaphorically, we want to say, is not named or denominated from the *res significata* of the name in question although it is referred to what is denominated from it: the thing which is spoken of metaphorically is not named properly because it does not fall under the range of the principal signification of the term in question. We shall have to return to this, of course, but first we will examine a case where, from different points of view, we can say either that a thing is being spoken of metaphorically (*improprie*) or analogically (*proprie*).

St. Thomas asks if light is found properly in spiritual things, but before replying invites us to consider that a name may be taken either according to its first imposition or according to subsequent usage. For example, "to see" is imposed to signify the activity of one external sense, but we also speak of the activities of the other senses as seeing, e.g. "See how warm this is" and "See how it tastes." Indeed, we speak of seeing in the case of intellectual activity itself: Blessed are the pure of heart, for they shall see God. So it is with "light."

> Nam primo quidem est institutum ad significandum id quod facit manifestationem in sensu visus; postmodum autem extensum est ad significandum omne illud quod facit manifestationem secundum quamcumque cognitionem. Si ergo accipiatur nomen luminis secundum primam impositionem, metaphorice in spiritualibus dicitur, ut Ambrosius dicit. Si autem accipiatur secundum quod est in usu loquentium ad omnem manifestationem extensum, sic proprie in spiritualibus dicitur. [34]

With respect to the *usus loquentium* invoked here, we must distinguish the mere use of a word—surely metaphor is a use of a word—from usage which suggests regularity and convention and thus results in the extension of the very meaning of the word. [35] Without such an extension of meaning, St. Thomas is saying, the use would be metaphorical. He elaborates this in a parallel text where he begins by distinguishing metaphor and analogy. Ambrose and Denis maintain that "light" is used only metaphorically of spiritual things and this seems true "because nothing per se sensible belongs to spiritual things except *metaphorically*, for though something can be *analogically* common to spiritual and corporeal things, something per se sensible cannot." Thus "light" is said of spiritual things "either equivocally or metaphorically." It is interesting to read how St. Thomas expresses the common ground between Ambrose and Denis, on the one hand, and, on the other, Augustine who held that light is found properly in spiritual things.

> Sciendum tamen quod transferuntur corporalia in spiritualia per quamdam similitudinem, quae quidem est similitudo proportionabilitatis; et hanc similitudinem oportet reducere in aliquam communitatem univocationis vel analogiae; et sic est in proposito: dicitur enim lux in spiritualibus illud quod ita se habet ad manifestationem intellectivam sicut se habet lux corporalis ad manifestationem sensitivam. Manifestatio autem verius est in spiritualibus; et quantum ad hoc, verum est dictum Augustini . . . quod lux verius est in spiritualibus quam in corporalibus, *non secundum propriam rationem lucis, sed secundum rationem manifestationis.*[36]

If *lux* has only a *ratio propria*, it is used metaphorically of whatever does not verify that notion. However, if we attend to the *res significata*, the denominating form, manifestation, it is possible to form a *ratio communis*: "whatever causes manifestation" and any mode of manifestation can then be named properly by the term *lux*. In order to grasp these extended meanings, we must have recourse to the proper notion, but these extended meanings are other denominations from the *res significata*. This is the *similitudo analogiae* which is distinguished from the *similitudo proportionabilitatis.*[37] We are now on the threshold of discovering the peculiar way in which metaphor involves a reference to the *ratio propria*, a way which does not amount to a different mode of signifying the same *rem significatam*. Notice how St. Thomas expresses himself in the following text. "Ea quae proprie de ipso (i.e. de Deo) dicuntur, vere in eo sunt; sed ea quae metaphorice dicuntur de eo per similitudinem proportionabilitatis ad effectum aliquem,

sicut ignis Deuter. IV, eo quod sicut ignis se habet ad consump-
tionem contrarii, ita Deus ad consumendum nequitiam."[38]
Here there is no similarity of nature, or in that from which the
name is imposed to signify; rather, the thing named metaphorically
has a property or effect similar to an effect or property of that
which the term properly signifies. As fire consumes fuel, God
consumes evil; as the lion acts boldly, so too does Socrates.
Obviously no metaphor would be involved in saying "Socrates is
bold." Only "Socrates is a lion" is taken to be metaphorical.
Thus, on the basis of "lion: bold: Socrates: bold," it is the
transfer of "lion" which constitutes the metaphor and the word
is not so transferred because of a new mode of signifying the
res significata—which is why what is named metaphorically,
cannot be properly supposed for by the name in question. It
may be, of course, that the effect is a sufficient sign of leonine
nature,[39] but it is not the *id a quo* in the sense of the *res significata*
of *lion*.

CONCLUDING SUMMARY

By way of summary we want to state (1) how metaphor is opposed
to analogy, (2) how analogy is a kind of metaphor, and (3) how
metaphor is a kind of analogy. As we have just seen, metaphor
consists of the application of the name of one thing to another.
Consequently, the metaphorical use of a term entails a reference
to the proper meaning of that term. If we are going to speak of
an explanation as casting light on a subject, what we are saying
depends for its intelligibility on our auditor's knowing what
light is, e.g. the sun, a desk lamp. It is that meaning which enables
us to say that something like light is operative in intellection
because it has an effect similar to light in the proper sense. In
its metaphorical use, it is not the denominating form of "light"
which comes into play, but an effect of what is denominated
from that form. The analogous name, as opposed to metaphorical
usage, involves a new way of signifying the *res significata*,
a new way in which something is denominated from that form.
As analogous it is denominated from that form, not *per prius*,
but with reference to what is first of all denominated from it

and to which appeal will be made to explain this new meaning. Thus, in analogical signification, while the same *res significata* is involved, there are various modes of signifying it, one of which will be primary, more familiar and proper. Thus, the rule that, in things named analogically, *ratio propria non invenitur nisi in uno* is universal; it is as true of the divine names and *being* as it is of *healthy*. In analogy, but not in metaphorical usage, there is an extension in the meaning of the word, the formation of another *ratio* of the name. This new *ratio*, like the *ratio propria*, will contain the *res significata*, but the mode will vary. It is just the judgment that the *res significata* permits of various *modi significandi* which explains Augustine's position on the propriety of using "light" to speak of spiritual things. Thanks to the recognition of the new way of signifying the denominating form, they are seen to fall under the distribution of the term. Metaphorical usage does not involve a new way of signifying the same form, a proportion to the *res significata* by way of the *ratio propria*; rather, the metaphor refers the thing so named to what is properly named by the term in question because of a similarity of effects or properties. What is named metaphorically is not denominated by the form of the name in question in a manner which, *secundum ordinem nominis*, involves reference to the mode involved in the *ratio propria* of the name. In this fashion, we can distinguish quite properly the metaphor from the analogous name and there is not the slightest need to introduce the notions of intrinsic and extrinsic denomination in the way Cajetan would.

Despite this formal distinction of metaphor and analogy, we can speak of analogy as a kind of metaphor. To do so, we must of course back off from the restricted meaning of metaphorical usage given in the preceding paragraph and go rather to the etymology, μεταφερεῖν, to transfer. Both metaphor in the narrow sense and the analogical extension of the meaning of a word involve a transfer of the word from a more usual and familiar context. This would seem to explain the passage we cited above concerned with the extension of "nature" to any essence whatever, where the extension in question seems to involve a new way of signifying the denominating form and yet is said to take place by way of metaphor. It could also be argued that the recognition of the analogical extension of the meaning of a term implies that the term had first of all been used metaphorically (in the narrow sense). Reflection on the metaphor could suggest that not only a similarity of effects is present, but a new way of being denominated from the form of the word. Thus metaphor in the narrow sense could be said to give way to analogy, but the analogy then recognized could still be called a metaphor in the sense of a transfer of the name from what saves its *ratio propria* to what saves the *res significata* in a different mode. Aristotle and St. Thomas, who maintain that sensible things are the connatural objects of our intellect and that whereby we come to know whatever else we know, see an unavoidable fittingness in our employment of the names we impose to signify material things to signify any other entities we come to know. As our knowledge of other entities is dependent on our knowledge of sensible things, so the process of naming will reflect the progress of our knowledge and we will have no choice but to extend or transfer the names of material things to immaterial things.

Can we say that metaphorical usage is a kind of analogy? There is certainly no doubt that metaphorical usage is often based on a proportional similitude. We pointed out earlier that, in the *Poetics*, Aristotle mentions one kind of metaphor which is based on an analogy; St. Thomas seems always to link metaphor with such proportional similitude. When speaking of metaphors applied to God, this is surely the only species of metaphor we can employ since the three other kinds are based on genus/species relations. It goes without saying that such proportional similarity is not what is meant by the analogous name. If the cup is to Dionysus what the shield is to Ares, we have a proportional similarity and there is of course as yet no question either of metaphor or of an analogous name. It is when the cup of Dionysus is spoken of as his shield, on the basis of the proportional similarity, that the matter of metaphor arises. If, with reference to its ground, such a metaphor is called analogical, well, we can see quite clearly what is and what is not meant.

We may add here, by way of an aside, that when an analogical extension of the meaning of a common term is based on such a proportional similarity, there is a pile-up of meanings of "analogy." That is, we could say that the analogy (i.e. analogous name) is founded on an analogy (i.e. proportional similarity). It would be confusion confounded to equate the analogical name with analogy in the sense of proportional similarity, since the latter is not itself an analogous name—it may found metaphorical usage, analogical extension of the meaning of a common name, or neither.

There is another way in which the metaphor may be called an analogy, this time in the sense of an analogous name. In the adverbial scale we spoke of earlier, we saw St. Thomas recognize a gradation in the manner of signifying the *res significata* of the common name which ranged from *propriissime* through *proprie* and *communiter*. *Communiter* and *minime proprie* seem sometimes to be equated with *metaphorice* by St. Thomas and the suggestion is given that metaphor differs from analogical extension of meaning in degree rather than in kind. There are several possible reasons for this suggestion. One is that such a distance has been traversed from the *ratio propria* that reference to it is almost lost and the word may seem to be used equivocally. Another reason would be that there is involved in metaphorical usage a reference to the *ratio propria*, although this is quite different from that involved in the extensions *proprie* of the name.

While we feel that we have arrived at a formal difference between the metaphorical use of a term and its analogical extension as well as reasons for calling analogous terms metaphors and vice versa, we would like to end by stressing the exploratory nature of our effort with respect to the total position of St. Thomas. There is much important work to be done if we are to grasp the scope and subtlety of St. Thomas' doctrine on language. To mention a few points of interest: the phrase *locutio figurativa* is broader than *locutio metaphorica*;[40] moreover, in speaking of the formula for consecration of the wine in the Mass, St. Thomas dwells on the metonymic and metaphorical import of the sentence.

Needless to say, if our essay is tentative with respect to Thomas, it is quite inadequate with respect to current discussions. Of these, the contributions of C. S. Lewis and Owen Barfield are of particular importance.[41] Perhaps our effort will help to renew interest in the older treatments of metaphor so that a fruitful encounter with contemporary views will be possible.

NOTES

1. Cf. *De nominum analogia* (ed. P. N. Zammit, O. P. and P. H. Hering, O. P., Romae, 1952), cap. 3.

2. *Metaphysics*, Delta, 4, 1051a11; St. Thomas, *ad loc.*, lectio 5, n. 823.

3. *Poetics*, chap. 21, 1457b9, 16.

4. *Op. cit.*, n. 25.

5. *Ibid.*, n. 26.

6. Cap. 7, n. 75. Cajetan doubtless has in mind here such remarks as that in *De veritate*, q. 7, a. 2, c.: "In his quae translative dicuntur, non accipitur metaphora secundum quamcumque similitudinem, sed secundum convenientiam in illo quod est de propria ratione eius cuius nomen transfertur."

7. *In I*[am], q. 13, a. 6, n. IV: "Ad hoc breviter dicitur, quod analoga inveniuntur duobus modis. Quaedam enim significant *ipsos respectus* ad primum analogatum, ut patet de sano. Quaedam vero significant *fundamenta* tantum illorum respectuum; ut communiter invenitur in omnibus vere analogis, proprie et formaliter salvatis in omnibus analogatis. Propositio ergo illa universalis in antecedente assumpta, intelligenda est universaliter in primo modo analogiae: ita quod sensus est, quod in omnibus nominibus quae de pluribus analogice, idest secundum diversos respectus, dicuntur, oportet poni unum. In quaestione *de Veritate* de secundo modo analogiae dixit oppositum. Et haec responsio est universalior ea quam alibi assignavimus, ex Qu. de Ver., quia ista responsio habet locum in analogis secundum proportionalitatem, metaphorice tamen dictis: in his enim etiam unum ponitur in ratione alterius." —As he had pointed out in his opusculum (n. 76): "Et propter hoc huiusmodi analoga prius dicuntur de his, in quibus proprie salvatur, et posterius de his, in quibus metaphorice inveniuntur, et habent in hoc affinitatem cum analogis secundum attributionem, ut patet."

8. *Op. cit.*, cap. 2, n. 14.

9. *In I*[am], q. 1, a. 9, n. 1.

10. *In I*[am], q. 13, a. 5, n. XIV, *in fine*.

11. *The Logic of Analogy* (The Hague: Martinus Nijhoff, 1961).

12. *I*ª, q. 13, a. 3, ad 3ᵐ.

13. *Ibid.*, a. 6.

14. *In IX Metaphys.*, lect. 14, n. 1773.

15. N. 1774.

16. *In V Metaphys.*, lect. 14, n. 974.

17. *In IX Metaphys.*, lect. 1, n. 1776. In n. 1780, St. Thomas gives a most explicit statement of what constitutes the community of analogy. "Unde manifestum est quod in definitione harum potentiarum, quae dicuntur respectu bene agere vel pati, includuntur rationes primarum potentiarum, quae dicebantur simpliciter agere vel pati: sicut in bene agere includitur agere; et pati, in eo quod est bene pati. Unde manifestum est, quod omnes isti modi potentiarum reducuntur ad unum primum, scilicet ad potentiam activam. Et inde patet quod haec multiplicitas non est secundum aequivocationem, sed secundum analogiam."

18. *I*ª, q. 16, a. 6, c.

19. *In I*ᵃᵐ, q. 16, a. 6, n. IV.

20. *Ibid.*, n. III.

21. Cf. Louis LaChance, O. P., *Philosophie du Langage* (Ottawa, Montreal: Les Éditions du Lévrier, 1943); Franz Manthey, *Die Sprachphilosophie des hl. Thomas von Aquin* (Paderborn: Ferdinand Schoeningh, 1937). The latter is a rather uninspired yet painstaking arrangement of textual citations (unfortunately by way of outmoded convention) under various headings; the former is popular and somewhat too personal to be considered an analysis of St. Thomas. What is wanted is a book which will combine the verve of Lachance and the scholarship of Manthey.

22. Cf. *I Sent.*, d. 2, q. 1, a. 2, where Thomas distinguishes "real" words, logical words and fictional words.

23. For textual justification of the preceding paragraphs, cf. the work mentioned in note 11 above.

24. *I Sent.*, d. 22, q. 1, a. 3, ad 2ᵐ.

25. "Aequivocatio inducitur ex diversa forma significata per nomen, non autem ex diversitate suppositionis: non enim hoc nomen *homo* aequivoce sumitur ex eo quod quandoque supponit pro Platone, quandoque pro Sorte. Hoc igitur nomen *homo*, et de Christo et de aliis hominibus dictum, semper eandem formam significat, scilicet naturam humanam,"—*IV Contra Gentiles*, cap. 49.

26. Cf. "The *ratio communis* of the Analogous Name," *Laval théologique et philosophique*, vol. XVIII, no. 1 (1962), pp. 9–34.

27. But what are we to make of those not infrequent cases where the same word is used as genus and to signify one of the species of that genus, e.g. "animal" as generic name but also used as the name of a species of animal? Since in the two cases "animal" is imposed from different *res significatae*, this is a case of equivocation.

28. "Sed dicendum est quod unum dividentium aliquod commune potest

esse prius altero dupliciter: uno modo, secundum proprias rationes, aut naturas dividentium; alio modo, secundum participationem rationis illius communis quod in ea dividitur. Primum autem non tollit univocationem generis, ut manifestum est in numeris, in quibus binarius secundum propriam rationem naturaliter est prior ternario; sed tamen aequaliter participant rationem generis sui, scilicet numeri: ita tamen est ternarius multitudo mensurata per unum, sicut et binarius. Sed secundum impedit univocationem generis. Et propter hoc *ens* non potest esse genus substantiae et accidentis: quia in ipsa ratione *entis*, substantia, quae est ens per se, prioritatem habet respectu accidentis, quod est ens per aliud et in alio."—*In I Periherm.*, lect. 8, n. 6.

29. *I*ᵃ, q. 33, a. 3, c.

30. *Ibid.*

31. Cf. e.g., *I*ᵃ-*II*ᵃᵉ, q. 22, a. 1, c.; *Q. D. de virtutibus in communi*, a. 7.

32. *In I de anima*, lect. 10, n. 157.

33. *Ibid.*, n. 160.

34. *I*ᵃ, q. 67, a. 1. On why sight of all the senses should be so extended, see *In I Metaphys.*, lect. 1, nn. 5-8.

35. Cf. *I*ᵃ, q. 29, a. 4, in fine corp., for a distinction between use and meaning.

36. *II Sent.*, d. 13, q. 1, a. 2; cf. *In Ioannem*, cap. 1, lect. 3, n. 96.

37. Cf. *II Sent.*, d. 16, q. 1, a. 2, ad 5m; Bernard Montagnes, O. P., *La doctrine de l'analogie de l'être d'après saint Thomas d'Aquin* (Louvain: Nauwelaerts, 1963). p. 75, n. 21.

38. *I Sent.*, d. 45, q. 1, a. 4, c. Cf. M. T.-L. Pénido, *Le rôle de l'analogie en théologie dogmatique* (Paris: Vrin, 1931), pp. 98–108.

39. ". . . effectus qui est signum alicuius secundum proprietatem in uno est signum eiusdem secundum similitudinem in altero, in omnibus quae metaphorice dicuntur."—*I Sent.*, d. 45, q. 1, a. 4, ad 2m.

40. Cf. *In Ephes.*, cap. 1, lect. 8; *IV Sent.*, d. 8, q. 2, a. 2, quest. 2.

41. C. S. Lewis, "Bluspels and Flalansferes," in *Rehabilitations and Other Essays* (London: Oxford University Press, 1939); Owen Barfield, "The Meaning of the Word *Literal*," in *Metaphor and Symbol*, edited by L. C. Knights and Basil Cottle, Butterworths Scientific Publications, London, 1960, pp. 48–63.

DISPLAYING LOGICAL AND FORMALISTIC METHODS

5

ON ANALOGY

I. M. Bochenski

1. INTRODUCTORY. The present paper is an attempt to clear up some of the problems involved in the traditional theory of analogy as presented by the Thomistic school. The two main ideas behind the formal developments offered here are: (1) analogy is an important discovery, worthy of a thorough examination and further development, (2) contemporary mathematical logic supplies excellent tools for such work. This essay is, as far as the author knows, the first of its kind;[1] it deals with a difficult subject in a sketchy way; what it contains is, therefore, not meant to be definitive truths, but rather proposals for discussion.

The approach to the problems of analogy used here is the semantic one. This is not the only method, but it would seem to be both the most convenient and the most traditional. As a matter of fact, it is difficult to see how equivocity, which is and must be treated as a relation of the same type as analogy, can be considered except by the semantic method. Also, St. Thomas Aquinas examined analogy in his question concerning divine names and the title of Cajetan's classical work is "*De Nominum Analogia.*"

It will be taken for granted that the reader has a good knowledge of classical texts of St. Thomas and Cajetan, and of the content of the *Principia Mathematica*;[2] no reference will be made to these works, except for some laws used in the proofs. Other more recent topics of mathematical logic needed for the theory, as, e.g., plural relations,[3] semantics,[4] etc., will be explained.

The main results of our inquiry are: (1) an exact definition of univocity, equivocity, and analogy of attribution; (2) proof of the principles of contradiction and of excluded middle for univocal and equivocal names; (3) a metalogical examination and exact translation of the formula "analogy itself is analogical"; (4) proof that a syllogism in *Barbara* with analogical middle terms, if analogy is defined according to the alternative theory, is a correct formula; (5) criticism of the alternative theory; (6) definition of analogy of proportionality by isomorphy; (7) proof that a syllogism in *Barbara* with analogical middle terms, if analogy is explained according to the isomorphic theory, is a correct formula; (8) a suggestion that contemporary Logic uses analogy.

Incidentally other results are reached, which may have a more general relevance: (1) the foundations of a semantic system, useful for Thomistic Logic, are sketched; (2) a generalised table of relevant semantic relations between two names is given; (3) the formal validity of a syllogism in *Barbara*, as opposed to its verbal correctness, is defined; (4) a rudimentary analysis of causality, as understood by Thomists, is supplied.

2. MEANING.   The fundamental notion of our theory is that of meaning, described by the following formula: "the name a means in the language l the content f of the thing x" (symbolically: "$S(a, l, f, x)$"). The situation symbolized by "$S(a, l, f, x)$" will be called a "semantic complex." In spite of its simplicity the semantic complex merits a detailed comment.

(1) By "name" we understand here a written word or other written symbol. It must be emphasized that a written symbol is just a black mark (a spot of dry ink) on paper. As such (*materialiter sumptum*) it is a physical object which occupies a given position in space and time. It may happen, therefore, that two names, e.g., a and b have the same graphical form (symbolically $I(a, b)$, where "I" suggests "isomorphy") but we cannot speak correctly of "the same" name which occurs twice, e.g. as middle term in a syllogism. In that case we have always two different names of the same graphical form.

(2) Every relation of meaning implies a reference to a language. This is obvious, for the same name may mean one thing in one language and something quite different in another. Moreover, it may have no meaning at all in another language. If the mention of a language is omitted in classical definitions, it is because the authors writing during the Middle Age and the Renaissance thought of the only one language used at that time, Latin.

(3) What we call "content" is what classical Thomists called "*ratio*." This *ratio* is always conceived as something determining the thing whose content it is; even in case of substantial contents (as "substance" and similars) we conceive them as such and St. Thomas explicitly teaches that in this case we always have to do with a quality in a broader meaning (including "substantial quality").

(4) Finally, the "thing" means the same as the "*res*" of the Thomists, namely the subject to which the content connoted by the name belongs. This is, at least if the logical analysis is pushed sufficiently far, an individual.

The relation S gives rise to several partial relations and partial domains. We are not going to investigate them here, as they are not relevant to our theory. We shall note, however, that the relation S allows some elegant definitions of some important semantic terms. Let $D_n'R$ be the class of all x_n such that there is at least one x_1, one $x_2 \cdots x_{n-1}$, one x_{n+1}, one $x_{n+2} \cdots x_m$ (m being the number of terms of R) such that $R(x_1, x_2, \cdots, x_n, \cdots, x_m)$. We shall call $D_n'R$ "the n-th domain of R." We put now:

2.1. $\quad$ nom $= {}_{Df}.D_1'S = {}_{D.f}\hat{a}\{\ (\exists\, l, f, x)\ S\,(a, l, f, x)\ \}$

2.2. $\quad$ lin $= {}_{Df}.D_2'S = {}_{Df}.\hat{l}\{\ (\exists\, a, f, x)\ S\,(a, l, f, x)\ \}$

2.3. $\quad$ rat $= {}_{Df}.D_3'S = {}_{Df}.\hat{f}\{\ (\exists\, a, l, x)\ S\,(a, l, f, x)\ \}$

2.4. $\quad$ res $= {}_{Df}.D_4'S = {}_{Df}.\hat{x}\{\ (\exists\, a, l, f)\ S\,(a, l, f, x)\ \}.$

The above definitions define the classes of names (*2.1*), languages (*2.2*), contents (*2.3*) and things (*2.4*).

3. ANALOGY A RELATION INVOLVING TWO NAMES. We contend that analogy, as well as univocity and equivocity, is not an absolute property of *one* name, but a relation involving *two* names at least. If this seems contrary to tradition, it is because of the use the classical authors made of the formula "the same name": they meant two names of the same form but spoke for the reason mentioned above (§2), of a single name. If, however, our considerations about the names are admitted, we are compelled to say that no single name is, strictly speaking, univocal, equivocal, or analogical. A single name may have a clear meaning or a confused meaning; but it has always *one* meaning only, and it is not possible to speak about identity or diversity of its meanings, which is required, if we have to define univocity, equivocity, or analogy.

4. THE 16 RELATIONS BETWEEN TWO SEMANTIC COMPLEXES. Now if our relations involve two meaning names, they must be relations between two semantic complexes; and as the nature of these relations depends on the relations holding between the terms of both complexes, they will be octadic relations, each complex being a tetradic relation. The general form of such relations will be consequently the following:

$$R(a, b, l, m, f, g, x, y),$$

where a and b are names, l and m languages, f and g contents, x and y things, while we have $S(a, l, f, x)$ and $S(b, m, g, y)$.

The question arises now, how many relevant relations are there of the above type. This depends, evidently, on the number of dyadic relations between the terms a-b, l-m, f-g and x-y. Such dyadic relations are very numerous, indeed, infinite in number; but for each couple two relations only are relevant, namely, $I(a, b)$ and $\sim I(a, b)$ for names; $l = m$ and $l \neq m$ for languages; $f = g$ and $f \neq g$ for contents; $x = y$ and $x \neq y$ for things. Thus there are 16 and only 16 relevant relations between two semantic complexes. The following table enumerates them:

No.	a, b	l, m	f, g	x, y	No.	a, b	l, m	f, g	x, y
1.	I	$=$	$=$	$=$	9.	$\sim I$	$=$	$=$	$=$
2.	I	$=$	$=$	$\neq$	10.	$\sim I$	$=$	$=$	$\neq$
3.	I	$=$	$\neq$	$=$	11.	$\sim I$	$=$	$\neq$	$=$
4.	I	$=$	$\neq$	$\neq$	12.	$\sim I$	$=$	$\neq$	$\neq$
5.	I	$\neq$	$=$	$=$	13.	$\sim I$	$\neq$	$=$	$=$
6.	I	$\neq$	$=$	$\neq$	14.	$\sim I$	$\neq$	$=$	$\neq$
7.	I	$\neq$	$\neq$	$=$	15.	$\sim I$	$\neq$	$\neq$	$=$
8.	I	$\neq$	$\neq$	$\neq$	16.	$\sim I$	$\neq$	$\neq$	$\neq$

This table should replace the traditional division of names into univocal, equivocal, and synonyms. As we are, however, not interested in the establishment of a full semantic theory, we shall not define all 16 relations, but only the first four which are directly relevant to the theory of analogy.

5. DEFINITION OF UNIVOCITY AND EQUIVOCITY These four (octadic) relations, which we shall name "R_1," "R_2," "R_3," and "R_4," are defined as follows:

5.1. $R_1 (a, b, l, m, f, g, x, y) \cdot$
$$= {}_{Df.} S (a, l, f, x) \cdot S (b, m, g, y) \cdot I (a, b) \cdot l$$
$$= m \cdot f = g \cdot x = y$$

5.2. $R_2 (a, b, l, m, f, g, x, y) \cdot$
$$= {}_{Df.} S (a, l, f, x) \cdot S (b, m, g, y) \cdot I (a, b) \cdot l$$
$$= m \cdot f = g \cdot x \neq y$$

5.3. $R_3 (a, b, l, m, f, g, x, y) \cdot$
$$= {}_{Df.} S (a, l, f, x) \cdot S (b, m, g, y) \cdot I (a, b) \cdot l$$
$$= m \cdot f \neq g \cdot x = y$$

5.4. $R_4 (a, b, l, m, f, g, x, y) \cdot$
$$= {}_{Df.} S (a, l, f, x) \cdot S (b, m, g, y) \cdot I (a, b) \cdot l$$
$$= m \cdot f \neq g \cdot x \neq y$$

5.1 is the definition of names which are semantically identical in spite of being (physically) two names. We may call them "isosemantic" names. *5.2* is the definition of univocal names: *quorum* (x and y) *nomen est commune* [i.e. $I (a, b)$], *ratio autem significata* (*f and g*) *est simpliciter eadem* (*f = g*). *5.3* is again the definition of names which have the same denotation, but a different connotation; we may term them "heterologic" from λόγος – *ratio*. Finally *5.4* defines the equivocal names: *quorum* (*x* and *y*) *nomen est commune* [i.e. *I*(*a, b*)], *ratio autem significata simpliciter diversa* (*f ≠ g*). In all cases *l = m*, i.e. both languages are identical. This being so, we may drop "*l = m*" and put "*l*" for "*m*" in the above definitions. The definitions of univocity and equivocity will now run as follows:

5.5. Un (a, b, l, f, g, x, y) ·
        $=_{Df} S(a, l, f, x) \cdot S(b, l, g, y) \cdot I(a, b) \cdot x \neq y \cdot f = g$
5.6. Ae (a, b, l, f, g, x, y) ·
        $=_{Df} S(a, l, f, x) \cdot S(b, l, g, y) \cdot I(a, b) \cdot x \neq y \cdot f \neq g$

We have used "*Un*" to suggest "*univoca*" and "*Ae*" to suggest "*aequivoca*"; we also changed, for technical reasons, the order of the two last factors.

The following laws, which are immediate consequences of *5.5*, will be needed in the latter parts of this essay:

5.7. Un $(a, b, l, f, g, x, y) \cdot \supset \cdot S(a, l, f, x)$

5.8. Un $(a, b, l, f, g, x, y) \cdot \supset \cdot S(b, l, f, x)$.

6. PARTIAL DOMAINS AND RELATA Each of our relations *Un* and *Ae* being heptadic, contains $\binom{7}{6} = 7$ hexadic, $\binom{7}{5} = 21$ pentadic, $\binom{7}{4} = 35$ tetradic, $\binom{7}{3} = 35$ triadic and $\binom{7}{2} = 21$ dyadic partial relations, together 119 (120 with the full relation). We may denote them by "*Un*" resp. "*Ae*" followed by two figures: one above, indicating the type of the partial relation (e.g. "*Un⁵*" for a pentadic partial relation of *Un*), another below, meaning the place which it occupies among partial relations of the given type—the whole between parentheses. E. g. "(Un_2^5)" will mean the second among the pentadic partial relations of *Un*.

Moreover, each of these partial relations gives rise, exactly as the whole relation does, to many partial domains and relata. The *n*-th domain of the relation *R* will be symbolized, as above (par. 2), by "$D_n'R$" and the *n*-th class of relata of *R* by "$sg_n'R$."

There are 120 such domains and 120 such classes of relata. We shall not define them all; the scope of the above remarks was only to show how ambiguous the common language is when we use it to speak about univocity or equivocity and, of course, about analogy.

We shall, however, use our notation in order to define the traditional terms "*univoca*" and "*aequivoca*." We need here first a definition of the following partial dyadic relations:

6.1. $(Un_{21}^2) =_{Df} \hat{x}\hat{y}\{ (\exists a, b, l, f, g) \, Un \, (a, b, l, f, g, x, y) \}$

6.2. $(Ae_{21}^2) =_{Df} \hat{x}\hat{y}\{ (\exists a, b, l, f, g) \, Ae \, (a, b, l, f, g, x, y) \}.$

We can now define the classes called "*univoca*" and "*aequivoca*" which we shall name "*uni*" or "*aeq*":

6.3. $uni =_{Df} F' \, (Un_{21}^2)$

6.4. $aeq =_{Df} F' \, (Ae_{21}^2).$

If this would appear too generic, we may use triadic relations, including the language as a term:

6.5. $(Un_{31}^3) =_{Df} \hat{l}\hat{x}\hat{y}\{ (\exists a, b, f, g) \, Un \, (a, b, l, f, g, x, y) \}$

6.6. $(Ae_{31}^3) =_{Df} \hat{l}\hat{x}\hat{y}\{ (\exists a, b, l, g) \, Ae \, (a, b, l, f, g, x, y) \}$

and consequently:

6.7. $unil =_{Df} D'_1 \, (Un_{31}^3) \cup D'_2(Un_{31}^3)$

6.8. $aeql =_{Df} D'_1(Ae_{31}^3) \cup D'_2(Ae_{31}^3).$

7. THE PRINCIPLES OF CONTRADICTION AND EXCLUDED MIDDLE
Other important laws of our theory are two formulae which will be called, respectively, "the law of contradiction" and "the law of excluded middle for univocal and equivocal names." We mean by the first that no two names can be univocal and equivocal in respect to the same language, couples of contents and of things. By the second we mean that if such names are not univocal, they must be equivocal, and conversely. It should be clearly understood that this is true only in respect of some determined contents meant by the names, moreover that these names must be of the

same form and the things they mean must be not-identical. For nothing prevents two names from being univocal in respect of $f - g$ and, at the same time, equivocal in respect of $h - j$, if $f \neq h$ or $g \neq j$; also, if the names do not mean the contents involved, they are neither univocal nor equivocal in respect of them. The last two conditions follow from our table (in our par. 4).

Consequently, we state our principles in the following form:

7.1. $(a, b, l, f, g, x, y) : S(a, l, f, x) \cdot S(b, l, g, y)$
$$\cdot I(a, b) \cdot x \neq y \cdot \supset$$
$$\supset \cdot \sim [Un(a, b, l, f, g, x, y) \cdot Ae(a, b, l, f, g, x, y)]$$

7.2. $(a, b, l, f, g, x, y) : S(a, l, f, x) \cdot S(b, l, g, y) \cdot I(a, b)$
$$\cdot x \neq y \cdot \supset$$
$$\supset \cdot Un(a, b, l, f, g, x, y) \vee Ae(a, b, l, f, g, x, y).$$

Proofs:[5]

(1) $p \supset \sim (pq \cdot p \sim q)$ (axiom)

(2) $p \supset \cdot pq \vee p \sim q$ (axiom)

(3) $\sim (f = g) \cdot = _{Df.} \cdot f \neq g$ (definition)

(4) $S(a, l, f, x) \cdot S(b, l, g, y) \cdot I(a, b) \cdot x \neq y: \supset$
$$\supset : \sim (S(a, l, f, x) \cdot S(b, l, g, y) \cdot I(a, b) \cdot x \neq y$$
$$\cdot f = g):$$
$$: S(a, l, f, x) \cdot S(b, l, g, y) \cdot I(a, b) \cdot x \neq y \cdot \sim (f = g):$$
by (1) putting $\dfrac{S(a, l, f, x) \cdot S(b, l, g, y) \cdot I(a, b) \cdot x \neq y}{p}, \dfrac{f = g}{q}$

(5) $= 7.1$

by (4), (3), 5.5 and 5.6 with the rule for adjunction of quantifiers.

(6) $S(a, l, f, x) \cdot S(b, l, g, y) \cdot I(a, b) \cdot x \neq y: \supset$
$$\supset : S(a, l, f, x) \cdot S(b, l, g, y) \cdot I(a, b) \cdot x \neq y \cdot f = g \vee$$
$$\vee \cdot S(a, l, f, x) \cdot S(b, l, g, y) \cdot I(a, b) \cdot x \neq y \cdot \sim (f = g)$$

by (2) with the same substitutions as for (4)

(7) $= 7.2$

by (6), (3), 5.5 and 5.6 with the rule for adjunction of quantifiers.

The law of excluded middle shows that the classical Thomists were right when they named their *analoga* "*aequivoca a consilio*," considering them as a subclass of the class of *aequivoca*, and that some modern Thomists are wrong when they put analogy as a third class coordinated to univocity and equivocity. Incidentally it may be remarked that the authors of the *Principia Mathematica* used an exact translation of the "*aequivocatio a consilio*" when they coined the expression "systematic ambiguity." As a matter of fact, they were treating of analogy.

8. ON THE GENERIC NOTION OF ANALOGY   Analogy will be, according to the above analyses, a heptadic relation between two names, a language, two contents and two things (at least). The names will be of the same form; the things must be different. How the contents are related we must still investigate. If we suppose that the answer to that question is expressed by "F," the generic definition of analogy will be the following:

8.1. $An(a, b, l, f, g, x, y) \cdot =$
$$= {}_{Df.} \cdot S(a, l, f, x) \cdot S(b, l, g, y) \cdot I(a, b) \cdot x \neq y \cdot F.$$

Moreover, using *7.2* we may say that analogy is either a kind of univocity or a kind of equivocity. According to the Tradition it is certainly not the first. Thus it must be the second. We may put therefore:

8.2. $An(a, b, l, f, g, x, y) \cdot = {}_{Df.} \cdot Ae(a, b, l, f, g, x, y) \cdot F.$

The question arises now, if there is a factor G such that F would be identical with the product of G with another factor, say H_n, G being identical in all kinds of analogy, H_n different for each; the definitions of the successive kinds of analogy would be constructed by putting in *8.2* for "F" first "$G \cdot H_1$," then "$G \cdot H_2$" and so on. If it be so, we could say that the name "analogy" is univocal; if not, i.e. if there could be no common factor G, it would be equivocal.

As a matter of fact some well known Thomists asserted that the name "analogy" is an analogical name, i.e. (according to

8.2) an equivocal one. We are not going to discuss this assertion, but limit ourselves to a correct formulation of it. This requires, however, some preliminary steps.

9. EXPANSION OF THE THEORY TO HIGHER LEVELS   We must first note that we are already dealing with a situation that is far more complex than that which is met in classical Formal Logic. As a matter of fact, all artificial symbols of any system of contemporary Formal Logic belong to the same semantic level, namely to the object language, i.e. each of them means some object, but none of them means a symbol of an object. But in the theory developed above we are using symbols belonging to a higher level, namely our symbols "*a*" and "*b*," which are names of names, i.e. symbols of symbols.

In order to supply the last sentence with a more definite meaning, let us introduce the following recursive definition: (1) the object language is the first level; (2) a language such that at least one term of it is a symbol of a symbol belonging to the *n*-th level, but none is a symbol of such term, is the *n* + 1 level; (3) a relation holding between objects of which at least one is of the *n*-th level, and none is of the *n* + 1 level, is of the *n*-th level.

It will appear that our *a*, *b* and also *S*, *Un*, *Ae* etc. are of the second level; consequently the *names* of these will belong to the third level. Now when we say that "analogy" is an analogical name, the word "analogy" is a *name* of *An*; thus it belongs to the third level. We have to investigate if and how are we allowed to extend our theory to that level, for everything we said until now was clearly situated on the second level.

Let us note first that the laws of the third level would be, as far as structure is concerned, exactly similar to these met on the second. For if we say that "analogy" is analogical, we mean that two names, say *A* and *B*, mean in our new language (which is, by the way, the third level), the relations An_1 and An_2 of the objects $(a_1, b_1, l_1, f_1, g_1, x_1, y_1)$ and $(a_2, b_2, l_2, f_2, g_2, x_2, y_2)$. The last two may be considered as classes; but there is nothing to prevent us from considering them as objects, as the relations An_1 and An_2 are true contents of them. Let us put "*X*" for the first and

"*Y*" for the second. We shall obtain the following exact formulation of the thesis "analogy is analogical":

$$AN\,(A,\,B,\,L,\,An_1,\,An_2,\,X,\,Y).$$

Here all symbols (except the parentheses and commas) are different from those used in the former paragraphs; and yet the structure is not only similar, but strictly identical with the structure of

$$An\,(a,\,b,\,l,\,f,\,g,\,x,\,y).$$

It is also clear that the whole of our previous analyses might have been repeated on the third level. We would reach a theory whose terms and meaning would be different from the theory we developed above, but whose structure would be completely identical.

This suggests an important remark. Analyses of such kind involve the use of the idea of structural identity, or isomorphy. Now, according to the theory we shall propose, this means analogy of proportionality. It seems, consequently, that we cannot treat adequately the problem of the generic notion of analogy without a previous examination of analogy of proportionality.

10. ANALOGY OF ONE-ONE ATTRIBUTION Among the several kinds of analogy there are only two that are really relevant: analogy of attribution and analogy of proportionality. Two names which are related by the first will be called "attributively analogous"; similarly, two names related by the latter will be called "proportionally analogous.'

We are starting with the first kind. Here again there is one relation called "*analogia unius ad alterum*"—in our terminology "one-one analogy" (symbolically "*At*")—and another called "*analogia plurium ad unum*," here "many-one analogy" (symbolically "*Atm*"). Let us begin with the first, which is the more fundamental.

We have two things, x and y and two contents, f and g; the names a and b are equivocal in regard to them, but there is still another characteristic: x is the cause of y or y the cause of x. Writing "$C(x, y)$" for "x is the cause of y" we shall have:

10.1. $At (a, b, l, f, g, x, y)$·
    $= _{Df.} \cdot Ae (a, b, l, f, g, x, y) \cdot C (x, y) \vee C (y, x).$

This is, however, rather unsatisfactory, for the connection of f and g is not shown, the relation of causality being not analysed. We cannot, of course, give a complete analysis of this highly complex notion here. We shall note only that the relation of causality is a pentadic relation which holds between two things, two contents and a peculiar dyadic relation between the things; e.g. the food is the cause of the health of the animal, if and only if there is a content f (health) present in the food (x) such that, if a peculiar relation R (here: of being eaten) is established between x and the animal (y), another content g (the health of the animal) appears in y. Writing "$C(f, x, R, g, y)$" for this relation we shall have:

10.2. $At (a, b, l, f, g, x, y)$ ·
    $= _{Df.} \cdot Ae (a, b, l, f, g, x, y) \cdot (\exists R) \cdot C (f, x, R, g, y) \vee$
        $\vee C (g, y, R, f, x).$

The alternative is necessary, according to the traditional doctrine, as there may be an analogy independently from the direction of causality.

11. ANALOGY OF MANY-ONE ATTRIBUTION The second kind of analogy of attribution is clearly derived from the first. The many-one analogy holds, namely, between two names a and b, if and only if there is a third name c, such that both a and b are attributively analogous (according to *10.2*) with c:

11.1. $Atm (a, b, l, f, g, x, y)$ ·
    $= _{Df.} \cdot (\exists c, h, z) \cdot At (a, c, l, f, h, x, z)$ ·
        $\cdot At (b, c, l, g, h, y, z).$

Let x be food, y—urine, z—animal, f, g, h—the contents called "health" of, respectively, x, y, z, and a, b, c—the names of these contents. There will be a many-one analogy of a in respect of b.

We may still distinguish four further subclasses of this class of analogical names, for in *11.1* we may have either

(1) $C(f, x, R, h, z) \cdot C(g, y, R, h, y)$ —or

(2) $C(f, x, R, h, z) \cdot C(h, z, R, g, y)$ —or

(3) $C(h, z, R, f, x) \cdot C(g, y, R, h, z)$ —or

(4) $C(h, z, R, f, x) \cdot C(h, z, R, g, y)$.

12.   CONDITIONS OF ANALOGY OF PROPORTIONALITY   There are, according to tradition, two conditions for this kind of analogy: the contents must be non-identical, i.e. we must have equivocity; still, the syllogism having as middle terms a couple of proportionally analogous names must be a correct formula. This is secured, according to classical writers, by the fact that these middle terms mean something "proportionally common" in both cases, or that there is an *analogatum commune* containing *in confuso* the contents meant by both names.

It seems at first, that these requirements are contradictory: for, if the meanings of the two names are quite different, one can hardly see how a syllogism with them as middle terms may be a correct formula. As a matter of fact, not only is there a logical theory capable of fulfilling both requirements without contradiction, but it seems even that there are *two* such theories. It seems, namely, that one theory is suggested by the "*proportionaliter commune,*" the other by the "*confuse.*" We shall call the former "isomorphic," the latter "alternative theory." As far as is known to the writer, St. Thomas used the isomorphic theory, while the alternative seems to be originated by Cajetan.

13.   THE ALTERNATIVE THEORY   The central idea of the alternative theory may be explained as follows: we have to do with three names; one of them means the content *f*, the other the content *g*, *f* and *g* being the *analogata particularia*; the third name means the *analogatum commune*, namely, the alternative of *f* and *g*, symbolically $f \cup g$. We shall give to that expression a sufficiently clear meaning by putting

13.1. $[f \cup g]x \cdot =_{Df.} \cdot fx \, v \, gx.$

A rather complex situation arises here because of admission of three names: this makes an expansion of our previous formulae to three complexes necessary, and the basic formula for analogy of proportionality becomes a relation of 10 terms. Once a definition of this form is established, the (heptadic) relations analogous to *Un* and *Ae* will appear as partial relations of the general one, and the verbal formulae as elliptic. We shall not, however, define this general relation in that way, as, for several reasons, to be explained later (par. 16), the whole alternative theory appears as inadequate. But we are going to investigate the validity of a syllogism in *Barbara* with proportionally analogous middle terms. For the use in that inquiry we define the analogy of proportionality (*Anp*) according to the alternative theory as a heptadic relation in the following way:

13.2.　　$Anp\,(a, b, l, f, g, x, y) \cdot$
　　　　　$=\,_{Df.} \cdot Ae\,(a, b, l, f, g, x, y) \cdot (\exists\,h) \cdot f = [g \cup h].$

This is a partial relation contained in the full relation of analogy described above.

14.　ON FORMAL VALIDITY OF SYLLOGISM　If we wish to investigate the validity of a syllogism with analogical middle terms we meet a serious difficulty unknown in current Formal Logic. For in current Formal Logic it is always supposed that a formula which is verbally valid is also formally valid; the reason of this supposition is that all terms used in current Formal Logic are univocal symbols. Here, however, the situation is different, as we have to deal with analogical names. We need, consequently, a distinction between the verbal and formal validity of a formula; moreover we need to know when a verbally valid formula is also formally valid. This is by no means a universal rule, as the case of the syllogism with equivocal and non-analogical middle terms shows. We are not going to investigate the problem in its full generality, but we will limit ourselves to a single case, the syllogism in *Barbara*.

We shall first construct two languages:

(1) A first-level univocal language. This will be the language of

the theory of classes, interpreted as a Logic of contents. In it the mode *Barbara* will run as follows:

$$f \subset g \cdot h \subset f \cdot \supset \cdot h \subset g.$$

(*2*) A second-level analogical language. This will contain all symbols used until now (small Latin letters being sometimes substituted by small Greek letters and indexes being added to them), with addition of the following: (i) "II"; a formula composed of "II" followed by "*a*," followed by "*b*" will be interpreted as meaning the formula "*a* $\subset$ *b*"; (ii) "+"; a formula such as "II + *a* + *b*" will be read: "a formula composed of II followed by *a*, followed by *b*"; (iii) "ϵ *T*"; "*F* ϵ *T*" will be read: "*F* is a true theorem."

The proofs will be developed in a second-level language, containing as subclasses the above two. We shall proceed as follows. Given the (second-level) premises *A* and *B* such that $A \epsilon T \cdot B \epsilon T$, we wish to prove that the (verbally correct) conclusion *C* (of the same level) is a true theorem, i.e. that $C \epsilon T$. We translate *A* and *B* into the first-level language, apply to the result the laws of classical Formal Logic and obtain a conclusion, which we re-translate into the second-level language; if we are able to obtain $C \epsilon T$ in that way, the formula "if $A T \epsilon \cdot B \epsilon T$, then $C \epsilon T$" is clearly a valid formula and the formal validity of the mode, whose premises are *A* and *B*, and the conclusion is *C*, is proved.

We put as a law of translation the intuitively evident:

14.1. $S(a, l, f, x) \cdot S(b, l, g, y) : \supset : \mathrm{II} + a + b \epsilon T \cdot \equiv \cdot f \subset g.$

With the help of *14.1* we can easily prove that a syllogism in *Barbara* with univocal middle terms is a formally valid formula; but we cannot prove it if the middle terms are either purely equivocal or attributively analogical. Alongside of *14.1* we shall need still another law of translation for cases where an existential quantifier is involved:

14.2. $(\exists h) \cdot S(a, l, [f \cup h], x) \cdot S(b, l, g, y) : \supset$
              $\supset : (\exists h) \cdot [f \cup h] \subset g.$

This seems to be also intuitively evident.

15. The validity of the syllogism in Barbara with analogical middle terms according to the alternative theory In such a syllogism the middle term of the major premise is analogical with regard to the middle term in the minor premise, the situation being this, that the former means alternatively the content meant by the latter *and* some other content. This syllogism, if in *Barbara*, is a valid formula. The proof is rather cumbersome, because of the existential quantifier; we shall however give here a developed sketch of it.

In the first place we need two theorems analogous to *5.7* and *5.8*. These may be proved as follows:

(1) $Anp\,(a, b, l, f, g, x, y) \cdot$
$\equiv \cdot Ae\,(a, b, l, f, g, x, y) \cdot (\exists h) \cdot f = [g \cup h]$
[by *13.2*]

(2) $\equiv \cdot S\,(a, l, f, x) \cdot S\,(b, l, g, y) \cdot I\,(a, b) \cdot x \neq y \cdot$
$\cdot f \neq g \cdot (\exists h) \cdot f = [g \cup h]$
[by (1) and *5.6*]

(3) $\equiv \cdot (\exists h) \cdot S\,(a, l, f, x) \cdot S\,(b, l, g, y) \cdot I\,(a, b) \cdot$
$\cdot x \neq y \cdot f \neq g \cdot f = [g \cup h]$
[by (2) and * *10.24 Principia Mathematica*.]

(4) $\equiv \cdot (\exists h) \cdot S\,(a, l, [g \cup h], x) \cdot S\,(b, l, g, y) \cdot I\,(a, b) \cdot$
$\cdot x \neq y \cdot f \neq g$
[by (3) and **13.12 Principia Mathematica*.]

(5) $\equiv \cdot (\exists h)\,S\,(a, l, [g \cup h], x) \cdot (\exists h)\,S\,(b, l, g, y) \cdot$
$\cdot (\exists h) \cdot x \neq y \cdot f \neq g$
[by (4) and **10.5 Principia Mathematica*.]

15.1. $Anp\,(a, b, l, f, g, x, y) \cdot \supset \cdot (\exists h)\,S\,(a, l, [g \cup h], x)$
[by (5) and "$p \equiv qr \cdot \supset \cdot p \supset q$"]

15.2. $Anp\,(a, b, l, f, g, x, y) \cdot \supset \cdot S\,(b, l, g, y)$
[by (5) and "$p \equiv qrs \cdot \supset \cdot p \supset r$," dropping the quantifier].

We enumerate now the five hypotheses of the syllogism in

Barbara with analogical middle terms, explained according to the alternative theory:

H1.	$\Pi + m_1 + a_1 \in T$
H2.	$\Pi + b_1 + m_2 \in T$
H3.	$Anp\,(m_1, m_2, l, \mu_1, \mu_2, x, y)$
H4.	$Un\,(a_1, a_2, l, \alpha_1, \alpha_2, z, t)$
H5.	$Un\,(b_1, b_2, l, \beta_1, \beta_2, u, v).$

The proof of "$\Pi + b_2 + a_2 \in T$" runs as follows:

(1)	$(\exists h)\,S\,(m_1, l, [\mu_2 \cup h], x)$	by H3 and 15.1
(2)	$S\,(a_1, l, \alpha_1, z)$	by H_4 and 5.7
(3)	$(\exists h) \cdot [\mu_2 \cup h] \subset \alpha_1$	by (1), (2), H1 and 14.2
(4)	$S\,(b_1, l, \beta_1, u)$	by H5 and 5.7
(5)	$S\,(m_2, l, \mu_2, y)$	by H3 and 15.2
(6)	$\beta_1 \subset \mu_2$	by (4), (5), H2 and 14.1
(7)	$\beta_1 \subset \mu_2 \cdot (\exists h) \cdot [\mu_2 \cup h] \subset \alpha_1$	by (6) and (3)
(8)	$(\exists h) \cdot \beta_1 \subset \mu_2 \cdot [\mu_2 \cup h] \subset \alpha_1$	by (7) and * 10.35 PM
(9)	$(\exists h) \cdot \beta_1 \subset \alpha_1$	by (8), "$f \subset g \cdot [g \cup h] \subset j \cdot \supset \cdot f \subset j$"
		and *10.28 PM
(10)	$\beta_1 \subset \alpha_1$	by (9)
(11)	$S\,(b_2, l, \beta_1, u)$	by H5 and 5.8
(12)	$S\,(a_2, l, \alpha_1, z)$	by H4 and 5.8
(13)	$\Pi + b_2 + a_2 \in T \cdot \equiv \cdot \beta_1 \subset \alpha_1$	by (11), (12) and 14.1
(14)	$\Pi + b_2 + a_2 \in T$	by (10) and (13)

Q.E.D.

16. CRITICISM OF THE ALTERNATIVE THEORY It has been shown that a syllogism in *Barbara* with analogical middle terms, defined according to the alternative theory, is a formally valid formula. This is, however, the only advantage of this theory. Not even all requirements of Theology and Metaphysics in regard to the syllogism can be met by means of it. For a syllogism of these sciences has not only analogical middle terms, but also analogical major terms; e.g. when we write "if every being is good, and God

is a being, then God is good," not only "being," but also "good" must be analogical. But this means, according to the alternative theory, that *H4* in par. 15 should be replaced by

$$Anp\,(a_1, a_2, l, a_1, a_2, z, \iota).$$

If so, instead of (3) we would obtain only

$$(\exists\,h) \cdot [\mu_2 \cup h] \subset [\alpha_2 \cup g]$$

which does not allow us to draw the conclusion (*14*). Neither can we try to invert the order of "*f*" and "*g*" in *15.1*; in that case the syllogism would become valid, but the major term in the conclusion would have an alternative meaning, which can hardly be admitted.

Moreover, the theory has other inconveniences. First, the very definition of analogy, as sketched in par. 13, is highly unsatisfactory. By saying that two names are analogical if and only if there is a third name meaning alternatively the contents meant by both, we do not show any intrinsic connection between the contents involved; and every couple of names would be analogical, according to that definition, for we can always introduce into our system a new name, defined precisely as meaning the said alternative. Secondly, there are serious gnoseological difficulties. The situation with which we have to deal is the following: two names are given, and while we know the meaning of the first by direct experience, we do not know in that way the meaning of the second. In order to be able to use that second name correctly, we must supply it with a meaning correlated in some way with the meaning of the first. Now the alternative theory allows nothing of the sort: it only says how we can deal with middle terms having alternative meanings, when both meanings are already known.

These remarks do not lead to the complete rejection of the alternative theory; but they seem to show that it is at least incomplete and should be completed by another theory. The present author believes that this was the position of Cajetan.

17. THE ISOMORPHIC THEORY This theory is based on the

following considerations: the "*proportionaliter eadem*" suggests that there is an identity, not between the contents meant by both analogical terms, but between some relations holding between the first (f) and its thing (x) on one side, the second (g) and its thing (y) on the other. The texts of St. Thomas Aquinas are clear enough here. The said relations are, however, not identical; this is also a traditional thesis, strongly emphasized by all classical Thomists. We may therefore admit, as a first approximation, that, while being non-identical, they are both contained in the same relation. The definition of analogy of proportionality would run, in that case, as follows:

17.1. $Anp\,(a, b, l, f, g, x, y) \cdot =\,_{Df.} \cdot Ae\,(a, b, l, f, g, x, y) \cdot$
$\qquad (\exists\,P, Q, R) \cdot fPx \cdot gQy \cdot P \neq Q \cdot P \subset R \cdot Q \subset R.$

This is, however, not satisfactory. For if *17.1* would be the definition of analogy of proportionality, there would be a material univocal element; analogy would allow us to transfer to the other name some material relations found in the meaning of the first. Now St. Thomas Aquinas and Tradition are quite clear as to the negation of such univocity. But *17.1* can be corrected by the affirmation that the common element in both relations is formal, i.e. consists in the isomorphy of these relations. The definition becomes:

17.2. $An\,(a, b, l, f, g, x, y) \cdot =\,_{Df.} \cdot Ae\,(a, b, l, f, g, x, y) \cdot$
$\qquad \cdot (\exists\,P, Q) \cdot fPx \cdot gQy \cdot PsmorQ.$

This is what we mean by "isomorphic theory." It is strongly supported by the fact that St. Thomas Aquinas uses for illustration of his doctrine mathematical proportionality, the only mathematical function he possessed and a function which makes one immediately think of isomorphy.

One may think, perhaps, that if this be analogy of proportionality, the meaning of our sentences about spirit, God, etc., would be extremely poor, indeed limited to some very few formal relations enumerated in the *Principia Mathematica*. But this is not so. It is true that we cannot, as yet, give exact formulations of many formal properties involved in relations used by Metaphysics and Theology; the reason, however, is not the lack of such formal properties, but the very undeveloped state of Biology and of other sciences, from which the Metaphysician and the Theologian must draw his analogical names (and contents). An immense progress in speculative sciences would arise out of a formalization of these disciplines. And yet, even in the actual state of knowledge, where only Mathematics, i.e. the poorest of all sciences, is formalized, we can show, e.g., the difference between the Principle and the Father by purely formal means—as, evidently, the first is transitive, the second intransitive.

18. THE EXISTENTIAL INTERPRETATION OF THE MODE BARBARA   If the isomorphic theory is admitted, a peculiar interpretation must be given to the mode *Barbara* with analogical middle terms. Let us consider the following substitution: "if all being is good, and God is a being, then God is good." According to the isomorphic theory the only common element meant by the two "being" and the two "good" is a product of some formal relations, say P in the first case and Q in the second. But if it is so, the major must be interpreted as follows: "for all x: if there is an f such that fPx, then there is a g such that gQy"; the minor will be interpreted in the same manner by the formula "for all x: if there is an h such that hRx, then there is an f such that fPx." From this we draw the conclusion "for all x: if there is an h such that hRx, then there is a g such that gQx." This would mean: "if there is an x such that h is the Divinity of x, then there is a g such that g is the Goodness of x." The law used here is:

18.1. $(x) \cdot (\exists f) fPx \supset (\exists g) gQx : (x) \cdot (\exists h) hRx \supset (\exists f) fPx :$
$\supset : (x) \cdot (\exists h) hRx \supset (\exists g) gQx.$

This is a correct formula of the Logic of predicates.

The remarkable result of the existential interpretation is that the Thomistic idea of analogy becomes sharply formulated in a very anti-univocal sense. For, we do not know, as a result of our reasoning according to *18.1*, anything except that there is something (undetermined as to the content) which has to God the set of quite formal relations Q. And yet, the talk about God's goodness is clearly meaningful; moreover rigorous demonstrations concerning it are possible.

19. THE VALIDITY OF THE SYLLOGISM WITH ANALOGICAL MIDDLE TERMS ACCORDING TO THE ISOMORPHIC THEORY   We are going to show now how, in such theory, a syllogism in *Barbara* is a formally valid formula. We meet here, however, two formal difficulties.

First we note that isomorphy, being a relation between two relations, cannot be, as such, treated as a relation in which these relations are contained; now this seems to be necessary if we wish to construct a correct syllogism with analogical middle terms, interpreted according to the isomorphic theory.

This difficulty may be, however, obviated in the following manner. Isomorphy implies the identity of a series of formal properties of the relations involved. These formal properties are different in each case of couples of isomorphic relations; but for each of them *in concreto* a product of such properties may be determined. E.g., in some cases both relations will be included in diversity and will be transitive; in other cases they will be intransitive and asymmetric, etc. Now each of these properties may be conceived as a relation in which the given isomorphic relations are contained. This can be done by introducing into the system the name of a new relation, which is treated as a primitive term, but whose meaning is determined by an axiom. E.g. for symmetry we will put a relation S and determine the meaning of "S" by the axiom $(x, y) : xSy \cdot \equiv \cdot xSy \equiv x\check{S}y$. The product of such relations would constitute the relation in which both isomorphic relations are contained.[6]

The other difficulty is strictly operational. It will appear that we shall need an expansion of our *17.2* in order that the name of the common relation R, in which the relations P and Q are contained, might be treated as an argument of "*Anp*." If so, a new relation must be defined, namely an octadic relation containing as terms, besides the seven stated in *17.2*, also R. We shall define it as follows:

19.1. $Anp\,(a, b, l, f, g, x, y, R) \cdot =\,{}_{Df.} \cdot Ae\,(a, b, l, f, g, x, y) \cdot$
$\cdot (\exists\,P, Q, R) \cdot f P x \cdot g Q y \cdot P \neq Q \cdot P \neq R \cdot Q \neq R \cdot$
$\cdot P \subset R \cdot Q \subset R \cdot \epsilon\,Form.$

By "*Form*" we mean the class of all formal relations, as described in § 17.

There will be three laws of translation, analogous to *14.1*:

19.2. $Anp\,(m_1, m_2, l, \mu_1, \mu_2, x, y, P) \cdot$
$Anp\,(a_1, a_2, l, \alpha_1, \alpha_2, z, t, Q) : \supset$
$\supset\,: \Pi + m_1 + a_1 \,\epsilon\,T \cdot \equiv \cdot (x) \cdot (\exists f) f P x \supset (\exists\,g)\,g Q x.$

19.3. $Anp\,(b_1, b_2, l, \beta_1, \beta_2, u, v, R) \cdot$
$Anp\,(m_1, m_2, l, \mu_1, \mu_2, x, y, P) : \supset$
$\supset\,: \Pi + b_1 + m_2 \,\epsilon\,T \cdot \equiv \cdot (x) \cdot (\exists\,h)\,h R x \supset (\exists f) f P x.$

19.4. $Anp\,(b_1, b_2, l, \beta_1, \beta_2, u, v, R) \cdot$
$Anp\,(a_1, a_2, l, \alpha_1, \alpha_2, z, t, Q) : \supset$
$\supset\,: \Pi + b_2 + a_2 \,\epsilon\,T \cdot \equiv \cdot (x)_4 \cdot (\exists\,h)\,h R x \supset (\exists\,g)\,g Q x.$

Our hypotheses are

H1. $\Pi + m_1 + a_1 \,\epsilon\,T$
H2. $\Pi + b_1 + m_2 \,\epsilon\,T$
H3. $Anp\,(m_1, m_2, l, \mu_1, \mu_2, x, y, P)$
H4. $Anp\,(a_1, a_2, l, \alpha_1, \alpha_2, z, t, Q)$
H5. $Anp\,(b_1, b_2, l, \beta_1, \beta_2, u, v, R).$

The proof of "$\Pi + b_2 + a_2 \,\epsilon\,T$" runs as follows:

(1) $(x) \cdot (\exists f) f P x \supset (\exists\,g)\,g Q x$ by *H3, H4, H1*, and *19.2*

(2) $(x) \cdot (\exists\,h)\,h R x \supset (\exists f) f P x$ by *H5, H3, H2*, and *19.3*

(3) $(x) \cdot (\exists\,h)\,h R x \supset (\exists\,g)\,g Q x$ by *(1)*, *(2)* and *18.1*

(4) $\Pi + b_2 + a_2 \,\epsilon\,T \cdot \equiv \cdot (x)\,(\exists\,h)\,h R x \supset (\exists\,g)\,g Q x$
                                                by *H5, H4* and *19.4*

(5) $\Pi + b_2 + a_2 \,\epsilon\,T$ by *(4)* and *(3)*
        Q.E.D.

20. ON ANALOGY IN RECENT LOGIC   While the classical Thomists used analogy in ontology and theology, but not in logic, recent writers seem to make a constant use of it in formal logic. We

noticed already that the authors of the *Principia Mathematica* re-invented the very name used for analogy by the Thomists (§ 7) and that analogy appears in the construction of semantics (§ 9). The last phenomenon is connected with the theory of types. It is known that, in order to avoid contradictions, we are bound to divide all objects treated by logic (or all logical expressions) into classes called "types." The formulae used in each type have quite a different meaning, but exactly the same structure as the formulae used in another. This means that the formal properties involved are identical, i.e. that we have to do with analogy, at least if the isomorphic theory is accepted.

The question arises as to why analogy has penetrated the domain of formal logic. The answer seems to be given by the theory of Prof. H. Scholz, who says that recent formal logic is nothing else than a part of classic ontology.[7] As a matter of fact, recent formal logic generally deals, not with rules, but with laws of being in its whole generality; most of the laws contained in the *Principia Mathematica*, e.g., as opposed to metalogical rules, are such laws. If this is so, it is not to be wondered at that some consideration must have been given to analogy, for "being" is an analogical term and so are the names of all properties, relations, etc., belonging to being as such.

One curious feature of these developments is that the highly trained mathematical logicians who had to speak about analogy, spoke about it in a very loose and inexact way. What, for example, the *Principia Mathematica* contains on the subject is far more rudimentary than the classic Thomistic doctrine. Yet, recent formal logic, once applied to the language itself, supplies superior tools for the elaboration of that notion. The present paper is believed to contain only a very small sub-class of the class of theorems on analogy, which may and should be elaborated by means of recent formal logic.

NOTES

1. The author is, however, indebted to the late Fr. Jan Salamucha and to J. Fr. Drewnowski who were the first to apply recent Formal Logic to Thomistic problems. The present essay may be considered as an attempt to formalize some of the opinions expressed by them. Cf. *Myśl katolicka wobec Logiki współczesnej* (Polish = The Catholic Thought and Contemporary Logic), Poznan 1937 (with French abstracts) and J. Fr. Drewnowski, *Zarys programu filozoficznego* (Polish = A sketch of a Philosophic Programme), Przeglad Filozoficzny, 37, 1943, 3–38, 150–181, 262–292, especially pp. 95–98. (There is a French account of this important work in *Studia Philosophica* [Lwow], I, 1935, 451–454.)

2. A. N. Whitehead and B. Russell, *Principia Mathematica*, 2nd ed., Cambridge 1925–1927.

3. Cf. R. Carnap, *Abriss der Logistik*, Wien 1929, pp. 43–45.

4. Cf. A. Tarski, *Der Wahrheitsbegriff in den formalisierten Sprachen*, Studia Philosophica (Lwow), I, 1935, 261–405.

5. The method used is that of the *Principia Mathematica*; therefore what we call a "proof" is rather a sketch of a proof. Rigorous proof could be, however, easily built along the lines given here. (This applies to all proofs contained in the present essay.)

6. The author is conscious that the proposed solution is highly un-orthodox; he would be glad to find anything better. It must be remembered, however, that the whole difficulty is purely operational; it seems intuitively evident that once there is a common property, the syllogism is valid.

7. H. Scholz, *Metaphysik als strenge Wissenschaft*, Köln 1941.

6

BEING, ESSENCE, AND EXISTENCE

Desmond Paul Henry

BY the use of many-link functors much of medieval philosophy and logic can be made intelligible in terms of modern logic. Since, following a suggestion of C. Lejewski (*LAS*248–250), the use of such functors as they occur in the Ontology of S. Lešniewski has already facilitated the interpretation of statements involving such terms as "*esse*", "*species*", and so on, in St. Anselm's writings (*HAN, HDG, HAR*), a tentative set of conjectures as to the sense of St. Thomas Aquinas's discourse concerning essence (*essentia*) and existence (*esse*) is now presented. Thanks to the flexibility and richness of Lešniewski's Ontology these conjectures are susceptible of further qualifications in order to bring them into line with the finer points of Aquinas's theory; in other words, there is nothing final about their every detail. Further, no attempt is made hereunder to reproduce features of Aquinas's thought apart from the topics in question; e.g. the distinction of substance from accident, and its accompanying notion that an accident is *magis entis quam ens* have not been accounted for hereunder. Sigla (as listed at the close of the paper) are immediately followed by appropriate numerical references.

Lešniewski's Ontology is a theory of *ens in quantum ens*, and so carries into effect, using the resources of modern logic, the project originally conceived in Aristotle's *Metaphysica* (*LR*150). It presupposes Protot
thetic (propositional calculus with functorial variables) and is also used as a basis for further theories such as

Mereology (theory of part and whole), Chronology (theory of time), and so forth. A general survey of Leśniewski's systems which underlines their interpreted, anti-formalist, and paradox-free nature, is to be found in *LLL*. In the account which follows the signs for proposition-forming functors which have propositions as arguments will be those of the Peano-Russell sort. Quantification is unrestricted, thereby allowing the dissociation of some-hood and existence, so that the latter can be accounted for in notation distinct from quantifier-notation: "∃ . . ." is hence read as: "For some......", and *not* as: "There exists an...... such that......" (Cf. *LLE* and 2 below). This makes Ontology particularly suitable for dealing with questions concerning *esse*. The primitive functor used in Leśniewski's 1920 axiom for Ontology is "ϵ", which is a proposition-forming functor for two arguments, the latter being names or name-like expressions (shared, unshared, or fictitious). A proposition of the form "$a \epsilon b$" is true if and only if *either* "a" and "b" each name only one and the same individual *or* "a" names only one individual which is one of several individuals named by "b"; e.g. "Cicero is Tully", "Elizabeth is queen", "The son of Sophroniscus is a philosopher". The informal extra-systematic characterisation of the primitive term can, of couse, be carried out in any manner which is judged effective (*LR*154–6). The 1920 axiom for Ontology is:

1. $[ab]: : a \epsilon b . \equiv : . [\exists c] . c \epsilon a : . [c]: c \epsilon a . \supset . c \epsilon b :$
$$[cd]: c \epsilon a . d \epsilon a . \supset . c \epsilon d$$

Rules for definition are briefly outlined in *LR*172–174, and will not be given here. First one of several possible functors of existence may be defined:

2. $[a]: ob(a) . \equiv . [\exists b] . a \epsilon b$

(The *definiendum* "ob( )" may be read as: "There exists exactly one......"). Singular and weak identities may be defined thus:

3. $[ab]: a = b . \equiv . a \epsilon b . b \epsilon a$

4. $[ab]: a \text{ o } b . \equiv . [c]: c \epsilon a . \equiv . c \epsilon b$

One can guarantee a name-like expression as the correlate of any verb by means of:

5. $[a]: a \in \text{trm} <\varphi> . \equiv . a \in a . \varphi(a)$

(where "φ" is, of course, a predicate (i.e. verb, functor) variable). In English "term satisfying........." can be used to read off "trm< >", which is the first of several many-link functors now to be defined. A definition of a many-link functor which, in contrast with 5, yields a verb corresponding to any name, is:

6. $[ab]: \text{Cl}\{b\}(a) . \equiv . a \circ b$

The natural-language correlates of "Cl{   }" are quite numerous: "Form the class of......" is one which is sometimes appropriate. Next, a form of "ϵ" which, unlike the primitive "ϵ" (1), takes verbs as its arguments, may be defined:

7. $[\varphi\psi]: : \varphi\epsilon\psi . \equiv : . [\exists a]: . \varphi(a) . \psi(a): . [b]: \varphi(b) . \equiv . a \circ b$

(Strictly speaking, the difference between the semantical category of this "ϵ" and that of the primitive "ϵ" should be marked by the adoption of some new form of parenthesis for the argument-places, but it is assumed that the diversity of argument-shapes in the expressions in which it occurs is sufficient to show forth the categorial diversity). The "is" defined in 7 is like that which is encountered in expressions such as "To run is to move", "Running is moving", "*Vivere est esse viventibus*", and so on. It will hereinafter be called the "high-order ϵ" (or "is") in order to distinguish it from the "lower-order" (primitive) "ϵ". Once 7 is available, higher-order functors analogous to those definable in terms of the lower-order "ϵ" may be defined or characterised. As an example of this possibility, consider the following definition of a lower-order "and" ("..... $\cap$ ......") whose arguments are names:

8. $[abc]: a \in b \cap c . \equiv . a \in b . a \in c$

An analogous higher-order characterisation of an "and" whose arguments are verb-like in nature is:

9. $[\varphi\psi\chi]: \varphi \in \psi \cap \chi . \equiv . \varphi \in \psi . \varphi \in \chi$

The higher-order "ϵ" also figures in the *definiens* of the following:

10. $\qquad [a\varphi]: a \, \epsilon \, \mathrm{el}(\varphi) \, . \, \equiv \, . \, [\exists b] \, . \, \varphi \, \epsilon \, \mathrm{Cl}\{b\} \, . \, a \, \epsilon \, b$

The *definiendum* "el( )" could here be read off as "element of the class determined by.....", but can equally well be used (as it is to be used below) in order to interpret the "having" of some essence or nature by *a*. It will also be useful to have at our disposal:

11. $\qquad [a\varphi]: \mathrm{Cl}\langle\varphi\rangle(a) \, . \, \equiv \, . \, \mathrm{Cl}\{\mathrm{trm}<\varphi>\}(a)$

wherein "Cl⟨ ⟩" is the many-link functor defined. Finally, it is clear that the "V" defined by the following will serve for the translation of the Latin "*ens*" ("being"), understood nominally, into the language of Ontology:

12. $\qquad [a]: a \, \epsilon \, \mathrm{V} \, . \, \equiv \, . \, a \, \epsilon \, a$

Indefinitely many more analogous senses of "ens" (as a participle) can be defined in terms of successively higher and higher orders of "ϵ".

The elucidation of Aquinas's uses of "*essentia*" and "*esse*" may be undertaken by considering the fact that he would accept the following three sentences as truths:

(1)　　　*albedo est quo album est album,*

(2)　　　*humanitas est quo homo est homo,*

(3)　　　*esse est quo substantia est ens.*

(See, for instance, *ACG* II 54, *AST* I q.3 a.3.) The important point to note here is the parallelism which shows itself between the essential cases (1) and (2), and the *esse* case (3). In view of this parallelism it is clear that if cases like (1) and (2) can be understood, then the key to the understanding of (3) will be available. Now in (1) and (2) *albedo* and *humanitas* are the essences which, as the two following Aquinate commonplaces demonstrate, are possessed by whites and men respectively:

(4)　　　*album est habens albedinem,*

(5)　　　*homo est habens humanitatem.*

And now, by generalising from (4) and (5), one can regard the following as an Aquinate thesis:

(6)   *omne ens est essentiam habens,*

(provided, of course, that its application is restricted to *entia per participationem* other than pure forms). (6) in its turn reminds one of the following well-known adage of St. Thomas:

(7)   *omne ens est esse habens.*

If, therefore, an elucidation of (6) is possible, then a key to the interpretation of (7), and hence to Aquinas's discourse concerning *esse* will be within our reach, given also the parallelism already evidenced in (1), (2) and (3) above.

The project outlined in the last paragraph imposes various tasks. First, we must attempt to situate abstract nouns (e.g. *albedo*, *humanitas*) within the terms made available by the language of Ontology. Given definitions 7 and 10 it is possible to relate such nouns to their more unproblematic corresponding non-abstract nouns (e.g. *albus*, *homo*) by means of the following frame:

(8) $[\varphi] :: \varphi \, \epsilon \, \psi \, . \equiv :. \, \varphi \, \epsilon \, \varphi :. \, [a] : a \, \epsilon \, \text{el}(\varphi) \, . \equiv . \, a \, \epsilon \, X$

Hereby, given, for instance, "*albus*" in the place of "X", one can assign a sense to "*albedo*", which would then stand correspondingly in the place of "Ψ". This treatment of abstract nouns presupposes that they are in fact more akin to verbs (i.e. values of "φ", "ψ", etc.) than nouns, and is due to C. Lejewski (cf. *LAS*). At the same time it is in entire accord with Aquinas's doctrine in his *In Boetii de Hebdomadibus* lec.2, n.21, wherein "*currere*" (a possible argument, verb-like in nature, of the higher-order "ϵ" which figures in (8)) is said to signify abstractly, as "*albedo*" does, and both are contrasted with "*currens*" and "*album*" respectively (i.e. possible arguments, nominal in nature, of the lower-order, primitive "ϵ" of Ontology). In view of these facts it is apparent that "el(ψ)" (cf. 10), wherein the sense of "ψ" has been related to that of "X" as shown in (8), suffices to represent Aquinas's sense of "*habens X-eitas*" (where "X-*eitas*" is the abstract noun corresponding to "X"). Now such abstract nouns in some way signify essences; in fact *"essentia"* is a quasi-common-name, which "refers" to *albedo, humanitas,* and the like; in relation to functors already defined (6, 7) *"essentia"* may be understood as "Cl" as it occurs in the following:

(9) $[\varphi] : \varphi \in \text{Cl} . \equiv [\exists a] . \varphi \in \text{Cl}\{a\}$

Thus, given that one of the various ways in which *"ens"* (as a name) may be rendered is by means of "V" (defined 12), the thesis *"omne ens est essentiam habens"* ((6) above), along with the obviously true converse, amounts to:

(10) $[a] :. [\exists\varphi] . a \in \text{el}(\varphi) . \varphi \in \text{Cl} : \equiv . a \in \text{V}$

On the assumption that the "φ" of "el(φ)" has been built up on the lines indicated in (8), and recollecting that "el( )" thus represents *"habens.....eitas"*, we see that (10) not only ensures that the values of "φ" are *essentia*, but also shows forth the correlation between *having an essence* and *being a being*, i.e. a totally unproblematic elucidation of the Aquinate position as regards the essential aspect of *entia per participationem* other than pure forms is now available. True, in the absence of further restrictions on the nature of the non-abstract nouns which can stand in the place of "X" in (8), the expression (10) has a wider sense than Aquinas would wish it to have; thus, were proper nouns (e.g. "Socrates", "this") eligible to take the place of the "X" mentioned, then Scotist individuating essences (*"Socrateitas," "haecceitas"*) would be comprised in the generalisation which (10) represents. An appropriate restriction in respect of (8) must therefore be imposed if (10) is to be understood in a strictly Aquinate sense.

The sense of (6) having thus been resolved, it now remains to discover a verb which will serve as a value of "φ" in (10), but which will convey the fact that it is *esse*, rather than an *essentia*, which is had by *a*. In this fashion the case parallel to (6), i.e. (7), will have been elucidated. One of Aquinas's own remarks gives an exact indication as to the verb needed: *esse cuiuslibet rei consistit in indivisione.......unumquodque sicut custodit suum esse, ita custodit suam unitatem* (*AST* I q. 11 a.1 c.). (The first part of this statement sounds like a deliberately amended version of Anselm of Canterbury's "*esse uniuscuiusque rei in definitione consistat*" (*ΛDG*152) which itself is a derivation from similarly worded statements in Boethius (*BDT*1196 C)). Clearly, at this point Aquinas has in mind a truth such as that conveyed by the following thesis of Ontology:

(11) $[ab]: . \, ob(a) . \supset : [cd] . \, c \,\epsilon\, a . \, d \,\epsilon\, a . \supset . \, c = d$

This thesis follows from the axiom 1 and definitions 2 and 3, and indicates the connection between exactly-one-hood and "indivision" which is in question here; it suggests also that "ob ( )" ("There exists exactly one......") is the verb required for our purpose. In order, however, to fit it as an argument of "el( )" as defined at 10, we need first of all to compound from "ob( )" a nominal form which can stand as a value of "*b*" in 10. This is quite easily done by the use of "trm< >" (defined 5) so that as the appropriate instance of 10 we have:

(12) $[a]: a \,\epsilon\, el(Cl\{trm<ob>\}) . \equiv . \, Cl\{trm<ob>\} \,\epsilon$
$$Cl\{trm<ob>\} . \, a \,\epsilon\, trm<ob>$$

Further, in view of definition 11 "Cl{trm<ob>}" may be contracted to "Cl⟨ ob ⟩", so that the left-hand side of (12), which is going to figure in the "*esse*" parallel of (10), will read "*a* ε el(Cl(ob))". Hence, using "Cl⟨ ob ⟩" as a value of "*φ*" in (10), we have the analogous thesis:

(13) $[a]: a \,\epsilon\, el(Cl⟨ ob ⟩) . \, Cl⟨ ob ⟩ \,\epsilon\, Cl . \equiv . \, a \,\epsilon\, V$

The second conjunct of this expression, in view of its thetic nature (cf. (9)) is clearly superfluous, so that as the required expression of *omne ens est esse habens* (along with its obviously true converse) one now has:

(14) $[a]: a \,\epsilon\, el(Cl⟨ ob ⟩) . \equiv . \, a \,\epsilon\, V$

Once again, this result accords exactly with Aquinas's remarks in *In Boetii de Hebdomadibus*, wherein "*esse*", "*currere*", and "*albedo*" (all verb-like) are contrasted with "*ens*", "*currens*", and "*album*" respectively (all nominal); in (14) "Cl⟨ob⟩" is the verb which corresponds with "*esse*" and "V" is the noun corresponding to "*ens*".

I would like to thank Dr. C. Lejewski for his advice in connection with the preparation of this essay.

ABBREVIATIONS

SIGLA

ACG	AQUINAS,	*Summa Contra Gentiles*
ADG	ANSELM,	*De grammatico* (Ed. SCHMITT)
AST	AQUINAS,	*Summa Theologica*
BDT	BOETHIUS,	*De Differentiis Topicis* (*Patr. Lat.* 64)
HAN	HENRY, D. P.,	St. Anselm's Nonsense (*Mind*, Vol. LXXI N.S., No. 285)
HAR	HENRY, D. P.,	An Anselmian Regress (*Notre Dame Journal of Formal Logic*, Vol. III, No. 3)
HDG	HENRY, D. P.,	*The* De grammatico *of St. Anselm*, Notre Dame University Press, 1964.
LAS	LEJEWSKI, C.,	Proper Names (*Aristotelian Society Supplementary Volume* No. XXXI, 1957)
LLE	LEJEWSKI, C.,	Logic and Existence (*British Journal for the Philosophy of Science*, Vol. 5, No. 18)
LLL	LUSCHEI, E. C.,	*The Logical Systems of Leśniewski* (Studies in Logic and the Foundations of Mathematics, Amsterdam, 1962)
LR	LEJEWSKI, C.,	On Leśniewski's Ontology (*Ratio*, Vol. I, No. 2)

7

OCKHAM'S SUPPOSITION THEORY AND MODERN LOGIC[1]

Gareth B. Matthews

READING Philotheus Boehner on medieval logic,[2] one may get the idea that medieval supposition theory is, in part, a kind of quantification theory. Up to a point this is a helpful idea to have. But one may also get the idea from reading Father Boehner that the main difference between modern quantification theory and the relevant portion of medieval supposition theory is a difference over the interpretation of universal propositions. This last idea, it seems to me, is quite wrong-headed. It needs to be done away with completely if one is to be at all clear about how medieval supposition theory is related to modern mathematical logic. I wish to do my part in doing away with it.

In his discussion of supposition theory Father Boehner has something to say about Peter of Spain, William of Ockham, and Walter Burleigh. But in comparing the medieval theory with modern logic Boehner seems most interested in the logic of Ock-ham. So, since I can also make my own points with reference to Ockham alone, I shall take Ockham's *Summa Logicae* as the medieval source for the remarks to follow.

I

Suppositio, according to William of Ockham, is a property of a categorematic term in its role as the subject or predicate of some specific proposition (*Summa Logicae* 1.63). Therefore, although supposition belongs to terms, it belongs to them only within some given proposition or other.

The supposition of the term "man" in the proposition

   (1) Some man is an animal.

can be shown, according to Ockham, by a "descent" (*descensus*) to singular propositions about individual men. Thus (1) implies

   (2) This man is an animal or that man is an animal or that man. . . .

Similarly the supposition of "man" in

   (3) All men are animals.

is shown by descent to the proposition

   (4) This man is an animal and that man is an animal and that man . . . .

So far we have considered only subject-term supposition. According to Ockham the predicate term of a proposition has supposition as well. The supposition of "animal" in

   (1) Some man is an animal.

is shown by descent to

   (5) Some man is this animal or some man is that animal or. . . .

And the supposition of "animal" in

   (3) All men are animals.

is shown by the descent to

   (6) Each man is either this animal or that animal or. . . .

The various kinds of supposition shown by the above descents all have names. But we need not concern ourselves with them here. It is enough to say that all the types of supposition represented above fall under the heading *common personal supposition*, and that Ockham recognizes other kinds of supposition as well.

Consider now the following claim of Father Boehner's:

A particular, affirmative, categorical proposition . . . is interpreted by the scholastics in exactly the same manner as by modern logicians [p. 29].

What Boehner has in mind is this. The usual modern formalization of a proposition like (1) would be the following:

(7) $(\exists x)(Fx \cdot Gx)$.

But (7) implies this:

(8) $Fx_1 \cdot Gx_1 \cdot \lor \cdot Fx_2 \cdot Gx_2 \cdot \lor \cdot \ldots$

And (8) is a suitable formalization of (2). Therefore, the inference from (7) to (8) in modern quantification theory parallels the suppositional descent from (1) to (2).

Boehner goes further. He says that Ockham considers (1) and (2) equivalent, on the grounds that Ockham says both that (1) implies (2) and that any one of the disjuncts of (2) implies (1). Moreover, Boehner seems equally confident that a modern logician would consider (7) and (8) equivalent (p. 30). So, again, (7) and (8) would seem to be modern parallels to (1) and (2).

A modern philosopher might want to argue that, although (8) implies (7), (7) does not imply (8) and therefore the two are not equivalent.[3] But certainly some modern philosophers have maintained the opposite—Frank Ramsey, for example, in "Facts and Propositions."[4] So we might say on Boehner's behalf that it is at least plausible to think that (7) and (8) are equivalent and, furthermore, the question as to whether they really are or not does not illuminate medieval supposition theory.

The claim that Ockham thought (1) and (2) equivalent is itself questionable, however. True, Ockham supposed that one can descend from (1) to (2) and ascend from any one of the disjuncts of (2) to (1). Still, he did not put the descent and the ascent together to make up an equivalence. But I do not wish to labor this point. Rather, I shall simply ignore Boehner's claim about equivalence and concentrate instead on the weaker, but still very interesting, claim (to be found in Boehner on page 41) that the inference from (7) to (8) parallels the suppositional descent from (1) to (2).

Here I want to call attention to a curious flaw in Boehner's argument. One of his reasons for insisting that medieval and modern logicians differ on the interpretation of the *A* proposition is that there is no parallel in modern logic to the *predicate*-term suppositional descent from

(3) All men are animals.

to

(6) Each man is either this animal or that animal or. . . .

Yet Boehner says nothing about predicate-term supposition in an *I* proposition, even though a similar difficulty is to be found there. In fact, one reason the inference from (7) to (8) is not really parallel to the suppositional descent from (1) to (2) is that the descent to (2) shows the supposition of the subject term "man" only. As we have already noted, "animal" in (1) has its own supposition, as shown by the descent to

(5) Some man is this animal or some man is that animal or. . . .

(7) cannot be expanded in the two distinct ways required to bring out both subject and predicate supposition. That is, "$Fx_1 \cdot Gx_1 \cdot \vee \cdot Fx_2 \cdot Gx_2 \cdot \vee \cdot \ldots$" has to do for "This man is an animal or that man is . . ." as well as for "Some man is this animal or that animal or. . . ." So Boehner's claim that a proposition like (1) is "interpreted by the scholastics in exactly the same manner as by modern logicians" is quite misleading.

We might, of course, set out to provide a quantificational parallel for each of the descents of Ockham's suppositional logic. By enriching our logical vocabulary to include an identity sign we could provide separate quantifications for the subject and predicate suppositions. Here is such a double quantificational formalization of (1):

(9) $(\exists x) [Fx \cdot (\exists y) (Gy \cdot x = y)]$
Something which is a man is identical with something which is an animal.

There is, perhaps, some warrant in Ockham for such use of the notion of identity, since Ockham does say that a particular affirmative proposition is true if, and only if, the subject and the predicate terms supposit for the same thing (*Summa Logicae* 2.3). But the main reason for preferring (9) to (7) as an approach to the understanding of Ockham's supposition theory is that (9) yields both of these:

(10) $Fx_1 \cdot (\exists y) (Gy \cdot x_1 = y) \cdot \vee \cdot Fx_2 \cdot (\exists y) (Gy \cdot x_2 = y)$
$\cdot \vee \cdot \ldots$

(11) $(\exists x) (Fx : Gy_1 \cdot x = y_1 \cdot \vee \cdot Gy_2 \cdot x = y_2 \cdot \vee \cdot \ldots)$

(10) and (11) suggest the difference between subject and predicate supposition which is shown by (2) and (5).

Even (10) and (11), however, although certainly better than anything we could get by expanding "$(\exists x) (Fx \cdot Gx)$," are nevertheless basically unfaithful to Ockham's theory of supposition. Let me try to show why this is so.

(10) can be put into words as follows:

(10*a*) x_1 is a man and x_1 is identical with something which is an animal, or x_2 is a man and x_2 is identical with something which is an animal, or. . . .

However, the proposition to which (10*a*) is meant to correspond, let us not forget, is

(2) This man is an animal or that man is an animal or. . . .

The demonstratives in (2), "this" and "that," pick out individual men. Their analogues in (10) and (10*a*), the subscripts on "x," pick out everything within the range of the values of the variables, non-men as well as men.

Of course (10*a*) and (2) are equivalent in truth value. For (10*a*) is a string of conjunctions in disjunction and only one of these disjuncts need be true to make the whole proposition true;

therefore we can simply disregard all disjuncts about x's which are not men. But this enormous wastage of disjuncts makes (10a) a misleading analogue to (2).

So far, then, we have found two reasons for denying that the I proposition is interpreted by modern logicians in the same way it was interpreted by Ockham. First, a single quantifier is normally all that is used in modern logic for an I proposition; but in order to parallel the two suppositional descents we should need two quantifiers. Second, and even more important, the modern parallel to suppositional descent involves a wastage of disjuncts. Let me enlarge a bit on this last point.

Ockham's supposition theory is, in part anyway, a kind of quantification theory. And his suppositional descent is an elimination of the quantification by expansion. In Ockham's theory it is the *subject and predicate terms that are considered to be quantified.* So "Some man . . ." is expanded into the disjunction "Man$_1$ . . . or man$_2$ . . . or . . ." and "All men . . ." is expanded into the conjunction "Man$_1$ . . . and man$_2$ . . . and. . . ."

In modern mathematical logic it is *variables that are quantified.* To eliminate a quantification by expansion we should have to go from "$(\exists x)\phi x$" to the disjunction "$\phi x_1 \vee \phi x_2 \vee \cdot \ldots$" and from "$(x) \phi x$" to the conjunction "$\phi x_1 \cdot \phi x_2 \cdot \ldots$" So one reason there can be no faithful rendering of suppositional descent in modern mathematical logic is this: since it is variables that are quantified in modern logic, any descent to singulars achieved by the elimination of quantifiers would have to be a descent to all x's, that is, to all the individuals within the universe of discourse. Regardless of whether a proposition is universal or particular, there could be no descent by elimination of quantifiers to, say, men and nothing else, as there is in supposition theory.

II

Boehner, as we have already noted, claims that medieval supposition theory is in agreement with modern logic on the interpretation of the I proposition (and presumably the O proposition). Where they differ, he thinks, is on the interpretation of universal propositions. In the last section I argued against Boehner's claim about the *I* proposition. In this section I want to consider the *A* proposition. I do not wish to deny that medieval supposition theorists, and Ockham in particular, differ with modern logicians on the interpretation of the *A* proposition. But I want to suggest that this difference is essentially related to a difference we have already noted in their respective approaches to the *I* proposition.

The usual form into which an *A* proposition is cast in modern logic is this:

(12) $(x)\,(Fx \supset Gx)$

From the viewpoint of Ockham's supposition theory (12) has the same fault as (7); that is, it has only one quantifier whereas there are two suppositions involved. The appropriate parallel to (9) is obvious, namely:

(13) $(x)\,[Fx \supset (\exists y)\,(Gy \cdot x = y)]$
    Anything that is a man is identical with something that is an animal.

The implicate of (13) we get as analogue for (10) is then this:

(14) $Fx_1 \supset (\exists y)\,(Gy \cdot x_1 = y) \cdot Fx_2 \supset (\exists y)$
                    $(Gy \cdot x_2 = y) \cdot \ldots$
    If x_1 is a man, then it is identical with something that is an animal; and if x_2 is a man, then it is identical with something that is an animal; and. . . .

Of course this is an implausible formalization of

(4) This man is an animal and that man is an animal and. . . .

Consider, moreover, the following schemata:

Put "*p*" for "Some man is an animal";
    "*q*" for "All men are animals";
    "r_i" for "This [or that] man is an animal."

(15) $p \supset \cdot r_1 \vee r_2 \vee \cdot \ldots$

(16) $q \supset \cdot r_1 \cdot r_2 \cdot \ldots$

(15) shows the descent from the particular proposition; (16) shows that from the universal proposition. Now here is a basic difficulty. Where the proposition for "p" is rendered as (9) and that for "q" as (13), no single proposition will follow for "r_i." For the "r_i" proposition which follows from (9) we have this:

(17) $Fx_n \cdot (\exists y)(Gy \cdot x_n = y)$

x_n is a man and x_n is identical with something that is an animal.

And for the "r_i" proposition which follows from (13) we have this:

(18) $Fx_n \supset (\exists y)(Gy \cdot x_n = y)$

If x_n is a man, then x_n is identical with something that is an animal.

The difficulty here is not that the universal proposition, according to modern quantification theory, carries no existential import. If that were the trouble, we could simply add an existential commitment to (13) in this fashion:

(19) $(\exists z) Fz \cdot (x)[Fx \supset (\exists y)(Gy \cdot x = y)]$

Something is a man and anything that is a man is identical with something that is an animal.

But the patch is of no help. Instead of (18) we now have this:

(20) $(\exists z) Fz \cdot Fx_n \supset (\exists y)(Gy \cdot x_n = y)$

Something is a man and if x_n is a man then x_n is identical with something that is an animal.

(20) is not, of course, the desired substitute for "r_i."

How are we to understand this situation? Are we to think that our inability to provide a quantified substitute for "r_i" in mathematical logic arises from the fact that modern logicians give the A proposition a so-called hypothetical interpretation?

That would be arbitrary for two reasons. First, the A proposition can also be given either a "conjunctive" or a "disjunctive" interpretation in modern logic. That is, "$\sim (\exists x)(Fx \cdot \sim Gx)$" and "$(x) \sim (Fx \cdot \sim Gx)$" and "$(x)(\sim Fx \vee Gx)$" are all equivalent to "$(x) (Fx \supset Gx)$."[5] Moreover, the I proposition can also be given a "hypothetical" interpretation. For "$\sim (x) (Fx \supset \sim Gx)$" and "$(\exists x) \sim (Fx \supset \sim Gx)$" are equivalent to "$(\exists x) (Fx \cdot Gx)$." Second, it is in any case just as much the "conjunctive" interpretation of the I proposition as it is the "hypothetical" interpretation of the A proposition which makes it impossible to provide a quantified substitute for "r_i" in mathematical logic. The point is that "$(x) (Fx \supset Gx)$" and "$(\exists x) (Fx \cdot Gx)$" differ, not just in quantification, but also in internal structure. And they differ in such a way that no equivalent of the one has the same internal structure as any equivalent of the other. It is arbitrary to blame this on the "$\supset$" in "$(x) (Fx \supset Gx)$."

Ockham can descend to "This man is an animal" from both "All men are animals" and "Some man is an animal" because he understands corresponding A and I propositions to differ only in the quantity of their respective terms. His view is plausible so long as we think of the subject and predicate terms as quantified. But if we quantify over variables instead, it turns out that we cannot plausibly interpret corresponding A and I propositions as differing in quantity alone. That is, if we try to fill out

(21) Everything is . . .

and

(22) Something is . . .

in such a way as to make them correspond to

(3) All men are animals.

and

(1) Some man is an animal

we may come up with completions such as these:

    (a) if a man then an animal.
    (b) either not a man or else an animal.
    (c) an animal unless not a man.
    (d) both a man and an animal.
    (e) not either not a man or not an animal.

But the completions that will do for making (21) into a reasonable approximation to (3) will not do for making (22) into a reasonable approximation to (1). Of the items above, (a), (b) and (c) will do the first job but not the second; (d) and (e) will do the second job but not the first. Our inability to make a single completion do both jobs shows that we cannot quantify over variables and still think of corresponding A and I propositions as differing only in quantity.

I conclude that the idea that Ockham and modern logicians agree on the interpretation of particular propositions but differ on the interpretation of universal propositions is both wrong and wrong-headed. It is wrong because in fact they differ on both counts. It is wrong-headed because, once one realizes that Ockham quantifies over terms whereas modern logicians quantify over variables, one can see that Ockham and the moderns are not free to agree on the interpretation of any catergorical propositions —whether A, E, I, or O.

NOTES

1. This essay owes much to the criticisms and the encouragement of Norman Kretzmann, Gerald Lilje, Harry Bracken, and Jaakko Hintikka.

2. *Medieval Logic* (Manchester, 1952). All page references, unless otherwise noted, are to this work.

3. For a recent argument along these lines see Gustav Bergmann's "Generality and Existence," *Theoria*, XXVIII (1962), esp. 7–8.

4. *The Foundations of Mathematics*, pp. 138–155. Although Ramsey later backed down on the claim that "$(x)Fx$" is equivalent to "$Fx_1 \cdot Fx_2 \cdot \ldots$" (see his "General Propositions and Causality" in the same volume), he apparently continued to hold the view that "$(\exists x)Fx$" is equivalent to "$Fx_1 \, v \, Fx_2 \, v \ldots$"

5. For the sake of simplicity I revert to single quantification here; the argument is not affected by the simplification.

8

THE FORMALITIES OF OMNISCIENCE

A. N. Prior

WHAT do we mean by saying that a being, God for example, is omniscient? One way of answering this question is to translate "God is omniscient" into some slightly more formalised language than colloquial English, e.g. one with variables of a number of different types, including variables replaceable by statements, and quantifiers binding these. In such a language, the common form of the statements

God knows that $2 + 2 = 4$
God knows that $2 + 2 = 5$
God knows that God knows that $2 + 2 = 4$

can clearly be given as

God knows that p,

and this is going to be useful in answering our opening question.

If there is no God, it would seem that all statements of the form just given are false; but even if there is a God, it would seem that some of them are. For example, God doesn't know that 2 and 2 are 5, for the simple reason that 2 and 2 *aren't* 5.

This example is sufficient to show that one way in which we might be tempted to translate "God is omniscient" simply will not do. I mean the translation

(1) For every p, God knows that p.

141

At least, this won't do if we want to mean something *true* by "God is omniscient". For it is a general rule that we may pass from a universal proposition to any singular instantiation of it, and one instantiation of (1) would be the false proposition

God knows that $2 + 2 = 5$.

And we know this to be false, not by any subtle or dubious theologising, but simply by the logic of knowledge as such—if anyone thinks that $2 + 2 = 5$, his state of mind isn't knowledge but error.

Still, the correction required to this first effort seems simple and obvious. When we say that anyone knows everything, it is surely understood that what we mean is that he knows everything that's true. So, as a second attempted translation of "God is omniscient" let us put

For every p, if it is *true* that p then God knows that p,
or more simply

(2) For every p, if p then God knows that p.

And it does seem that all the instantiations of *this* proposition are things which a believer in God's omniscience *would* wish to maintain. For example

If $2 + 2 = 4$ then God knows that $2 + 2 = 4$
If $2 + 2 = 5$ then God knows that $2 + 2 = 5$
If God knows everything then God knows that God knows everything.

These are "instantiations" of (2) in the sense that they are formed by simply dropping the initial quantifier and putting some actual statement for the variable "p" at the two places where it occurs, the same statement at each place. There are also "instantiations" of (2) in a slightly more complicated sense, and all of these are, I think, propositions which a believer in God's omniscience would wish to maintain. These more complicated instantiations of (2) are ones like

(3) For every x, if x + 2 = 4 then God knows that x + 2 = 4.

It is easy to see how we get instantiations of (2) like this. In place of the two "p's" after the quantifier in (2) we put, not actual statements, but *forms* of statements still containing variables, and we replace the initial quantifier "For every p" by another one containing whatever variables occur in the replacement for "p".

Here is another example of the same sort: Suppose we write "fx" for any statement about x, e.g. "f(Plato)" for any statement about Plato. Then the proposition

(4) For every f, if f (Plato) then Gods knows that f (Plato)

would mean that God knows everything there is to know about Plato, and this too would be an instantiation of (2). So also would

(5) For every f and x, if fx then God knows that fx,

which asserts in plain English that God knows everything about everything.

Again, suppose we introduce a variable d which stands for any expression which, attached to a statement, forms a statement, for example, "It is not the case that—", "Johnny believes that—", and so on. Thus a formula like "d(2 + 2 = 5)" can stand indifferently for such statements as

> *It is not the case that 2 + 2 = 5*
> *Johnny believes that 2 + 2 = 5*
> *I wish it were the case that 2 + 2 = 5*

and so on; and also for such statements as

> *1 + 1 = 3 and 2 + 2 = 5*
> *Either my name is Percy or 2 + 2 = 5*
> *If my name is not Percy then 2 + 2 = 5*

and, for that matter, for such statements as

> *If 2 + 2 = 5 then 2 + 3 = 6*
> *Either 2 + 2 = 5 or my name is Percy*
> *That 2 + 2 = 5 is less surprising than that my name is Percy,*

in which the expression substituted for "d" and making a statement by being attached to "2 + 2 = 5", isn't attached to "2 + 2 = 5" by being *prefixed* to it but rather by being as it were wrapped around it. And among the instantiations of the proposition (2) is this:

(6) For all d, if d (2 + 2 = 5) then God knows that d(2 + 2 = 5).

This could be a way of translating something rather puzzling that some of the schoolmen used to say, namely that there *is* a sense in which God knows even false propositions;[1] for He *understands* them just as completely as He understands true propositions, and of course as part of this complete understanding He understands or knows that they are false. He knows, we might say, all truths into which the idea of 2 and 2 being 5 in any way enters, e.g. the truth that it is not the case that 2 + 2 = 5, that some idiotic boy believes that 2 + 2 = 5, and so on.

But now we must raise a deeply controversial point. In this statement that for every p, if p then God knows that p, are we to understand this verb "knows" as a verb in the present tense, or are we not? Many very reputable philosophers, e.g. St. Thomas Aquinas, have held that God's knowledge is in some way right outside of time, in which case presumably the verb "knows" in our translation would have to be thought of as tenseless. I want to argue against this view, on the ground that its final effect is to restrict *what God knows* to those truths, if any, which are themselves timeless. For example, God could not, on the view I am considering, know that the 1960 final examinations at Manchester are now over; for this isn't something that He or anyone could know timelessly, because it just isn't true timelessly. It's true now, but it wasn't true a year ago (I write this on August 29th, 1960) and so far as I can see all that can be said on this subject timelessly is that the finishing-date of the 1960 final examinations is an earlier one than August 29th, and this is *not* the thing we know when we know that those exams are over. I cannot think of any better way of showing this than one I've used before,[2] namely, the argument that what we know when we know that the

1960 final examinations are over can't be just a timeless relation between dates because this isn't the thing we're *pleased* about when we're pleased that the exams are over. In any case it seems an extraordinary way of affirming God's omniscience if a person, when asked what God knows *now*, must say "Nothing", and, when asked what He knew yesterday, must again say "Nothing", and must yet again say "Nothing" when asked what God will know tomorrow.

Of course if we take the "knows" in our translation to be the ordinary present-tense "knows", then we must regard the "is" in the thing it's a translation *of*, namely "God is omniscient", as the ordinary present-tense "is", and if we want to translate the belief that God's omniscience is a permanent and unalterable thing we must expand our (2) to this:

> (7) It is, always has been, and always will be the case that for all p, if p then God knows that p.

We may further note that even with respect to what God is said in both formula (2) and formula (7) to know *now*, the statements over which the variable "p" may range include not only present-tense but past-tense and future-tense ones, and tenseless ones also, if any such there be. For example, we can infer by instantiation from both (2) and (7) the following propositions:

> If there were living organisms a million years ago, God knows that there were living organisms a million years ago;

and

> If there will be living organisms a million years hence, God knows that there will be living organisms a million years hence.

Omniscience as here defined, in other words, covers *fore*-knowledge of whatever will be, that is, *knowledge at every moment of whatever at that moment will be.*

But now I want to raise a subtler point. Is the believer in God's omniscience committed to the following proposition:

(8) For all p, if (it is the case that) p, God has always known that it would be the case that p,

(for example, if I now scratch my head, God has always known that I would scratch my head on this occasion)? The first thing to be said about this proposition is that it *isn't* a simple logical consequence of God's omniscience in the sense of our proposition (7). It does follow from proposition (7) that

(9) If, at any time, it was the case at that time that it would be the case that p, then God knew at that time that it would be the case that p.

But this is not enough to give us proposition (8), unless we supplement it by

(10) For all p, if (it is the case that) p then it has always been the case that it would be the case that p.

If (10) is true, and God is omniscient in the sense of proposition (7), then (8) is true. And contrariwise if (10) is false, then (8) must be false also. For if (10) is false, that means that in some cases in which it *is* the case that p, it nevertheless *hasn't* always been the case that p would be the case, and if this hasn't always *been* true, then clearly neither God nor anyone can have *known* it to be true. So that at this point everything really depends on whether for every p that *is* the case, it has always been the case that it would come to pass that p, or as I sometimes loosely put it, whether whatever *is* the case *has always been going to be* the case. This proposition, together with God's omniscience, *does* yield the conclusion that with respect to whatever is now the case, God has always known that it would be the case; but that conclusion, i.e. our proposition (8), does *not* follow from God's omniscience alone. And my own view would be that, whatever may be the case with the doctrine of God's omniscience itself, proposition (8) is not true, nor is proposition (10). And on both these points, I mean the denial of the logical proposition (10) and even of the theological proposition (8), I rather think that, for what this is worth, I have St. Thomas Aquinas on my side, though this involves some very tricky questions of exposition.

Let's look, anyhow, at a bit of what Thomas has to say about these matters in his *De Veritate*, Question 2, Article 12, "Whether God knows singular future contingents".[3] He begins by stating some twelve arguments for the negative, of which I think the most persuasive is the seventh, which begins like this: Given any true proposition of the form "If p then q", if the antecedent p is absolutely necessary, then the consequent q must be absolutely necessary also. The point of this *necessarium absolute*, and the sort of necessity with which Thomas is contrasting it, is obvious enough. If I make a statement of the form "If p then necessarily q", I may not mean that from the truth of p we can infer that q is in itself a *necessary* truth, i.e. I may not mean "If p then necessarily-q"; I may only mean that the truth of q—it could quite well be the *contingent* truth of q—*necessarily follows* from the truth of p, i.e. I may only mean "If p then—necessarily q". This is not an absolute but a merely conditional necessity of q; in fact not really a necessity of q at all, but only a necessary connection between q and something else. Nevertheless we can legitimately infer the necessity of q in itself if we are given not only its necessary following from p, but also the necessity of p in itself. What necessarily follows from something necessary is itself necessary. That's the first premiss that Thomas's imaginary objector uses here, and Thomas himself, we shall find, quite explicitly assents to it.[4]

Now here, the objector goes on, is a true proposition of the form "If p then q": "If anything is known to God, then that thing will be". This perhaps needs filling out a little; it is clear from the context that what the objector has in mind is any proposition of the general form "If it has come to God's knowledge that X will happen, then X *will* happen". But the antecedent of this, at least if it's true at all, is necessary, if only becase it's *past*, and so beyond anyone's power to prevent—*quod fuit, non potest non fuisse*, "What has been, cannot now not have been".[5] So anything that follows from this necessary, i.e. now-unpreventable, truth, must itself be now-unpreventable. From this in turn it follows—the corollary is too obvious for Thomas to bother drawing it explicitly—that whatever *isn't* now-unpreventable *hasn't* yet come to God's knowledge. That's against proposition (8); it is clear that a similar argument could be used to show, against proposition (10), that whatever *has already come to be* part of what is to come is now unpreventable, and so whatever isn't yet unpreventable hasn't yet come to be part of what is to come.

The general point of this type of argument might be brought out by using a few symbols. Suppose we use "X = Y" to assert that the propositions X and Y are logically equivalent, i.e. inferable from one another; this equivalence having the usual properties of symmetry (if $X = Y$, $Y = X$) and transitiveness (if $X = Y$ and $Y = Z$, $X = Z$) and also the property that if $X = Y$ then $f(X) = f(Y)$, where f is any logical function, e.g. "Not". Let us, further, include among logical functions of a proposition p the functions "Necessarily p" (or "Now-unpreventably p"), symbolised as "Lp"; "It was the case n time-units ago that p", written "Pnp"; "It will be the case n time-units hence that p", written "Fnp"; and "God knows that p", written "Gp" It is easy to show that if we have the logical equivalence

$$Pnp = LPnp$$

("It was the case that p if and only if it now-unpreventably was the case that p") and any logical equivalance of the form

> (i) $X = PnY$,

we can prove

> (ii) $X = LX$

for we have $X = PnY = LPnY = LX$. Thus if we have

> (iii) $p = PnGFnp$

("p is the case if and only if God knew n time-units ago that p would be the case n time-units later"; i.e. approximately proposition (8)), then we have

$$p = PnGFnp = LPnGFnp = Lp;$$

while if we have

(iv) p = PnFnp

("p is the case if and only if it was the case n time-units ago that p would be the case n time-units later"; i.e. approximately proposition (10)), then we have

p = PnFnp = LPnFnp = Lp.

And if we have

(v) p = Gp

("p if and only if God knows that p"), then we can derive (iii) from (iv) and *vice versa* (my earlier point about the deductive equivalence of (8) and (10), given God's omniscience); for by (v), Fnp = GFnp, and so PnFnp = PnGFnp.

I wish I knew where Thomas got this seventh objection from. It was developed very powerfully *after* Thomas by the fifteenth-century anti-Occamist Louvain philosopher Peter de Rivo;[6] and Peter de Rivo knew, but so far as I can discover Thomas did not know, Cicero's *De Fato*, in which a very similar argument is put into the mouth of Diodorus the Megarian.[7] In the absence of any better theory, I would suggest that perhaps Thomas himself constructed this argument against the theological proposition (8) on the pattern of the analogous argument against the logical proposition (10) which he found in Aristotle's *De Interpretatione*, and enlarged upon (and so far as I can see accepted) in his commentary on that work, Book I, *Lectio* 13. But wherever Thomas got the argument from, it seems to me, with one slight modification that I'll discuss later, entirely conclusive. Thomas treats it, too, with the respect it deserves, and brushes aside three ways of dealing with it which he considers inadequate before putting forward an answer of his own.

There are some, he tells us, who argue that the antecedent of this conditional, despite its expressing a truth about the past, is contingent. For, these people say, it has a reference to the future, and that sort of truth about the past isn't always unpreventable—we do sometimes say truly that a thing was going to happen, and then when the time comes it doesn't. Thomas admits this sense of "going to happen"—we do sometimes say that a thing was going to happen when we mean that everything was so to speak pointing that way—but even in this sense of "going to happen", Thomas points out, if it's ever true that a thing was going to happen, then it cannot by that time not have been going to happen in that sense, even though perhaps by this time it isn't happening and it's clear that it never will.

Others, again, say that the proposition "It has come to God's knowledge that X will happen" is contingent because it's a compound proposition with a contingent component, like "Peter is a white man"—Peter cannot but be a man, but he needn't be white, and so needn't be a white man. To this Thomas replies that the necessity or contingency of a proposition doesn't depend on the character of its subject-matter but on the nature of the main "link" in its construction; e.g. "I believe that man is an animal" and "I believe that Peter is running" are equally contingent though the thing believed is necessary in the one case and contingent in the other. I'm not sure that this rule of Thomas's always works; with simple conjunctions like "Peter is an animal and Peter is running" the modality of the whole *does* depend up to a point on the modality of the bits; but the point perhaps is that what we have here isn't that sort of combination but rather the sort in which there is definitely a principal clause ("It has come to God's knowledge—") and a subordinate one, and here the pastness and consequent "necessity" of the principal clause does seem to settle the matter.[8]

While I think Thomas was right on the main point here, I ought to mention that this is what was called in question by most of the writers subsequent to him who considered this argument and were not satisfied with his handling of it; for example, the fifteenth century Occamists. They held that an element of futurity even in a subordinate clause could destroy the sort of necessity which normally attaches to past-tense truths, and in fact made such truths essentially future in sense even if past in form.[9] If, to construct a new example, my own future choice and nothing else can cause me to start smoking tomorrow, then my own future choice and nothing else can cause it to *have been* the case yesterday that I would start smoking in two days' time from then; and this fact that is directly about yesterday and only indirectly about tomorrow, if it is a fact at all, is as much a contingent fact as the one that is directly about tomorrow. Nor have Occamists hesitated to ascribe a like contingency to God's foreknowledge. But I must confess to a difficulty here. I think I can attach intelligible senses to the phrases "was *true* yesterday" and "was *the case* yesterday" which give the Occamist results; but I cannot find any such sense for " was *known* yesterday". I can by my free choice, not exercised until tomorrow, cause a person's *guess*, made yesterday, to have been a correct one (I do this simply by deciding to do what he guessed I would); and I can by the same act convey the same retrospective verification to another person's guess, made right now, that the first person's guess *was* a correct one. It is so to speak still open to this latter guess, despite its past-tense subject matter, either to turn out to have been correct or to turn out not to have been correct; its present correctness, if it does turn out to have been correct, is thus entirely contingent. But while contingent futures, and contingent future-infected pasts, can in this way be correctly or incorrectly guessed, I cannot see in what way they can be "known"; or to put it another way, I cannot see in what way the alleged knowledge, even if it were God's could be more than correct guessing. For there would be *ex hypothesi* nothing that could *make* it knowledge, no present *ground* for the guess's correctness which a specially penetrating person might perceive.[10] So if we talk this way, while we do get my proposition (10) in a rather trivial way, I don't think we get my proposition (8), because I don't think we get the thing that ties the two together, namely God's omniscience, except in the weak sense that He *knows whatever is knowable*, this being no longer coextensive with what is true. This conclusion (that you don't get omniscience this way) seems confirmed by the fact that Ockham, who I suppose was the classical exponent of the point of view I've just been sketching, was driven to assert that "it is impossible to express clearly the manner in which God knows future contingencies".[11]

Returning now to Thomas: he goes on to consider a third way of answering this "seventh objection", namely by arguing that a necessary antecedent of a true conditional *can* have a contingent consequent, as in, for example, "If the sun shines this tree will flower". The sun cannot but shine; but something *could* interfere with its influence on the tree so that it doesn't flower after all. Only where the connection between antecedent and consequent is immediate, without the possibility of anything intervening to frustrate it, does the rule really hold. So it is argued; but Thomas argues on the contrary that it is only where there is no possibility of frustration that the conditional is strictly true. "If the sun shines the tree will flower" is for this reason *not* true; if it *were* true, the necessity of its antecedent *would* be conveyed to its consequent.

Once again I think Thomas is right, but there is something that ought to be added here to obviate a misunderstanding. Some writers on these topics have thought it important to insist that no sort of knowledge, not knowledge of what is to come any more than knowledge of what has been, actually *causes* the truth of that which is known. Thomas doesn't insist on this, I think because in the case of divine knowledge he doesn't believe it is true. Personally I do think it is true, but not very relevant to the argument we are considering. For a conditional proposition such as "If it has come to God's knowledge that X will be, then X will be", doesn't require for its truth, or for its conveying necessity from its antecedent to its consequent, that its antecedent should *causally bring about* its consequent. It is enough that the former cannot be the case without the latter being the case, regardless of why this is so. And in fact if we like to say that it is because X will be that it can be known that it will be, rather than *vice versa*, this means more than ever that X's future coming to pass is beyond prevention, since it has already *had consequences* which its opposite could not have (I take this point from Jonathan Edwards,[12] who reproduced this Objection 7 in the eighteenth century for a different purpose—not to show that God cannot know future contingencies, but to show that, just because God does know all the future, none of it can *be* contingent).

What, then, with all these lines of escape stopped up, are we left with? Nothing, Thomas thinks, but to accept the objector's conclusion; only with a careful elucidation of the exact sense in which it is true. Here I must do a little re-translating of his Latin. Above, I have used the phrase "has come to God's knowledge" to render Thomas's *est scitum a Deo*, because this translation brings out the pastness of the *scitum*, on which the objection as stated so heavily depends. But in fact what is *scitum a Deo* is necessarily so whether this *scitum* expresses a *past* fact or an *eternal* one, and this point is explicitly admitted by Thomas when he restates this objection in the *Summa Theologica*, Part I, Question 14, Article 13 (Objection 2). His answer to the argument, however, requires him to insist that what is in fact expressed, so far as we may suppose the antecedent to be true at all, is not proper pastness but eternity. And his answer consists in simply admitting that what is known to God *is* unalterable in the form in which God knows it; for God does not see the future contingent fact as future but as present. It is, he says, nearer the truth to say that if God knows a thing it *is*, than that if He knows it, it *will* be. At an earlier point, where he is neither stating nor answering an objection but simply setting out his own view, he argues thus: The contingent, considered as future (*ut futurum est*) cannot be the object of any sort of knowledge which cannot fall into falsehood; so since the divine knowledge neither does nor can fall into falsehood, God could not possibly have any knowledge of future contingencies if He knows them *as* future. Divine *fore*knowledge of such events is, in fact, out; as He knows them, they are not still to to come, but already there. This (which is what I had in mind when I said earlier that Thomas denies not only the logical proposition (10) but even in a way the theological proposition (8)) is a doctrine taken over from Boethius; its import is perhaps illuminated by the comment of an earlier follower of Boethius, namely Anselm, who observes that the unchanging "presence" which on this view all things have to God, is in some ways less like our own present than our past. Looking back over what *has* happened, we can distinguish what was bound to happen as it did from what could have happened otherwise, though of course none of it

can now, by the time we look back on it, have happened otherwise. It is in some such way as this that God distinguishes neces-
sities and contingencies even though there is no contingency left
in the latter in the form in which they reach His gaze.

For myself, I cannot wholly agree either with the objection or
with Thomas's answer to it. I do agree with both that in some
sense in which we *can* alter the future we *cannot* alter the past.
But there is an objection to this that the future is precisely whatever it is that does come to pass after our alleged alteration has
taken place, so what we alter *isn't* the future after all, and the
real future can no more be altered than the past can. What I want
to say to this—and as far as it goes I think it is Thomist doctrine
too—is that nothing can be said to be truly "going-to-happen"
(*futurum*) until it is so "present in its causes" as to be beyond
stopping; until that happens, neither "It will be the case that p"
nor "It will be the case that not p" is strictly speaking true. What
Thomas says is that neither of them is true *determinate*; and what
this appears to mean is that though they somehow share truth
and falsehood between them, neither is as yet definitely attached
to either proposition rather than the other.[13] I don't myself
now think—though I once did—that this complication is necessary; it is enough to distinguish (as Thomas did not) between
the form "It will be that it is not the case that p" (which commits
one to the futurition of Not-p) and the form "It is not the case
that it will be that p" (which could also be true if it is simply as
yet undetermined whether it is p or not-p that the future holds).
Writing "F" for the simple "It will be that", "N" for "Not", and
"AXY" for "Either X or Y", I would say that we have at this
stage

$$NAFpFNp$$

("Neither it-will-be-that p nor it-will-be-that not-p".) And this
state of affairs we can alter, changing it to

$$AFpFNp$$

when it is in our power to decide one way or the other and we do
so. But what is past cannot be thus altered, for it is *always* the

case that either p *has been* the case or Not-p has, i.e. we always have

$$APpPNp,$$

and there can be no question of changing from this to its opposite or *vice versa*. Moreover, with respect to any specific past time, say n time-units ago, we have

$$APnpPnNp,$$

but for some future times we have, on the contrary,

$$NAFnpFnNp.$$

Let us now put "MFnp" for the assertion that p is one of the things that *can* happen n time-units hence, and take this to mean that it *isn't* yet settled that p will *not* be the case at that time; i.e.

(vi) $MFnp = NFnNp.$

We can similarly define "It can be that p *has* happened n time-units ago", MPnp, as NPnNp; but there is a very big difference between this case and the preceding. For "It *isn't* the case that p was then *not* the case" is true only of those times of which it *is* the case that p then *was* the case,[14] i.e. we have

(vii) $MPnp = Pnp,$

whereas "It isn't (yet) the case that p will then not be the case" can be true of "thens" of which it isn't yet the case, either, that p will then *be* the case, i.e. we do *not* have as a law

$$MFnp = Fnp.$$

So I want to say that "It can be that X" is logically equivalent to the simple X where X is a past-tense proposition, but not where it is a future-tense. Thomas and his objector would, I think, agree with this, but they say, further, that "It *must* be that X" is equivalent to the simple X where X is in the past tense and not where it is future; and this difference I cannot myself obtain in any straightforward way.[15] What I have succeeded in formalising is in fact not quite the Aristotelian-Thomist account of this whole situation, but a slight modification of it that you get in C. S. Peirce, who says that the past is the region of "brute fact" while the future divides into the necessitated, for which alone we have either Fnp or FnNp, and the merely possible, for which we have neither.[16]

Still, with this position also the proposed distinction between past and future can be shown to break down if we equate p either with PnFnp or with PnGFnp, at least if we also admit (as all writers that I know of do) that

$$\text{(viii)} \quad p = \text{FnPnp},$$

i.e. a proposition *is* true if and only if it *will* be the case at any given time hence that it *was* the case that interval of time before. For on these assumptions we have

$$
\begin{aligned}
\text{MFnp} &= \text{NFnNp (vi)} \\
&= \text{FnPnNFnNp (viii)} \\
&= \text{FnNPnNNFnNp (vii)} \\
&= \text{FnNPnFnNp (NNp = p)} \\
&= \text{FnNNp (iv)} \\
&= \text{Fnp (NNp = p)}
\end{aligned}
$$

("= FnNPnGFnNp" may be inserted after the 4th line by (v) and removed by (iii).) Intuitively, the argument proceeds thus: Suppose it is now possible that a certain thing, say p, should come to pass n time-units hence. Then it *will* be true when that time comes (whatever actually happens then) that this thing *was* possible now. That is, it *will* be false then that the thing *was* at this present time booked to fail to come to pass. But if this will be false then, it will also be false then that it *is* failing to come to pass (for on the hypothesis that we are considering, if it were then failing to come to pass, it *would* now have been going to fail). But if it will then be *false* that it *isn't* coming to pass, it will be *true* that it *is* coming to pass. That is, from the mere possibility of a future event we can by these steps infer that it will actually occur. On this view also, then, the reality of future contingency is incompatible with our proposition (10), and by the same type of argument with proposition (8).

There is an interesting, and formally rather beautiful, relation between the "tense-logic" here advocated and the "Occamist" tense-logic mentioned earlier as an alternative to Thomas's. We can formalise the Occamist system by having one set of variables, say "p", "q", "r", etc., for statements generally, and a special further set, say "a", "b", "c", etc., restricted to statements with no trace of futurity in them. We might then have "a = La" as a law but not the more general "p = Lp" and not even "Pnp = LPnp", though we would have "Pna = LPna". Certain functions of the "A-variables" would be substitutable for them in laws (would constitute "A-formulae"), others not. For example, "Pna" as well as the plain "a" (and "Na") would count as an A-formula, and be substitutable for "a" in laws, but "Fna" would not, nor would "PmFna", though both of these would be substitutable for "p". ("Pna" would be an A-formula because formed by prefixing "Pn" to an A-formula, but "PmFna" would not, because the formula to which the "Pm" is here prefixed isn't one.) "LFna" and "LPmFna" are of course well-formed, and propositions of this form could some-times be true; and there is a case for counting as an "A-formula", i.e. as not having *proper* futurity, any formula at all that begins with "L", even ones like "LFna". (Such assertions "haven't proper futurity" because whether it is or is not necessary that Fna must depend solely on factors now in being, which either do or do not now leave open an alternative future, n time-units hence, to a.) And earlier I have in effect sketched a case for taking the same line with "G", and for having in this sort of system the law "a = Ga", but not "p = GP".

The laws of this system would include both "NPnp = PnNp" ("It is not the case that p was then so, if and only if it was then the case that not-p") and "NFnp = FnNp" ("It is not the case that p will then be, if and only if it will then be that not p"), and of course the substitutions of "a" for "p" in these. But whereas they will include "NLPna = LPnNa" (by the law "a = La", the fact that "Pna" and "PnNa" are A-formulae, and a preceding equivalence, these giving us the chain "NLPna = NPna = PnNa = LPnNa"), they will not include "NLFna = LFnNa" (the chain breaks because "Fna" and "FnNa" are not substitutable for "a" in "a = La").

Suppose now we remove the Occamist's functor "F" from the system and replace it by another "F" equivalent to the Occamist's "LF". Assuming that there is no way of forming "non-A" propositions out of the A ones except by the use of the Occamist "F", in this new system none but A-propositions will be formulable, so no variables need be used but A-variables; or if you like, the P-variables can be treated as A-variables. Because we had "a = La" in the old system, we will have "p = Lp" in the new one; in fact there will be no use in it for the operator "L". And we will have "NPnp = PnNp" in the new system as in the old; but we will *not* have "NFnp = FnNp", for the new "F" is the old "LF", and we didn't have "NLFna = LFnNa". We will, though, now have "p = Gp", since we had "a = Ga" in the old.

This "new" system is in fact precisely the "Peircean" or near-Aristotelian system advocated above. So it could be said, and indeed it has been said (e.g. by Professor Shorter), that the system advocated is merely the Occamist one robbed of its means of expressing contingent truths. I would reply that in an important sense of "truths" there are no contingent truths; once a thing reaches the status of a "truth" there can be no going back on it; though there are contingencies", i.e. matters of which it is not yet true either that they will be the case or that they will fail to be the case. This is of course a terminological difference rather than one of substance, but being a difference as to what we shall count as a "truth", it affects what we mean by "God knows all truths", and so could (and in my view should) affect what truth-value we attach to this statement.

There is, we may observe at this point, an even more direct way of getting "p = Lp" than the method of Thomas's Objection 7. For the schoolmen commonly contrasted the contingency of the future with the necessity not only of the past but also of the present —not only what *has been* the case cannot now not have been the case, but what *is* the case cannot now not *be* the case. But is it plausible to say that the functor "It is the case that—" makes no difference to the truth or falsehood of *anything* to which it is prefixed, so that *all* propositions are equivalent to ones which are of the present tense in their principal clause? Thomas seems to admit this when, commenting on *De Interpretatione* 16 b 17–19, he equates *est praeteritum* and *fuit praesens*, and *est futurum* and *erit praesens*—putting "Sp" for "It is the case that 'p' ", we have "Sp = p" and in particular "SPp = Pp = PSp" and "SFp = Fp = FSp". And this, given "Sp = LSp", gives "Fp = SFp = LSFp = LFp", thus breaking down the above difference between future and present. The Occamist answer to this is presumably to replace "p" by "a" in the law "Sp = LSp" (there is then no need for him to alter "p = Sp"); the Peircean admits the conclusion but gets the reality of future and unreality of present and past contingency in another way.

As to Thomas's own answer to his real or imaginary objector, I can only say this: I simply cannot see how the presentness, pastness or futurity of any state of affairs can be in any way relative to the *persons to whom* this state of affairs is known.[17] What makes this quite impossible to stomach is precisely the truth that both Thomas and his objector insist on, namely that the future has an openness to alternatives which the past has not; such openness is just not the sort of thing that can be present for one observer and absent for another—either it exists or it doesn't, and there's an end to it; and so either a thing has already occurred or it hasn't, and there's an end to *that*. But the presentness, pastness or futurity of states of affairs does of course vary with *time*, i.e. it is itself a tensed matter—what *was* future or present, *is* now and *will be* past, and so on.[18] So I don't understand what is meant by saying that contingent future occurrences are neither contingent nor future *as* God sees them, though I do understand what would be meant if it were said that they are neither contingent nor future *when* God sees them. How, in fact, could God *know* a state of affairs to be present and beyond alteration, until it *is* present and beyond alteration (for if He sees it as present when it is not, surely He is in error)? But to know that something is so when it is so, is surely not *fore*knowledge. So when I try to set out to myself what Boethius and Thomas—and later on, Peter de Rivo (and even Peirce[19])—are saying here, I find that either I cannot understand what I am saying, or I slip into something which I certainly *can* understand, but which is surely too trivial altogether to express the intention of these writers. Still, with this trivial thing, so far as it goes, I do agree; I agree, that is, that God, or let us say any omniscient being, knows what is happening when it is happening; and of course I agree also with the negative admission of Thomas and of Peter de Rivo that God *doesn't* know future contingencies literally *when* they are still future and contingent, and that it is impossible that He or anyone else should know them in this way. But (and this is what Thomas himself says[20]) this is only because there is not then any truth of the form "It will be the case that p" (or "It will be the case that not p"), with respect to this future contingency p, for Him to know; and *nihil potest sciri nisi verum.*

NOTES

1. See, e.g., Ockham, *Tractatus de Praedestinatione*, etc., ed. P. Boehner (Franciscan Institute, 1954), pp. 56, 101B.

2. A. N. Prior, "Thank Goodness that's Over," *Philosophy*, Jan. 1959, p. 17. Cf. C. D. Broad. *Examination of McTaggart's Philosophy*, Vol. II, Part I, pp. 266–7.

3. Directly on the maxim that *id quod est verum in praesenti, semper fuit verum esse futurum*, it is worth glancing at *Summa Theologica*, Part I, Question 16, Article 7, Obj. 3 and answer.

4. Stock sources for this law in Aristotle are *An. Pr.* I, Ch. 15, 34a, 23, and *An. Post.* I, ch. 6, 75a, 1–11.

5. The main stock source for this is the *Nicomachean Ethics*, VI, 1139 b. See also *De Caelo*, I, 283 b 13.

6. See L. Baudry's excellent collection of texts, *La Querelle des Futurs Contingents* (*Louvain* 1465–1475), Vrin, 1950; e.g. p. 70.

7. Cicero, *De Fato*, vii, 14.

8. On these two very different ways in which a proposition may be compounded out of past-tense and future-tense elements, see Peter de Rivo in Baudry, *op. cit.*, p. 339.

9. See Ockham himself on this, *op. cit.*, pp. 5–6, C, and Ferdinand of

Cordova in Baudry, *op. cit.*, p. 159. For what seems to be a very similar view, see Ryle's *Dilemmas*, "It Was to Be."

10. I owe much in this paragraph to Professor J. M. Shorter. Cf. also, on the negative point, Jonathan Edwards on the Will, Part II, Sect. XII, Observation II. But this is a frequently repeated Thomist point too—that there can logically be no *knowledge* of the future, for one who is still awaiting its actualisation, but what he can gather from its already present causes. (See, e.g., *De Malo*, xvi, 7.)

11. Ockham, *op. cit.*, p. 15.

12. Edwards, *op. cit.*, Observation III, Corollary I, discussion of Whitby. My attention was first drawn to this Section in Edwards, and the resemblances between its opening argument and Thomas's Objection 7, by Mr. J. C. Thornton.

13. See, especially, the latter part of Part I, *Lectio* 13, in his *Peri Hermeneias* commentary.

14. At least the theory of future contingencies provides no exceptions to this. For the possibility of other exceptions, see *Summa Theologica*, Part I, Question 16, Article 7, Objection 4, and answer; and my own *Time and Modality*, Ch. 4, and "Identifiable Individuals," *Review of Metaphysics*, June 1960, pp. 692, 695-6.

15. For the difficulty here, see my *Time and Modality*, p. 97.

16. Collected Papers of C. S. Peirce, 5, 459.

17. Cf. Scotus, as given in Ockham, *op. cit.*, p. 53 and n.

18. Cf. McTaggart, *The Nature of Existence*, Ch. XXXIII, Sects. 305, 330; and my own "Time after Time", *Mind*, April 1958, pp. 244-6.

19. C. S. Peirce, *op. cit.*, 4, 67.

20. *De Veritate*, Question 2, Article 13, Objection 1 and answer.

DISPLAYING MORE TRADITIONAL METHODS

9

THE AUGUSTINIAN ARGUMENT FOR THE EXISTENCE OF GOD

John A. Mourant

THE one definitive attempt by Augustine to demonstrate the existence of God occurs in the second book of his *De Libero Arbitrio*, one of his early philosophical dialogues. There are anticipations of the argument in the *De diversis quaestionibus*, LXXXIII, a brief outline of it in the *De vera religione*, and possible implications for a demonstrative argument in other writings, notably the *Confessions*. In this paper I wish to suggest first various reasons why Augustine never attempted a more systematic and extended demonstration. This will entail not simply an examination of the structure of the argument of the *De Libero Arbitrio*, but a consideration of other suggestions and implications for a proof and some attention to the whole orientation of Augustine's thought, both philosophical and theological. Only by viewing the argument in these contexts and with its special relevance for the Augustinian epistemology can we arrive at a correct evaluation of the Augustinian demonstration.

First, we may make some fairly well-known observations on the general orientation of Augustine's thought. Augustine was primarily and almost wholly the theologian rather than the philosopher. Actually, the philosophical interests of Augustine are largely restricted to the first several years after his conversion. This is amply supported by the evidence of his writings. Of all his works, only some eight or nine out of a total of eighty-three may be regarded as strictly philosophical. And none of these can be compared in extent, profundity, or originality with such great treatises as the *De Trinitate*, the *De Civitate Dei* and the *De Genesi ad litteram*. All his philosophical works were composed over a short period of time and before his ordination as a priest. The *De Magistro* is the last of the philosophical works and with its concluding account of Christ as the teacher within forms the natural transition to the *Utilitate Credendi* which is his first work after ordination. Bardy regards it as his adieu to philosophy and comments:

> Des ce livre, le prêtre d'Hippone tourne résolument le dos à la libre recherche, à l'investigation rationelle des problemes vitaux. Que pourrait donner la plus belle des philosophies à celui qui jouit des lumières de la foi chrétienne?[1]

We may well speculate why Augustine did not pursue his philosophical inquiries further. The answer is essentially twofold. First, there was the depth of his own religious experience, the intensity of his conversion and as its consequent the very real and solid conviction that God exists. Personally he had no need to demonstrate to his own satisfaction the existence of God. Second, the life of Augustine became increasingly occupied with ecclesiastical matters and the need to explain to others than philosophers the truths of revelation. Especially in the later years of his life, there was the ever increasing need to combat the views of the heretics. Since both heretics and believers accepted without question God's existence and many of the truths about God, there were no philosophical issues but rather the problems of biblical exegesis and theological interpretations. The religious polemics of the day demanded the development of a theology rather than philosophical explanations. For Augustine God is pre-eminently present in the truths he has revealed; there is no question of whether God "must" exist or "ought" to exist. The fact is that God does exist. In a letter to Evodius (c. 414) regarding certain problems Evodius has posed, Augustine writes:

You also have some help in the book on religion;[2] if you would review it and look into it, you would never think that reason can prove the necessity of God's existence, or that by reasoning it can ever be established that God must necessarily exist. In the science of numbers, which we certainly make use of in everyday life, if we say seven plus three ought to be ten, we do not speak exactly. It is not: they ought to be ten—they are ten.[3]

The emphasis on the primacy of Augustine's theological interests receives further justification from another source. In the *Retractiones*, as is well known, Augustine went to considerable effort to review his principal writings and to make whatever necessary corrections were required both of his statements on doctrine and on philosophy. Yet in all the *Retractiones* the emendations on philosophical issues are proportionately few and occur primarily where the consequences of Platonism conflict with Christian belief. Even in the *De Libero Arbitrio* Augustine's main concern in the *Retractiones* is with the problem of grace. No mention or supplementation is made of the philosophical issues. Generally, then it would seem that the absorbing interests and demands of theology, the polemics of the day, and the burdensome and ever increasing administrative duties left Augustine with little of the enthusiasm and the time with which he once engaged in philosophical argument. Also, it may be observed that there is nothing in the *Retractiones* comparable to the *De Principiis* of Origen, no great philosophical synthesis summing up his concluding opinions.

Above all, the basic motivation for Augustine's apparent unconcern with a more systematic exposition of an argument for God's existence than that found in the *De Libero Arbitrio* may be attributed to his more absorbing conviction that the approach to the existence of God must proceed always from faith, that without faith we cannot have understanding. His own experience as revealed in the *Confessions*—an experience that might be described as an existential argument—shows that the existence of God is not so much a matter of reason but rather of faith. The God of faith exists in our memory, He is ever present to our intellect, He is the source of our love and our life, a Being experienced rather than achieved through reason. The accomplishment of reason is to establish God as a transcendental being for the better understanding of the world and the place of man. But the actuality of God is more a matter of the religious experience of the individual than a matter of dialectic. And God's existence is so evident in faith that it may be said that this has the effect of rendering the argument of the *De Libero Arbitrio* more of an explication of the existence of God than a demonstration. Some would contend that the argument proceeds too easily and even rather naively from the existence of truth to Truth itself. But for Augustine this is not a deficiency in the argument nor an unwarranted inference; rather it is because in his eyes the identification of truth with Truth itself as God is so self evident as to need little more justification or argument. Persuasion is not merely a matter of logic. Augustine does not feel called upon to go beyond what to him becomes merely a simple intuition of the existence of God. An intuition that actually stems from his faith and is made more apparent to reason through that faith. In a somewhat analogous fashion in one of his sermons on faith, he observes that nature itself is a miracle that constantly exemplifies the work of God. But the very evidence of God in nature becomes apparent only with the attainment of faith.

> Men wondered that our Lord God Jesus Christ filled so many thousands with five loaves; and yet they do not wonder that through a few grains the whole earth is filled with crops. When the water was made wine, men saw it, and were amazed; what else takes place with the rain along the roof of the vine? He did the one, He does the other; the one that thou mayest be fed, the other that thou mayest wonder.[4]

Rather than a belief in God following demonstratively or inferentially from the evidence of nature, the evidence of God in nature becomes evident and a source of wonder and conviction to the individual who first possesses faith. This is perhaps the principal reason for the rejection by Augustine of any approach to God from the empirical evidence of the external world. Such evidence, he feels, cannot lead through reason to faith nor to a knowledge of God's existence. For faith is grace and comes from God. Hence just as God first loves us, so that we may love Him; just as He first chooses us, so that we may choose Him; so, He first knows us and extends the grace and illumination of His knowledge to us, so that we may know Him. For Augustine, there is strictly speaking no teleological argument for God's existence, since our understanding of nature as teleological is consequent upon our faith and explicated in the light of that faith. The *crede ut intelligas* pervades the whole ontology and epistemology of Augustine.

Finally, since it is peculiarly the function of reason to explicate faith, any argument for the existence of God needs merely to clarify or to make more explicit what we already accept upon faith. To Augustine the argument of the *De Libero Arbitrio* accomplished just that; hence he felt no urgency to develop a more thoroughly demonstrative argument. Also, with his primary interest in theology, it becomes Augustine's purpose to explicate not merely the existence of God, but to employ reason for the explication of all the truths that God has revealed and to establish these truths against unbelievers and for the edification of the faithful. The revealed truths of God are manifold whereas the revealed truth that God exists is but one truth. In this connection it is relevant to note the observation of Grabowski that Augustine is really much more concerned with the need to clarify the nature of God rather than to prove His existence.

In all his proofs for God's existence from reason, Augustine presupposes that the mind already knows from faith what is examined by reason. Moreover, the principal purpose for the using of reason in probing into the concept of God is to bring out the purity and the excellence of the divine attributes rather than to demonstrate the actual existence of the Supreme Being.[5]

And in any consideration of the requirements of demonstrative arguments, it is well to keep in mind that Augustine was by profession a rhetorician and that it is the function of the rhetorician to persuade rather than to demonstrate. Aside from an early interest in philosophical dialogue, Augustine's principal literary vehicle was to be the sermon, the letter, and the theological treatise.

Turning now to the structure of the argument in the *De Libero Arbitrio* a brief summary of the demonstration may be outlined. In refutation of the sceptics, Augustine begins by establishing the possibility of knowledge, initiating a method that was to be followed more narrowly later by Descartes. Analyzing next the nature of knowledge, Augustine proceeds from a consideration of the knowledge attained by the senses and the function of such knowledge to a consideration of the function of the intellect and the kinds of truths it attains. Describing the essential characteristics of both mathematical and moral truths he points out that they possess the characteristics of being eternal, immutable and necessary. From this the inference is then drawn that that which is eternal, immutable and necessary cannot be regarded either as created by the mind of man or as existing innately within the mind of man. This entails that such truths are objective intelligible realities transcendent to or "above" the human mind. As such they are dependent upon God and in some sense may be identified with God Himself as eternal, necessary and immutable truth. In a word, the existence of such truths as immutable, necessary and eternal leads to the intuition that God exists as truth itself. As Augustine puts it:

> Well, then, if we could find something which you not only do not doubt to be, but also to be more excellent than our reason itself, will you hesitate to call that, whatever it is, God?[6]

To which Evodius assents:

> it does not please me to name God that to which my reason is inferior, but rather than to which nothing is superior.[7]

Sciacca gives the following summary of the argument:

Nous pouvons désormais donner la formule précise de la preuve:
L'être intelligent connaît des vérités nécessaires, immuables, absolues; l'être intelligent, contingent et fini, ne peut créer, ni recevoir
des choses, par le moyen des sens, les vérités absolues dont il a
l'intuition; la Vérité en soi, nécessaire, immuable, absolue, qui est
Dieu, existe donc. Ou bien, sous une autre forme (qui est plus
proprement augustinienne): il n'y a rien en l'homme ou dans le
monde qui soit au-dessus de l'esprit: or l'esprit a l'intuition des
vérités immuables et absolues, qui sont au-dessus de lui; la Vérité
immuable, absolue et transcendante, qui est Dieu, existe donc.[8]

Boyer puts the argument more succinctly:

Ainsi le raisonnement fondamental de saint Augustin revient à ce
syllogisme; S'il est quelque chose au-dessus de notre raison, Dieu
existe. Or, il est quelque chose au-dessus de notre raison. Donc
Dieu existe.[9]

Boyer contends that Augustine establishes the major premise on
the basis of the existence of degrees of being in nature and the
minor premise in the following manner:

La vérité possède une réalité positive. Or cette réalité est, dans sa
forme pure, supérieure à notre raison. Il y a donc une réalite supérieure à notre raison.[10]

That truth has such a positive reality is evident from Augustine's
discussion of the nature of intelligible reality as exemplified
especially in the truths of ideas and numbers.[11]

Granting the existence and the reality of such immutable,
necessary, and eternal truths and the ability of the individual to
grasp such truths, just what does the argument actually prove?
Has the transition from such truths to God as Truth itself been
effectively demonstrated? Actually, there seems to be a missing
premise here, a premise which would enable us to argue from
such truths as effects to God as a cause. The use of a causal principle suggests the Cartesian argument that there is an idea of God
in the mind and that the mind then infers from this idea of God

as an effect the necessity of positing God as an existing being and the cause of such an idea. But Augustine does not suggest the use of the causal principle in this way. Furthermore, this line of argument makes a presupposition which is alien to the Augustinian approach and which Augustine rejected several times, namely, that the mind possesses innate ideas. Augustine will argue that God is certainly present to the mind and to the memory of man, but always present as "above" man, as a being whose existence is intuited or discovered with the truths that are present to the mind of man.

Implicit in the structure of this argument and stemming in good part from his Platonic background, there appears to be a kind of analogical argument. Augustine argues that just as there are common objects of sense perception, so there are common and universal truths present to the minds of all men. So, too, God in whom all these truths subsist as a common source is present to all men and the means by which man obtains a knowledge of truth. The analogy appears to proceed from the common objects of sense to the common intelligible objects to the common transcendent and super-intelligible object which is God. Putting the analogical character of the argument in another way, just as there is an interior sense which exercises a kind of regulative function over the individual senses, so there are the rules of number and wisdom which exercise a regulative function over mathematical and ethical knowledge. And transcending all forms of knowing will be God who illuminates all minds and is Truth itself in comparison to these lesser truths and forms of knowledge. In an analogous sense God might be considered to exercise a regulative function over all knowledge.[12]

The Thomistic emphasis on the cosmological type of argument has led some commentators to discover more in the emphasis on causality in the writings of Augustine than is warranted. To this has been added some confusion or misconception as to the actual approach that Augustine takes to God, so that his theodicy is given a Thomistic cast. Certainly, the notion of causality appears frequently in the Augustinian quest for God, but this need not imply any explicit formulation by Augustine of a cosmological argument. Boyer seems to think differently and contends that "Saint Augustin a donc ramené l'argument cosmologique à l'argument ideologique." Many passages[13] from Augustine are cited in support of this thesis. In the *City of God*, for example, Augustine declares:

> Sans parler de la voix des prophéties, le monde lui-même par sa mutabilité, par sa mobilité admirablement ordonnées, et par les formes très belles de tout le visible, proclame silencieusement, en quelque sorte, et qu'il a été fait, et qu'il n'a pu être fait que par Dieu ineffablement et invisiblement grand, ineffablement et invisiblement beau.[14]

Other passages[15] of a similar nature may be readily discovered in Augustine, but it seems incorrect to interpret them as substantiating a cosmological type of argument. In the first place, they are not arguments and they are not demonstrative. Portalié's quotations from the *Confessions* represent more the testimony of nature rather than an argument. Secondly, as in the passage from the *City of God*, they frequently follow from some explication of faith or are clearly subordinated to such an explication. Thirdly, to discover causation in nature is one thing and to use it as a logical argument is another. Actually, it would be more in order for Augustine to arrive at a principle such as the uniformity of nature, more as a consequent of his faith than as any induction from experience. Also, the knowledge of causes and effects in nature is in the nature of *ratio scientiae* and such truths lack the marks of eternality, immutability and necessity. Hence, there can be no inference from such truths to the truths of *ratio sapientiae* to which "belongs the intellectual apprehension of the eternal." For Augustine the empirical approach never leads to the highest wisdom nor even to the highest form of knowledge. The orientation of Augustinian thought is always from a more strictly rationalistic or idealistic position in which sense knowledge is subordinated to reason. It is a mistake, therefore, to impose the Thomistic approach to God's existence upon the Augustinian analysis. Augustine discovers God as present to the mind of man, but does not argue by means of a *demonstratio quia* from the effects in nature to God as the cause of those effects.[16] Rather Augustine sees all things as images and vestiges of God after he has discovered God within and present to himself.

Observe that this is a discovery of God[17] rather than a demonstration of His existence. In this way Augustine avoids a criticism that has always been directed against the empirical arguments for God's existence, namely, that they presuppose more in the conclusion than was contained in the premises. To the contention of Gilson, who seems to be in accord with Boyer on this point, that "L'itineraire normal d'une preuve augustinienne va donc du monde à l'ame et de l'ame à Dieu,"[18] we might reply that the normal itinerary of the Augustinian approach to God's existence is from the soul to God and from God's presence to the soul to his discovery in nature. For how can I recognize the existence of God in nature unless He had first revealed Himself to me? The Augustinian approach or "way" to God is primarily then an explication of what has already been achieved through faith. The identification of the eternal and immutable truths which we discover present to the mind with God is made possible only after God has first revealed Himself to us through faith. Strictly speaking, then, there is no cosmological argument for Augustine, but only the knowledge that creation is an effect of God, that the rules we find in nature have their origin in the rules of the mind, rules given to the mind by God. The order is from God to creation, from the discovery of God as present to the mind of man to the knowledge that God has ordered nature.[19]

Although such a discovery of God cannot be attained by some form of cosmological proof, this does not mean that God is wholly inaccessible to man. Rather, it might be said somewhat paradoxically, that we can best discover God by first realizing that such a discovery is not a matter of reason or scientific knowledge. We discover God by apprehending Him as the source of all truth, but discovery does not mean the comprehension of God. Such a quest for God means that you must

return unto yourself. The dwelling place of truth is the inner man.
And if you discover your own nature as subject to change, then go

beyond that nature. But remember that, when you thus go beyond it, it is the reasoning soul which you go beyond. Press on, therefore, toward the source from which the light of reason itself is kindled.[20]

God thus becomes an object of discovery to the inner man, whereas the world of nature presents the *vestigia* or traces of God in the universe known only indirectly to the mind of the believer but apprehended directly in their manifestations to sense. For God is the source by which all knowledge is illuminated. Note that the injunction "to go beyond the reasoning soul," seems to emphasize that the activity of reason is restricted to this world, but that a kind of intuition takes us beyond any inferential stages to the discovery of God. Perhaps we might say that in the argument of the *De Libero Arbitrio*, the sensible world of contingent beings is the occasion for an intuition of the eternal truths, just as the intuition of such eternal and immutable truths becomes the occasion for the intuition of God as truth itself.

Yet what is the more precise relation of such truths to God? To what extent are such truths identifiable with the nature of God? If they are distinct from God and merely transcendent in the Augustinian sense of being above the human mind, then apparently we have not actually attained God Himself but merely the highest possible image of Him. On the other hand, to insist upon the identification of such truths with God as truth itself or as being in some sense contained within the divine mind can lead rather easily to an ontologism. This is certainly a debatable point in the Augustinian philosophy and it is possible on the basis of Augustinian texts to make out equally good cases for and against such a position. The solution of this problem as well as the exact status of such intelligible realities as the eternal and immutable truths would entail a comprehensive analysis of the Augustinian theory of the divine illumination. Such an analysis, however, would not lead to a definitive demonstration for the existence of God. The result of the argument seems to be, then, that we have an intuition or a discovery of God as present to the human mind, a presence reflected in or perhaps occasioned by the immutable truths of numbers and morals that we are capable of grasping through the medium of the divine illumination.

On the other hand, it has been argued that there are the elements of an ontological argument present in the writings of Augustine. In the argument of the *De Libero Arbitrio* it would be rather difficult to draw out anything very explicit, but a commentary of Augustine's on Psalm LXXII, 28, seems to suggest something like an ontological argument:

> reason recognizes that there is nothing between the soul and the body which is superior to the body and inferior to the soul. And that which is superior to every animating principle, we call that God. And whoever conceives it is united to it: because that which one conceives is true, while that which one believes is not (for that reason) true. Thus that which is true, without being present to the senses or the intellect, that can be but an object of faith and not of sensation or intelligence. Thus, the being who conceives God is united to God. Thus the rational soul conceives God, because it conceives that which is immutable and does not change. But both soul and body admit of change; thus that which is immutable is evidently superior to that which is not, and nothing is superior to the rational soul except God. If then it conceives something immutable, it is that without any doubt that it conceives. And it is Truth itself; and because the rational soul unites itself by knowledge, and this is the good of the soul, it is just to admit that this is the sense of the words: "But it is good for me to adhere to my God."[21]

Parts of this statement seem close to Anselm without being explicitly the Anselmian argument. What Anselm shows is that if we conceive God in a certain way—as a being than which nothing greater can be conceived—that such a conception of God leads necessarily to His existence. The most that Augustine seems to bring out is that to conceive God is to be united to Him and that we do conceive Him as immutable and also as he says elsewhere as necessary and eternal. What seems to be lacking in the Augustinian statement is the Anselmian contention that to conceive of such a necessary being logically implies the existence of such a Being. Augustine may have considered such a logical step but certainly did not take it. He is more cautious and content simply to say that to conceive of such a necessary and immutable being (Truth) unites us with God or enables us to intuit or discover God.

Sciacca apparently agrees that there is no ontological argument present in Augustine:

> le processus rationnel va de l'existence réèlle des esprits finis et contingents à l'existence réèlle de l'Esprit infini et absolu qui est Dieu—ou bien, de la *réalité positive* de la Véritée en soi ou de l'Intelligence infinie. Il ne s'agit donc pas de procéder de l'idée de Dieu à l'existence de Dieu, mais du donné réèl qu'est l'être pensant fini et contingent à la réalité absolue *de* Dieu, qui le fait être comme être pensant.[22]

Given certain expressions and statements in the writings of Augustine that seem to anticipate an ontological argument, we may well ask why a man of Augustine's intellectual genius apparently did not see the logical inference that might take him from the conception of a being exceeding all others in our understanding to the actual existence of such a being. In part the answer lies in what has already been brought out, namely, that for Augustine the existence of God is discovered or intuited by the individual rather than demonstrated. In other words for Augustine any formal demonstration or proof of God's existence is unnecessary for God already exists and is present to the individual. This point may be further elaborated in the light of a remark made by Augustine in reply to a letter (circa 414 A.D.) from Bishop Evodius. The latter had asserted among other things in his letter that "reason itself demonstrates that God exists or must necessarily exist." On this point Augustine comments:

> If you will recall points which you know well, or, if I mistake not, you once did know well, although you may have forgotten them, which I wrote after conferring and discussing with you in my treatises either on the greatness of the soul or on free will, you will find therein the answers to your problems, without help from me;

that is, of course, if you apply the labor of your mind to draw the conclusions from the points which are there made clear and definite. You also have some help in the book on religion (*De vera religione*); if you would review it and look into it, you would never think that reason can prove the necessity of God's existence, or that by reasoning it can be established that God must necessarily exist. In the science of numbers, which we certainly make use of in every day life, if we say seven plus three ought to be ten, we do not speak exactly. It is not: they ought to be ten—they are ten.[23]

The necessity of God's existence for Augustine is a necessity that characterizes His existence but in no sense determines it. It is a necessity similar to that which characterizes the eternal and immutable truths of morals and mathematics. Such truths possess necessity as one of their attributes but they do not exist in virtue of any necessary inferential warrant on our part. To say, then, that God must exist or necessarily exists is to confuse necessity as an aspect of the divine nature with necessity as a modal function. For Augustine any statement that God ought to exist or must exist would appear to place a certain determination upon God's existence. But God's existence is such that it must be completely free from all determinations.

Furthermore, to assert that God must exist raises some possibility of a doubt regarding His existence, for modal judgments lack the certitude of assertoric judgments. In the eyes of Augustine there is nothing more certain than God's existence. Consequently, His existence is just as evidently and immediately known as are the eternal and immutable truths present to our minds. In neither case is any necessary inference required for the truth of their existence. Furthermore, the certitude of our belief in God's existence is the result of the grace of God and not of any inferential warrant. We believe that God exists so that we may understand that He exists. We do not understand or require the necessity of God's existence in order that we may believe in His existence.

Hence, any so-called "proof" of God's existence in Augustine should be regarded more as an explication of what is already true in fact and known as such through faith. The proof for the existence of God might be said to do little more than to confirm what we already know; it is reason's way of strengthening the conviction of faith. Restricting the meaning of proof to its older connotation of "testing," we could say that the function of any proof for the existence of God is that of confirming that which we hold on faith and through authority. The reference in Augustine's letter to the *De vera religione* should be interpreted in this light rather than in the notion that there is any foreshadowing in this work of the proof offered in the *De Libero Arbitrio*. As an apologetic treatise the *De vera religione* is more concerned with the evidences for the true religion and as such is more a confirmation of God's existence than a demonstration of His existence.

The development, then, of any form of ontological argument to prove the necessity of God's existence would have seemed almost redundant to Augustine. For God clearly and already exists and is present to the mind of man. The sole function of any so-called rational demonstration is merely the explication and confirmation of what is already known by faith and experience. That God is Truth itself is reason's way of explicating God's presence to the soul.

Finally, it appears to me that a part of the persuasiveness of the argument of Augustine stems from the use of certitude in its various forms and the analogies that might be elicited here. The highest certitude is that of faith. The discovery of other certitudes might be said to support in a lesser degree the highest certitude which we already possess in faith, just as the uses of reason and the acquisition of knowledge might be said to explicate and to support the truths of faith. Better, perhaps, the kind of assent we give to the truths of reason points the way to a need for a higher certitude. For no matter how firm the assent of the mind to the truths of reason, the mind remains restless in its certitude. The truths of faith, on the other hand, yield the firmest assent because that assent is caused by the will. The lesser forms of certitude merely reflect that quiet certitude based upon an adherence to the Truth which is God. Just as all knowledge finds its source in the divine illumination, so all certitude finds its source in the ultimate certitude of faith. Without his Christian faith, we might hazard the guess that Augustine would probably have become an Academician.

Of the various forms of certitude, the most familiar is the one Augustine uses at the outset of his demonstration in the *De Libero Arbitrio* and which follows upon the attempt to doubt our existence. Here Augustine argues not merely that man knows himself as a thinking being, but as a living, feeling, sensing being.[24] The certitude in this case is not merely an intellectual one, but rather what might be termed an existential certitude. Such a certitude is basic to the other forms that we have indicated, namely, the certitude found in the truths of mathematics and morals. Also, we should not overlook another form of intellectual certitude—those exemplified in the disjunctives that Augustine is so fond of using in the *Contra Academicos*. After noting that differences among philosophers do not preclude wisdom and truth he declares:

> I hold it to be truly certain that there is only one world or that there are many worlds: if more than one that their number is either finite or infinite. . . . Likewise, I know that this world where we are owes its order either to the nature of bodies or to some providence; that it has always existed and will always exist; or that it had a beginning and will never end; or that it had no beginning in time and will have an end; or that it had a beginning and will not last forever. And I have much knowledge of similar problems of physics, for these disjunctives are true, and no one can confuse them with any likenesses to falsity.[25]

Long familiarity with the Cartesian approach should not deceive us here. For such intellectual truths to Augustine lack the fundamental content of an existential certitude, and they are not inferential steps leading to a proof of God's existence. Even though Augustine does not explicitly say so, such truths would be mere empty tautologies having their source in the wider certitude that is linked to the whole existence of man and not simply to one faculty of his being. Furthermore, they are subordinated to the certitude of moral truths and these in turn lack meaning unless integrated with the spiritual structure of man's being. Moral truths would have as little content as the will would have direction unless ordered to the grace of God.

The assertion that all such truths are immutable, eternal and necessary involves again the difficulty of relating such truths to a finite subject. How can man, as a finite being, subject to time and change, actually know of truths that are beyond time and change, unless in some way he has a prior knowledge of the meaning of eternity, immutability and necessity? Clearly, there seems to be no empirical way of arriving at truths with these characteristics. And since Platonic reminiscence must be rejected, it would appear that any recognition of such truths must be consequent upon some form of intellectual grace, such as faith and the divine illumination.

Hence, just as the forms of certitude converge on the highest certitude and through it take on meaning, so the various rational approaches converge upon that which is given and understood through faith. This explains perhaps why a person may follow the reasoning in an argument for God's existence, although he has not the faith which would enable him to establish the identity of the end of reasoning with the beginning of faith. He may even accept a proof for God's existence, and yet remain unpersuaded. As Fr. Luijpen expresses it:

> we observe that it is impossible for man ever to recognize the validity of the proof of God, if he has not previously recognized his existence in its religious dimension, i.e., as directedness to God. Of this directedness the proof that there is a God is only the learned expression. The proof presupposes one's religiousness. It does not produce this disposition, but on the contrary is produced by it.[26]

It has been outside our purpose to pursue all the possible inquiries involved in Augustine's quest for God.[27] Our analysis has been limited primarily to the argument from truth. It must be evident, however, that the inadequacies and difficulties of the argument are more than adequately supplemented by Augustine's profound conviction through faith that God exists. Actually the

Augustinian approach to God rests far more upon an existential argument for God's existence rather than upon the limited demonstration of the *De Libero Arbitrio*. In fact, the whole life and doctrine of Augustine is representative of an existential argument which moves from that troubled and restless existence of Augustine to the moral demand and need for a God who would give meaning to his existence. The philosophical explication of the conversion is the achievement of God as that transcendental being who makes Himself known to us by what He does to us. It can never be overlooked in any interpretation of Augustine that God exists as a moral necessity for man—that to attain God we must first become moral. As Augustine himself puts it:

> Oh God, ... whom no one finds unless he is first purified.[28] *And*: It is certainly perverse and preposterous to desire to see the truth so that you may purify your soul, which should rather be purified that you may see.[29]

To conclude, an existential necessity rather than a logical necessity leads us to God. The attainment of God is dependent on our necessity of being good and to be good depends on God. The paradox of moral action leads more determinately than any proof to the necessity of God's existence. In part this is evident even in the very argument of the *De Libero Arbitrio* where the moral truths occupy a higher position than the mathematical truths. For Descartes, the mathematician, the highest certitude lies in mathematics and upon the paradigm of such ideas he moves to God. For Augustine, and his insight is greater, man is fundamentally a moral being and it is through the demands of such a nature that man moves with the grace of God to the existence of that Being in whom we live and move and have our being. God is not a problem to be solved by logical argument or scientific discovery. He is a mystery to be apprehended through faith.

> He is more truly thought than expressed; and He exists more truly than He is thought.[30]

NOTES

1. *Oeuvres de Saint Augustin, XII. Les Revisions*, Introduction, Paris, Desclée de Brouwer et Cie, 1950, p. 130. (Unless otherwise noted all references will be to this edition of the writings of Augustine.)

2. *De vera religione.*

3. *Letter 162, Fathers of the Church* edition of the Writings of St. Augustine, Volume II, translated by Sister Wilfrid Parsons, New York, 1953, p. 375.

4. *Sermon CCCVI*, A Library of the Fathers of the Holy Catholic Church, edited by John Henry Parker, Oxford, 1845.

5. Grabowski, Stanislaus J. *The All-Present God*, Herder, St. Louis, 1954, p. 58.

6. *De Libero Arbitrio*, ch. 6, 14.

7. *Loc. cit.*

8. Sciacca, M. F., *L'existence de Dieu*, Paris, Aubier, 1950, p. 109.

9. Boyer, C., *L'idée de Vérité dans la philosophie de Saint Augustin*, Paris, Beauchesne, 1940, p. 65.

10. *Ibid.*, p. 65.

11. On the reality of mathematical truths, see not only the *De Libero Arbitrio*, but also the remarks in the *Confessions*, X., 12, 19.

12. This seems to be Augustine's meaning in the *City of God*, XI, 27, when he refers to that spiritual light which "illumines our mind and makes us able to judge correctly of all other things. For the faculty of judgement is in proportion to our capacity for this light."

13. *De Genesi ad litteram*, lib. 4, c. 32, n. 49. Migne, t. 34. col. 316–17; *Ennarrat. in ps.* 144, n. 13. Migne, t. 37. col. 1878; *Sermo* 141, c. 2, n. 2. Migne, t. 38. col. 776; *De Trin.*, lib. 12, c. 5, n. 5. Migne, t. 42, col. 1001.

14. *Essais sur la doctrine de saint Augustin*, Beauchesne, Paris, 1932, p. 61.

15. Portalié suggests that there is a metaphysical proof in the following passages from the *Confessions*: "I have questioned the earth . . . and the sea . . . and the depths . . . and they have answered: 'Look above us . . . He made us.' " (*Conf.* X., 6, 9). Or: "Behold, the heavens and the earth exist. They cry out that they were made, for they are changed and undergo variation. Whatever has not been made and nevertheless exists, has nothing in it which did not exist before; this is what change and variation mean. They also cry out that they did not make themselves . . ." (*Conf.* XI., 4, 6)—*A Guide to the Thought of Saint Augustine* by Eugène Portalié, SJ, translated by Ralph J. Bastian, SJ—Chicago, Henry Regnery, 1960, p. 126.

16. Boyer states, *loc. cit.*, that Augustine does not explicitly recognize the principle of causality, but must be supposed to have admitted it.

17. Not a discovery of God in the sense of comprehending His nature, for as he states in the *De Ordine*, 18, 47: "the soul has no knowledge of God save the knowledge that it knows Him not." None of the categories of reason are sufficient to enable us to attain a real knowledge of God.

18. Quoted by Boyer, *op. cit.*, p. 76.

19. The Augustinian "way" has also been described in the following terms: "L'attitude méditative, existentielle, donne à l'augustinisme son point de départ et, en un sens le principe unifacteur de toute la doctrine. Car si *'toute s'explique par Dieu,'* Augustin cherche et découvre Dieu en son âme par introspection ou, plus exactement, il s'élève au-dessus de son âme ou il cherche la Vérité béatifiante, pour la trouver enfin en elle-même au-dessus de son âme"—F. J. Thonnard, "Méthode Rationelle en Augustinisme" in *Études Augustiniennes*, VI., i. 17.

20. *De Vera Religione*, 39, 72.

21. *83 Div. Quaest.*, Q. 54.

22. *Op. cit.*, p. 110.

23. *Letter 162, op. cit.*

24. In addition to the account in the *De Libero Arbitrio* there is the very explicit passage in the *De Trinitate X.*, 10, where he declares: "When a mind is bidden to know itself, it knows that this is said to itself, to a self that is, lives, and understands. Further, men know that they will, and they know that no one can will who does not exist and does not live. Also they know that they have memory. All these come to mind quite apart from the knowledge that is received from without."

25. *Contra Academicos*, III., 10, 23.

26. Luijpen, William A., OSA, *Existential Phenomenology*, Duquesne University Press, Pittsburgh, 1960, p. 68.

27. Thus the interesting and Neo-Platonic inspired types of the ascension of the soul to God which Augustine is fond of delineating fairly frequently in his writings, e.g. *Confessions VII*, xvii, 23; *De Doctrina Christiana II*, vii, 9–12; and *De Quantitate Animae XXXIII*, 70–79. But such approaches to the discovery of God are not demonstrative arguments for His existence and they raise the larger question of Augustine's mysticism which merits more consideration than can be given in the present study.

28. *Soliloques*, I, 1, 3.

29. *De Utilitate Credendi*, XVI, 34.

30. *De Trinitate VII*, iv, 7.

10

COMMON NATURE: A POINT OF COMPARISON BETWEEN THOMISTIC AND SCOTISTIC METAPHYSICS

Joseph Owens

NO matter how much it throws the study out of correct historical perspective,[1] an investigation today of any major question in the metaphysics of John Duns Scotus can hardly avoid a comparison or a contrast with the corresponding position in the writings of St. Thomas Aquinas. Modern interest in Scholastic metaphysics inclines more or less inevitably to revolve around the two most outstanding of the mediaeval thinkers, Aquinas and Scotus. Efforts have been made to show that the two are in substantial agreement on fundamental issues, differing only in details or in mode of expression.[2] The predominating tendency, however, is to see a radical difference between their respective metaphysics. The present article seeks to examine the doctrines of the two mediaeval writers on a basic metaphysical issue, the doctrine of essence just in itself and apart from the universality that it has in the human intellect and the individuality that it possesses in the outside world. The purpose is to see if the teaching found in the two thinkers is at all compatible metaphysically or if on the other hand it reveals a diversity that is fundamental and a gap that is unbridgeable.

On this point, fortunately, the historical framework for the comparison is available in clear-cut lines. Both writers develop their doctrines of essence taken just in itself against a background already laid down by Avicenna. Both follow the general divisions of the Arabian thinker, and both use to a large extent the terminology taken from the Latin translation of his works. Hence, even though the two doctrines on this point are not formally confronted with each other in the works of Duns Scotus, they are nevertheless presented in both writers against a common background that should be of considerable help in examining their agreement or diversity.

I. THE AVICENNIAN ESSENCE

First, it will be advantageous to take a brief glance at the Avicennian doctrine of the essence just in itself. The teaching is outlined in texts like the following:

> animal est in se quoddam, et idem est utrum sit sensibile aut sit intellectum in anima. In se autem hujus nec est universale nec est singulare. Si enim in se esset universale, ita quod animalitas, ex hoc quod est animalitas, est universale, oporteret nullum animal esse singulare, sed omne animal esset universale. Si autem animal ex hoc quod est animal esset singulare, impossibile esset esse plus quam unum singulare, scilicet ipsum singulare cui debetur animalitas, et esset impossibile aliud singulare esse animal.[3]

Basing his reasoning on the evident facts of predication, Avicenna is showing very clearly that a nature or essence, for instance "animal," is of itself neither singular nor universal. The notion "animal" is predicated, say of a horse. A horse is an animal. If the notion "animal" involved in itself universality, then a particular horse, because it is an animal, would be universal. If on the other hand the notion "animal" in itself required singularity, then it would be identified with one particular instance only, and could not be predicated of any other individual.

The conclusions are manifestly based upon what is experienced in predication. They show that the animality in the individual horse perceived through sensation, and the animality in the universal understood through the intellect, is the same animality. It is something that just in itself does not involve either universality or singularity. Neither universality nor singularity is essential to it. Rather, both universality and singularity, and anything else not contained within the very notion of animality, are all accidental to it. Avicenna states this expressly:

> Animal autem in se est quoddam intellectum in mente quod sit animal, et secundum hoc quod intelligitur esse animal non est nisi animal tantum. Si autem praeter hoc intelligitur esse universale aut singulare aut aliquid aliud, jam intelligitur praeter hoc quoddam, scilicet id quod est animal, quod accidit animalitati.[4]

Examining these considerations from a metaphysical viewpoint, and with express reference[5] back to the logical treatment, the Arabian shows that the nature expressed in the definition is just in itself neither one nor many, and neither existent in the mind nor existent in reality:

> Equinitas etenim habet deffinitionem quae non eget universalitate. Sed est cui accidit universalitas, unde ipsa equinitas non est aliquid nisi equinitas tantum. Ipsa enim ex se nec est multa nec unum nec est existens in his sensiblibus nec in anima.[6]

Unity, therefore, is a conception that has no place in regard to a nature taken just in itself. Only when the nature is seen in conjunction with something accidental to it, can the question of unity be placed:

> Cum ergo subiectum quaestionis posita fuerit ipsa humanitas secundum quod est humanitas veluti aliquid unum, et interrogaverint nos secundum aliquod contrariorum dicentes, quod aut est unum aut multa, tunc non erit necesse respondere aliquod illorum. Ipsa enim humanitas ex hoc quod est ipsa humanitas est quiddam praeter aliquid illorum in cuius diffinitione non accipitur nisi humanitas tantum. Sed si proprietas eius est esse unum vel multa, sicut proprietas quae eam sequitur, tunc sine dubio appropriabitur per hoc,

sed tamen ipsa non erit ipsum appropriatum ex hoc quod est humanitas; ergo ex hoc quod ipsa est humanitas non est ipsum unum vel multum, sed est aliud quiddam cui illud accidit extrinsecus.[7]

To ask whether the nature taken just in itself is one or many is to ask a question that allows no direct reply, because it is not properly placed. The question of unity can be asked and answered only after the nature is considered as appropriated to a condition accidental to it as such. The nature just in itself has no unity. Yet this denial of unity does not at all imply that it is a plurality. The very question, rather, cannot be applied to it. Hence, if one asks whether humanity as humanity is different in Plato from humanity in Socrates, one is asking about humanity in an absolute sense, that is, in a sense that has freed it from any of the accidental conditions that may follow upon it. So one has to answer no to the question, the denial being understood in this absolute sense. Humanity in Socrates is not different from humanity in Plato. But this answer does not exclude numerical difference. It does not at all imply that Socrates and Plato are the same individual. They have the same nature, humanity, but they are numerically different. The numerical differences are extrinsic to the humanity as such, and so do not prevent it from being the same humanity, as humanity, in both individuals:

Unde si quis interrogaverit an humanitas quae est in Platone ex hoc quod est humanitas sit alia ab illa quae est in Socrate, et necessario dixerimus non, non oportebit consentire ei, ut dicatur: ergo haec et illa sunt una numero; quoniam negatio illa absoluta fuit, et intelleximus in ea quod illa humanitas ex hoc quod est humanitas est humanitas tantum. Sed hoc quod ipsa est alia ab humanitate quae est in Socrate quiddam extrinsecum est. Ipse vero non interrogavit de humanitate nisi ex hoc quod est humanitas. Cum autem dixit, humanitas quae est in Platone ex hoc quod est humanitas, iam posuit ei respectum ex hoc quod est humanitas; attribuit ergo ei respectum extraneum ab ea, cum dixit, quae est in Platone, aut quae est illa quae est in Platone.[8]

There can be no question, then, of applying the notion of unity to a nature just in itself. A nature can be called "one" only after it is considered in a respect that is extrinsic to it as such. Unity is accordingly an accidental property, lying outside the nature taken just in itself:

Unitas autem est proprietas quae cum adiungitur equinitati fit equinitas propter ipsam proprietatem unum. Similiter etiam equinitas habet praeter hanc multas alias proprietates accidentes sibi.[9]

This denial of unity in the nature as such is found unqualified in Avicenna. It is not restricted to one kind of unity, individual unity, at least expressly. Avicenna in this connection makes no mention of any other kind of unity that would be immune from his present conclusions. He speaks as though numerical unity is the only unity with which he is concerned. He shows no interest in leaving open the way for an exception to be made in regard to some other kind of unity that might belong to the nature as such without involving numerical unity. He does not make any explicit denial of the possibility of such a doctrine, but at the same time he does not positively teach it. He speaks as though to deny individual unity to the nature as such is to deny unity to it without feeling any necessity to leave room for further qualification.

Does the same reasoning, however, hold in regard to the being of the nature as such? Is its being, like its unity, something accidental to it? Does the denial of being in sensible things and being in the intellect mean also a denial of all being whatsoever in the nature as such? Certainly, in the text already quoted,[10] being in reality and being in the intellect are expressly treated in the same way as unity and plurality. Elsewhere, however, the nature itself is seen with a priority of its own in being when compared with its being in reality and its being in the intellect:

... poterit autem animal per se considerari, quamvis sit cum alio a se; essentia enim eius est cum alio a se, ergo essentia eius est ipsi per se. Ipsum vero esse cum alio a se est quiddam quod accidit ei vel aliquid quod comitatur naturam suam sicut haec animalitas et humanitas; ergo haec consideratio, scilicet ex hoc quod est animal praecedit in esse, et animal quod est individuum propter accidentia sua, et universale quod est in his sensibilibus, et intelligibile sicut simplex praecedit compositum, et sicut pars totum; ex hoc enim esse nec est genus nec species nec individuum nec unum nec multa. Sed ex hoc esse est tantum animal et tantum homo, nec comitatur illud sine dubio esse unum vel multa, . . .[11]

So in the Latin translation of Avicenna, the nature or essence taken just in itself appeared as a kind of being, an *esse* that is prior to being in reality and to being in the mind. By virtue of this being (*ex hoc esse*) the nature is merely what it is in itself, merely animal, for example, or merely man. By virtue of this being it is neither one nor many, neither individual nor universal. Such being is not viewed expressly as giving rise of itself to any unity. It is a being that of itself renders the nature neither one nor many, neither existent in sensible things nor existent in the intellect. It is a being that will have to coincide entirely with nature or essence, for it implies nothing that is accidental to the essence. In fact, Avicenna calls it the proper being of essence. It is the *certitudo* of the thing, the essence itself: "Et hoc est quod fortasse appellamus esse proprium; nec intendimus per illud nisi intentionem esse affirmativi, quia verbum ens signat etiam multas intentiones, ex quibus est certitudo qua est unaquaeque res; et est sicut esse proprium rei."[12]

The essence taken just in itself has then its own proper being, which is not the being of the thing in reality nor its being in the intellect. These latter two are accidental to it, while the proper being is essential to it. The Avicennian essence or nature, accordingly, as found described in Latin translation, is something that of itself has being but not unity. After the development of the general doctrine on the transcendent properties of being that had taken place among the Latin thinkers of the thirteenth century, the Avicennian teaching on essence could hardly be left in the status that allowed a nature being but denied it unity. Where being was found, a corresponding unity must also be present. Where unity was altogether lacking, to that same extent would there be dearth of being. A mediaeval Latin thinker, working in this Avicennian background after the middle of the thirteenth century and developing the doctrine more profoundly, would have to make his choice. He would either have to accept the denial of unity in the essence at its face value and neglect the Avicennian teaching on the proper being of that essence, or else he would be forced to allow the essence its own proper being or entity and so would have to set up a unity corresponding to that entity, qualifying or explaining away the Avicennian assertions that unity does not apply to the nature taken as such. This is the point that is crucial in the texts of St. Thomas and Duns Scotus as they develop their respective doctrines of essence as such against the common background seen in the Arabian theologian.

In regard to terminology, one might note that in the translation of Avicenna the Latin term *commune* is used synonymously with *universale*.[13] Nor does the Latin text make the term *universale* exclude altogether a sense in which it is synonymous with the nature just in itself, and distinct from the universal in its true sense.[14]

II. THE COMMON NATURE
IN ST. THOMAS AQUINAS

In the early treatise *De Ente et Essentia* St. Thomas Aquinas develops his notion of essence in a quite noticeable Avicennian framework.[15] After having shown how the nature that is predicated of the individual is taken in abstraction without precision,[16] St. Thomas notes that the nature or essence so accepted can be considered in two ways. First, there is the absolute consideration, the consideration of it just in itself, and in this consideration it is neither one nor many:

Natura autem uel essentia sic accepta potest dupliciter considerari. Uno modo secundum rationem propriam, et hec est absoluta consideratio ipsius, et hoc modo nichil est uerum de ea nisi quod conuenit sibi secundum quod huiusmodi, . . . Vnde si queratur utrum ista natura sic considerata possit dici una uel plures neutrum

concedendum est, quia utrumque extra intellectum humanitatis, et
utrumque potest sibi accidere. Si enim pluralitas esset de intellectu
eius, nunquam posset esse una cum tamen una sit secundum quod
est in Socrate. Similiter si unitas esset de ratione eius, tunc esset una
et eadem Socratis et Platonis et non posset in pluribus plurificari.[17]

The reasoning of St. Thomas is based upon the facts of predication
and follows the general lines of that of Avicenna in the texts
quoted above.[18] It uses the same examples of humanity and Plato
and Socrates, and the term "absolute" in its application to the
nature just in itself, the nature as freed from all subsequent
conditions. The study of predication shows that unity and plurality
are both outside the nature considered absolutely or just in
itself, and both are accidental to it—*utrumque potest sibi accidere*.
The Avicennian framework is undeniable. But one point of
difference, at least in expression, is rather striking. The consideration of essence just in itself is not expressed as something that
involves a proper *being* of the essence, but is a consideration
according to the proper *ratio* of that essence. It is an absolute
consideration of the essence, rather than a proper being of the
essence. The text seems to be framed carefully in a way that
avoids any implication of *being* in the essence absolutely considered. It can accordingly go on to place unity outside that nature
without embarrassment from any implicit commitment of being
upon which unity would necessarily follow.

Such is the absolute consideration of the nature. On the other
hand, nature or essence can be considered as it has being. Its
being may be two-fold. It may exist in singular things, or it may
exist in the mind. But neither way of being belongs to the nature
considered just in itself. Accordingly, the nature absolutely
considered abstracts from all being whatsoever, though without
prescinding from any being to which it is open:

Hec autem natura habet duplex esse: unum in singularibus et aliud in
anima; et secundum utrumque consequitur dictam naturam accidens,
et in singularibus habet eciam multiplex esse secundum singularium
diuersitatem. Et tamen ipsi nature secundum primam considerationem suam, scilicet absolutam, nullum istorum esse debetur.

Falsum enim est dicere quod essentia hominis, in quantum homo, habeat esse in hoc singulari; quia si esse in hoc singulari conueniret homini in quantum est homo, et numquam esset extra hoc singulare; similiter eciam si conueniret homini in quantum est homo non esse in hoc singulari, numquam esset in eo. Set uerum est dicere quod homo in quantum est homo non habet quod sit in hoc singulari uel in illo uel in anima. Ergo patet quod natura hominis absolute considerata abstrahit a quolibet esse, ita tamen quod non fiat precisio alicuius eorum. Et hec natura sic considerata est que predicatur de indiuiduis omnibus.[19]

In this text the Avicennian position that nature as such is existent in neither sensible things nor the mind[20] is followed closely enough, but the conclusion drawn is that the nature absolutely considered abstracts from any being whatsoever—*a quolibet esse*. No room seems left for a proper being of the essence as such. This is quite in accord with St. Thomas' doctrine elsewhere, which regards every aspect of being as coming to the essence from without, and none whatsoever as belonging to it just in itself.[21] It brings the denial of unity in the nature absolutely considered into full conformity with the already accepted Scholastic teaching on the transcendent properties of being. Where a transcendent property like unity is denied, there being also must be denied. Were any being present, a corresponding unity would necessarily follow.

Further, the text goes on to state that the nature absolutely considered is what is predicated of all individuals. This doctrine is worthy of serious note. It follows directly upon the assertion that the nature so considered abstracts from all being whatsoever, though without precision. The connection of the two statements should be apparent enough. Predication requires identity of subject and predicate. It asserts that the one is the other. If the nature to be predicated of the individual had of itself any being whatsoever, it could not actually be predicated, for the required identity in reality would be rendered impossible. Any being of its own would at once set up the nature as a reality distinct in some real way from the individuating principle, and so would prevent the identity necessary for predication. Predication requires a genuine identity in reality between nature and individual. Such identity is possible because of the entire lack of being in the essence considered absolutely just in itself and in abstraction from any existence. The two doctrines, accordingly, go together. If the nature just in itself is assigned a proper being of its own, then the nature just in itself cannot be what is predicated of the individuals. If on the other hand the nature just in itself is what is predicated, in strict cogency that nature has to be considered as devoid of all being in itself, and the Avicennian denial of unity has to be followed up with a corresponding denial of all being to it when it is taken as just in itself.

The doctrine of a nature that can exist in the two-fold way and that is predicated of the individuals continues in the later Thomistic works. For instance, St. Thomas, using the two senses of the term "universal" that were allowed in the Avicennian background,[22] writes:

> Universale potest accipi dupliciter. *Uno modo* potest dici universale ipsa natura communis, prout subjacet intentioni universalitatis. *Alio modo* secundum se. . . . Ista autem natura, cui advenit intentio universalitatis, puta natura hominis, habet duplex esse: unum quidem materiale, secundum quod est in materia naturali; aliud autem immateriale, secundum quod est in intellectu. . . .
>   Sic igitur patet, quod naturae communi non potest attribui intentio universalitatis nisi secundum esse quod habet in intellectu: . . . Ipsae autem naturae, quibus accidit intentio universalitatis, sunt in rebus. Et propter hoc, nomina communia significantia naturas ipsas, praedicantur de individuis.[23]

The nature just in itself, the nature that is predicated of individuals and that may receive being in reality and being in the mind, is designated in this text as the "common nature." The expression may be found used in that sense in works of St. Thomas through the different periods of his teaching career.[24] It denotes the essence or quiddity of the thing, and is signified by the definition. The distinction in reality of essence from being, a distinction consistently maintained throughout the Thomistic writings, makes possible the predicability of the common nature in regard to all the individuals.

III. THE COMMON NATURE
IN DUNS SCOTUS

In three parallel places[25] Duns Scotus treats explicitly and at length of the nature taken just in itself. In all three he is concerned with the problem of individuation. He aims to show that a nature or essence, except that of God, is not of itself individual, but is common. To be individual it requires something outside itself as such, a mode that is accidental to it. This doctrine he develops in the Avicennian framework that the nature just in itself is something neither individual nor universal, and to which individuality and universality are both accidental. Using the same example as the Arabian, equinity,[26] Scotus writes:

> Modus ponendi est Avicennae 5 Metaphys. cap. 1. *Equinitas est tantum equinitas*, hoc est, ex se non habet hoc *esse* singulare, nec *esse* universale; sed natura potest habere *esse* sub universalitate, ut in anima, et potest habere majorem unitatem realem quam specificam; ideo neutrum est ex se, . . .[27]

Of itself, then, an essence or nature is neither singular nor plural, just as in Avicenna. However, the unity that Scotus is denying the common nature[28] is a unity that is greater than specific unity. This greater unity, obviously, is the unity found in the individual as individual. Such unity does not belong to the nature as such. So much the Avicennian background makes clear. But Scotus is qualifying the excluded unity in a way that leaves room for a unity that is lesser than individual unity and that is not excluded from the nature as such. In fact, his first effort in the process of showing positively that a material substance is not of itself individual is to establish the presence of this real though lesser than individual unity in things. It is found in things apart from any working of the human intellect. It receives the technical name *unitas minor*, lesser or minor unity.

A number of arguments are used to show the presence of this real though minor unity in things.[29] First, a real measure with its own real unity is required for things that constitute a species. That measure and so that unity have to be prior to the individuals in the species. Such unity is therefore prior to and different from numerical unity. Then, any comparison, similarity, equality, contrariety, and so on, must have a real unity as a foundation. This unity cannot be numerical unity, for nothing that is numerically one can be similar or equal to itself. If all real unity were numerical, all diversity would be equal and the intellect could not abstract anything more common from Plato and Socrates than it could from Plato and a line, and the universal would be a pure figment of the mind.[30] Similarly, the senses distinguish different *kinds* of things, even when they fail to distinguish those things as numerically different. They distinguish things, therefore, according to a specific unity.[31] Finally, even if there were no intellect, fire would cause fire. There would be a real formal unity between the two, and so the generation would still be univocal. The intellect through its consideration, therefore, does not make the generation univocal, but merely recognizes that it is such.

The burden of all these arguments is that there has to be a real basis for comparison among individuals, so that the universals will not be pure figments of the mind and the value of human science destroyed. This requires a specific unity of individuals, a specific unity that is really present in the things and that is independent of any work of the human intellect. The minor unity, however, is never found in reality outside the existent individuals.[32] In the real individual the nature acquires a unity that is proper to the individual, over and above its own minor unity. So in any individual the nature has a two-fold unity; first, a unity that belongs to it not of itself but only on account of the individual in which it is found, and secondly, another and lesser unity that belongs to it of itself: "Et sic dupliciter dicitur illa unitas minor, una, quia essentialiter est una unitate minori numerali, et tamen denominative est una numero, quia in hoc uno numero."[33]

Denominatively, then, the humanity that is in one individual differs from the humanity in another individual, for each is denominated *one* from the numerical unity of the respective individuals. This difference, however, is not at all incompatible with the specific unity of human nature as such, a unity that includes all human nature wherever it is found, and that is really present as a unity outside the mind:

> Respondeo, si loquamur realiter, humanitas quae est in Socrate, non est humanitas quae est in Platone, et est realis differentia ex differentiis individualibus unitive contentis, inseparabilibus hinc inde. Si autem circumscribamus differentiam hinc inde, sic ut nec natura intelligitur una maxima unitate in se, sed tantum illa unitate minori, quae est communis; sic nec est divisa ab humanitate Platonis divisione numerali, nec aliqua, quia non specifica, . . . [34]

To try to conceive the common nature as existing separately from the individuating mode would be attempting to conceive a contradiction, for when really existing the nature is part of a composite that contains the individual difference unitively. Conceived as existing without that individuating mode the common nature would be thereby conceived as an individual, for what really exists is individual. The nature accordingly would be conceived as common and not common, as individual and not individual. If in spite of the self-contradictory character of the objection, however, one wishes to urge the question, Scotus answers that if the individual differences were *per impossibile* struck away, then the humanity that is in this individual and the humanity that is in the other individuals would thereby merge into one real humanity, for there would be nothing to differentiate them.

This means that the community of nature is a real community outside the mind, and is the real foundation of all universal predication and scientific knowledge.[35] It does not at all imply that the common nature exists as common outside the mind, for it exists in reality only as already individuated. But does the doctrine require that the common nature have a proper being of its own, a being that is in some way prior to real existence as well as to existence in the intellect? Does the real minor unity involve a corresponding real being?

Certainly, according to the general principle that unity follows upon being, to have a real unity outside the mind the nature should have an entity of its own, differing from individual being just as much as minor unity differs from major unity. Minor unity will necessarily presuppose a corresponding entity, for unity follows upon entity: "Sicut unitas in communi per se consequitur entitatem in communi, ita quaecumque unitas per se consequitur aliquam entitatem; . . ."[36] The community of nature, in fact, is present according to the proper entity and unity of the nature just in itself:

> Et ideo concedo quod quarenda est causa *universalitatis*, non tamen quaerenda est causa communitatis alia ab ipsa *natura*; et posita communitate in ipsa natura secundum propriam entitatem et unitatem, necessario oportet quaerere causam *singularitatis*, quae superaddit aliquid illi naturae cujus est.[37]

Community, then, is placed by Scotus in the nature itself prior to any individuation or universality. The community pertains to the proper entity and the proper unity of the nature just in itself. Against the Avicennian background there could hardly be any difficulty in regarding the nature as having a proper entity of its own, for Avicenna had given the nature its own proper being. But what of the Arabian's categorical denial of unity to that nature? This has to be explained as referring to numerical unity only, just as the denial of universality is restricted to the complete sense of universality as effected by the intellect:

> Qualiter autem potest hoc intelligi, potest aequaliter videri per dictum Avicennae, V. *Metaph.*, ubi vult quod *equinitas sit tantum equinitas, nec ex se una, nec plures, nec universalis, nec particularis.* Intellige, non est ex se una unitate numerali; nec plures, pluralitate opposita illi unitati; nec universalis actu, eo modo quo aliquid est universale factum ab intellectu, non ut obiectum intellectus; nec est particularis de se; licet enim nunquam sit realiter sine aliquo istorum, non tamen est *de se* aliquod istorum, sed est *prius naturaliter* omnibus istis.[38]

As in Avicenna the *esse proprium* of the essence enjoyed a priority over its being in reality and its being in the mind, so the Scotistic common nature, though it can never exist except in the individual in reality or in the universal in the intellect, nevertheless has its own quidditative entity that is prior to numerical unity or plurality and to singularity or universality. Of itself it is the object of the intellect and the object of metaphysical consideration. As such it has sufficient being to give rise to the truth of quidditative propositions:

> Et secundum istam prioritatem naturalem est *quod quid est et* per se obiectum intellectus, et per se ut sic consideratur a Metaphysico, et exprimitur per definitionem; et propositiones *per se primo modo* sunt verae ratione *quidditatis* sic acceptae. . . .[39]

A corresponding truth as well as a corresponding unity follow accordingly upon the nature taken just in itself. These transcendent properties have to be based upon a proper entity of the nature. Accordingly, the Scotistic common nature will not be predicable of the individual:

> Tamen in creaturis est aliquod commune unum unitate *reali* minori unitate *numerali*; et illud quidem commune non est ita commune quod sit *praedicabile* de multis, licet sit ita commune quod non repugnet sibi esse in alio quam in eo in quo est.[40]

The complete identity in reality of nature with individual that was found in St. Thomas Aquinas[41] is lacking here. The one is not the other:

> non potest haberi in actu universale, quo ipsum est dicibile de alio sic, *hoc est hoc*, nisi per intellectum. . . . Tamen non potest secundum istam realem unitatem minorem esse simul hoc et hoc, . . .[42]

Because it has an entity of its own, distinct from the individuality, the Scotistic common nature is not completely identified in reality with the individual, and so cannot be predicated of the individual. Predication requires an identity that allows one to say "this is this." The common nature does not have that identity with the individual in Duns Scotus, as it had in St. Thomas. In St. Thomas, there is no real distinction between the thing and the nature absolutely considered, for the nature absolutely considered is not in itself a reality. In Scotus, however, the one individual thing is composed of different realities, and so exhibits a distinction unknown in the philosophy of St. Thomas. No matter how much the individual is one thing, it can be distinguished for Scotus into different realities:

> potest distingui, quantumcumque sit *una res,* in *plures realitates formaliter distinctas,* quarem haec formaliter non est *illa,* sed haec est formaliter entitas *singularis* et illa est entitas *naturae* formaliter.[43]

The specific entity of the common nature is, accordingly, formally distinct from the other entity that constitutes the individuation. Each is of itself an entity, each is a reality. The formal distinction, no matter what it may be elsewhere in the philosophy of Duns Scotus, is here expressly a distinction between two realities and two entities.[44] The thing remains numerically one, and contains unitively both the nature and the individuating entity.[45] Though the thing is one, the realities that compose it are more than one, independently of any consideration of the human intellect. The formal distinction is here sufficient to prevent the real identity of nature and individual that is necessary for predicating the common nature of the individual thing.

IV. CONCLUSION

In both St. Thomas and Duns Scotus the common nature is the essence taken just in itself as neither particular nor universal, neither one nor many, neither existent in singulars nor existent in the mind. In both thinkers the doctrine is developed against the Avicennian background that essence is of itself indifferent to all these qualifications. In Avicenna, however, the essence as such had been described as having a being of its own but no unity of its own. It is on this point that the Thomistic and Scotistic doctrines show their fundamental divergence. In St. Thomas the denial of unity is accepted without qualification. Accordingly, the common nature cannot have any proper being of its own. The *esse proprium* of the Avicennian essence does not appear in the Thomistic development. Because it has no being of its own whatsoever, the essence when taken without precision can be predicated of every individual that comes under it. It has no being at all that could make it different in reality from the individual in which it is found. It can be perfectly and adequately identified in reality with any and every individual that comes under it, for it presents no being of its own that would render it at all different from any one of them, or that would make it in any way a different thing when it is known and so becomes existent in the mind. In this way the common nature for St. Thomas is predicable of the individual and is completely identified with it in reality. There can be no distinction in reality whatsoever between individual and nature in Thomistic metaphysics.

For Duns Scotus, on the contrary, the Avicennian denial of unity to the common nature is qualified. Only numerical unity is denied to it as such. A unity lesser than numerical, minor unity, is found in the common nature as the necessary basis for universality and for specific resemblance and diversity. This minor unity follows upon a corresponding entity of the common nature, an entity that is positive in itself and formally distinct in reality from the individuating mode. It is true that the common nature never exists outside the individuals and outside the mind, yet when existent either in the mind or in the individuals it always remains formally distinct in its own entity from both the individuality and the universality. The result is that the Scotistic common nature can never be predicated of the individual, for it can never be completely identified with the individual in the way required by predication.

From the metaphysical viewpoint, therefore, the fundamental difference between the two doctrines of essence is clear-cut. For St. Thomas, a finite essence just in itself has no being or entity whatsoever. A finite essence always remains other than any being it may possess. For Scotus, an essence just in itself has a positive entity of its own. Upon this entity there follow in a finite essence a minor unity and a formal distinction from the individuating entity. Neither this minor unity nor this formal distinction can even be conceived in terms of Thomistic philosophy. Similarly the requirement of unitive continence to make the individual one with its nature is alien to Thomistic thought. The notion of unitive continence can arise only when the nature is in reality distinct in some way from its individuating principle, and the two have to be united in reality to form something numerically one. Only in infinite being are nature and individuality identical, as for St. Thomas only in God do essence and being coincide.

On the doctrine of essence, then, the two great mediaeval thinkers show a radical difference of thought, presenting a gap that cannot be bridged. For St. Thomas finite essence has of itself no being, it is other than being. For Scotus the essence as such has its own proper entity, but a finite essence is different in reality from its individuating mode. In St. Thomas, the basic metaphysical distinction in creatures falls between essence and being. In Scotus, it falls between essence and individuality. This fundamental difference has far reaching consequences in the development of the two doctrines. On the Thomistic basis the objectivity of human cognition is assured by the complete lack of being in the essence of the sensible thing that is known. In itself the thing remains exactly the same when it becomes existent in the intellect, for of itself it has no being that could render it in any way different. The thing that exists in reality outside the mind remains exactly the same thing when it acquires being in the mind. For Scotus, the common nature has its own proper unity prior to both existence in reality and existence in the mind, and so offers a real basis for the universal mode of human cognition. In St. Thomas, real composition in the angels is shown by the distinction between their essence and their being. In Scotus, the real composition is established by the distinction between their essence and their individuating mode. For St. Thomas, the Anselmian argument for the existence of God is invalid because it does not start from really existent things. For Scotus, the existence of infinite being is demonstrated from the quiddity or possibility of things. The essence as such has an entity of its own, and so can be the starting-point for the demonstration of infinite being. In St. Thomas, the finite essence has of itself no being, and so cannot be the starting-point of a procedure that is to arrive at the primary being. In these and other similar problems the radical difference between the notions of essence makes itself sharply felt throughout the two respective metaphysical procedures.

NOTES

1. "Chercher à comprendre les positions fondamentales du Docteur Subtil n'est aucunement le situer dans son temps. L'intérêt du philosophe ne peut pas ne pas faire tort ici à la vérité de l'histoire." E. Gilson, *Jean Duns Scot* (Paris, Vrin, 1952), p. 10.

2. Instances may be found cited in Johannes Kraus, *Die Lehre des Johannes Duns Skotus von der Natura Communis* (Freiburg, Schweiz, 1927), p. 3. As an instance in contemporary American study: "It is the personal opinion of the author that the doctrine of St. Thomas and that of Duns Scotus are fundamentally compatible." Allan B. Wolter, *The Transcendentals and their Function in the Metaphysics of Duns Scotus* (Washington: Catholic University of America Press, 1946), p. 31, n. 2.

3. Avicenna, *Logica*, III (Venice, 1508), fol. 12r1.

4. *Ibid*.

5. *Metaph.*, V, 1B (*ed. cit.*), fol. 86v2.

6. *Metaph.*, V, 1A; fol. 86v1.

7. Loc. cit., fol. 86v2.

8. *Metaph.*, V, 1B; fol. 86v2.

9. *Metaph.*, V, 1A; fol. 86v1.

10. Supra, n. 6.

11. *Metaph.*, V, 1C; fol. 87r1.

12. *Metaph.*, I, 6C; fol. 72v1.

13. E.g.: "Equinitas ergo ex hoc quod in diffinitione eius conveniunt multa est communis. Sed ex hoc quod accipitur cum proprietatibus et accidentibus signatis est singularis." *Metaph.*, V, 1A; fol. 86v1. ". . . sine conditione communis aut proprii aut unius aut multi, . . ." *Ibid.*, V, 1C; fol. 87r1. ". . . de animali ex hoc quod est animal non debet praedicari proprietas nec communitas, nec est verum dicere quod de animali ex hoc quod est animal debet non praedicari proprietas vel communitas." *Ibid.*, V, 1D; fol. 87r2. ". . . manifestum est ergo non esse possibile ut una natura habeat esse in his sensibilibus,

ita ut in actu sit universalis id est ipsa una sit communis omnibus . . ." *Ibid.*, V, 2B; fol. 87v1.

14. ". . . ergo universale ex hoc quod est universale est quoddam, et ex hoc quod est quiddam cui accidit universalitas est quiddam aliud; . . ." *Metaph*, V, 1A; fol. 86v1.

15. The Avicennian background is pointed out in detail by M.-D. Roland-Gosselin, *Le "De Ente et Essentia" de S. Thomas d'Aquin* (reprint, Paris: Vrin, 1948), pp. 9–28.

16. *De Ente et Essentia* (ed. Roland-Gosselin), c. II; pp. 12.5–23.7.

17. *De Ente*, c. III; pp. 24.1–25.4.

18. Supra, nn. 3–8.

19. *De Ente*, c. III; pp. 25.9–26.11.

20. Cf. text supra, n. 6.

21. E.g.: ". . . ita quod quamcumque rationem essendi aliquid habeat, non sit sibi nisi a Deo, se defectus essendi sit ei a seipso." *In II Sent.*, d. 37, q. 1, a. 2, Solut.; ed. Mandonnet, II, 946. ". . . illud quod habet esse ab alio, in se consideratum, est non ens, si ipsum sit aliud quam esse quod ab alio accipit; . . ." *De Pot.*, III, 13, ad 4m; ed. Mandonnet, *Quaest. Disp.*, II, 97a.

22. Cf. text supra, n. 14.

23. *In II de An.*, lect. 12, (ed. Pirotta) nos. 378–380. Cf.: *De Pot.*, V, 9, ad 16; ed. Mandonnet, *Quaest. Disp.*, II, 203–204. *CG*, I, 26. *In VII Metaph.*, lect. 13, (ed. Cathala) nos. 1570–1571.

24. Cf.: ". . . natura communis recipitur in aliquo, et fit hoc aliquid." *In I Sent.*, d. 8, q. 4, a. 1, ad 2; ed. Mandonnet, I, 219. "Natura communis, si separata intelligatur, non potest esse nisi una: quamvis habentes naturam illam plures possent inveniri." *CG*, II, 52; ed. Leonine, XIII, 387a31–33. ". . . per additionem alicuius materialis natura communis individuatur ad hanc hypostasim." *CG*, IV, 40; ed. Leonine, XV, 139a27–29. ". . . natura enim communis est quam significat definitio indicans quid est res; unde ipsa natura communis, essentia vel quidditas dicitur. Quidquid ergo est in re ad naturam communem pertinens, sub significatione essentiae continetur: . . . Si enim quidquid est in substantia particulari ad naturam communem pertineret, non posset esse distinctio inter substantias particulares ejusdem naturae. Hoc autem quod est in substantia particulari praeter naturam communem,. . ." *De Pot.*, IX, 1c: ed. Mandonnet, II, 300a. "In substantiis vero simplicibus nulla est differentia essentiae et subjecti, cum non sit in eis materia individualis naturam communem individuans; . . ." *Ibid.*, p. 300b. ". . . (natura enim communis de se non subsistit nisi in singularibus); aliud est quod per principia individuantia supposita naturae communis ab invicem distinguuntur." *De Pot.*, IX, 5, ad 12: *ed. cit.*, II, 316a. "Secundum vero quod supponitur alicui naturae communi, sic dicitur res naturae; sicut hic homo est res naturae humanae; . . ." *ST*, I, 29, 2c. "Unitas autem sive communitas humanae naturae non est secundum rem, sed solum secundum considerationem; unde iste terminus homo non supponit pro natura communi, nisi . . ." *ST*, I, 39, 4,

ad 3. ". . . natura communis distinguitur et multiplicabitur secundum principia individuantia, . . ." *ST*, I, 76, 2, ad 3. "Intelligitur enim natura communis seclusis principiis individuantibus, . . ." *ST*, I, 76, 2 ad 4 "Nam *cogitativa* apprehendit individuum, ut existens sub natura communi; quod contingit ei, in quantum unitur intellectivae in eodem subjecto; unde cognoscit hunc hominem prout est hic homo et hoc lignum prout est hoc lignum. *Aestimativa* autem non apprehendit aliquod individuum, secundum quod est sub natura communi, . . ." *In II de An.*, lect. 13, (ed. Pirotta) no. 398.

However, the expression "common nature" is not restricted by St. Thomas to the technical meaning of specific nature as such. It is used by him in senses wider than the specific, e.g.: ". . . natura communis habeat aliquod esse in unoquoque eorum . . ." *In I Sent.*, d. 19, q. 5, a. 2, ad 1m; ed. Mandonnet, I, 492. ". . . naturam communem entis . . ." *CG*, I. 65; ed. Leonine, XIII, 179a42–43. ". . . naturam communem cum omnibus . . ." *ST*, I, 84, 2c.

25. *Op. Ox.*, II, 3, 1–6; ed. Quaracchi, II, 223–276. *Rep. Par.*, II, 12, 3–8; ed. Vives, XXIII, 20–41. *Quaest. Metaph.*, VII, 13; ed. Vives, VII, 402–426. These are the pertinent *loci* in the printed works.

26. The example "humanity" is also taken as found in Avicenna: "Ad illud Avic. de *humanitate*, dico, quod per hoc quod *equinitas est tantum equinitas*, ly *tantum* non excludit illa quae sunt de per se ratione *equinitatis*, cuiusmodi est *entitas rata*, sed excludit illa quae sunt per se *passiones entis*, ut unum, actu, etc. . . ." *Op. Ox.*, I, 3, 5, no. 13; Quar., I, 394 (no. 440a). Cf. *ibid.*, no. 7; p. 389 (no. 435a).

27. *Rep. Par.*, II, 12, 5, no. 11; Vives, XXIII, 30b. Cf. text infra, n. 38.

28. Scotus uses "common nature" as a technical expression very rarely: "Item, quae conveniunt individuis, ut agere, generari, etc. aut insunt eis per naturam communem, aut per differentias individuales; si primo modo, tunc primo insunt universali; . . ." *Quaest. Metaph.*, VII, 13, 19; Vives, VII, 419b. ". . . quidquid per se inest uni individuo, cuius simile inest alii individuo, inest per naturam communem, . . . *Ibid.*, no. 22; p. 422b. ". . . sic natura cui intellectus tribuit intentionem speciei, quae dicta est esse in re, est communis, . . ." *Ibid.*, no. 19; p. 420a. The notion "common," though, is clearly and forcefully contrasted with the notion of "universal" in the complete sense: ". . . est ergo in re commune, quod non est de se *hoc*, et per consequens ei de se non repugnat esse *non hoc*. Sed tale commune non est universale in actu, quia deficit ei illa indifferentia, secundum quam completive universale est universale, secundum quam scilicet ipsum idem aliqua identitate est praedicabile de quolibet individuo, ita quod quodlibet sit ipsum." *Op. Ox.*, II, 3, 1, no. 9; Quar. II, 231 (no. 238). Yet the use of the term "common" in the full sense of "universal" is not entirely excluded: ". . . loquitur de communi *praedicabili*, non praecise de communi quod determinatum est de facto, licet non repugnet sibi esse in alio, quale commune praecise potest poni in creatura realiter." *Ibid.*, p. 232. Cf. text infra. n. 40.

Conversely, Scotus allows the use of the term "universal" to designate the nature taken absolutely: "Primo modo dicitur natura absolute sumpta *universale*, quia non est de se haec, et ita non repugnat sibi ex se dici de.multis. Secundo modo non est universale, nisi sit actu indeterminatum, ita quod unum intelligibile numero sit dicibile de omni supposito, et illud est complete universale. *Quaest. Metaph.*, VII, 18, no. 6; Vives, VII, 456–457. "Sed *singulare* addit aliquam *entitatem* supra entitatem *universalis*, . . ." *Op. Ox.*, II, 9, 1 & 2, 3, no. 10; Quar., II, 451 (no. 497).

However, the regular contrast in this respect in Duns Scotus is that of the "common" with the individual and the universal. Even though Scotus does not use the technical expression "common nature" as frequently as does St. Thomas, the peculiar importance of the doctrine designated by that name has given the common nature a fundamental place in the vocabulary of Scotistic tradition: ". . . den Skotisten hingegen galt sie jederzeit als Grundpfeiler ihres Systems." J. Kraus, *Die Lehre des Johannes Duns Skotus von der Natura Communis*, p. 143. ". . . the doctrine of *Natura Communis*—the main bastion of Scotist theory of knowledge and metaphysics." Theodore Crowley, in *Philosophical Studies* (Maynooth), III (1953), 136.

29. *Op. Ox.*, II, 3, 1, nos. 3–6: Quar., II, 225–228 (no. 233). *Rep. Par.*, XII, 5, nos. 8–10; Vives, XXIII, 29–30; *Quaest. Metaph.*, VII, 13, nos. 10–12, and 18, nos. 1–2; Vives, VII, 410–412 and 453.

30. "Sic nec omnis unitas realis minor unitate numerali est universalis, sed est unitas naturae praesuppositae operationi intellectus, et ideo intellectus movetur magis ad abstrahendum unum conceptum specificam a Socrate et Platone, quam a Socrate et lapide, . . ." *Rep. Par.*, XII, 5, no. 13; Vives, XXIII, 31b. ". . . et ita omnia essent *aeque distincta*, et tunc sequitur quod non plus potest intellectus abstrahere a Socrate et *Platone* aliquod commune quam a Socrate et *linea*, et esset quodlibet universale purum figmentum . . . si tantum est in hac re unitas realis numeralis, *quaecumque entitas* est in re, illa est ex se *una numero*; ergo istud et illud secundum omnem entitatem in eis sunt *primo diversa*, et in nullo aliquo modo convenientia." *Op. Ox.*, II, 3, 1, nos. 5–6; Quar., II, 227–228 (no. 233).

31. ". . . entitas autem singularis non est propria ratio gignendi phantasma, sed tantum entitas naturae praecedens illam entitatem singularem." *Op. Ox.*, III, 14, 3, no. 9; Vives, XIV, 529a. ". . . ergo illud primum objectum habet aliquam unitatem realem, non unitatem singularitatis, quia tunc nihil, nisi hoc singulare videretur; nec universalitatis, quia objectum visus praesupponitur omni actui rationis, universale non." *Quaest. Metaph.*, VII, 13, no. 11; Vives, VII, 411b.

32. "Sicut tamen in aliis unitive contentis non est separatio realis, nec etiam potentialis; sic natura cui intellectus tribuit intentionem speciei, quae dicta est esse in re, est communis, sicut commune est potentiale in re, nunquam separabitur ab alia perfectione unitive secum contenta, vel ab illo gradu, in quo accipitur differentia individualis . . . contradictio includitur, quod separetur

propter unitivam continentiam." *Quaest. Metaph.*, VII, 13, nos. 19–20; Vives, VII, 420a.

33. *Rep. Par.*, II, 12, 5, no. 13; Vives, XXIII, 32a. Cf. *Op. Ox.*, II, 3, 5 & 6, no. 10; Quar., II, 265–266 (no. 286).

34. *Quaest. Metaph.*, VII, 13, no. 21; Vives, VII, 421b. Cf. text from Avicenna, supra, n. 8. This full explanation of the community given to a nature by minor unity is found only in the earlier work, and is a good instance of Gilson's remark: "Lorsqu'on étudie la pensée de Duns Scot sur un point important de philosophie et surtout lorsqu'on cherche à discerner la formation de sa doctrine, on se trouve toujours ramené quel que soit l'ouvrage dont on soit parti, à chercher ce qu'il a déjà dit dans ses *Quaestiones in metaphysicam Aristotelis*." "Avicenne et le Point de Départ de Duns Scot." *Archives d'Histoire Doctrinale et Littéraire du Moyen Age*, II (1927), 91.

35. For opinions on whether this community of nature is to be called positive or negative, cf. J. Kraus, *Natura Communis*, pp. 65-68. From the standpoint of individual reality, the community of course appears as negative, and is explained by indifference to being in this or that singular thing. But from the viewpoint of the common nature itself, which is prior to that of individuality, the entity and minor unity of the nature as such are positive, and accordingly the community caused by that minor unity would appear to be positive.

36. *Op. Ox.*, II, 3, 5 & 6, no. 9; Quar. II, 264 (no. 285a). Cf. ". . . cuicumque enim gradui reali entitatis, correspondet realis unitas." *Quaest. Metaph.*, VII, 13, no. 19; Vives, VII, 420a. ". . . sicut *unum* convertitur cum ente, ita omnis modus *unius*, cum aliquo gradu entis, cui est proprius . . ." *Ibid.*, no. 9; p. 410a.

37. *Op. Ox.*, II, 3, 1, no. 10; Quar., II, 232 (no. 240). Cf.: ". . . et secundum illam entitatem habet *unitatem* sibi proportionalem, . . . illa unitas est *propria passio* naturae secundum suam entitatem primam, . . . *Ibid.*, no. 7; p. 230 (nos. 235d–236). ". . . cum in qualibet unitate minore unitate numerali sit dare entitatem *positivam*, quae sit ratio per se illius unitatis. . . ." *Op. Ox.*, II, 3, 2, no. 4; Quar. II, 236 (no. 248).

38. *Op. Ox.*, II, 3, 1, no. 7; Quar. II, 228–229 (no. 235a). Scotus explains Avicenna's way of speaking on the ground that a *propria passio* is not included in the formal aspect of the nature: "Ad *Avicennam* dico quod praecisissime considerat *quidditatem* inquantum nihil includit quod non pertinet *ad per se rationem* quidditatis eius; et hoc modo *equinitas* est tantum equinitas, et nec una nec plures, quantumcumque unitas eius non sit alia res addita, sed necessario consequatur istam entitatem, sicut et omne ens secundum quamcumque, entitatem consequitur propria unitas, non tamen ista unitas est intra *formalem rationem* quidditatis ut quidditas est, sed est quasi *passio* consequens quidditatem, et omne tale apud eum vocatur *accidens*." *Op. Ox.*, II, 3, 4, no. 20; Quar. II, 256 (no. 272). Cf. text supra, n. 26.

39. *Op. Ox.*, II, 3, 1, no. 7; Quar. II, 229 (no. 235a). Cf.: ". . . *natura* est

prius naturaliter quam *haec* natura, et *unitas* propria consequens naturam ut *natura* prior est naturaliter unitate eius ut *haec* natura, et sub ista ratione est de ea consideratio metaphysica et assignatur definito eius et sunt propositiones *per se primo modo: . . .*" *Op. Ox.*, II, 33, 5 & 6, no. 10: Quar. II, 265 (no. 286). "Prima ergo intellectio est naturae ut el non cointelligitur aliquis modus, . . ." *Op. Ox.*, II, 3, 1, no. 7; II, 229 (no. 235b). This entity of the common nature is described as a positive entity: ". . . nullus negat entitatem *positivam* esse rationem unitatis specificae, a qua entitate positiva sumitur ratio differentiae specificae . . . cum in qualibet unitate minore unitate numerali sit dare entitatem *positivam*, quae sit ratio per se illius unitatis. . . ." *Op. Ox.*, II, 3, 2: no. 4; II, 236 (no. 248). It is the proper and primary entity of the nature ". . . nec est ex se *haec* intranee, nec secundum entitatem propriam necessario inclusam in ipsa natura secundum primam entitatem suam." *Op. Ox.*, II, 3, 1, no. 7; II, 230 (no. 236). Scotus has no hesitation in speaking of an *esse quidditativum* and an *esse possible* ". . . non de existentia, sed de esse quidditativo." *Quaest. Metaph.*, I, 1, no. 49; Vives, VII, 37a. "Secundo modo consideratur absolute secundum *esse quidditativum*, et sic insunt ei praedicata essentialia." *Super Universalia Porphyrii*, XI, no. 2; Vives, I, 136a. ". . . de esse quiditative sive de esse possibili, non autem de existentia actuali." *Op. Ox.*, I, 2, 1 & 2, no. 56; ed. Vaticana, II, 162, 6–7.

40. *Op. Ox.*, II, 3, 1, no. 9; Quar., II, 231–232 (no. 238b).

41. Cf. supra, n. 19.

42. *Rep. Par.*, II, 5, 12; Vives, XXIII, 31a. Cf.: "Unde dico, quod species non praedicat totam naturam individui integraliter, sicut nec genus speciei." *Quaest. Metaph.*, VII, 13, no. 13; Vives, VII, 413a. ". . . sed non est idem cum individuo, sed quodammodo pars ejus, cum individuum addat super eam, formam individualem, ut dictum est." *Ibid.*, no. 15; p. 414b.

43. *Op. Ox.*, II, 3, 5 & 6, no. 15; Quar., II, 270 (no. 289). The distinction follows upon the proper unity and entity: "Contra, illud quo aliquod ens habet entitatem, eo, tamquam fundamento proximo unitatis, est unum unitate correspondente tali entitati, et per consequens distinctionum [sic] a quocumque ente non habente hanc unitatem; . . ." *Quodl.*, III, no. 11; Vives, XXV, 122a.

44. If the notion "really distinct" is reserved for a distinction between two individual things, then it cannot be applied to the Scotistic formal distinction: "Furthermore, the individual difference and the nature are not distinct as *res* and *res*, that means, they are not really distinct." P. Boehner, "Scotus' Teaching according to Occam, II. On the *Natura Communis*." *Franciscan Studies*, VI (1946), 365. In this respect it has been called real *secundum quid*. ". . . the formal distinction belongs to the category of real distinctions not *simpliciter* but *secundum quid*, and hence one has a plurality of distinct realities." M. J. Grajewski. *The Formal Distinction of Duns Scotus* (Washington: Catholic University of America Press, 1944), p. 101. However, the fact that in this instance the formal distinction falls between entities does not at all require

that in other instances it should likewise fall between entities, e.g., in the transcendentals or the divine attributes.

45. The nature does not contain the individuating mode unitively, nor the individuating mode the nature, but the one thing contains both: ". . . natura non continet unitive gradum illum, sed compositum ex natura, ct illo gradu." *Quaest. Metaph.*, VII, 13, no. 20; Vives, VII, 420b.". . . ista proprietas individui nunquam est res alia a forma specifica, tamen semper est non idem formaliter, licet aliquid possit continere unitive utrumque." *Rep. Par.*, II, 12, 8, no. 3; Vives, XXIII, 37b. "Sed in proposito nec entitas specifica includit per identitatem entitatem *individualem*, nec e converso, sed aliquod tertium tantum, cuius ista ambo quasi sunt *primo per se partes*, includit ambo ista *per identitatem*; et ita tollitur ista compositio pcrfcctissima quac est ex *re* et *re*, non tamen omnis; universaliter enim quaecumque natura non est *de se haec*, sed determinabilis ad essendum *haec*, sive determinetur per aliam *rem*, quod est impossibile in quocumque, sive per aliam *realitatem*, non est *simpliciter simplex*." *Op. Ox.*, II, 3, 5 & 6, no. 16; Quar., II, 271 (290a).

On the sources for Scotus' doctrine of universality and the interpretations given it by modern commentators, see T. Barth, "Individualität und Allgemeinheit bei J. Duns Skotus," *Wissenschaft und Weisheit*, XX (1957), 106–112.

11

THE TWICE-REVEALED AVERROES

Harry A. Wolfson

AVERROES was revealed twice to European philosophy: first in the thirteenth century and then in the sixteenth century. In this essay I shall try to recall to our minds the circumstances which had led to each of these revelations and to discuss the problems which they each gave rise to.

I shall first take up the revelation in the thirteenth century.

In the second half of the eighth century, for reasons which need not here be gone into, a fervid activity of translating works on philosophy from the Greek into Arabic was started in Islam. It lasted for about two and a half centuries. During that time, among the many works translated, were almost all the works of Aristotle and many of his Greek commentaries. The study of these translations led to original writings on philosophy, beginning with the works of al-Kindi (d. 820) and ending with those of Averroes (d. 1198). Most of these philosophic works written originally in Arabic consisted of independent systematic treatises; but those of Averroes consisted mainly of commentaries on Aristotle. Of these commentaries, five were written in three forms, known as Long, Middle, and Epitome; ten only in two forms, Middle and Epitome; two only in the form of the Epitome: and one only in that of the Middle.[1] In addition to these, there are many short treatises by Averroes on special topics in Aristotelian philosophy,[2] among them his treatise *De Substantia Orbis*.

211

his *Quaestiones in Physica*, and his lost *Treatise on the Prime Mover*.[3] Without counting these short treatises and the doubtful commentary on *De Plantis*, and counting *Parva Naturalia* as one and including Porphyry's *Isagoge*, there are thirty eight commentaries of Averroes on Aristotle.

With the Christian reconquest of Toledo in 1085, a school of translators from the Arabic into Latin was established there shortly after 1130 under the patronage of its archbishop. Before the close of the century, certain Arabic translations of Aristotle and of Greek commentaries on Aristotle, as well as of original Arabic works on philosophy, were translated from the Arabic into Latin.[4] These translations created a demand for other translations from the Arabic. And so in the second decade of the thirteenth century, less than twenty years after the death of Averroes, there began a systematic attempt to translate his commentaries into Latin. The translators who dedicated themselves to this task were Michael Scot and Hermann the German. Both of them had started their work in Toledo and then, either both or only Michael, drifted into the court of Frederick II, the then patron of translations from the Arabic. They produced translations of four of the five long commentaries, those on the *Physica*, *De Caelo*, *De Anima*. and *Metaphysica*. These contained also Latin translations of the Arabic translations of the Greek text of Aristotle, according as they were quoted in these commentaries of Averroes. They produced also translations of the Middle commentaries on four works: *Poetica*, *De Caelo*, *De Generatione et Corruptione*, and *Ethica Nicomachea*; and also a translation of the Epitome of *Parva Naturalia*.[5] A third translator, a contemporary of these two, was William of Luna, who translated Averroes' Middle commentaries on the *Isagoge* of Porphyry, the *Categories*, and *De Interpretatione*; and also his Middle commentaries on *Analytica Priora* and *Analytica Posteriora*.[6] To these three may be added Theodorus Antiochenus, also of the court of Frederick II, who translated Averroes' Prooemium to his Long Commentary on the *Physics*.[7]

The reception of these translations of Averroes' commentaries by Christian philosophers may be described by a term currently in vogue as ambivalent.[8] They praised him as commentator but damned him as theologian. For Averroes occasionally, in his exposition of Aristotle on innocuous problems of philosophy, digresses to pay his respect to certain touchy problems of religion. Already in the thirteenth century, while he was hailed by William of Auvergne (1228–1249) as "the most noble philosopher" (*philosophus nobilissimus*),[9] by St. Thomas as "the Commentator" (*Commentator*),[10] and by Dante as "he who made the grand commentary (*il gran commento*),"[11] he was decried by all of these, as well as by others, for certain heretical views. Special books were written against him and time and again was he publicly condemned. Toward the end of the thirteenth century, Giles of Rome, in his work, *Errores Philosophorum*, devotes a special chapter to the errors of Averroes.[12]

I should like to discuss some of these errors, and to discuss them not for their own sake, as problems of philosophy and theology, but rather as examples illustrating two predicaments, the predicament of language and the predicament of the apperceptive mass, which every student of the history of the transmission of ideas so often encounters in the course of his studies. The manner in which Averroes was received by the Schoolmen is a good illustration of these two predicaments. Transferred as he was from the Arabic world with its Islamic background to the Latin world of mediaeval Christianity, Averroes' vocabulary and pronouncements often invoked in the minds of his new readers associations and meanings springing from an accumulated mass of knowledge quite different in origin and composition. For our purpose here I have selected the first three statements contained in the first of the twelve errors which Giles of Rome found in Averroes.

Here is one statement. To quote: "Because he reviled all law, as is clear from book II of the *Metaphysics* and also from book XI, where he reviles the law of the Christians, that is our Catholic law, and also the law of the Saracens, because they maintain the creation of the universe and that something can be produced out of nothing."

The statement is verbally correct. In his commentary on the *Metaphysics* XII, Comm. 18, in the 1574 Junta edition of Aristotle's works, vol. 8, p. 305 F, Averroes explicitly says that "the *Loquentes* of the three laws which exist today" believe in creation *ex nihilo*, and that he rejects it. It is also true that the *Loquentes* of the three laws or religions maintained creation *ex nihilo*. In Christianity, Patristic and Scholastic philosophers maintain it. Jewish philosophers of the Arabic period, for the most part, describe creation as being *ex nihilo*. In Islam one of the early creeds, the Fikh Akbar II, which may have originated in the middle of the tenth century, says in Article 5: "Allah has not created things from a pre-existing thing."[13] Still, Giles' statement that Averroes, by his denying creation *ex nihilo*, was reviling the Muslim religion just as he was reviling the Christian religion, is not an accurate statement, for the status of the belief in creation *ex nihilo* in Islam was different from that in Christianity and consequently for a Muslim at the time of Averroes to have denied creation *ex nihilo*, as it was rigidly understood in Christianity, and to substitute for it another theory of creation, was not the same as for a Christian at the time of Giles of Rome to come out with such a denial and to substitute for it another theory of creation.

Let us briefly analyze the problem of creation as it emerges from the discussions of this problem in the Arabic philosophic literature. The problem falls into three parts.

First, irrespective of the question whether the present world existed as it now is is from eternity or whether it had come into existence after it had not existed, there is the question whether the world is self-sufficient and causeless or whether it is in some sense dependent upon a cause. The answer, on the basis of the Koran, is that the world is dependent upon a cause, whom the Koran calls God and who is described as Creator.

Second, there is the question whether a Muslim is bound to accept the chronology of the Hebrew Scripture, whereby the age of the present world can be determined by adding to the Christian era either 3760 years, according to the Jewish reckoning, or 5503 years, according to the Patristic reckoning, or 4004 according to Archbishop Ussher's reckoning.[14] The answer is no. The Hebrew scriptural chronology is not mentioned in the Koran, and so a Muslim may believe that the present world is millions of years old. But the Koran does mention that Adam was the first man, and so a Muslim must believe that all mankind is descendant from one man. Accordingly, one of the Twelve Shiite Imams is reported to have said that "millions of Adams passed away before our father Adam" and the Sufis are reported to have said that "forty thousand years before our Adam there was another Adam."[15] Mas'ūdī, speaking for Islam in general, declares that religious philosophers among the Muslims say that "demonstrations may establish the creation of the world" as well as the belief that "the beginning of men is from Adam" but that "it is impossible for us to determine and count up the years," adding that "God has informed us in His Book that He created Adam . . . but He has not furnished us any information with regard to the extent of time that has elapsed since then."[16]

Third, there is also the question whether in the Koran there is an explicit mention of creation *ex nihilo*. The answer is no. Quite the opposite, the Koran says something to the effect that God created the heaven out of smoke (41: 10). Thus as early as the ninth century the question whether the world was created *ex nihilo* or out of a preexistent matter appeared in Islam, as I have shown,[17] under the guise of the discussion of the philosophic problem whether the "nonexistent" is "nothing" or "something," and as late as the twelfth century there was still a discussion as to the meaning of the "smoke" out of which according to the Koran, God created the heaven. Zamakhsharī says that the smoke proceeded from the waters under the throne of God, which throne was one of the things created before the heavens and the earth.[18] Averroes, however, uses this verse to prove that the heavens were created from something eternal.[19]

Orthodox Islam, indeed, decided in favor of creation *ex nihilo* and the phrase *ex nihilo* became standardized, but, standardized though it became, it was interpreted differently, so that a philosopher like Alfarabi, who believed that the world was eternally emanated from the essence of God by the will of God, described that belief of his as a belief in creation *ex nihilo*.[20] And it can be shown, I think, that, while orthodox Islam would reject Alfarabi's interpretation of *ex nihilo*, it would not brand it as heretical. For this I can cite no better authority than Algazali, the great champion of Muslim orthodoxy. In his discussion of the problem of creation, Algazali argues especially against those who believe in the eternal emanation of the world from God by necessity, and it is this view which is branded by him as being "opposed to the religion of the Muslims."[21] He does not discuss the view of the eternal emanation of the world from the will of God and, though he would undoubtedly reject it on the ground of its assertion of the coëternity of the world with God, but his rejection of it, as his rejection of the coëternity of the world with God in general, would be on purely philosophic grounds, for it is to be noted that nowhere in his argument against the mere conception of the eternity of the world, without the added conception of necessity, does he repeat his statement that it is "opposed to the religion of the Muslims."[22] This leniency on the part of Muslim orthodoxy toward such a conception of the coëternity of the world with God is based, I venture to suggest, upon a conception of eternity in its relation to God which is distinctive of orthodox Islam. Eternity, to Muslim orthodoxy, is not a property which is peculiar to God alone, and consequently not everything that is eternal must *ipso facto* be God. It is on this ground that orthodox Islam, despite its insistence upon the absolute unity of God, could justify its belief in the reality of eternal attributes existing in God. It is also on this ground that orthodox Islam, while rejecting the belief in an eternal world, even when conceived of as depending upon the will of God for its existence, could still tolerate such a belief and not consider it as inconsistent with the belief in the absolute unity of God.

As for Averroes, he rejects, indeed, the view that the world is coëternal with God in the sense that it is eternally emanated from God. To him, the world is coëternal with God in the sense that it is eternally moved by God. But this its being eternally moved by God is described by him in religious terms as being eternally "created" (*muḥdath*) by God and, while he disagrees with the orthodox conception of creation *ex nihilo*, he still uses this expression as a description of his own view, insisting that he uses that expression in its right meaning.[23] Similarly, while he denies creation as an act of divine will in the sense in which orthodoxy uses that expression, he still uses that expression as a description of his own view, insisting, again, that he uses it in its right meaning.[24] On logical grounds, I imagine, Algazali would have rejected this view of Averroes, but, on strictly religious grounds, he would have no objection to it. And what is true of "the law of the Saracens," Islam, is true also of the third of "the three laws," Judaism, with regard to the doctrine of creation *ex nihilo*.[25]

The situation in Christianity was different. Whatever reference or allusion there is in the New Testament to the creation of the world, it reflects the Old Testament teaching. In the Old Testament story of creation, there is no explicit statement that creation was *ex nihilo*. Still the Fathers from the earliest times insisted upon creation *ex nihilo*. The proof-text upon which they base their view is II Maccabees vii. 28. But that proof-text does not say that God created heaven and earth ἐκ μηδενός, that is, "out of nothing"; it says that God created them οὐκ ἐξ ὄντων, "not out of things existent," and, as in philosophic Greek οὐκ ὄν or μὴ ὄν may mean matter, the proof-text quoted may mean that He created heaven and earth out of pre-existent matter.[26] The Fathers of the Church, however, had a good theological reason for insisting upon creation *ex nihilo*. The doctrine of the Trinity, which from the earliest time maintained the equality of the first two persons as God and which gradually came to maintain the equality of all the three persons as God, required the denial of the existence of anything coëternal with the triune God. For the belief in the equality of all the three coëternal persons as God meant to the Fathers that eternity spells deity and hence that nothing which is not God could be eternal. It is by this argument that Tertullian rejected the belief in the creation of the world out of a pre-existent eternal matter as urged by Hermogenes.[27] It is for this reason, too, I imagine, that Johannes Scotus Erigena, who interpreted creation *ex nihilo* as a sort of Neoplatonic emanation out of God himself, explaining that God is called *nihil* because of His incomprehensibility and ineffability and of the impossibility of describing Him by any terms,[28] still does not conceive of the creation of the world as an eternal process but maintains that this visible world of changing qualities and quantities and all the other accidents had a temporal beginning.[29]

And so, when Giles of Rome says that Averroes by his belief in the eternity of the world reviled not only the Christian religion but also the Muslim religion, he was passing judgment upon Averroes from an apperceptive mass which is peculiarly Christian and was not shared by Muslim thinkers. In Christianity, creation *ex nihilo* was already an established principle; in Islam, as well as in Judaism, it was still a debatable subject, even though orthodoxy in both these religions was upholding it.

Here is a second statement by Giles of Rome. To quote again: "These vituperations are to be found also in the beginning of book three of the *Physics*, where he holds that some people, because of the contrary habit (*consuetudinem*) of the laws, deny self-evident principles, such as the principle that nothing can be produced out of nothing." What Giles is here accusing Averroes of saying may be restated as follows: "Some people", namely the *Loquentes* of the three religions, to whom, as we have seen, he ascribes elsewhere the belief in creation *ex nihilo*, have arrived at this belief because of their "habit" to follow their respective "laws," and thus, believing as they do in creation *ex nihilo*, they deny the self-evident principle of *ex nihilo nihil fit*.

The reference here to "book three of the *Physics*" should be, as has been pointed out by the editors Koch and Riedl, "book three of the *Metaphysics*," referring to a passage in Averroes on *Metaphysics* II, Comm. 14, p. 34, I-K, which is a comment on Aristotle in *Metaphysics* II, 3, 995a, 3–6.

Let us see what Aristotle says in that passage, what Averroes means in his comment on it, and what Giles makes of that comment.

In the original Greek text, Aristotle says: "How great a force habit (σύνηθες) is, the laws (ος νόμοι) make manifest, for in the law the fanciful and the childish, through force of habit, have more influence than our knowledge of them."

Averroes, in his comment on this, says as follows: "And this happens not only in the laws (*in legibus*) but also in the primary notions (*prima cognita* = τὰ πρῶτα νοήματα), as it happens to men who for the first time heard the science of the *Loquentes*, for those *Loquentes*, on account of habit (*propter consuetudinem*) deny the nature of being and truth and deny also necessity in existence and assume that everything is possible."

I shall try to show that Giles misunderstood the meaning of two expressions used in this comment of Averroes. First, he misunderstood the meaning of the expression *in legibus*. Second, he misunderstood the meaning of the expression *prima cognita*.

Let us first take up his misunderstanding of the expression *in legibus*.

The term *lex* in the Latin translation of Averroes' Long Commentary on the *Metaphysics* stands for the following two Arabic words:

(1) *millah* "religion." This use of *lex* occurs in such expressions as "opinio Loquentium in nostra lege et lege Christianorum"[30] and "Loquentes trium legum quac hodie quidem sunt."[31]

(2) *nāmus*, which is only a transliteration into Arabic characters of the Greek νόμος "law." This use of *lex*, in its plural form *leges*, occurs in the Latin phrase *in legibus*, which translates the Arabic *fī al-nawāmis*,[32] which in turn reflects the Greek οἱ νόμοι[33] in the original passage of Aristotle, upon which Averroes commented in the passage now under consideration. Quite evidently the Latin *in legibus* in Averroes' comment is used in the sense of "laws" and not in the sense of "religions."[34]

Giles, however, misled by the frequent use of the term *leges* in the Latin translation of Averroes in the sense of "religions," took it in this passage also to mean religions, and hence he takes this passage of Averroes as a gibe against those whom he elsewhere calls "the *Loquentes* of the three laws which exist today."

Let us now take up his misunderstanding of the meaning of Averroes' expression *prima cognita* "primary notions."

What Averroes means by "the primary notions" and by his statement that "the *Loquentes*, on account of habit deny the nature of being and truth and deny also necessity in existence and assume that every thing is possible" may be established by passages, all available to Latin readers, which expound the Kalam's denial of causality and its explanation of the regularity in the succession of events observed in nature as being due to what they call habit ('ādah, consuetudo)[35] a view with which we have now all become acquainted through Hume's argument against causality.[36] Averroes, in his refutation of this view, argues that the denial of causality would lead to a denial of "the nature of being"; but, he continues, it is "self-evident," that is, it is a "primary notion," that each existent thing has "a nature."[37] From all this it is quite evident, then, that when Averroes says here that the Loquentes, on account of "habit," denied the "primary notion" and denied also the "nature of being," the reference is to their denial of causality and not to their affirmation of creation ex nihilo. On this point, it may be noted, all the Schoolmen, including Giles himself, with the only exception of Nicolaus of Autrecourt, agree with Averroes in rejecting the view of the Loquentes.

And so, because of his misunderstanding of the allusions in the text of Averroes, Giles found heresy in a statement of his, which, if he had understood it properly, he would have applauded.

And here is a third statement in Giles' condemnation of Averroes. To quote once more: "And what is worse, he derisively dubs us and other upholders of the law Loquentes, as if to say babblers and people who are moved [to talk] without reason."

No reference to any passage in Averroes, where this alleged error of his is to be found, is given by Giles. The reference, as has been suggested,[38] is undoubtedly to a passage in Averroes on Metaphysics III, Comm. 15, p. 55 B, which bears upon a text in Aristotle's Metaphysics III, 4, 1000a, 5 ff.

Let us then see what Averroes actually says in his comment on that text of Aristotle.

In the text which occasioned Averroes' comment, Aristotle raises the question whether the principles of perishable things and imperishable things are the same or different. He quotes the opinion "of the school of Hesiod and the theologians (θεολόγοι)." He refutes their opinion, and describes both the school of Hesiod and the theologians as having "thought only of what was plausible to themselves, but treated us with disdain" or as "using words which are familiar to themselves, yet what they have said . . . is above our comprehension." Now in the Arabic translation of the text of Aristotle quoted by Averroes the Greek expression πάντες ὅσοι θεολόγοι is rendered by a phrase which should be literally translated into Latin by "omnes qui loquuntur in rebus divinis, i.e., all those who speak of matters divine.[39] The Latin translation, however, instead of "omnes qui loquuntur in divinis" uses the expression "omnes loquentes in divinis."[40] Then also in Averroes' comment on the text, the Arabic should be translated into Latin to read "intendit per *ei qui loquuntur in divinis* ei qui loquuntur sermonem extra intellectum hominis." Instead, the Latin translation reads: "intendit per *loquentes in Divinis* loquentes sermonem extra intellectum hominis" (p. 55 B). Now the change from *ei qui loquuntur* to *loquentes* is significant. For the term *loquentes*, through the Latin translations of the works of Averroes and Maimonides, became a technical term referring to the Muslim theologians known as the Mutakallimūn. Moreover, the term *Loquentes* was extended by Averroes to include both Jewish and Christian theologians, as when, for instance, he speaks of "the *Loquentes* of the three laws which exist today" (*Loquentes trium legum, quae hodie quidem sunt*)[41] or "the *Loquentes* in our law and the law of the Christians" (*Loquentes in nostra lege et lege Christianorum*).[43] Similarly Maimonides extends the meaning of *Loquentes* to include "the sages of the [Christian] Greek *Loquentes*" (*scitae a sapientibus Graecarum Loquentium*).[43] And so the statement of Averroes in his comment on Aristotle, which in its original Arabic is merely a reproduction of Aristotle's characterization of Greek myth-makers, was misunderstood by Giles and taken to refer, as he says, to "us and other upholders of the law," that is to say, to Christian, Muslim, and Jewish theologians. It is interesting to note that a similar mistake is made by Renan when he says that in "*Met.* XII, Cap. vi" (1071b, 27 = Averroes, Text. 30, p. 314 H; Comm. 30 p. 315 E), θεολόγοι is translated by Averroes "*Motecallemin*" [= *Loquentes*].[44] The Latin translation there of that Greek term is both in the Text and in the Commentary "Loquentes in Divinis," which, without the printer's capitalization, does not mean the Muslim "*Mote-callemin.*"

Besides this misunderstanding, which is due to the predicament of language, this passage of Giles contains another misunderstanding, which is due to the predicament of the apperceptive mass.

When Giles came upon Averroes' reference to the *Loquentes* of the Christians, he naturally associated these *Loquentes* with the Fathers of the Church. Consequently, when he came upon Averroes' references to "our *Loquentes*" or "the *Loquentes* of the Saracens" or "the *Loquentes* of the three laws," he assumed that the position of the *Loquentes* in Islam was similar to that of the Church Fathers in Christianity. When, therefore, he thought that Averroes derisively dubbed the *Loquentes* babblers and people who speak without reason, he naturally described him as one undermining the authority of the upholders of both these two religions. But here is where Giles was mistaken: he viewed an internal squabble in Islam from a Christian perspective. The position of the *Loquentes* in Islam is not the same as that of the Church Fathers in Christianity. The Church Fathers are those who formulated the fundamental Christian doctrine during the first six Oecumenical Councils. It was they who purged Christianity of the various heresies, and they are constantly cited by the later mediaeval Schoolmen in whatever question of faith that may come up. The term "Holy Fathers," which was first applied by St. Basil to the traditional 318 representatives of the Church who assembled at Nicea, was subsequently applied to all those representatives of the church who flourished to about the middle of the eighth century. Nothing like it is the position of those called *Loquentes* in Islam. If there is any body of religious authorities in Islam corresponding to the Church Fathers in Christianity, it is those who are referred to as the *aṣḥāb*, "the companions" of the Prophet, and the *tabi'yyūn*, "the followers," and the *salaf*, "the ancients." All these are distinguished from the *Mutakallimūn*, the so-called *Loquentes* of the Latin translations from the Arabic. By the time of Averroes, the *Mutakallimūn* were spoken of as being of two kinds. There were the Muʻtazilite *Mutakallimūn* and

there were the Ash'arite *Mutakallimūn*. The former were condemned as heretical. As for the latter, while by the time of
Averroes they were already established as the exponents of orthodoxy, they did not gain that recognition, without having first been
attacked by orthodoxy. The term "*Mutakallimūn*" did not mean
to the Muslims at the time of Averroes what the term "Fathers of
the Church" meant to Christians. And so when Averroes, as a
Muslim, spoke rather derogatorily of the *Loquentes*, he was unlike
a Christian of the same period who would speak derogatorily of
the Church Fathers.

So much for the first revelation of Averroes.

Taking up now the second revelation, let us again begin by
reminding ourselves of the circumstances which have brought
about this second revelation.

Despite the repeated condemnation of Averroes for his real or
imaginary heresies, his commentaries were widely read and studied
and copied. Moreover, they were imitated. The very same persons
who damned him for his heresy—Albertus Magnus, Thomas
Aquinas, and even Giles of Rome—followed his example and
wrote commentaries on Aristotle in his style and manner; and
they constantly quoted him. These new commentaries on Aristotle by Schoolmen, despite their freedom from religious error,
did not replace Averroes. They only created a greater interest
in Aristotle, and with it in Averroes. By the fourteenth century
Averroes came to be recognized as the Commentator *par excellence*, and this reputation he continued to enjoy during the
fifteenth century.[45] Then a boost came for the commentaries of
Averroes from a source unexpected. Nicolaus Leonicus
Thomaeus, a celebrated Greek scholar who taught Aristotle at
Padua, publicly declared that, with the exception of the Greek
commentators, Averroes was the most admirable (*exquisitissimus*)
interpreter of Aristotle.[46] Then also, a way was found of removing
the sting of heresy from the works of Averroes. In 1495 Niphus
published an edition of Averroes' works fringed with antidotal
notes. All this led to a demand in the sixteenth century for a
complete translation of Averroes.

But by that time, in Europe, it was hard to find copies of the original texts of Averroes' commentaries. Huet (1630–1721) quotes Scaliger (1540–1609) as saying that there was no Arabic copy of Averroes in Europe and that he saw only the various Latin translations, which by that time already existed in print. Huet then adds:[47] "But I myself have seen an Arabic Averroes, which was formerly brought hither, out of the East, by Postellus; and which one would wonder that Scaliger would never hear of, he who was his intimate friend and correspondent in learning." The Arabic Averroes referred to is Averroes' Middle Commentary on the *Organon*, now in Leyden,[48] which contains besides the six books of the *Organon* also the *Rhetoric* and *Poetics*, thus eight of Averroes' thirty-eight commentaries. Since that time, it may be remarked, research in European libraries has discovered one copy each of the Middle Commentary on *De Caelo* and the Long Commentary on *Metaphysics*, again in Leyden, and two copies of the Epitome of the *Organon*, one in Paris and one in Munich, but both of them are in Hebrew characters.

Besides the scarcity of the original Arabic texts of Averroes in Europe, there were at that time in Europe very few people who could translate Arabic philosophic texts. Fortunately, the Jews, who had been expelled from Muslim Spain with the coming of the Almohades at about the middle of the twelfth century, carried with them the works of Averroes to the new countries where they found refuge, Northern Spain and Southern France. Some of these Arabic works, transliterated into Hebrew characters, are still to be found in European libraries. Then, less than a century later, in 1232, these Arabic works of Averroes began to be translated into Hebrew, and in the course of ninety years all of his commentaries, with the possible exception of two, were translated into Hebrew. It is through Latin translations from these Hebrew translations that Averroes revealed himself again to European philosophy. In the sixteenth century editions of Latin translations of Aristotle, those of the Juntas and Cominus de Tridino, which contain also Latin translations of thirty-four of the thirty-eight commentaries of Averroes and of some of his other works, twenty-six of these thirty-four translations were made from the Hebrew, six of them replacing older translations made in the thirteenth century directly from the Arabic.[49] Similarly, his other works contained in the Junta edition, namely, *De Substantia Orbis*, *Destructio Destructionum*, and *Epistola de Intellectu* were translated from the Hebrew, though, again, of some of these works there existed older translations made in the thirteenth century directly from the Arabic. Of chapters 57–59 of *Colliget* V the new translation from the Hebrew is printed by the side of the older Latin translation from the Arabic.

The reception with which Averroes was now met after his second revelation was of a different kind. The old cry of heresy no longer came from the Schoolmen. A new cry was now raised by the Hellenists, questioning the usefulness of Averroes' commentaries. Two conflicting views were expressed. Here are representative examples. On the one hand, the Spanish scholar Juan Luis Vives (1492–1540) said:[50] "He has gained the name of Commentator, though he is very far from explaining his author Aristotle or deserving that title. This would have been too great a task for one of an extraordinary genius, much more for him who had but a moderate one, nay, to say the truth, a mean one. For what qualifications had he for undertaking a commentary on Aristotle? He had no knowledge of antiquity, nor of its several doctrines and sects with which Aristotle everywhere abounds." He then goes on to point at certain errors made by Averroes. But, on the other hand, the German scholar Gerhard Johann Vossius (1577–1649) said:[51] "He was called the Commentator *par excellence*, who, without knowing anything of Greek, penetrated so felicitously into the mind of Aristotle."

These are wholesale condemnation and wholesale praise. A more judicious opinion is given by Bartholomaeus Keckermann (1571–1609), who made a special study of Averroes' works on the *Organon*. He says:[52] "In the *Posterior Analytics*,[53] it appears, Averroes has performed an excellent work, and such as deserves to be immortal. *The Epitome of Logic*,[54] which he wrote [not in the form of a running commentary on a text], is most praiseworthy for many reasons, and his *Logic*[55] is extraordinary (*quaesita*). None of the ancient interpreters seem to hit the sense of Aristotle so happily as this Arabian."

I am not going to debate the question whether Averroes was not often wrong in his interpretation of Aristotle. One may readily admit it. But so were his Greek commentators, Alexander, Themistius, and Simplicius, also often wrong in their interpretations of Aristotle and, to judge by reviews that appear in learned journals on every new book on Aristotle, commentators on Aristotle are still often wrong. Many years ago, on the basis of my studies of Averroes' commentaries and the Hebrew supercommentaries on them, I arrived at this conclusion: "Contrary to the prevalent opinion among students of the history of philosophy, the translations of Aristotle both in Arabic and Hebrew have preserved to a remarkable degree not only clear-cut analyses of the text of Aristotle's works but also the exact meaning of the terminology and forms of expression. The literalness and faithfulness with which the successive translators from one language into another performed their task, coupled with a living tradition of Aristotelian scholarship, which can be shown to have continued uninterruptedly from the days of the Lyceum through the Syriac, Arabic, and Hebrew schools of philosophy, enabled [mediaeval readers] to obtain a pretty accurate knowledge of Aristotle's writings. That knowledge, to be sure, was traditional and one-sided, but the tradition upon which it was based, like the various traditional interpretations of the Bible text before the rise of independent critical scholarship, was clear and definite and suffered comparatively little corruption."[56] The more I followed the history of the transmission of philosophy through translations the more firmly convinced I became of the continuity of an oral tradition accompanying every translation, which served as a sort of oral commentary upon each translation, explaining all the new shades of meanings that were imported into the words of the language of the translation from the language from which they were translated.

Perhaps I could best illustrate this point by a concrete case study. As subject for this case study I shall take a passage of a Latin translation made from the Hebrew translation of one of the commentaries of Averroes—a passage which deals with a problem involving certain technical terms in Greek and certain constructions peculiar to Greek, which are untranslatable into Arabic. I shall act as a sort of supercommentator on Averroes' commentary. First, I will introduce the problem dealt with in the passage in question. Then I will quote the passage in Latin, followed by an English translation. Finally, in my exegesis I will explain what I have done in my translation and why I have done it.

The passage which I have selected is from Averroes' *Epitome of the Organon*. The Latin text is from the Junta edition of 1574–75. The underlying Hebrew text is from an edition of the Hebrew of the *Epitome of the Organon* published at Riva di Trento in 1559. The Arabic text has not yet been published, but it is extant in two manuscripts in Hebrew characters. I have purposely made no effort to secure a photostat of the Arabic text, as I wanted to use this case study also as a test of how far one could go in translating and interpreting texts of Averroes on the basis of the Latin and Hebrew translations where no Arabic texts are extant.

Here is the introductory statement concerning the problem dealt with in the passage to be quoted from Averroes:

From several places in his writings we gather that Aristotle distinguishes between the following three forms of logical propositions:

(1) $\check{\epsilon}\sigma\tau\iota$ $\tau\nu\varphi\lambda\acute{o}_2$ $\check{\alpha}\nu\theta\rho\omega\pi os$, Man is blind.[57]
(2) $o\mathring{\upsilon}\kappa$ $\check{\epsilon}\sigma\tau\iota$ $\delta\acute{\iota}\kappa a\iota os$ $\check{\alpha}\nu\theta\rho\omega\pi os$, Man is not just.[58]
(3) $\check{\epsilon}\sigma\tau\iota\nu$ $o\mathring{\upsilon}$ $\delta\acute{\iota}\kappa a\iota os$, $\check{\alpha}\nu\theta\rho\omega\pi os$, Man is not-just.[59]

Ammonius, on the basis of certain statements in Aristotle, describes these three types of propositions respectively as "privative" ($\sigma\tau\epsilon\rho\eta\tau\iota\kappa\grave{\eta}$), "negative" ($\mathring{\alpha}\pi o\varphi a\tau\iota\kappa\grave{\eta}$), and "indefinite" ($\mathring{\alpha}\acute{o}\rho\iota\sigma\tau os$),[60] the last of which, through a mistranslation of Boethius,[61] is known in Western philosophy as "infinite." With regard to privative and negative propositions, Aristotle draws the following distinction. The negative proposition "A is not seeing" may be used even in cases where the subject "A" is an inanimate object which by nature is incapable of seeing.[62] The privative proposition "A is blind" can be used only in cases where the subject "A" is a living being who by nature is capable of seeing but it happens to be deprived of sight.[63] There is nothing in his writings, however, to indicate as to whether, with respect to that distinction drawn by him between negative and privative propositions, the indefinite proposition belongs to the one or to the other.

The uncertainty as to whether a proposition with a separable negative particle preceding the predicate is regarded by Aristotle as a privative or as a negative proposition becomes all the greater when we find that a proposition with an inseparable negative particle prefixed to the predicate is treated by him both as a privative and as a negative proposition. Thus a proposition of the type of "man is toothless ($\nu\omega\delta\delta\varsigma$)" is explicitly described by him as a privative proposition.[64] Similarly from his statement that "the brutes are not to be described as either temperate ($\sigma\omega\phi\rho\rho\nu\alpha$) or as intemperate ($\dot{\alpha}\kappa\delta\lambda\alpha\sigma\tau\alpha$)"[65] it is to be inferred that the predicate "intemperate" is used here as a privation, for, if it were used as a negation, it could be predicated of brutes, since by nature brutes are incapable of temperance. The same may be inferred from his statement that the terms "just" ($\delta i\kappa\alpha\iota\varsigma$) and "unjust" ($\ddot{\alpha}\delta\iota\kappa\varsigma$) are contraries between which there is an intermediate, so that the subject may be described as being at once "neither just nor unjust."[66] Here, too, the predicate "unjust" is used as a privation, for, if it were used as a negation, then "unjust" would be "contradictories" ($\dot{\alpha}\nu\tau\iota\phi\dot{\alpha}\sigma\epsilon\iota\varsigma$) and not "contraries" ($\dot{\epsilon}\nu\alpha\nu\tau i\alpha$),[67] and consequently the statement that the subject may be described as being at once "neither just nor unjust" would be wrong, for it would infringe upon the Law of Excluded Middle.[68] But, then, such statements as "a voice is invisible ($\dot{\alpha}\delta\rho\alpha\tau\varsigma$)"[69] and "a unit . . . is quantitatively indivisible ($\dot{\alpha}\delta\iota\alpha i\rho\epsilon\tau\varsigma$)"[70] and "is positionless ($\ddot{\alpha}\theta\epsilon\tau\varsigma$)"[71] are quite evidently used by Aristotle as negations.

In one place, *Metaphysics* V, 22, predicates with alpha privative, such as $\ddot{\alpha}\nu\iota\sigma\sigma\nu$, "unequal," $\dot{\alpha}\delta\rho\alpha\tau\sigma\nu$, "invisible," and $\ddot{\alpha}\tau\sigma\mu\tau\sigma\nu$, "uncutable," are each called "privation," but are each described as being used either in the technical sense of negation or in the technical sense of privation, depending upon the nature of the subject of which they are predicated.[72] Of the same tenor is also the statement that "the immobility (ἀκινησία) of that to which motion belongs [by nature] is rest (ἠρεμία),"[73] the implication of which is that the immobility of that to which motion does not belong [by nature] is not rest but rather something which is a negation of both motion and rest. In consequence of this view, the term "immobile," when used in a proposition in which the subject is "man," would be a privation but, when used in a proposition in which the subject is "God," would be a negation. This distinction, it may be remarked, would not explain why, in the statement quoted above, the term "intemperate" predicated of brutes is used as a privation.

Both these uses of predicates with the alpha privative are to be found in post-Aristotelian philosophy. Thus the Stoics use the proposition "the man is inhumane (ἀφιλάνθρωπος)" as an illustration of what they call "privative,"[74] and, in Boethius, the typical example of a privative proposition is the proposition *est iniustus* [= ἄδικος] *homo*.[75] In Philo, Albinus, Plotinus, and the Church Fathers, however, various terms with alpha privative are predicated of God in the sense of negation.[76] Arabic students of Aristotle's works could not get any information from the above-quoted "man is toothless (νωδός)" as to how Aristotle used this type of proposition, for in the Arabic translation of the *Categories*, the Greek term νωδός, which is negative both in form and in meaning, being composed of the negative prefix νη and ὀδούς, "tooth," is translated by the Arabic *adrad*, which is positive in form, though negative in meaning. However, from the reading in the Arabic translation of the passage in *Metaphysics* V, 22, quoted above, Arabic students of Aristotle could learn that *lā musāwin* and *lā mubṣar*, which are the equivalents respectively of the Greek ἄνισος, "unequal," and ἀόρατος, "invisible," are used as negations, whereas *lā munkaṭi'*, which is the equivalent of the Greek ἄτμητος, "uncutable," is used either as a negation or as a privation, and so are these terms explained by Averroes in his Long Commentary on the *Metaphysics*.

In the case of this kind of proposition, then, from the fact that Aristotle himself says that it may be used either as negation or as privation, we may reasonably assume that those whom we have quoted as using it either in the one or in the other of these two senses only happen to have occasion to use it in that one particular sense, without thereby excluding the possibility of its use in the other sense.[79] In the case, however, of propositions in which the predicate is preceded by a separable negative particle, concerning the use of which no information is to be found in Aristotle, we note two opposite views among post-Aristotelian philosophers, one by Western philosophers and the other by Averroes, who represents an older Arabic tradition.

The Stoics are reported to have described a proposition, which Aristotle would call "indefinite," as a "privative proposition,"[80] but it is not certain whether they meant it to be taken as an interpretation of Aristotle, or whether they meant it to be taken as a view of their own. So also in Hobbes *homo est non lapis*, which, according to Aristotle, should be described as an indefinite proposition, is described as a negative proposition,[81] but here, again, it is not certain whether this was meant to be in opposition to Aristotle, or whether it was meant to be an interpretation of Aristotle, or whether unknowingly Hobbes confused an indefinite proposition with a negative proposition. Quite certain it is, however, that the use by Kant of what he calls infinite judgment, such as "the soul is not-mortal,"[82] as the equivalent of Aristotle's negative judgment was not meant to be an interpretation of Aristotle, for what he calls negative judgment, such as "the soul is not mortal,"[83] is not used by him as the equivalent of Aristotle's negative judgment but rather as the equivalent of Aristotle's privative judgment. But I imagine it would be heretical to say that Kant unwittingly distorted an old logical distinction; it would be more canonical to say that he discovered an original profound logical distinction. In Averroes, however, Aristotle's indefinite propositions are presented without much ado as privative propositions. Thus commenting on the passage in *De Interpretatione* where Aristotle distinguishes between the negative proposition "man is not just" and the indefinite proposition "man is not-just," he adds: "When we say man is not just, the statement may apply both to a man who is wicked and to a man who is neither wicked nor just, that is, an uncivilized man or boy.

But when we say 'man is not-just,' the statement applies only to a man who is wicked, for our predicate 'not-just' signifies a privation, and privation is the remotion of a habit from a subject in which it would naturally exist at a time when it would naturally exist in it."[84]

But here Averroes and other Arabic writers, dealing with this type of proposition, hint at a certain difficulty which they try to solve in anticipation. The difficulty may be stated as follows. In Greek, the difference between a negative proposition and an indefinite proposition, as may be gathered from the examples used by Aristotle,[85] consists in the difference in the position of the negative particle in the proposition. In a negative proposition, such as οὐκ ἔστι δίκαιος ἄνθρωπος, the negative particle is placed before the copula, whereas in a privative proposition, such as the proposition ἔστιν οὐ δίκαιςἄνθρωπος, the particle is placed before the predicate. This is all well and good in Greek, where the copula, with but a few exceptions, is always used. But in Arabic the copula is as a rule omitted. How then could the difference between the two kinds of propositions be expressed? Thus the three Arabic words *Zayd lā basīr*, "Zayd not seeing," may stand either for the negative proposition "Zayd is not seeing" or for the privative proposition "Zayd is not-seeing."

Here is the Latin text in which Averroes deals with the problem:

Et earum sunt remotivae, et sunt illae, quarum praedicatum est nomen vel verbum imperfectum: sicut si dixerimus Socrates est non sanus: et hoc est in orationibus, quae non usitantur in lingua Arabum. . . . Vis autem nominum inperfectorum in idiomatibus, quae utuntur eis, est vis nominum privativorum, quia dictum nostrum non videns est in gradu dicti nostri caecus: et dictum nostrum non sanum est in gradu dicti nostri aegrum. Quoniam autem non fuerunt ista nomina in lingua Arabum, fuit dictio negationis apud eos ex dictionibus ambiguis, quia ipsi aliquando proferunt ipsam simpliciter, et volunt per eam rem privationis, et aliquando volunt per eam negationem absolutam. Et hoc est, quod cogit homines huius artis loqui per nomina remotiva, quia nos dum non cavemus ea, et imponemus eis istam impositionem, possible est quod erremus, et accipiamus quod est imperfectum loco negationis, et contra.[86]

And here is an English translation in which I put within parentheses Latin terms which I did not translate literally and within brackets explanatory comments which are not to be found in the Latin text underlying the translation:

"Some propositions are transposed (Latin: *remotivae*) and these are those propositions in which the predicate is an indefinite (Latin: *imperfectum*) noun or verb, as when we say, for instance, 'Socrates is [*non sanus*; Hebrew: *lo bari'* = Arabic: *lā ṣaḥīḥ*, used in the sense of] not-healthy.' This occurs in propositions which are not used in the Arabic language. . . . The force of indefinite (Latin: *imperfectorum*) terms in those languages in which they are used is the force of privative terms, for, when we say [*non videns*; Hebrew: *lo ro'eh* = Arabic: *lā baṣīr*, which consists of two words] 'not' and 'seeing' [it may mean 'not-seeing' and as such] it is of the same order as when we say 'blind,' and similarly, when we say [*non sanus*; Hebrew: *lo bari'* = Arabic: *lā ṣaḥīḥ*, which consists of two words] 'not' and 'healthy' (it may mean 'not-healthy' and as such] it is of the same order as when we say 'sick.' Inasmuch as these [indefinite] terms do not exist in the Arabic language, the negative particle [*lā*, 'not,' in the Arabic proposition *lā baṣīr*] is regarded by Arabic logicians as a sort of ambiguous particle, for sometimes they use it in an unrestricted sense [as, e.g., in the expression 'is not-seeing'] and mean thereby privation, and sometimes [they use it differently, as in the expression 'is not seeing'] when they mean thereby absolute negation. It is this consideration that has compelled men of this art [of Logic in the Arabic language] to speak of 'transposed terms' (Latin: *nomina remotiva*), for, if we are not careful about predicates preceded by a negative particle and do not think of the possibility that they may have two meanings, we may err and take some such predicate as indefinite [and hence as a privation], when it should be taken as a negation, and similarly the other way around."

Here is my exegetical supercommentary:

It will be noticed that in my English translation I have rendered the Latin *remotivae* by "transposed" and the Latin *imperfectum* by "indefinite." There is a good reason for these renderings.

Both these Latin terms are possible translations of the underlying Hebrew terms, (1) the Latin *remotivae* of the Hebrew
musarim; (2) the Latin *imperfectum* of the Hebrew *bilti
nishlam* or *bilti magi'a*. Since, however, the context requires
that these two terms, or at least one of them, should reflect
Aristotle's ἀόριστος, "indefinite," as used by him in *De Interpretatione*, I assumed that behind one of these terms, at least,
there would be an Arabic term used as a translation of that Greek
term of Aristotle. Fortunately the old Arabic translation of *De
Interpretatione* is available in two printed editions.[87] There the
Arabic for ἀόριστς is *ghayr muḥaṣṣal*, which would ordinarily
mean "not caused to result," "not attained." Inasmuch as these
are respectively the ordinary meanings of the Hebrew *bilti
nishlam* and *bilti magi'a* underlying the Latin *imperfectum*, we
may assume that the underlying Arabic of these Hebrew terms is
ghayr muḥaṣṣal, which, as we have already seen from the Arabic
translation of *De Interpretatione*, is the conventionalized Arabic
rendering of the Greek ἀόριστος. On the basis of this I have substituted in my translation the English "indefinite" for the Latin
imperfectum.

Since the Latin *imperfectum* proved to stand for the Arabic
ghayr muḥaṣṣal, the other Latin term, *remotivae*, would have to
stand for some other Arabic term. But what is that Arabic term?
Here our search would have to start from the Hebrew term
musarim of which Latin *remotivae* is a translation. And so I began
to look for the term *musar* in Hebrew works which were translated from the Arabic and of which the Arabic was available in
print. I could not find that word in any published Hebrew work
of that type.[88] But I found it in a copy of an unpublished Hebrew
translation of Algazali's *Maqāṣid al-Falāsifah*[89] in the library of
the Jewish Theological Seminary.[90] There the Arabic underlying
the Hebrew *musar* is *ma'dūlah*. Now the term *ma'dūlah*, as techni-
cally used in logical terminology, has been variously interpreted.
John Hispalensis, of the twelfth century, in his Latin translation
of Algazali's *Maqāṣid*, as may be gathered from a quotation in
Prantl's *Geschichte der Logik* II[2] (1885), p. 273, n. 60, translated
it *privativa*. But this cannot be connected etymologically with

ma'dūlah. Horten in *Die spekulative und positive Theologie des Islams* (1912), p. 203, translates it *infinita*. This, too, cannot be connected etymologically with *ma'dūlah*. Goichon, in her *Lexique de la langue philosophique d'Ibn Sīnā* (1938), §411, translates it *equivalente*. This has an etymological connection with *ma'dūla*, for *ma'dūlah* comes from a word which means "to be equal," but there is no term in Greek philosophy meaning "equivalent" to be used in the sense in which the Arabic term seems to be used here in this context. What is needed here is a Greek term, under-lying this Arabic term, which should have been used as an equiv-alent of the term ἀόριστος, "indefinite," as used by Aristotle in connection with the subject under discussion. So we went to look for such a term, and lo and behold! Alexander of Aphrodisias in his commentary on *Analytica Priora*, of which there existed an Arabic translation,[91] quotes Theophrastus as having used the expression πρότασις κατὰ μετάθεσιν,[92] "proposition by transposi-tion," that is to say, a proposition in which the negative particle was transposed from a place before the copula to a place before the predicate, as the equivalent of the expression "indefinite proposition." All we needed now was to show how *ma'dūlah* could be used as a translation of κατὰ μετάθεσιν. This was easy, for the verb *'adal*, of which *ma'dūlah* is a passive participle, means not only "to be equal" but also "to deviate." Thus *ma'dūlah* means "deviated" and as such we may assume it was used in the sense of "transposed" as a translation of κατὰ μετάθεσιν. Similarly the Hebrew term *musarim*, of which the Latin translation is *remotivae*, may also mean "turned away" and hence "deviated" and "transposed." Moreover, another unpublished Hebrew trans-lation of Algazali's *Maqāṣid*, of which, again, there is a copy in the library of the Jewish Theological Seminary, translates *ma'dūlah* by *noṭeh*,[93] "turning away," and hence "deviated" and "transposed."

Averroes must have had all this in the back of his mind. He thus speaks of "those languages" in which "indefinite terms" are used, that is to say, in which the copula is used, so that by position of the negative particle one could tell whether the prop-osition is negative or indefinite. And thus he speaks also of the

Arabic language in which "indefinite terms" are not used, so that
there is no way of telling whether certain Arabic propositions are
negative or indefinite. What languages he had in mind in his
reference to those languages which use "indefinite terms" may be
gathered from a parallel passage in Avicenna, which would seem
to be the source of the passage of Averroes quoted above. In that
parallel passage, Avicenna, after stating that in Arabic the copula
is sometimes omitted, refers to "certain languages" in which the
copula is always used, and of these languages he specifically
mentions "Persian," a language which he knew and of which he
quotes a sentence as an illustration.[94] The other language of the
"languages" referred to by Avicenna was undoubtedly Greek,
which he did not know, but about which, on this particular point
there must have been a living tradition among students of Aristotle's *Organon*, with which he was acquainted. Accordingly,
"those languages" referred to by Averroes, we may assume, are
Greek and Persian, neither of which he knew.

In Arabic, then, there were two terms to designate what Aristotle calls "indefinite" propositions, (1) *ghayr muḥaṣṣal* and (2)
ma'dūlah, the former being a translation of ἀόριστος used by
Aristotle himself; the latter being a translation of κατὰ μετάθεσιν,
quoted by Alexander from Theophrastus. The Arabs, as we may
gather not only from the passage here of Averroes but also from
passages of Avicenna[95] and Algazali,[96] adopted the term *ma'dūlah*
as a description of the indefinite proposition. They must have
followed Alfarabi who said that "propositions whose predicates
are *ghayr muḥaṣṣalah* are called *ma'dūlāt*."[97] To those Arabic
philosophers, a single word was preferable to a phrase. Moreover,
the phrase *ghayr muḥaṣṣal* merely told them that a proposition
was "indefinite"; the term *ma'dūlah* told them how to recognize
a proposition as "indefinite"; it is "indefinite" when it is "transposed." Thus, for instance, in such a proposition as *Zayd lā baṣīr*,
literally consisting of three words, "Zayd not seeing," when the
copula "is" is mentally supplied before "not," the proposition is
negative; but when later it is mentally transposed to before
"seeing" the proposition thereby becomes "indefinite."

This is what Averroes means by his statement in the latter part of his passage that "it is this consideration that has compelled men of this art [of logic in the Arabic language] to speak of transposed propositions," where he then goes on to explain in effect how by mentally transposing the mentally supplied copula one could tell that a proposition is "indefinite," that is, "privative," rather than "negative."

This, then, is an example of what is needed for an understanding of a text of Averroes, especially if one has only the Latin translation before him. No wonder that there were different opinions about the value of Averroes after his second revelation.

I have spoken of two revelations—revelations which took place at an interval of four hundred years. In 1931, about four hundred years after the second revelation of Averroes, there was a third revelation. It took place when our Academy adopted its plan for the publication of a *Corpus Commentariorum Averrois in Aristotelem*. There is, however, a difference between the third revelation and its two preceding ones. The first revelation involved translations only. The second revelation involved translations and printing only. The third revelation, as projected in the plan, involves three series of edited texts, each text in each of the three series equipped with three critical apparatuses and a quadrilingual glossary, and supplementary to all these a fourth series of translations with commentaries. The brief exegesis of the Latin passage in Averroes which I have acted out before you will explain why this third revelation of Averroes had to take this elaborate form.

In speaking of the first two revelations, I dealt with their achievements and their receptions. But I feel there must have been a story, a human story, behind the achievements, the story of Michael and Hermann and William and Frederick and Abraham de Balmes and Joannes Franciscus Burana and Jacob Mantinus and the Juntas and Cominus de Tridino. For we of the Academy know that there is a story, a human story, behind the volumes, so splendidly published in our *Corpus*—the story of scholars who, without the patronage of a Frederick, voluntarily gave up their evenings and week-ends, year after year, for the preparation of the thousands of minute items that make up the elaborate and complicated apparatuses and glossaries of their editions; the story of

a provost and a dean of a university who allowed us the use of a
certain fund under their care for the publication of certain
volumes; the story of the president of a foundation who always
came to our assistance when we had to meet the printer's bill;
and the story of a business man who at a luncheon, after con-
sulting with one of our editors on a matter on which he needed
some advice, said: Now that you have done something for me,
what can I do for you? And he did. He came just in the nick of
time to enable us to publish one of our most expensive volumes.
I hope that some future speaker at a future meeting of the Academy, perhaps at the celebration of the completion of the *Corpus*
fifty years, or a hundred years, hence, in reporting on the achievement and the reception of this third revelation of Averroes, will
also tell the story, the human story, behind the achievement.

POSTSCRIPT

After the original publication of this paper, I secured, through
the courtesy of the Mediaeval Academy, a microfilm of the Munich
manuscript of the Arabic text of the Epitome of the *Organon*.
It verified all my conjectures as to the Arabic terms underlying
the Hebrew, and hence also the Latin, translation.

NOTES

1. Cf. M. Bouyges, "Inventaire des textes arabes d'Averroès, *Mélanges de
l'Université Saint-Joseph, Beyrouth*, VIII (1922), pp. 13 ff.

2. Cf. Steinschneider, *Die hebräischen Übersetzungen*, §§91–107.

3. Cf. H. A. Wolfson, "Averroes' Lost Treatise on the Prime Mover,"
Hebrew Union College Annual, XXII, 1 (1950–51), 683–710.

4. Cf. Steinschneider, "*Die europäischen Übersetzungen aus dem Arabischen*," *Sitzungsberichte d. Wiener Akademie*, CXL (1905), 1–84, under
"Gerard von Cremona" (pp. 16 ff.) and "Johannes Hispalensis" (pp. 40 ff.).

5. *Ibid.*, under "Hermannus Alemannus" (pp. 32 f.) and "Michael Scotus"
(pp. 55 ff.).

6. *Ibid.*, under "Wilhelmus de Lunis apud Neapolim," p. 80; G. Lacombe,
Aristoteles Latinus, I, pp. 101–2, 207–10.

7. *Ibid.*, p. 79; *ibid.*, p. 104.

8. Cf. Renan, *Averroès et l' Averroïsme*, 2nd ed. (1861), pp. 205 ff.

9. *Il de Universo* II, 8 (*op.* 1574, p. 851, col. 2).

10. *Sum. Theol.* I, 3, 5 obj. 2.

11. *Inferno* IV, 144. The expression *gran commento* does not simply mean the Great or Long Commentary as distinguished from the "Middle" Commentary or "Epitome," for in the translations of that time these distinctions were not stressed.

12. Cf. *Giles of Rome: Errores Philosophorum*, edited by Josef Koch and translated by John O. Riedl (1944).

13. Cf. Wensinck, *The Muslim Creed*, pp. 94, 190.

14. Cf. my paper, "The Veracity of Scripture in Philo, Halevi, Maimonides, and Spinoza," *Alexander Marx Jubilee Volume* (1950), pp. 622 ff. and in my *Religious Philosophy* (1961), pp. 237 ff.

15. Quoted by Muhammad Ali in his *Translation of the Holy Quran* (Lahore, 1928), p. lxxv.

16. Mas'ūdī, *Les Prairies d'Or*, IV, 110–111 (texte et traduction par C. Barbier de Meynard, 1865).

17. "The Kalam Problem of Nonexistence and Saadia's Second Theory of Creation," *Jewish Quarterly Review*, N.S., XXXVI (1946), 371–391.

18. Quoted by Sale in a note to his translation of the Koran 41: 10.

19. *Faṣl al-Maqāl*, p. 13, ll. 6–7 and 11–12 (ed. M. I. Müller, under the title of *Philosophie und Theologie von Averroes*, 1859; German translation, 1875).

20. Cf. my paper, "The Meaning of *ex nihilo* in the Church Fathers, Arabic and Hebrew Philosophy and St. Thomas," *Mediaeval Studies in Honor of J. D. M. Ford* (1948) p. 358.

21. *Tahāfut al-Falāsifah* III (ed. Bouyges 1927), §2, p. 96, ll. 1–4 and III, §16, p. 102, l. 13 (English translation in *Averroes: Tahāfut al-Tahāfut*, by Simon van den Bergh (1954), pp. 87 and 96; also in *Al-Gahasali: Tahāfut al Tahāfut*, by Sabih Ahmad Kamali (Lahore, 1958), pp. 63 and 68.

22. *Ibid.* III, §§ 17–28, p. 103, l. 4–p. 109, l. 14 (English: van den Bergh, pp. 96, 97, 98–99, 99–100, 101, 102; Kamali, pp. 68–73).

23. *Tahāfut al-Tahāfut* III (ed. Bouyges, 1930), §§34–38, p. 162, l. 7–p. 165, l. 3 (English: van den Bergh, pp. 96–97, 97–98).

24. *Ibid.* III, §§23–24, p. 157, l. 11–p. 158, l. 12 (English: van den Bergh, pp. 93–94).

25. Cf. my *Philo.* I (1947), pp. 302–303, 324, and my paper, "The Platonic, Aristotelian, and Stoic Theories of Creation in Halevi and Maimonides," *Essays in Honour of Chief Rabbi, the Very Rev. Dr. J. H. Hertz* (1942), pp. 427–442.

26. Cf. *art. cit.* above (n. 19), p. 379.

27. *Adversus Hermogenem*, ch. 4.

28. Cf. *art. cit.* (above n. 20), pp. 357–358.

29. *De Divisione Naturae* III, 15 (Migne, *P.L.*, CXXII, 665–666).

30. *In XII Metaph.*, Comm. 18, p. 304f.

31. *Ibid.*, p. 305 f.

32. *In II Metaph.*, Text. 14, p. 34 I (Arabic *Tafsīr mā ba'd aṭ-ṭabi'at*, ed. Bouyges, 1938, p. 43, l. 1).

33. *Metaph.* II, 3, 995a, 4.

34. Comment 14 of the Latin translation under discussion is not a translation of the corresponding Comment 14 in the published Arabic text (pp. 43–44). It is an abridgement of it. But the term *nāmūsiyyah* occurs in the Arabic original (p. 43, l. 9).

35. The most likely source from which Schoolmen could have learned of the *Loquentes*' explanation of causality by "habit" (*consuetudo*) is the Latin translation of Maimonides' *Guide of the Perplexed* I, 73 (72), Propositions 6 and 10.

36. Cf. my paper, "Causality and Freedom in Descartes, Leibnitz, and Hume," *Freedom and Experience, Essays Presented to H. M. Kallen* (1947), pp. 108 ff. and in my *Religious Philosophy* (1961), pp. 196 ff.

37. *Tahāfut al-Tahāfut*, Phys. I (XVII), §5, p. 520, l. 9–p. 521, l. 2 (English p. 318).

38. Cf. n. 41, on p. 17, of Koch and Riedl's edition of *Errores Philosophorum*.

39. Arabic of Averroes, *In III Metaph.*, Text. 15, p. 247, l. 2.

40. Latin, *ibid.*, Text 15, p. 54 C.

41. *In XII Metaph.*, Comm. 18, p. 305 f.

42. *Ibid.*, p. 304 f.

43. *Deux seu Director dubitantium aut perplexorum* I, 70, fol. XXIX v, ll. 4–5 (Paris, 1520).

44. *Op. cit.*, n. 2 on pp. 104–105.

45. Cf. Renan, *op. cit.*, p. 317.

46. *Ibid.*, pp. 385–86.

47. Pierre Daniel Huet, *De Claris Interpretibus*, p. 185, which is the second part of his *De Interpretatione Libri Duo* (1860).

This quotation and also quotations in notes 48, 49, 50 below are from Pierre Bayle's *Dictionary Historical and Critical* (*Dictionnaire Historique et Critique*), I, 552–556 (London, 1734). The quotations as well as the references have been checked and, whenever necessary, revised. For this quotation see Bayle, p. 558, n. 83.

48. Cf. Bouyges, *op. cit.* (n. 1 above), p. 10, No. 5.

49. Cf. pp. 93–94 in my paper "Revised Plan for the Publication of a *CORPUS COMMENTARIORUM AVERROIS IN ARISTOTELEM*," *Speculum*, 38 (1963).

50. Joannes Ludovicus Vives, *De Causis Corruptarum Artium* V, 3, in *Opera Omnia*, VI (1785), 192 (Bayle, p. 552, n. 5).

51. Gerhard Johann Vossius, *De Philosophia et Philosophorum Sectis*, Liber II (1657), p. 90 (Bayle, p. 552 c).

52. Cf. Keckermann, *Systema Systematum*, Part I: *Recognita Logica*, Tract. II, Cap. 2, no. 32 (1613), p. 17 (Bayle, p. 558, n. 87).

53. Of the *Posterior Analytics* there are three Latin translations of the greater part of Book I and two translations of the rest of the work, all of them made from the Hebrew and all of them printed in parallel columns, taking up a volume of 568 folios in the Junta edition of 1574–75. The Arabic test is not extant.

54. This refers to Averroes' *Epitome of the Organon*, which contains Porphyry's *Isagoge* at the beginning and the *Rhetoric* and *Poetics* at the end.

55. This probably refers to Averroes' *Quaesita varia in Logica* and *Epistola Una*, translated from the Hebrew, which in the Junta edition follows the *Epitome in Libros Logicae Aristotelis*.

56. Cf. my *Crescas' Critique of Aristotle* (1929), p. 7.

57. *Categ.* 10, 12a, 31–33.

58. *De Interpret.* 10, 19b, 27–28.

59. *Ibid.*, 28.

60. *Ammonius De Interpretatione*, ed. A. Busse (1897), "Index Verborum," sub πρότασις.

61. Boethius on *De Interpretatione*, Secunda Editio III, c. 10 (ed. C. Meiser, II, 277–278).

62. Cf. *Alexander in Metaphysica*, ed. M. Hayduck (1891), p. 327, ll. 18–20.

63. *Categ.* 10, 12a, 27–34.

64. *Categ.* 10, 12a, 31–33.

65. *Eth. Nic.* VII, 7, 1149b, 31–32.

66. *Categ.* 10, 12a, 20–25.

67. *Anal. Post.* I, 2, 72a, 12–14.

68. *Metaph.*, IV, 7, 1011b, 23–24.

69. *Phys.* III, 5, 204a, 13–14; V, 2, 206b, 10–11; *Metaph.* XI, 10, 1066a, 36.

70. *Metaph.*, XIV, 2, 1089b, 35–36.

71. *Ibid.* V, 6, 1016b, 30.

72. *Ibid.*, V, 22, 1022b, 32–1023a, 4.

73. *Phys.* III, 2, 202a, 4–5.

74. Diogenes, VII, 70.

75. Boethius, *op. cit.*, Prima Editio, II, c. 10 (Vol. I, p. 133); Secunda Editio, III, c. 10 (Vol. II, p. 277).

76. Cf. *Philo*, II, pp. 111, 153–154, 158–160.

77. Cf. *Categ.* 10, 12a, 34, in *Organon Aristotelis in Versione Arabica Antiqua*, ed. Badawi, p. 41.

78. Book V, Text. et Comm. 27 (cf. above n. 32).

79. This will explain why in his *Epitome of the Metaphysics* Averroes uses Arabic terms reflecting Greek terms with alpha privative in senses which are only negations (cf. pp. 177–178 in my paper "Infinite and Privative Judgments in Aristotle, Averroes, and Kant," *Philosophy and Phenomenological Research*, 8 (1947).

80. Diogenes, VII, 69; οὐχὶ ἡμέρα ἐστίν.

81. *Opera Latina* (1839), I, 31.

82. *Logik*, §22; *Kr. d. rein. Vern.*[1], p. 70.

83. *Ibid.*

84. Middle Commentary on *De Interpretatione* (*Aristotelis Opera* [Venice, 1574], Vol. I, 1, p. 86 A): "Nam cum dicitur, homo non est iustus, verificatur de homine iniusto et de homine qui non est iniustus neque iustus, qui sive est incivilis vel puer. Sed cum dicitur, homo est non iustus, significat privationem. Privatio autem est ablatio rei ab aliquo, qui nata est inesse, tempore quo nata est in inesse ei."

85. *De Interpret.* 10, 19b, 27–28.

86. *Epitome of De Interpretatione* (*op. cit.*, Vol. I, 2, p. 41, I).

87. *Die Hermaneutik des Aristoteles*, ed. Isidor Pollak (Leipzig, 1913); *Organon Aristotelis*, ed. 'Abdurraḥman Badawi (Cairo, 1952).

88. Klatzkin's *Thesaurus Philosophicus Linguae Hebraicae*, under *musar* quotes only the passage of the *Epitome* here under discussion, and *musar* is translated there *privative*.

89. Cairo, n.d., p. 22, l. 17.

90. MS. Adler, 1015, p. 23a.

91. Cf. Steinschneider, *Die arabischen Übersetzungen aus dem Griechischen* (1897), p. 41.

92. *Alexander in Priora Analytica*, ed. M. Wallies (1883), p. 397, l. 2; cf. Prantl, *Geschichte der Logik*, I (1885), 357–358, nn. 30–33; Zeller, *Die Philosophie der Griechen*, II, 2[2] (1862), 158, n. 4.

93. MS. Adler, 131, p. 9b.

94. *Kitāb al-'Ishārāt wa'l-Tanbīhāt*, ed. J. Forget (1892), p. 27, l. 20–p. 28, l. 1. French translation: *Livre des Directives et Remarques* by A.-M. Goichon (1951), p. 127. Cf. also Algazali, *Maqāṣid*, p. 22, ll. 13–14, where reference is made to the use of the copula in Persian.

95. *Op. cit.*, p. 27, l. 9; p. 28, l. 9 (French, pp. 125 and 128).

96. *Op. cit.*, p. 22, l. 17.

97. *Alfarabi's Commentary on Aristotle's DE INTERPRETATIONE*, ed. W. Kutsch and S. Marrow, p. 106, l. 17.

12

OCKHAM AND THE TEXTBOOKS: ON THE ORIGIN OF POSSIBILITY

Allan B. Wolter

THE neophyte in scholastic philosophy can scarcely avoid receiving a distorted view of Ockham's doctrines if he reads the neo-scholastic textbooks used in most of our seminaries and colleges today. To illustrate this contention, we have selected the question of the origin of possibility. We have examined thirteen typical textbooks whose publication dates roughly cover the period of the past two generations.[1] Each of these works has enjoyed a great measure of popularity among seminary and college professors in its day, and practically all have gone through several editions or reprintings. Yet, in none of these works could we find a fair or an accurate presentation of Ockham's position. Careful examination seemed to reveal that, in general, the older the work, the less erroneous the statements it contained. This progressive misrepresentation of the Venerable Inceptor could be explained plausibly on the ground that the more recent authors simply copied from the earlier works. Most of the authors do not bother to quote any text in Ockham where the opinion they attribute to him is to be found. Five, however, do give us a reference, and in all five cases the text referred to is the same, namely question two of the 43rd distinction of the first book of the Commentary on the Sentences. Because of the difficulty in obtaining this work, we have appended to this essay a corrected edition of this question based on the best manuscripts.[2] If the reader of this essay will but compare the doctrine Ockham presents in this question with the position that the textbook authors ascribe to him, we feel sure he will come to the same conclusion that we did, namely, that those responsible for our textbooks did not even make an effort to read the text of Ockham to which they referred their students.

We shall give first a brief analysis of the contents of this question in Ockham, and then compare the Ockham of the text with the Ockham of the textbooks.

I. ANALYSIS OF THE QUESTION

The problem discussed is this. Are things impossible because God cannot make them, or is it rather that God cannot make them because they are impossible? In this question, the conjunction "because" is intended to express some priority of nature. Whether Henry of Ghent was the first to formulate this particular problem or not, at least his question and the solution he gave to it became the starting point for a similar discussion by at least three of the later scholastics, Duns Scotus, William Ockham, and Peter Aureoli.[3] The last two have developed their doctrines independently of each other, but both Ockham and Aureoli first give Henry's position and then Scotus' before presenting their own.

1. Solution of Henry of Ghent

Briefly, Henry's answer to the problem is this. The possibility of creatures has its origin in the omnipotence of God; impossibility on the contrary originates with creatures. Hence, creatures are possible because God can make them, whereas God cannot make what is self-contradictory because it is impossible. In other words, we must attribute omnipotence to God before we can attribute possibility to a creature. But with impossibility, it is just the other way around. We do not attribute impossibility to a creature, Henry tells us, because we have first attributed some impotency to God, for impotency is not something real or positive in God; it is a negation.

The guiding principle for Henry's solution to this problem is one which Ockham quotes quite literally: "Si vero illud quod attribuitur Deo secundum rationem sui nominis significat aliquid quod non est dignitatis simpliciter, etsi tale Deo attribuitur, hoc non est secundum se et primo, sed quia aliquid attribuitur creaturae et ex respectu ejus ad Deum, illud Deo attribuitur."[4] Whatever is not purely and simply a perfection (*aliquid dignitatis simpliciter*) is not attributed to God primarily or as such. To this category belongs, first of all, every so-called relative perfection, for instance, the notions of creator, or cause, etc. which imply relations to creatures. Secondly, all privations or negations are included, such as God's impotence with regard to the impossible.

But is not omnipotence itself a relative perfection? Does it not imply a relation to creatures? Here Henry introduces a distinction. God's omnipotence or active possibility, he tells us, can be considered in two ways: subjectively, or in relation to the subject in which it is found; objectively, or in reference to the object or term which can be produced. The same is true of passive possibility. It may be considered subjectively, or in reference to the creature which is said to be possible; again, it may be considered objectively, or in reference to the active potency which is capable of producing it in being. Though only a conceptual distinction exists between the objective and subjective phase of any given potentiality, be it active or passive, still this suffices to speak of an order existing between the various phases of active and passive potentiality.

In general, the subjective phase has a priority over its corresponding objective phase. Furthermore, whatever is of positive perfection in a creature is derived from the perfection of God. Hence, says Henry, the following order obtains. If we consider God's power or omnipotence subjectively, i.e. in relation to himself, we find that it involves no imperfection but is a perfection pure and simple. Therefore, according to the Ghentian norm, it must be attributed to God "secundum se et primo." Secondly, the passive potentiality or possibility of the creature, subjectively considered, is derived somehow from God's omnipotence. Thirdly, this same passive potentiality can be considered objectively, or in relation to God, as the active power or source of its possibility. This relation to God is real (*secundum rem et esse*). But because of this real relation of the creature to God, we must attribute a corresponding relation in God towards the creature. The latter, however, will not be a real relation, but merely a conceptual one (*secundum rationem et dici*). This latter relation is God's omnipotence in so far as it implies a reference to creatures.

It is in this way, then, that Henry saves his principle that all so-called relative perfections, like privations or negations, are not attributed to God primarily or as such but only secondarily. That is to say, the correlative perfection is primarily attributed to creatures; but because these same creatures bear a real relation to God, God is given a new name to express his relation to creatures. Thus God is called "Lord" because creatures exist which are his servants.

Hence, Henry's conclusion is that, absolutely speaking, active possibility or omnipotence is attributed to God prior to attributing possibility to creatures; whereas impossibility is first attributed to such fanciful creatures as the chimera or other "impossibles" before attributing any impotency to God in their regard.

But as both Scotus and Aureoli have noted, Henry apparently retracted this opinion some two years after he had first proposed it.[5] For in his 8th Quodlibet Henry asserts that not only are things possible because God can do them, but what is impossible is so because God cannot do it. In other words, both active possibility and impossibility are prior in God to any corresponding passive possibility or impossibility in creatures. As Henry himself puts it: "Non est verum dicere de impossibili simpliciter, quod Deus non potest illud facere, quia non potest fieri, sed potius non potest fieri quia Deus non potest facere, sicut et in affirmativa non dicitur Deum possibile aliquid facere, quia illud possibile est fieri, sed econverso quia Deus potest illud facere, ideo possibile est fieri aut objective aut subjective."[6]

Here we have the opinion commonly attributed to Ockham as we shall see more in detail later. The fact that Ockham quotes

Henry against Henry in his first argument against the Ghentian's earlier opinion, might lead one who did not bother to read this question of Ockham through to the end to believe that the Venerable Inceptor subscribed to the same opinion. Though even here it is difficult to see how this misinterpretation could arise, for the argument is clearly *ad hominem*. The point he wishes to make is, not that we must attribute to God's omnipotence a priority over intrinsic possibility, but that the principle used by Henry to reach his first position is false, namely that every relative attribute is affirmed of God only because we have previously affirmed a correlative attribute of creatures. Henry, Ockham insists, has already abandoned this principle, for on the basis of his second position, Henry would have to say that the contrary is true, namely that such relative terms are ascribed to creatures because their correlative terms have already been ascribed to God.[7] And in this connection Ockham does not contend, as is patently evident to anyone who reads on to the end of the question, that either one of two such correlative terms, as active power and passive possibility, has any priority over the other. On the contrary, the very fact that Henry ascribes the priority at one moment to God and at another to the creature merely accentuates the truth that these notions are genuine correlatives; neither can be defined independently of the others; neither has any antecedence over the other. Hence, to put it positively, we have as much right to say that things are possible or impossible because God can or cannot do them as we have to say that God can or cannot do things because they are possible or impossible respectively. Or to put it more correctly in a negative formulation as Ockham himself does in his own solution to the problem, we have no right to say that either proposition is true if the conjunction "because" is intended to indicate some kind of ontological priority.

2. Solution of Duns Scotus

Like Aureoli, Ockham, after citing and criticizing Henry's opinion, presents that of Scotus. The solution of John Duns to this question is based upon his conception of the "creatural ideas" in the mind of God. Unlike St. Thomas[8] or Henry of Ghent,[9] Scotus does not admit that the relationship of imitability of the divine essence *ad extra* in some specific way is by nature prior to the formal conception of the creature as a thought object. That is to say, he does not believe that the divine intellect is determined objectively to form the distinct idea of a creature because it sees that the divine essence can be imitated in such and such a way. This conception gives the creature some kind of fundamental existence in the divine essence as a *relatio rationis* which is by nature prior to, and is the ontological reason for, the divine knowledge. Scotus argues at great length against this thesis.[10] While it is not our intention to give his arguments in detail, we might note that his position is dictated by these dominant thoughts. We cannot speak of a relation of imitability without first bringing in the two terms of the relation which are the divine essence and the creatures. If we insist with Scotus "quod relatio non naturaliter cognoscitur nisi cognito termino,"[11] then to say that God sees his essence as imitable is to say that he already has a clear knowledge of both his essence and the creature which are the two terms of the relation. And since the terms are by nature prior to the relation, we cannot assign to the relation of imitability in a specific way an ontological priority over the formal knowledge of the creature, as the opinion of St. Thomas and Henry would have us do. Furthermore, since the creatural term, either in itself or in something that is not formally the divine essence as such, is required as an ontological determinant of the "quasi-passivus" divine intellect, "hoc videtur vilificare intellectum divinum, quia tunc esset passivus respectu aliorum objectorum cognitorum."[12]

Scotus' own escape from this difficulty was to fall back on an idea that has appeared in various forms throughout the history of Christian philosophy, namely the conception that the creatural ideas are to be regarded as quasi-termini of the "creative" activity of the intellect of God. They are not actually created, for that would be to give them real or actual existence. No, the meaning here is that the divine intellect, by knowing a creature, gives that creature an *esse objectivum* or *esse intelligibile* so that the creature may be said to exist as a thought object.

It is this doctrine that Scotus introduces into his solution of the question at hand. Various *instantia naturae* can be distinguished. In the first instance of nature, Scotus tells us, the creature is produced in intelligible *esse* by the divine intellect. In virtue of this we may speak of the creature as having a certain whatness or quiddity. Now, because this quiddity is what it is, that is to say, because it possesses just this and no other formal nature, it is compatible with real existence, and yet does not actually require it. Hence, Scotus tells us, in this second instance of nature, the creature possesses of itself *esse possibile* or possibility.[13]

With regard to impossibility, Scotus notes that the so-called "impossible" is a figment (*figmentum*) which consists of two or more positive entities, each of which is possible in itself but is of such a nature that it cannot be combined with the others in the unity of a single being. In a word, the impossible is an attempt to combine two incompatible notions. The result, according to Scotus, is not a true notion, but a figment that possesses a unity in name only. If we ask then for the ultimate reason for the impossibility of such a "thing," we shall find it formally in the nature of the two or more elements we are seeking to combine. He tells us: "Just as God, by his intellect, produces a possible in *esse possibili*, so he produces two formally different beings in *esse possibili* and these things produced are in themselves formally incompatible to the extent that they cannot exist simultaneously as one thing nor can a third something be composed of them. But this incompatibility which they possess formally, they have of themselves and they have it in some way from that which produced them as from a principle. And the impossibility of the figment as a whole follows from this incompatibility of these elements which it includes. And from this impossibility of the figment in itself and from the incompatibility of its parts, results its impossibility in relation to some agent."[14]

Hence, for Scotus both possibility and impossibility are due (*ex se*) to the formal nature of the thing in question, yet if we reduce this inner or intrinsic possibility to its first extrinsic principle, we must admit, according to him, that the possible depends (*principiative*) upon the intellect as upon a principle. Hence the classic Scotist formula, that things are possible "formaliter" of themselves, but depend "principiative" on the divine intellect.

Ockham's first counter-argument to Scotus gives the clue to his fundamental criticism. The fact that something is known does not permit the converse inference, therefore, as known, it is or exists. Or to put it another way, the mere fact that a thing is known does not give the thing in question a new "existence" or *esse intelligibile* within the knower. All that the known object acquires by being known is a certain extrinsic denomination.[15]

Ockham at one time admitted such a "fictum theory" in regard to the human intellect, but later he abandoned the theory that the content of the concept is a quasientity within the accidental reality or quality of the concept itself. Consequently, if Ockham will not admit of such an intelligible *esse* as a diminutive sort of entity midway between nothingness and actual existence, then it follows that he will deny any kind of production in regard to such an *esse intelligible*. Hence, he denies all such productivity to the divine intellect as well. Whence his conclusion: "Ergo creatura in tali esse intelligibili non producitur."[16]

This fits into the pattern of his general criticism of Scotus' attempt to explain God's knowledge of creatures. Perhaps no scholastic has attempted such an elaborate divine psychology as has Duns Scotus. His distinction between God's manner of knowing his own essence and that of creatures, or between God's knowledge of what is contingent and what is necessary, has led Scotus to break down God's mental life, as it were, into so many formalities or rationes and then reconstruct these formally or conceptually distinct elements to establish a certain "ordo naturae."[17] But as Vignaux has aptly expressed it: "Si l'on entend par psychologie une décomposition de la pensée et une mise en ordre de ses éléments, le nominalisme exclut toute psychologie divine."[18]

Ockham has emphasized the divine simplicity to such an extent that he refuses to have anything to do with Scotus' "instantia naturae," as though God's knowledge of his own essence were somehow prior by nature to God's knowledge of creatures. "Talia instantia non sunt ponenda et ita impossibile est dari primo aliquod instans in quo prius intelligatur essentia quam creatura."[19] Nor is there any point in establishing an order within God's knowledge of creatures, for instance between his knowledge of their necessary acts or their free or contingent acts, between their past, present, or future. For "Deus intelligit omnia quaecumque intelligit unico actu indistincto."[20]

This knowledge of God is given with his essence; it is not something produced. "Ipsa cognitio creaturae est omnino incausabilis imo etiam omnino improducibilis."[21] Consequently, Ockham abandons any attempt to explain how God knows things, particularly future contingents.[22]

From all this it follows that Ockham's conception of the divine creatural ideas will differ radically from that of either Scotus or St. Thomas. To discuss his position on this point fully would unduly prolong this essay. Still we must give a brief summary at least if we would understand his notion of the possible.

3. Ockham's Conception of the Divine Ideas

As Vignaux has noted, Ockham's position in regard to the ideas or intelligibles represents a return to that of Peter Lombard.[23] The saints indeed loved to speak of the creature's existence in God as an idea or intelligible. The Master of the Sentences already cautioned his readers that this expression must be correctly understood. Ockham quotes this passage, adding his own approval: "Ex hoc ergo sensu omnia dicuntur esse in Deo et omne quod factum est dicitur esse vita in ipso, non ideo quia Creator sit creatura, vel quia ista temporalia essentialiter sunt in Deo, sed quia in eius semper sunt scientia quae vita est. Ecce hic habetur expresse quod creaturae non sunt in Deo essentialiter, sed sunt in Deo sicut obiecta cognita, et quod ipsa non sunt vita in Deo sed quod scientia in qua fuerunt tamquam obiecta cognita est in Deo vita."[24]

In question five, distinction thirty-five of the first book of the Sentences, Ockham puts this query: "Utrum [Deus] intelligat omnia alia a se per ideas eorum?" His answer to this question indicates the fundamental divergence of his conception of the divine ideas from that of Aquinas for instance.

The divine ideas are not the *rationes cognoscendi ipsas creaturas.* A *ratio cognoscendi* is a general term for anything that is somehow necessarily required for a knowledge of something. Thus it could be that which moves the intellect as an efficient cause to the act of knowledge, or it could be the act of knowledge by which something is known, or it could be that which receives the knowledge subjectively, as for instance the created intellect or soul in man as the recipient of the ideas or concepts, or, finally, it could be some other necessary condition required for the knowledge of the thing in question.

Now, all of these possibilities are excluded in regard to God. First of all, God's knowledge of creatures is as uncaused as his essence itself. Hence, the ideas of creatures cannot effectively cause this knowledge. Neither can the ideas be the knowledge itself God has of the creatures, for God's knowledge, like his essence, is one, indivisible, simple; the ideas are many. Neither can it be the third, because the divine essence or intellect is not recipient of its knowledge but is formally its knowledge. Finally, if the ideas were a condition for the divine knowledge, they would have to be either the divine essence itself, which is impossible because the essence is one and simple while the ideas are multiple and divisible, or they would have to be something really distinct from God or some *entia rationis.* But God's knowledge is conditioned neither by anything really distinct from himself nor by any *entia rationis.* Hence, the ideas cannot be the *rationes cognoscendi creaturas.* God has but one *ratio cognoscendi*, his infinitely perfect and simple essence.

Neither are the ideas posited as some kind of creatural likenesses which represent creatures to the divine intellect, for this view falls heir to some of the same difficulties as the above. "Dico quod non sunt ideae ponendae tamquam similitudines repraesentantes intellectui divino ipsas creaturas, quia illae similitudines non possunt esse divina essentia cum illa sit omnino implurificabilis. Nec est quod sint entia rationis quia nullum tale requiritur, nec ad producendum nec ad cognoscendum [creaturas]."[25]

Basing himself on St. Augustine, Ockham insists that the divine ideas are posited primarily as exemplars, to which God as it were looks in producing the particular creature in question. And the reason for requiring such an exemplar is that God is not a blind creator, but *rationabiliter operans*.[26]

If then we were to give a strict logical description of the divine idea, how would we delineate it? Viewed precisely, Ockham tells us, the "idea" is not a thing as such, that is to say it does not possess a "quid rei." It is a term or concept which we employ to signify something. It is not an absolute but a connotative or relative term. In other words, it does not signify something only directly or *in recto*, but it directly signifies one thing and in addition connotes *in obliquo* the thing signified plus something else. As such it may be described as follows: "Idea est aliquid cognitum a principio effectivo intellectuali ad quod activum aspiciens potest aliquid in esse reali producere."[27]

The idea then is something which an intellectual or rational efficient cause knows and to which he looks in producing it in actual existence. Now, such a notion or description does not designate directly or *in recto* the divine essence as such, for the things are many, whereas the divine essence is one and simple. Neither does it apply to any relation this divine essence might have towards creatures. No such real relation exists, for it is commonly admitted that while creatures may bear a real relation to God, God does not have any real relation to anything distinct from himself. Nor is there any conceptual relation that could be designated by this term. Hence, the only thing to which this term directly applies is the creature itself. "Dico quod ista descriptio non convenit ipsi divinae essentiae nec alicui respectui rationis, sed ipsimet creaturae."[28]

It is the creature itself which God knows. He knows each and every creature that ever will exist or ever could exist. He knows it perfectly. He knows it individually. He knows it from all eternity, before it ever comes into existence. And before he

actually creates it, he knows it, and knows it as non-existent.[29]
This knowledge is in no way dependent on the reality of the
creature, but it is something God possesses in virtue of his
divine essence. Hence, the only explanation we can give for it,
and this is not properly an explanation, is that God is God.
"Ex hoc ipso quod Deus est Deus cognoscit-omnia."[30]

Hence, it is the "creatura producibilis" that is designated by
the term "idea." Or as Ockham puts it in logical language:
"Idea importat ipsammet creaturam in recto et etiam ipsammet
in obliquo, et praeter hoc importat ipsam divinam cognitionem
vel cognoscentem in obliquo; et ideo de ipsammet creatura est
praedicabilis ut ipsa sit idea; sed non est praedicabilis de agente
cognoscente vel cognitione quia nec cognitio nec cognoscens est
idea sicut nec exemplar."[31]

As with the *esse intelligibile*, so with the *idea*. These terms
designate the creatura itself. They are extrinsic denominations
given to the creature by the fact that it is known by God from all
eternity. But this does not give the creature some kind of real
existence in God as in a subject; all we can say of the creature is
that it is an object of divine knowledge. This does not say that it
exists in God as an object but only that God knows it, and that
from all eternity. "Sequitur quod ideae non sunt in Deo subiective
et realiter, sed tantum sunt in ipso obiective tamquam quaedam
cognita ab ipso, quia ideae sunt ipsaemet res a Deo producibiles."[32]

It is the notion of Scotus, which gives the creatural idea an
esse obiectivum or *esse intelligibile* as the quasi-product of the
poetical activity of God's intellect, that Ockham is attacking in
his first counter-argument. The other arguments of Ockham
against specific points of Scotus' doctrine do not interest us,
with the exception perhaps of the fourth. His criticism here of
Scotus' distinction between the first instance of nature, where the
creature is produced in *esse intelligibile*, and the second instance
of nature, where the creature is said to be possible, is again
indicative of Ockham's refusal to elaborate a divine psychology.

4. Ockham's Solution to the Question

Having criticized both Henry and Duns Scotus, Ockham can

present his own solution to the original question very briefly. Correlative terms, like cause and effect, or active and passive potentiality, belong to the class of reciprocals which Aristotle says "come into existence simultaneously."[33] That is to say, they are such by nature that we cannot define the one without defining at the same time the other. Hence Ockham's conclusion: since omnipotence in God implies, as its correlative, that something can be made, and conversely, since something can be made implies that God can make it, it follows that we cannot attribute active possibility to God before we attribute passive possibility to the creature, or vice versa. Active potency and passive possibility are by nature simultaneous; neither can be said to be the cause or the ontological antecedent of the other. "In omnibus relativis quae vocantur relativa secundum potentiam activam et passivam vel causam et effectum, semper correlativa sunt simul natura. Et ideo quia sunt simul natura et mutuo se inferant, neutrum est magis causa alterius quam econverso. . . . Et ita universaliter quando est aliqua consequentia mutua, tenens praecise per naturam correlativorum non est una propositio magis causa alterius quam econverso. Et quando quaeritur an primo conveniat Deo non posse facere impossibile quam conveniat impossibili non posse fieri a Deo, dico quod non prius convenit Deo non posse facere impossibile quam convenit impossibili non posse fieri a Deo. Nec etiam prius competit impossibili non posse fieri quam Deo non posse facere impossibile."

Ockham's answer to the question is clear. If we ask: Are things possible because God can create them, or can God create them because they are possible? Ockham replies that neither proposition is true if by "because" we understand some priority of nature. In short, it is a meaningless question.

II. OCKHAM OF THE TEXTBOOKS

If we compare Ockham's position as revealed in the text with that attributed to him by our neo-scholastic textbooks, we discover quite a contrast. In twelve of the thirteen textbooks we have examined, Ockham is presented as the defendant of the thesis that the internal possibility of a created being depends on the divine power. Thus for instance in a recent edition of Hickey, we read: "Occam et nonnulli alii intrinsecam rerum possibilitatem a divina potentia pendere autumarunt, ita ut res esse possibiles dixerint quia Deus potest eas producere."[34]

Theoretically, Ockham's position is distinguished from that attributed to Descartes (rightly or wrongly, we do not wish to say), namely that the internal possibility depends on the free will of God in the sense that God could arbitrarily make what is possible impossible and vice versa. Practically, however, the average student is left with the impression that there is but little difference between the two.[35] This is brought out, for instance, by the following quotation: "Some philosophers, among them William of Ockham (Comment. in L. I Sent. dist. 43 q. 2), defended the doctrine that intrinsic possibility depends ultimately on God's power. . . . Why would things be intrinsically possible, i.e., why are their constitutive elements compatible and non-contradictory? Because God's omnipotence can produce them. And why are other things intrinsically impossible, i.e., why are their elements incompatible and contradictory? The only answer can be, because God's omnipotence cannot produce them. The ultimate ground for intrinsic impossibility would thus be the lack of power in God. If God had more power, the impossibles would also be intrinsically possible. But that is patently false. God possesses power in an infinite degree; therefore, no things should be intrinsically impossible, if it were merely a question of God's power. In that case it should be within God's power to produce a being which is finite and infinite at the same time, which exists and does not exist at the same time, which is rational and irrational at the same time, which is living and dead at the same time. But to make an assertion like this, means to invalidate the Principle of Contradiction and that means to destroy the foundation of all being and knowledge; skepticism must follow such a view."[36]

We have chosen this textbook for three reasons. First, it is a work that is enjoying a very great deal of popularity at the present time in Catholic colleges and universities of the United

States, and some seminary professors have even suggested that it be translated into Latin for use in our seminaries. Secondly, it gives a fair summary of the arguments generally used by the other texts we have examined. Thirdly, it does what most of the other textbooks do not do; it gives the exact reference to the passage in Ockham where we are supposed to discover this doctrine, namely in the text we have analyzed and printed in full at the rear of this article. But when we turn to this text of Ockham, what do we find?

First of all, we discover the surprising fact that Ockham does not even discuss the problem of the source or priority of intrinsic possibility in this question. This becomes quite clear if we analyze what is meant by "intrinsic possibility." As Father Bittle is kind enough to explain to his readers, it consists in the compatibility or non-contradictory character of a thing's essential notes. In other words, it is what St. Thomas calls the absolute possibility of a thing, in contradistinction to relative possibility, which is commonly referred to as extrinsic possibility, i.e. the relationship a thing bears to that which can produce it.[37] In some ways, this term "absolute possibility" is more exact, because "possible" as opposed to the "impossible" (i.e. what consists of self-contradictory or incompatible notions), as Aristotle tells us, involves no reference to an active power or potency.[38]

Ockham, however, is clearly not speaking of absolute, but of relative possibility. This is evident from his own solution. He speaks of those relative notions "quae vocantur relativa secundum potentiam activam et passivam," a clear reference to the second class of relative terms according to Aristotle's division.[39] In fact even the example used by Ockham is borrowed from the Stagirite. Such notions, Ockham tells us, are correlatives according to Aristotle and as such are "simul natura et mutuo se inferant." Ockham goes further and explicitly refers us to Aristotle's discussion on the simultaneity of such correlative notions.[40]

Further proof, if such were needed, that Ockham is not considering intrinsic or absolute possibility but extrinsic possibility is that he uses the term "factibile" rather than "possibile" in discussing the problem of priority. In addition, if we read the text of his own solution carefully, do we not discover him making a distinction between what our neo-scholastics would call intrinsic possibility or impossibility and that which is extrinsic? Thus he writes: "Et quando quaeritur an primo conveniat Deo non posse facere impossibile quam conveniat impossibili non posse fieri a Deo, etc." The "impossibile" is regarded as the subject to which is attributed "non posse fieri a Deo." But what is the "impossible" if not that which is intrinsically impossible, and the "non posse fieri a Deo" but the relative aspect we call extrinsic possibility? Now, the whole problem of priority or non-priority is discussed with regard to this relative aspect. And the same is true of the possible. "Et eodem modo dico de affirmativis, quod non prius convenit Deo posse facere possibile vel creaturam quam creaturae posse fieri a Deo."

A second point generally made by the authors of our textbooks is that intrinsic possibility according to Ockham depends on the divine omnipotence as on its cause or ontological antecedent. Now, even if we ignore the failure to distinguish between intrinsic and extrinsic possibility and assume for the benefit of our neo-scholastic authors that Ockham is speaking of the former instead of the latter, we still fail to see how they concluded that for him things are possible because God can cause them. It was Henry of Ghent, not Ockham, who espoused this theory. And in his second formulation, the Ghentian even went so far as to add that things are impossible because God cannot make them.

Could it be perhaps that someone read this text so hurriedly that he attributed Henry's opinion to Ockham? Such a hypothesis hardly seems possible in view of Ockham's clear statement that absolutely no priority of nature exists between such correlative notions. They are "simul natura . . . secundum Philosophum . . . Et ideo quia sunt simul natura et mutuo se inferant, neutrum est magis causa alterius quam econverso."

Another, and perhaps more plausible source of the error, is the assumption that the later authors instead of reading Ockham simply copied from the earlier writers without fully comprehending their various nuances of meaning. For in general, as we noted in the beginning, the older works contain less errors than the later ones. Liberatore, for instance, does not explicitly accuse Ockham of teaching that internal possibility depends on the omnipotence of God, but states simply that the Ven. Inceptor banishes internal possibility and leaves only external possibility. Urraburu, among the older authors, likewise does not specify which possibility depends on the omnipotence of God, but states simply that all possibility is to be traced back to this source according to a view "attributed" to Ockham. Schiffini, in explaining this "dependence," suggests two alternatives, namely: first that the very possible is an effect of the divine power; and second, that the possible is called such in reference to the divine power. This last alternative would be closer to Ockham's opinion in the sense that correlatives mutually imply one another and, hence, cannot be defined independently of each other. But even such a statement is misleading on two counts: first, it does not restrict such a description to the extrinsic possibility or to what Ockham would call the "factibile"; second, it does not indicate that the converse statement is equally true, namely that the divine power is called omnipotence in reference to the possible.

But what interests us in Schiffini's statement is that he does make a distinction between what is (*esse*) and what is called (*dici*). Later works (e.g. Donat and Frick) simply combine the two. Donat tells us for instance that, according to Ockham, "hoc solo, quod Deus aliquid facere possit, id dici et esse possibile." Still later works drop the *dici* entirely, as for instance, Coffey, Farges, and Bittle. It is this progressive misrepresentation that leads one to believe that later authors depended on the earlier for their interpretation of Ockham and made no attempt to read the original text to which some at least referred their readers.

Ockham and Intrinsic Possibility

So far our analysis has been more or less negative. That is, we have shown that Ockham is not treating the problem of intrinsic possibility primarily. But the reader may ask: "What is Ockham's positive position? What does he hold regarding the source of intrinsic possibility?"

In answering this question, a few things should be borne in mind. First of all, as we noted before, St. Thomas prefers to use the term "absolutely possible" instead of intrinsically possible. In fact, as far as we can determine, Aquinas never seems to employ the terminology of "intrinsic" and "extrinsic" with regard to possibility.[41] The closest he comes to "intrinsic" is to refer to the "absolute possibile" as that which is possible "secundum seipsum." In using this terminology, St. Thomas is following Aristotle, as he explicitly tells us.[42]

Now, if we read Aristotle[43] and St. Thomas, we discover a difference between their treatment of intrinsic possibility and that of the neo-scholastics. This difference, though slight, is not without significance. Where the neo-scholastics speak of the intrinsic possibility of a thing as a compatibility or lack of contradiction in its essential notes, St. Thomas and Aristotle speak of "absolute possibility" (or impossibility) only in connection with propositions. Thus Aquinas says: "Dicitur autem aliquid possibile vel impossibile absolute, ex habitudine terminorum; possibile quidem quia praedicatum non repugnat subiecto, ut Socratem sedere; impossibile vero absolute quia praedicatum repugnat subiecto, ut hominem esse asinum."[44]

This is not to imply that we cannot combine the subject and predicate of the proposition in a single concept, for the scholastics generally agree that where the elements combined do not mutually contradict each other they can be grasped by a simple act of apprehension. But the point we wish to make is that possibility and impossibility in this case are basically modalities of propositions about a given subject. Consequently, when we ask for the ontologic source of such a possibility, we should keep in mind that, formally speaking, we are inquiring after the source of a logical entity and not a real quality or perfection which inheres in the thing as such.

Secondly, we note that this intrinsic possibility or impossibility can be said to pertain to things of themselves. Thus St. Thomas says: "Sciendum est ergo quod impossibile quod dicitur secundum nullam potentiam, sed secundum seipsum, dicitur ratione discohaerentiae terminorum. . . ."[45]

Finally, we note that St. Thomas uses this notion of the "absolute possibile" to define God's omnipotence. In the *Summa Theologica*, for instance, he writes: "Si quis recte consideret, cum potentia dicatur ad possibilia, cum Deus omnia posse dicitur, nihil rectius intelligitur quam quod possit omnia possibilia, et ob hoc omnipotens dicatur. Possibile autem dicitur dupliciter, secundum Philosophum in V *Metaph*. Uno modo per respectum ad aliquam potentiam; sicut quod subditur humanae potentiae, dicitur esse possibile homini. Non autem potest dici quod Deus dicatur omnipotens quia possit omnia quae sunt possibilia naturae creatae, quia divina potentia in plura extenditur. Si autem dicatur quod Deus sit omnipotens, quia potest omnia quae sunt possibilia suae potentiae, erit circulatio in manifestatione omnipotentiae; hoc enim non erit aliud quam dicere quod Deus est omnipotens, quia potest omnia quae potest. Relinquitur igitur quod Deus dicatur omnipotens, quia potest omnia possibilia absolute, quod est alter modus dicendi possibile. Dicitur autem aliquid possibile vel impossibile absolute, ex habitudine terminorum; possibile quidem, quia praedicatum non repugnat subiecto, ut Socratem sedere; impossibile vero absolute quia praedicatum repugnat subiecto, ut hominem esse asinum."[46]

If we read Ockham, we find substantially the same position as that of St. Thomas. In answer to the objection that "esse possibile" is something that a creature has received from God, Ockham reminds his objector that possibility is not a real something which inheres in a creature. "To be possible" is something predicable of a creature; it is a logical modality that has been elevated to the status of a predicate. Hence we would be speaking more exactly if we said that a creature is possible not because "esse possibile" pertains to it, but because it can exist in the world of reality. "Nec est proprius modus loquendi dicere quod esse possibile convenit creaturae, sed magis proprie debet dici quod creatura est possibilis non propter aliquid quod sibi conveniat sed quia potest esse in rerum natura."[47]

While everything real which a creature has must be attributed to God as to a principle, this is not true of such logical entities as are predicated about them. Only in the sense that the rational creature, who formulates such propositions as "man is possible" or "it is impossible that man be a donkey," owes its total being, both substantial and accidental, to God as to a first principle, can we say that such predications are from God. "Dicendum quod quidquid creatura habet reale tamquam aliquid sibi inhaerens, habet a Deo tamquam a principio; sed non quidquid convenit sibi in praedicatione habet principiative a Deo nisi illo modo quo Deus habet tales praedicationes a Deo, quia tales praedicationes quando sunt in actu et realiter, tunc sunt a Deo."[48]

Properly speaking then, this absolute or intrinsic possibility is not something that a creature has by reason of some relation to an active potency in God. It is something which the creature has of itself. "Et ideo esse possibile convenit creaturae ex se non realiter tamquam aliquid sibi inhaerens, sed vere est possibile ex se sicut homo ex se est non asinus."[49] Not indeed that this "esse possibile" is something real pertaining to the creature, but in the sense that the creature can be. As Ockham put it in the quotation cited above: "Nec est proprius modus loquendi dicere quod esse possibile convenit creaturae, sed magis proprie debet dici quod creatura est possibilis non propter aliquid quod sibi conveniat, sed quia potest esse in rerum natura."

Finally, Ockham, like St. Thomas, recognizes that to define omnipotence by the "factibilia" and the "factibilia" by omnipotence is a circle that explains nothing. Hence, he too defines the omnipotence of God in terms of what does not involve a manifest contradiction. "Credo in Deum Patrem omnipotentem, quem sic intelligo, quod quodlibet est divinae potentiae attribuendum quod non includit manifestam contradictionem."[50]

To conclude, we must confess that we find Ockham's notion of so-called intrinsic possibility in substantial conformity with St. Thomas' express statements on this point. Both are good Aristotelians.

But what of the ultimate origin of this intrinsic possibility? What of the formulation adopted by Thomists and found in our contemporary textbooks? "Possibilia fundantur in essentia divina; sed constituuntur formaliter in ordine ideali per intellectum divinum," as one Thomist puts it.[51]

Here we must confess that though we have read much in St. Thomas, we have been unable to discover any explicit text where he attempts to reduce "absolute possibility," as he calls it, formally to the divine intellect and fundamentally to the divine essence. In St. Thomas' own discussions, "absolute possibility" is treated as its name implies, namely as a logical entity, as something to be found formally in a proposition and not in God. Even when pressed to explain how the world was possible before its actual creation, he does not reduce its intrinsic possibility to something in God. Only on the ground of extrinsic possibility can we relate it to God. "Dicendum quod antequam mundus esset, possibile erat mundum fieri, non quidem aliqua potentia passiva, sed solum per potentiam activam. Vel potest dici, quod fuit possibile non per aliquam potentiam, sed quia termini non sunt invicem discohaerentes, huiusmodi scilicet propositionis: 'Mundus est.' Sic enim dicitur esse aliquid possibile secundum nullam potentiam ut patet per Philosophum in 5 Metaph."[52]

It is true that God knows all creatures from the beginning of the world and consequently prior to their actual creation. Hence, God knows what is possible and that from all eternity. But St. Thomas does not say that this knowledge formally constitutes the possible as possible; neither does he say that the divine essence, as imitable ad extra, is to be regarded as the ontologic foundation for the possible. What Thomists have done, rightly or wrongly, is to connect St. Thomas' teaching on the creatural ideas with the notion of intrinsic or absolute possibility. Now it was Scotus, not St. Thomas, who connected these two notions explicitly. And it was Scotus who gave to the possible sort of "existence" in God an "esse intelligibile" as we have seen. Is the present "Thomistic" teaching on the origin of possibles another instance of the influence of Scotism on the doctrine of St. Thomas?

With Ockham, however, there is no possibility of tying up the teaching of the origin of the "divine ideas" with the absolute possible, for the "ideas" are not something found in God properly speaking. They are the creatures themselves and not the divine essence. They are objects of God's eternal knowledge, but this does not give them any "existence" in God. They are not the *ratio cognoscendi creaturas*, as they are for St. Thomas.

But in concluding, we might point out that if intrinsic possibility is a logical entity, we can say of the "possible" that, like the "idea," it is a connotative term which *in recto* signifies the creature itself and *in obliquo* connotes this same creature as the subject of the predication "potest esse." If we ask, where is this fact that a given creature, say Peter, is possible, first recognized, Ockham would unhesitatingly answer: In God! For God knows every possible creature from all eternity. He knows it by an intuitive knowledge before he ever creates it. Furthermore, he tells us that only what is incapable of existing in the world of reality is not an object of this intuitive eternal knowledge. As he puts it: "Dico quod contradictio est quod visio sit et quod illud quod videtur non sit in effectu, nec esse possit. Ideo contradictio est quod chimaera videatur intuitive; sed non est contradictio quod id quod videtur nihil sit in actu extra animam dummodo possit esse in effectu vel aliquando fuit in rerum natura. Sic est in proposito. Unde Deus vidit ab aeterno omnes res factibiles et tamen tunc nihil fuerunt."[53]

In other words, anything that our modern neo-scholastics call intrinsically possible, i.e. anything whose being is such that it would imply no contradiction if it existed, is seen by God from all eternity as possible. This knowledge of God is absolutely one with his essence; hence, if we ask, why is it that God has this knowledge of the possibles? Ockham would answer: Because God is God. "Ex hoc ipso quod Deus est Deus, cognoscit omnia."[54]

ORDINATIO (SENT.) I, DIST. 43

Quaestio secunda

A   Secundo quaero utrum prius conveniat Deo non posse facere impossibile quam impossibili non posse fieri a Deo.

Quod prius conveniat Deo non posse facere impossibile videtur: Quia prius convenit Deo facere possibile quam possibili posse fieri a Deo; igitur eodem modo prius convenit Deo non posse facere impossibile quam impossibili non posse fieri a Deo. Antecedens patet: Quia omne quod convenit Deo, prius convenit sibi quam aliquid conveniat creaturae, igitur quam cuicumque alteri a Deo; igitur cum Deo conveniat posse facere possibile fieri, prius hoc conveniet sibi quam conveniat cuicumque alteri posse fieri a Deo. Consequentia patet quia pro quocumque instanti vel signo convenit Deo posse facere possibile fieri, pro eodem instanti sibi convenit non posse facere impossiblie fieri; igitur, etc.

Ad oppositum: Nihil quod importat indignitatem convenit primo Deo; sed non posse facere impossibile fieri importat indignitatem quia importet privationem vel negationem; igitur, etc.

[Opinio Henrici Gandavensis]

B   Ad quaestionem dicitur[1] quod, quando aliquid, quod attribuitur Deo secundum rationem sui nominis, significat aliquid quod non est dignitatis simpliciter, non secundum se primo attribuitur Deo, sed quia aliquid quod non est dignitatis attribuitur creaturae ex respectu eius ad Deum, ideo illud Deo attribuitur. Et huiusmodi sunt nomina quae dicunt respectum in Deo ad creaturas, quae ideo Deo attribuuntur, quia creaturae habent respectum ad ipsum, secundum quod Deo attribuitur esse dominum quia ex tempore habet servum. Et ideo attribuitur Deo posse aliquid super creaturam active, quia creatura est in se possibilis ad recipiendum in se actionem creatoris.

Dicitur tamen, quod posse tam activum Dei quam passivum creaturae potest dupliciter considerari, scilicet respectu sui subiecti vel respectu sui obiecti. Si posse Deo consideretur primo modo, sic est prius quam posse creaturae qualitercumque consideretur, quia posse sic consideratum dicit dignitatem simpliciter. Secundo modo non dicit dignitatem simpliciter, et ideo non competit sibi nisi quia posse passivum competit creaturae respectu Dei. Et ideo dicit, quod absolute loquendo non est posse passivum in creatura, nisi quia est posse activum in Deo. Ut cum quatuor sint respectus secundum posse, scilicet duo secundum posse activum, unus videlicet quo posse Dei comparatur ad Deum ut cuius est, alius ut comparatur ad creaturam ad quam est, et duo secundum posse passivum, scilicet unus quo comparatur ad creaturam cuius est, alius secundum quem comparatur ad Deum ut ad quem est, in ipsis est talis ordo, quod a posse Dei

---

[1] *Quodl.* 6, q. 3.

activo secundum se est posse passivum in creatura secundum se, quod concomitatur posse passivum creaturae respectu Dei, et ex posse passivo creaturae respectu Dei dicitur Deus posse active respectu creaturae.

[Contra opinionem Henrici]

c   Contra istam opinionem potest argui per ipsummet alibi,[2] quia alibi dicit, quod sicut non dicitur Deum impossibile aliquid facere, quia illud impossibili est fieri, sed econverso, quia impossibile est Deum hoc facere, ideo impossibile est hoc fieri, ita dicitur in affirmativa, quod quia possibile est Deum hoc facere, ideo possibile hoc facere, quia possibile est hoc fieri. Ex isto patet quod prius competit Deo posse facere respectu creaturae quam competat creaturae posse passivum respectui Dei, ergo eodem modo prius competit Deo non posse facere impossibile quam impossibili non posse fieri a Deo. Et ex isto patet manifeste quod ipse habet dicere, quod non quodlibet quod dicit respectum ad creaturam attribuitur Deo, quia creaturae habent respectum ad ipsum, sed magis econverso ideo attribuuntur creaturae talia respectiva, quia alia respectiva attribuuntur Deo.

Praeterea, non magis attribuitur aliquid Deo quod dicit respectum ad creaturam, quia creatura habet respectum ad ipsum, quam aliquid attribuitur causae creatae, quia effectus suus habet respectum ad ipsam; sed tale quid non attribuitur causae creatae, quia effectus habet respectum ad ipsam, ergo etc. Minor patet, quia cum causa creata secundum ipsum habeat respectum realem, sequitur quod prius mutaretur causa ad respectum realem, quam effectus produceretur.

Si dicatur, quod non est simile de causa creata et de Deo, quia Deus non refertur realiter sed tantum secundum rationem, causa autem creata refertur realiter, et ideo non est simile.—Hoc non sufficit, quia non plus repugnat respectui reali oriri ex alio respectu quam respectui rationis, ergo non plus repugnat, quod ex respectu effectus oriatur respectus causae creatae quam Dei, cum minus tam secundum rem quam secundum rationem recipiat Deus a creatura quam causa creata ab effectu suo.

Similiter, si ex uno respectu reali non oritur respectus realis sibi correspondens, eadem ratione ex respectu rationis non oritur respectus rationis sibi correspondens; sed respectu creaturae ad

[2] *Quodl.* 8, q. 3.

Deum est respectus rationis, quia non realis, cum illud quod non est non referatur realiter; ergo ex isto respectu non oritur respectus rationis Dei ad creaturam.

Praeterea, contra aliud quod dicitur, quod posse Dei activum est prius posse creaturae passivo et quod dicit dignitatem simpliciter.— Contra: Impossibile est activum, qualitercumque consideretur, dummodo sit activum, quin respectu alicuius dicatur activum, ergo necessario illud posse activum respectu alicuius est posse activum, sed non respectu Dei, quia Deus non causat nec agit Deum, ergo necessario est respectu creaturae; ergo posse activum Dei, qualitercumque consideretur, dicitur respectu creaturae, ergo non competit sibi nisi quia dicitur ad ipsam per primum dictum, ergo non dicit dignitatem simpliciter per idem dictum.

Confirmatur, quia dicit quod sunt hic duo respectus in posse activo, sicut sunt duo in posse passivo, unus scilicet respectu Dei. Tunc quaero: Quomodo iste respectus est respectu Dei? Aut tamquam respectu fundamenti, aut respectu termini. Si tamquam respectu fundamenti, ergo habet alium terminum, et non nisi creaturam, ergo ille respectus terminatur ad creaturam, ergo non primo competit Deo nec importat dignitatem simpliciter. Si sit respectu Dei tamquam respectu termini, ergo cum activum dicatur ad passivum, sequeretur, quod Deus esset passivus, quod est impossibile. Et ita manifeste patet, quod in ista propositione repugnantia includuntur.

[Opinio Scoti]

D   Aliter dicitur,[3] quod prima ratio impossibilis non est ex parte Dei, sed quia illud est impossibile simpliciter propter repugnantiam eius ut fiat. Quod declaratur sic: Impossibile simpliciter includit incompossibilia, quae ex rationibus suis formalibus sunt incompossibilia, et ab eo sunt principiative incompossibilia, a quo principiative habent rationes suas formales. Et ideo iste est processus, quod primo intellectus divinus producit rem in esse intelligibili in primo instanti naturae, in secundo instanti naturae habet seipsa formaliter esse possibile, et sicut Deus suo intellectu producit possibile in esse possibili, ita producit utrumque incompossibilium, quae includuntur in impossibili, in esse formaliter possibili, et illa producta seipsis formaliter sunt incompossibilia, ut non possint simul esse unum nec

---

[3] Cfr. Scot. *Ox.* I, d. 43, q. u.

aliquid tertium ex eis; et istam incompossibilitatem, quam habent ex
seipsis formaliter, habent principiative ab eo qui ea produxit in esse
possibili; et istam incompossibilitatem eorum sequitur incompossi-
bilitas totius significati; et ex illa sequitur impossibilitas respectu
cuiuscumque agentis: et ibi terminatur totus iste processus, et non
ad negationem possibilitatis in Deo.

[Contra opinionem Scoti]

E   Contra aliqua hic dicta potest argui primo, quia non videtur bene
dictum, quod intellectus divinus producit creaturam in esse intelligibili, quia illud quod per aliquem actum nullum esse formaliter
recipit, sed tantum denominatur denominatione extrinseca, non
producitur per talem actum; sed creatura per hoc quod intelligitur
a Deo nihil formaliter recipit, sed tantum denominatur quadam
extrinseca denominatione, sicut obiectum intellectus creati non
produciter per hoc quod intelligitur, sed tantum denominatur
quadam extrinseca denominatione; ergo creatura in tali esse intelligibili non producitur.

Praeterea, aut creatura producitur in esse intelligibili praecise, quia
intelligitur, aut quia prius nihil fuit, aut quia prius non erat intelligibile. Non propter primum, quia tunc divina essentia vere produceretur in esse intelligibili, cum vere intelligatur, et tunc quilibet intelligens
Deum produceret Deum in esse intelligibili. Nec propter secundum,
quia etiam quando intelligitur creatura, nihil est, quamvis sit intel-
lecta. Nec propter tertium, quia essentia divina ante intellectionem
suam non fuit intelligibilis.

Praeterea, secundum istum numquam producitur aliquid in esse
intelligibili, nisi quia aliquid producitur in esse reali; sed secundum
istos creatura, quando producitur per intellectum divinum, non
producitur nisi in esse intelligibili; ergo aliquid aliud producitur in
esse reali; sed nihil potest dari—patet inductive.

Praeterea, quod dicitur, quod in primo instanti naturae producitur
in esse intelligibili et in secundo instanti habet esse possibile—
Contra: Accipio primum instans naturae, in quo intellectus praecedit
esse intelligibile creaturae, et quaero: Aut in illo instanti creatura est
possibilis, aut non est possibilis. Si est possibilis, ergo est possibilis,
antequam producatur in esse intelligibili. Si non est possibilis, ergo
sibi repugnat esse.

Praeterea, quod dicitur, quod status est in illo processu ad impossi-
bilitatem respectu cuiuscumque agentis sine respectu correspondente

in Deo—Contra: Sicut omni respectui creaturae in esse possibili ad Deum correspondet aliquis respectus in Deo ad creaturam in esse possibili, ita negationi respectus correspondebit negatio respectus in Deo ad impossibile; ergo non est ibi status.

Si dicatur, quod respectui creaturae in esse possibili ad Deum non correspondet respectus in Deo—Contra: Aut ille respectus creaturae in esse possibili est realis, aut est respectus rationis. Non realis, quia non habet fundamentum reale; ergo est respectus rationis qui fit per actum intellectus comparantis creaturam ad Deum, secundum istum; sed ita potest intellectus comparare Deum ad creaturam sicut econverso; ergo ita potest esse respectus in Deo ad creaturam sicut econverso, ergo etc.

[Opinio propria]

F   Ideo aliter dico ad quaestionem, quod generaliter cum relativo, si convenienter assignetur, correspondet aliquod correlativum, et in omnibus relativis, quae vocantur relativa secundum potentiam activam et passivam vel causam et effectum, semper correlativa sunt simul natura. Et ideo, quia sunt simul natura et mutuo se inferant, neutrum est magis causa alterius quam econverso. Sicut quia pater et filius sunt simul natura illo modo, quo loquitur Philosophus in Praedicamentis capitulo De ad aliquid de simultate naturae, non plus filius est filius quam pater est pater quam econverso, nec etiam plus filius est, quia pater est, quam econverso, nec filius habet patrem, quia pater habet filium, nec econverso. Et ita universaliter, quando est aliqua consequentia mutua tenens praecise per naturam correlativorum, non est una propositio magis causa alterius quam econverso.

Et quando quaeritur, an primo conveniat Deo non posse facere impossibile quam conveniat impossibili non posse fieri a Deo, dico quod non prius convenit Deo non posse facere impossibile quam convenit impossibili non posse fieri a Deo. Nec etiam prius convenit impossibili non posse fieri quam Deo non posse facere impossibile.

Et eodem modo dico de affirmativis, quod non prius convenit Deo posse facere possibile vel creaturam quam creaturae posse fieri a Deo, sed simul natura eo modo, quo secundum Philosophum factivum et factibile sunt simul natura, hoc est non prius est aliquid factivum quam aliquid est factibile, nec econverso.

Et si dicatur, quod quidquid creatura habet, a Deo habet, ergo esse possibile convenit sibi a Deo, sed esse factivum non convenit Deo ab alio sed a se; prius autem convenit aliquid alicui quod convenit sibi a se quam illud quod convenit sibi ab alio; ergo prius convenit Deo esse factivum quam creaturae esse factibile, ergo non simul.— Dicendum, quod quidquid creatura habet reale tamquam aliquid sibi inhaerens, habet a Deo tamquam a principio; sed non quidquid convenit sibi in praedicatione, habet principiative a Deo, nisi illo modo quo Deus habet tales praedicationes a Deo, quia tales praedicationes, quando sunt in actu et realiter, tunc sunt a Deo. Et ideo esse possibile convenit creaturae ex se non realiter tamquam aliquid sibi inhaerens, sed vere est possibile ex se sicut homo ex se est non asinus. Et ideo talia argumenta non valent nisi de convenienti realiter, quomodo totum habet partes et accidentia sua; nec est proprius modus loquendi dicere, quod esse possibile convenit creaturae, sed magis proprie debet dici, quod creatura est possibilis non propter aliquid quod sibi conveniat, sed quia potest esse in rerum natura.

[Ad argumentum principale]

G   Ad argumentum principale dico, quod non prius est Deus factivus quam creatura est factibilis, immo ita primo est creatura factibilis, sicut Deus est factivus.

NOTES

1. M. Liberatore SJ, *Institutiones Philosophicae*. 2 ed. Prati, 1883, v.I, p. 320; S. Schiffini SJ, Instit. *Philosophicae in Compendium Redactae*. Augustae Taurinorum, 1889, p. 207; J. J. Urráburu SJ, Instit. Phil. Vallisoleti, 1891, v. II, p. 670; J. Rickaby SJ, *General Metaphysics* (Stonyhurst Philos. Series). 3 ed. London, 1898 (reissue 1909), p. 178; C. Willems, *Instit. Phil. Treveris*, 1906, v. I, p. 419; J. Donat SJ, *Summa Philosophiae Christianae*, 3 ed. Oeniponte, 1914, v. III, p. 57; P. Coffey, *Ontology*. London, 1914, p. 95; C. Frick SJ, *Ontologia* (Cursus Philosophicus in usum scholarum II). 5 ed. Friburgi Brisg., 1921, p. 76; G. Eßer SVD, *Metaphysica Generalis*, Techny, Ill., 1933, p. 81; A. Farges et D. Barbedette, *Cours de Philosophie Scholastique*. 19 ed. Paris, 1935, v. II, p. 145; J. Gredt OSB, *Elementa Philosophiae Aristotelico-Thomisticae*. 7 ed. Friburgi Brisg., 1937, v. II, p. 115; C. Bittle OFM.Cap., *The Domain of Being*. Milwaukee, 1939, p. 74; J. S. Hickey O.Cist., *Summula Philosophiae Scholasticae*, 9 ed. Dublini, 1942, v. I, p. 349.

2. For a list and description of the Mss used see P. Boehner, "The Text Tradition of Ockham's Ordinatio," in: *New Scholasticism*, XVI (July, 1942), 206–209.

3. Henry of Ghent, *Quodlibet* 6, q. 3 (Venetiis, 1608), t. I, 333 v: "Utrum impossibile quod attribuitur Deo respectu creaturarum ut quod Deus non possit facere in creaturis vel in rebus contradictoria esse simul, oriatur causaliter ex parte creaturae ut quod non potest fieri in creaturis, quia Deus non potest illud facere an potius econverso?" Duns Scotus, *Opus Oxoniense*, I, d. 43, q. unica (Vives, 1893) X, 728: "Utrum prima ratio impossibilitatis rei fiendae sit ex parte Dei vel ex parte rei factibilis?" William Ockham, *Ordinatio* (*Sent.*) I, d. 43, q. 2: "Utrum prius conveniat Deo non posse facere impossibile quam impossibili non posse fieri a Deo?" Peter Aureoli, *Sent.* I, d. 42, pars 2, art. 3 (Romae, 1596), 993: "An omnipotentia Dei sit causa quod res sint possibiles, vel econverso: quod est inquirere an res sint possibiles quia Deus potest facere, et impossibiles, quia non potest, vel potius econverso, ideo Deus non possit quod res sunt impossibiles."

4. Henry, *Quodl.* 6, q. 3, t. I, 333va.

5. Paulus dates the 6th Quodlibet in the Advent season of 1281 or the Easter tide of 1282; the 8th is placed in the Advent of 1284. Cf. Henri de Gand, Paris; Vrin, 1938, p. XVn.

6. *Quodl.* 8, q. 3, t. II, 7va.

7. Ex isto patet manifeste quod ipse habet dicere quod non quodlibet quod dicit respectum ad creaturam attribuitur Deo quia creaturae habent respectum ad ipsum, sed magis econverso; ideo attribuuntur creaturae talia relativa quia alia respectiva attribuuntur Deo (Text, C.).

8. *Summa Theol.* I, q. 15, a. 2; also q. 14, a. 6.

9. *Quodl.* 5, q. 3; t. I, 230 rss.

10. *Oxon.* 1, d. 35, q. unica.

11. *Ibid.*, n. 10; X, 549a: "Et ista via (sc. ipsius Scoti) videtur tenere istam propositionem quae videtur probabilis, quod relatio non naturaliter cognoscitur nisi cognito termino. Sed nec intellectus camparat ad aliquid nisi naturaliter prius cognito termino, quam propositionem non potest alia via tenere [sc. Henrici et Thomae] quia oportet quod dicat quod illa relatione, qua comparat istam intellectionem, comparet essentiam ad aliquid non prius cognitum naturaliter."

12. *Ibid.*, n. 5; 540a.

13. *Oxon.* 1, d. 43, q. unica, n. 5; X, 734a: Per ipsam potentiam sub ratione qua est omnipotentia, non habet objectum quod sit primo possibile, sed per intellectum divinum producentem in primo instanti illud in esse intelligibili, et intellectus non est formaliter potentia activa, qua Deus dicitur formaliter omnipotens, et tunc res producta ab intellectu divino in esse tali, scil. intelligibili in primo instanti naturae, habet seipsa esse possibile in secundo instanti naturae, quia seipsa formaliter non repugnat sibi esse, et seipsa formaliter repugnat habere esse necessarium ex se, in quibus duobus stat tota ratio possibilis, in quibus correspondet rationibus potentiae activae.

14. *Ibid.*, n. 6; 734b s.

15. Non videtur bene dictum quod intellectus divinus producit creaturam

in esse intelligibili, quia illud quod per aliquem actum nullum esse formaliter recipit, sed tantum denominatur denominatione extrinseca, non producitur per talem actum. Sed creatura per hoc quod intelligitur a Deo nihil formaliter recipit sed tantum denominatur quadam extrinseca denominatione (Text E).

16. *Ibid.*

17. Confer for instance Scotus' elaborate description of the order in God's knowledge, *Quodl.* q. 14, n. 14; XXVI, 52a–54a.

18. "Nominalisme," in: *DictThCath* XI, col. 762.

19. *Sent* I, d. 35, q. 4, D.

20. *Ibid.*

21. *Sent.* I, d. 35, q. 5, F.

22. *Ibid.*, d. 38, q. 1, M: Tenendum est quod Deus evidenter cognoscit omnia futura contingentia sed modum exprimere nescio.

23. *Op. cit.*, col. 761.

24. *Sent.* I, d. 36, q. 1, H.

25. *Ibid.*, d. 35, q. 5, F.

26. *Ibid.*: Ideo dico quod ideae sunt ponendae praecise ut sint exemplaria quaedam ad quae intellectus divinus aspiciens producat creaturas cuius ratio est, quia secundum beatum Augustinum ubi supra, propter hoc praecise ponendae sunt ideae in Deo, quia Deus est rationabiliter operans. Unde dicit beatus Augustinus quis audeat dicere Deum omnia irrationabiliter condidisse, quasi ad rationabiliter operantem non solum requiratur virtus productiva et operativa, sed etiam exemplar ad quod aspiciat in operando; et ideae non sunt ipsa virtus productiva vel causativa producentis; ergo sunt ipsa exemplaria, et ita ut sint exemplaria sunt ponenda.

27. *Ibid.*, D.

28. *Ibid.*, E.

29. Recall Ockham's doctrine regarding God's intuitive knowledge of nonexistents. *Quodl.* 6, q. 6. See also P. Boehner, "The Notitia Intuitiva of Non-Existents According to William Ockham," in: *Traditio*, 1 (1943), 223–275; Vignaux, in: *DictThCath* XI, col. 768.

30. *Sent.* I, d. 35, q. 5, R.

31. *Ibid.*, E.

32. *Ibid.*, G.

33. *Categ.*, c. 7, 7b 15 ss.

34. *Op. cit.*, I, p. 349.

35. J. Rickaby, *op. cit.*, p. 174: "Of previous writers, Descartes might have singled out Ockham to lend some countenance to his views." See also Willems, *op. cit.*, p. 420, esp. his fifth argument ex absurdis.

36. C. Bittle, *The Domain of Being*, pp. 74–75.

37. *Summa Theol.* I, q. 25, a. 3; *ibid.*, q. 46, a. 1, ad 1; confer also Zigliara, *Summa Philosophica*, 10 ed. (Paris, 1895), v. I, p. 350.

38. *Meta.* V, c. 12. 1019b 35.

39. *Ibid.*, c. 15, 1021a 15 ss.

40. *Categ.*, c. 7, "De ad aliquid."

41. Cfr. *Summa Theol.* I, q. 25, a. 3c; *ibid.*, q. 46, a. 1, ad 1; *De Potentia*, q. 1, a. 3c; *ibid.*, q. 3, a. 1, ad 2; *ibid.*, a. 14c; *ibid.*, a. 17, ad 10; *Sent.* I, d. 42, q. 2, a. 3, etc.

42. *Summa Theol.*, 1. c.

43. *Meta.* V, c. 12. 1019b 22 ss.

44. *Summa Theol.* I, q. 25, a. 3c; confer also *De Potentia*, q. 3, a. 17, ad 10, etc.

45. *De Potentia*, q. 1, a. 3c.

46. *Summa Theol.* I, q. 25, a. 3c.

47. Ockham, Text F.

48. *Ibid.*

49. *Ibid.*

48. *Ibid.*

50. *Quodl.* 6, q. 6.

51. Hickey, *op. cit.*, p. 352.

52. *De Potentia*, q. 3, a. 17, ad 10; *Summa Theol.* I, q. 46, a. 1, ad 1.

53. *Quodl.* 6, q. 6.

54. *Sent.* I, d. 35, q. 5, R.

13

OCKHAM, BURIDAN, AND NICHOLAS OF AUTRECOURT

Ernest A. Moody

THE PARISIAN STATUTES OF 1339 AND 1340

I. Ockhamism at Paris: The Problem

In the *Chartularium Universitatis Parisiensis*, under the dates September 25th, 1339, and December 29th, 1340, we find two statutes of the Faculty of Arts which are described as defense measures against the incursion of Ockhamist teachings into the Parisian university. The first of these statutes, while not condemning any doctrines, prohibits the "dogmatizing" of the teachings of William of Ockham, on the ground that his writings had not been authorized as admitted texts, and had not been examined for possible errors. The statute of 1340, on the other hand, explicitly condemns certain statements and practices, but does not attribute them to Ockham's doctrine or method. Nevertheless this decree does mention Ockham's name in a final paragraph, stating that the provisions of the previous year's statute are to remain in force.[1]

Does this statement mean that the statute of 1340, like that of the previous year, was aimed at doctrines stemming from William of Ockham? The historians of mediaeval philosophy have so interpreted it, and have been led thereby to the conclusion that the whole series of doctrinal condemnations of the following decade, specifically envisaging the teachings of Nicholas of Autrecourt and of John of Mirecourt, were anti-Ockhamist measures. On the assumption that the 1340 statute was aimed at Ockhamism, this conclusion is *prima facie* plausible, because it can be shown that at least one of the statements reproved by the 1340 statute had been made by Nicholas of Autrecourt, who in turn was the object of an official condemnation issued in 1346, his books being burned in Paris in 1347.[2]

The characterization of Nicholas of Autrecourt as an Ockhamist thus seems to find historical justification in the connection between the measures taken against Nicholas in 1340, 1346, and 1347, on the one hand, and the statute of 1339 on the other, which forbade the "dogmatizing" of Ockham's doctrines. This connection itself, however, rests entirely on the assumption that the last sentence of the 1340 statute, which calls attention to the fact that the previous year's statute is still in force, justifies the conclusion that the 1340 statute was itself directed against Ockhamist teachings. Since this assumption is by no means necessitated by the wording of the 1340 statute, and leads moreover to strange paradoxes when we attempt to account for other definite historical facts, it seems worth while to examine the relevant evidence in the case, and to consider the possibility of a totally different significance which can be ascribed to the final sentence of the 1340 statute.

Such an examination is of considerable importance for our understanding of the history and influence of Ockham's philosophical ideas and methods. If the scepticism of Nicholas of Autrecourt was the consequence and fruit of the doctrines of Ockham as a matter of historical fact and not merely as a theory of philosophical interpretation, the characterization of Ockham's doctrine as a destructive and corrosive force in late mediaeval philosophy can lay claim to a foundation in the facts of history.[3] It then becomes necessary to find an explanation for the fact that a group of influential and constructive thinkers, John Buridan, Nicholas Oresme, Albert of Saxony, John Gerson, and Peter d'Ailly, have always been regarded as "nominalists" and of the

Ockhamist school. This paradox is revealed in a concrete historical problem connected with the statute of 1340. John Buridan, who was rector of the university in that year, signed this statute which we know to have been directed, at least in part, against Nicholas of Autrecourt. Who, then, was the Ockhamist? Was it Nicholas, the destroyer and sceptic, against whom the statute was directed? Or was it Buridan, the defender of natural knowledge and initiator of a fruitful and stable period of scientific progress at Paris?

Michalski, taking note of Buridan's sincere and vigorous opposition to Nicholas of Autrecourt as evidenced in Buridan's own writings, concluded that he could not have been so much of an Ockhamist as had been supposed, and that in the 1340 statute he was expressing his opposition to the philosophical principles of Ockham. A similar view is taken by Gilson, who likewise seeks to preserve the Ockhamism of Nicholas of Autrecourt, by curtailing that of Buridan.[4]

But what evidence is there, in the historical facts accessible to us, for the assumption that Nicholas of Autrecourt was an Ockhamist? The extant writings of Nicholas, as Gilson himself concedes, give no indication of any direct doctrinal connection between Nicholas of Autrecourt and Ockham.[5] The writings of John Buridan, by contrast, exhibit direct influence of Ockham's teachings on almost every page, and, despite the modifications and differences to be noted between the teachings of the two men, these writings substantially justify the long established tradition which links the names of Buridan and the other "nominalists of Paris" with that of Ockham.[6] Hence the association of Nicholas of Autrecourt with Ockhamism seems to rest primarily on the hypothesis that the Parisian statute of 1340, which was directed against Nicholas, was an anti-Ockhamist measure. If this hypothesis turns out to be unjustified in the light of the relevant facts and documents, there will remain little tangible foundation for the customary characterization of Nicholas of Autrecourt as an Ockhamist. And in that event the problem of accounting for the position of John Buridan as opponent of Nicholas, and for the undisturbed ascendancy and prestige of the nominalist group

fathered by Buridan during the subsequent decades, will be fully
resolved.

The relevant documents, from which we can build up a picture
of the historical situation at Paris in the years 1339 and 1340,
include the two statutes of those years, the writings of Nicholas
of Autrecourt, the writings of John Buridan, and, finally, the
writings of William of Ockham which are thought to have
occasioned the controversies which gave rise to the statutes. The
clue to the whole problem, hitherto overlooked, is clearly suggested
in the writings of Nicholas of Autrecourt; for these writings reveal
the existence of a sustained and lively debate concerning one of
the most controversial and distinctive doctrines of William of
Ockham, carried on between Nicholas of Autrecourt and the
Franciscan Bernard of Arezzo. An examination of the statutes of
1339 and 1340, in the light of the situation revealed in Nicholas'
letters to Bernard, and in connection with relevant writings of
Ockham and of Buridan, can provide us with a much clearer
picture of the events giving rise to these statutes, and of the
significance to be attached to the final paragraph of the statute of
1340.

II. The Statute of 1339: Nicholas of
Autrecourt and Bernard of Arezzo

The statute of 1339 is a disciplinary measure, and not a condemnation of any specific doctrines or theses. It is in two main
paragraphs, the first of which prohibits the "dogmatizing" of the
doctrines of William of Ockham on the ground that his writings
had not been officially approved as texts *in usu scholarum*, while
the second paragraph complains of the tumults raised by auditors
at the disputations, and forbids them to argue without special
permission fron the Master holding the disputation. The main
provisions of the statute are as follows:

> Since therefore, by our predecessors, who were not unreasonably
> concerned as to the books to be read publicly or privately among us,
> there was issued a certain ordinance which we have sworn to observe;
> and because we ought not to read certain books not admitted by them
> or in common use elsewhere; and since in these times not a few persons
> have presumed to dogmatize the doctrine of William called Ockham,

in public, and also by holding secret assemblies on this subject in private places—despite the fact that this doctrine had not been admitted by those in authority, nor acknowledged elsewhere as customary, nor examined by us or by others to whom this might pertain, for which reason it does not appear to be free from suspicion—; for this reason we, mindful of our well-being, and considering the oath which we made to observe the above mentioned ordinance, decree that no person shall presume to dogmatize the said doctrine, by listening to it or lecturing on it publicly or in private, or by holding assemblies for disputation concerning the said doctrine, or by citing it in lectures or disputations. . . .

Furthermore, since it is clearly evident to us that in the disputations which take place in the rue de Fouarre, such abuse has developed, that Bachelors and others present at the said disputes dare to argue on their own authority, showing very little reverence toward the Masters who are disputing, and making such a tumult that the truth of the conclusion being debated cannot be arrived at, so that the said disputations are not in any way fruitful for the listening Scholars: we therefore decree that no Master, Bachelor or Scholar, should argue without the permission and license of Master holding the disputations. . . .[7]

The two paragraphs of his decree of 1339, taken together, give us a rather clear picture of the state of affairs leading to the issuance of the statute. A lively controversy, revolving around doctrines of William of Ockham, had swept through the Faculty of Arts, to the extent that everyone, from the Masters down to the beginning students, was taking sides and heckling or interrupting during the regular "solemn disputations" held in the rue de Fouarre. Since it takes two armies to make a battle, it is reasonable to suppose that this controversy over Ockham's doctrines had split the university into two factions, pro-Ockhamist and anti-Ockhamist. The statute of 1339 seems chiefly concerned to restore order and discipline, without taking sides in the controversy itself—a fact which perhaps indicates the the pro-Ockhamist faction was relatively strong, and included in its number some of the more influential and respected members of the faculty. John Buridan may well have been one of these, since his writings, many of which represent lectures he had been giving since 1327 or earlier, show very marked influence of the doctrines and logical method of William of Ockham. From this we can at least draw one conclusion—if John Buridan had been peacefully teaching Ockhamist philosophical doctrines for twelve or fifteen years prior to 1339, we cannot ascribe the outbreak of controversy and disorder on the Faculty of Arts, in 1339 to any *sudden* incursion of Ockhamist teachings into the university.

It is the writings of Nicholas of Autrecourt which give us a clue to the nature of the controversy of 1339. Of these, there are extant only his letters to Bernard of Arezzo and to the Egidius who had come to Bernard's support in his debate with Nicholas, and two other writings recently edited by Father J. R. O'Donnell —the treatise *Exigit ordo executionis*, and a question *Utrum visio creaturae rationalis beatificabilis per Verbum possit intendi naturaliter*. In addition, there are two schedules of reproved theses of Nicholas, issued at Avignon in 1346, published in the *Chartularium* and reprinted by J. Lappe in his edition of Nicholas' letters.[8] Of most direct interest for our problem are these letters, and certain portions of the *cedulae* of retractation. A study of these will reveal the nature of the controversy over Ockhamism which gave rise to the disciplinary statute of 1339.

In his first letter to Bernard of Arezzo, Nicholas of Autrecourt tells us very explicitly what doctrines were being defended by Bernard, and attacked by him.

> For I read in a certain book which you were reading in the school of the Friars Minor, the following propositions which you conceded, to whoever wished to uphold them, as true. The first, which is set down by you in the first book of the Sentences, Dist. 3, Qu. 4, is this: *Clear intuitive cognition is that by which we judge a thing to exist, whether it exists or does not exist.* Your second proposition, which is set down in the place mentioned above, is of this sort: *The consequence, 'An object does not exist, therefore it is not seen,' is not valid; nor does this hold, 'This is seen, therefore this exists.'* . . . The third proposition set down in the same place is this: *Intuitive cognition does not necessarily require the existing thing.*[9]

Now these theses, which on Nicholas' testimony were being defended by the Franciscan Bernard of Arezzo, in the Franciscan school at the university, are theses for which William of Ockham is famed, and for which he is attacked even in our own time, as he was in his time. Indeed, Bernard's third proposition is verbally the same as one which was taken from Ockham's works by the Avignon commission appointed by Pope John XXII to examine his doctrines.

> Further, he asserts that intuitive cognition is not of itself necessarily of the existent any more than of the non-existent, and does not any more refer to existence than to non-existence. Every absolute thing distinct in place and subject from another absolute thing can, by divine power, exist when the other absolute thing is destroyed. But intuitive vision, both sensitive and intellectual, is an absolute thing distinct in place and subject from the object seen, so that if I see intuitively a star existing in the heavens, this intuitive vision, whether sensitive or intellectual, is distinguished in place and subject from the object seen. Therefore this vision can remain, the star being destroyed.[10]

Recent efforts to prove that Ockham was a sceptic have been based precisely on this doctrine that intuitive cognition does not necessarily require the existence of its object.[11] Nicholas of Autrecourt took the same point of view as these recent critics of Ockham, and used very much the same method of argument in seeking to show that his position leads to scepticism. For Bernard, like Ockham, asserted that it is only when the intuitive cognition is caused supernaturally, or by God alone without any secondary cause, that its existence does not require the existence of its object. And Bernard, like Ockham, held that we can validly judge, on the basis of an intuitive cognition, that its object exists as present before us, by the principles of *natural* causation, even though it is supernaturally possible for God to produce such an intuitive cognition in us without mediation of the object. Nicholas himself tells us this, in quoting Bernard's argument in order to refute it.

> But perhaps you will say, as it seems to me you wanted to suggest in a certain disputation over at the Preaching Friars, that, although from the fact of seeing it cannot be inferred that the object seen exists, when

that seeing is produced by a supernatural cause or conserved by it; nevertheless when it is produced precisely by natural causes, with the general influence of the first agent, concurring then it can be inferred.

Contra: When from some antecedent, if produced by some agent, a certain consequent could not be inferred by a formal and evident inference; then from that antecedent, no matter by what thing it be produced, that consequent could not be inferred.[12]

Bernard's distinction between an intuitive cognition as *naturally* caused by its object, in which case the object must exist, and an intuitive cognition caused *supernaturally* without the existence of the object, is one which Nicholas of Autrecourt will in no manner admit. It is, however, a distinction made very explicitly by Ockham, in the following passage from his commentary on the second book of the *Sentences*.

So it appears, then, that by intuitive cognition we judge a thing to exist when it exists, and this generally, whether the intuitive cognition be caused naturally, or supernaturally by God alone. For if it be caused naturally, then it cannot exist, unless the object exists as present and within a determinate distance.... If however it be supernatural, as for example if God should cause in me an intuitive cognition of some object existing at Rome, I could immediately judge, through having this intuitive cognition of it, that that which I see and intuit, is existent, just as well as if that cognition were had naturally. If you say that the object is not in this case present nor at a suitable distance, I reply: Although intuitive cognition cannot be caused naturally except if the object is present at a determinate distance, nevertheless it can, supernaturally.[13]

These passages are illuminating, not only because they show that Nicholas of Autrecourt was in definite opposition to the doctrine of Ockham, as defended by Bernard, but because they make evident the fundamental point of opposition, on which hinges the decision as to whether it was Nicholas who was undermining the metaphysical foundations of knowledge, or Ockham and Bernard. This fundamental issue is whether the criterion of necessity and evidence, on which the natural sciences are to be based, must be absolute and of a strictly transcendental order like the principle of contradiction, or whether it is of a qualified or conditional order involving the distinction between the *naturally possible* and the *supernaturally possible*. Nicholas of Autrecourt holds rigorously to the first view, arguing that *if* we admit that an effect (be it intuitive cognition or any other natural occurrence) can be supernaturally produced without its natural cause, then we have no right to posit natural causes for any effects whatever. Bernard of Arezzo, following Ockham and indeed following the traditional scholastic view, denies this consequence, and admits an order of natural evidence and necessity *secundum quid* or *ex suppositione naturae*. That this was the basic philosophical issue, underlying the controversy between Nicholas and the defenders of Ockham, receives interesting confirmation from the works of John Buridan, whose refutations and criticism of Nicholas of Autrecourt will be considered in due course.

Our inquiry has revealed, so far, the following definite facts. First, that in the year 1339 there existed, in the Faculty of Arts, a lively controversy over the doctrine of William of Ockham, carried on so generally, and with so much spirit and excitement, that it was upsetting the discipline of the university and causing tumultuous free-for-all debates at the disputations in the rue de Fouarre. Secondly, we have been able to identify Bernard of Arezzo as a defender of the Ockhamist position, and Nicholas of Autrecourt as a critic and opponent of the position of Ockham represented by Bernard. Finally we may conclude that although the statute of 1339 does not take sides on the controversy in its doctrinal aspect, it could be interpreted as something of a rebuke to Bernard of Arezzo, who apparently had been guilty of "dogmatizing" Ockham's doctrine, and to that extent it may have seemed like an encouragement to Nicholas of Autrecourt. If he took it as such, it was his error and misfortune, as we shall learn from our examination of the statute of the following year, issued in December 1340.

III. The Statute of 1340: Buridan, Ockham, and Nicholas of Autrecourt

In the year 1340 John Buridan became Rector of the University of Paris. In his capacity as Rector, he signed the statute of December 29th, 1340, which, in very strong language, denounced certain members of the Faculty of Arts for their "pernicious subtleties," for "seeking to be wiser than is fitting," and for introducing a practice of construing the texts of all the "authors" in their bare literal sense without taking account of the authors' intentions. As its introductory paragraph clearly shows, this statute of 1339 is not merely a disciplinary measure, applying generally to all members of the Faculty, but a condemnation of specific statements and methods being asserted or employed by some definite individual, or group, within the Faculty.

> Each one is duty bound, to the best of his ability, to avoid errors and in every way to block the path leading to them, especially when, by reason of such errors, knowledge of the truth may disappear. Now it has recently come to our attention that many in our Faculty of Arts have given themselves over to the pernicious subtleties of certain ones, and, not basing themselves on a firm rock, but seeking to be wiser than is fitting, are striving to sow certain unhealthy seeds from which intolerable errors, not only in philosophy but also with respect to divine Scripture, may in the future arise. Wherefore, wishing to combat this so pestilential disease, we have brought together, as best we could, the impious foundations and errors of those (certain ones), concerning which we issue the following regulations. . . .[14]

What are these errors? The main body of the statute contains six counts, most of them condemning the practice of interpreting and evaluating statements of philosophic authors according to their purely literal or grammatical sense, and without construing them in the sense obviously intended by the author. In each case, after laying down the specific prohibition, the statute adds its own explanation, following on a *quia* or *quoniam*, of the logical ground for its objection to the practice in question. It has been assumed by most of the historians of mediaeval philosophy, as it was assumed by the editors of the *Chartularium* when they supplied a title for this statute, that the methods of textual interpretation to which the statute objects, are those of William of Ockham. The most obvious basis for this assumption is the fact, previously mentioned, that this statute, in its last sentence, reminds the members of the Faculty of Arts that the previous year's statute prohibiting the "dogmatizing" of Ockham's doctrine, is to remain in force. That this is not the correct interpretation of that sentence, is the thesis of this paper; but the presence of the sentence in the statute does account for the assumption, which has been generally made, that the statute as a whole is anti-Ockhamist.

There is, nevertheless, one positive and definite indication, in the body of this statute, of one of the persons whose teaching practices it condemned. The sixth count of the indictment gives us this clue, as follows:

> Further, that no one should assert, without a distinction or exposition, that Socrates and Plato, or God and a creature, are nothing; because those words sound very badly if taken at face value, and because such a proposition has one sense that is false, namely if the negation implicit in this word 'nothing' is understood to apply not only to being, in its singular sense, but also to beings taken plurally.[15]

Now we find, in the revocation by Nicholas of Autrecourt of his errors and heretical statements, made at Avignon in 1346, the following sentence:

> Further, I said in a certain disputation that God and a creature are not anything.—False and scandalous according to the way the words sound.[16]

This serves to identify Nicholas of Autrecourt as one of the group being attacked by the statute, as indeed the editors of the *Chartularium* recognized by making the identification in a footnote. Now in view of the fact, revealed by our examination of Nicholas' controversy with Bernard of Arezzo, that Nicholas had been opposing the Ockhamist theses defended by Bernard, this identification of Nicholas as one of those condemned by the 1340 statute gives a *prima facie* improbability to the assumption that this statute was directed against the Ockhamist group in the Faculty of Arts. A further difficulty with that assumption, already mentioned, is the fact that the statute was signed by Buridan, who has always been regarded as at least a "moderate Ockhamist," and who, as we shall see, was definitely opposed to the position taken by Nicholas of Autrecourt against Bernard of Arezzo. So the tangible evidence provided by the document, and by John Buridan's having signed it, is against the assumption that it is an anti-Ockhamist measure.

What about the internal evidence provided by the other five counts of the statute? Do the methods of textual interpretation, therein condemned, find any support in what Ockham himself has to say on the subject? This is surely a relevant consideration, though few seem to have taken the trouble to consult Ockham's writings in order to learn the answer.[17] Let us then examine these five items of the statute, and compare them, one by one, with relevant statements of Ockham. The first item of the statute reads as follows:

> That no Masters, Bachelors, or Scholars lecturing in the Faculty of Arts at Paris shall dare to say, concerning any famous proposition of the author whose book they are reading, that it is unconditionally false, or that it is literally false, if they believe that the author, in stating it, had a true understanding; but that they should either concede it, or distinguish the true sense from the false sense; because the propositions of the Bible, for the same reason, would have to be denied by such literal interpretation, which is dangerous. And because discourse does not have any force, except by institution and by the common usage of authors or other people, therefore the force of discourse is such as the authors commonly use it and as the subject matter requires, since words are to be interpreted through the subject matter.[18]

What is forbidden, in the above paragraph, is obviously not the practice of distinguishing between the literal meaning of a sentence, and the meaning intended by the author, but rather the practice of failing to take any account of this distinction, and of judging the truth of the sentence by the literal criterion alone. Anyone familiar with Ockham's writings is bound to recognize that such a distinction of senses, as is recommended by this statute, was habitually made by Ockham. But he does not only practice this method of interpreting authors by their intentions, or by the truth of the subject matter, rather than by their mere words—he also preaches it.

> The third utility of logic is the ability to perceive the force of words and the proper manner of speech. For by this art one can easily know what is asserted by the authors in a literal sense, and what not in a literal sense but according to a common usage of speech; or what, according to the intention of the speaker, is asserted literally, and what is asserted metaphorically—which is of the greatest importance for all those who study the sayings of others, because he who takes all the statements of the authors in a literal sense or according to the force of the word, falls into many errors and inexplicable difficulties.[19]

The second clause of the 1340 indictment reads as follows:

> Further, that no one shall say that every proposition, which would be false according to the personal supposition of the terms, is false without qualification or by the force of words; because this error leads to the previous error, for authors frequently use other suppositions.[20]

The meaning of this sentence may be obscure to those unfamiliar with the distinctions of the suppositions of terms, as established by Peter of Spain's *Summulae logicales* in the 13th century, which was used as a standard text-book of logic in the universities. Three suppositions were usually recognized: a term in a proposition will have "personal supposition" when it is taken as standing for the things it means, as when we say "Man is an animal"; it is taken with "simple supposition" if taken as designating the concept, intention, or "idea" *by* which its meaning is instituted, as when we say " 'Man' is a universal"; it is, finally, said to have "material supposition" when taken to stand precisely for itself as a word, as when we say " 'Man' is a three-letter word." These three modes of supposition were recognized by Ockham, by Buridan, and by all the scholastics of the time. The notion that no proposition is true which is not true if construed with *suppositio personalis*, may possibly have been upheld by Nicholas of Autre-court; it was certainly not upheld by Ockham. The following statement from his logical commentary makes this clear enough.

> And ignorance of the intention of Aristotle in this book makes many modern people err, who believe that he wishes many things here stated to be understood for things, which however he wishes to be understood for words only, and proportionally for intentions or concepts in the soul.[21]

The third count, in the 1340 statute, reproves those who fail to distinguish the senses of a proposition quoted from a text, and thereby lead their pupils into error.

> Further, that no one shall say that no proposition is to be distinguished; because this leads to the above mentioned errors, since if a pupil accepts one meaning of a proposition, and the teacher understands another, the pupil will be under a false impression, until the proposition is distinguished. Likewise if one party to a debate takes one meaning, and the respondent understands another meaning, the disputation will be purely verbal, if no distinction is made.[22]

The quotations already given from Ockham should suffice to show that he is in favor of making distinctions between diverse senses of a proposition, and a glance at any of his works should convince anyone that he practiced what he preached. The following quotation from his *De sacramento altaris* is relevant to this third count of the 1340 statute, and, in its reference to the bad results of applying literal criteria to the interpretation of Scripture, to the first count of the statute, as well.

> And it is not unfitting to expound their statements (i.e., those of the doctors), since many statements of Holy Scripture as well need exposition also; because many things are not true according to the literal force of the word, but according to the meaning which we ought to have, they are most true.[23]

The fourth prohibition of the 1340 statute makes a similar point, and concludes with a reference to Aristotle which appears in almost the same words in a passage from Ockham's *De sacramento altaris* concerned with the same subject. The statute reads as follows:

> Further, that no one shall say that no proposition is to be conceded unless it is true in its literal sense; because to say this, leads to the aforesaid errors, since the Bible and the authors do not always use words according to their proper sense. Therefore one ought rather to attend to the subject matter, than to the proper forms of speech, in affirming or denying statements; for a disputation concerned with the forms of speech, and accepting no proposition other than in its proper sense, is nothing but a sophistical disputation. Dialectical and doctrinal disputations, which aim at discovery of the truth, *have very little concern for names*.[24]

Turning to Ockham, we read the following:

> And therefore Aristotle cared very little about the manner of speech, from which the fact was noted, as appears in the first book of the *Physics*, that *he had very little concern for names*. And hence many fall into diverse errors, on account of the fact that they interpret the texts of the ancients according to the literal sound, and according to the proper forms of speech, which however the ancients did not intend.[25]

The fifth item of the prohibition is reminiscent of an often quoted, and even more often misunderstood, passage from Ockham's *Commentary on the Sentences*, and at first sight it seems to justify the theory that the statute is directed against Ockhamist doctrine.

> Further, that no one shall say that there is no knowledge of things which are not signs, that is, which are not terms or statements; because in the sciences we use terms for things, which we cannot carry with us to the disputations. Hence we have knowledge concerning things, even though it is by means of terms or statements.[26]

The passage in Ockham, of which this sentence is reminiscent' has often been quoted, by Prantl and other historians, as an indication of Ockham's "nominalism." If it is examined, however, according to the principle of trying to grasp the intention of the author, rather than that of taking a sentence out of its context and construing it verbally, it will be seen that Ockham's position is not that which the above item of the statute condemns, but is on the contrary the position acknowledged by the authors of the statute and used by them in explaining the sense in which knowledge is of things other than signs. The passage from Ockham occurs in the course of his discussion of the distinction between *scientia rationalis*, or logic, and *scientia realis*, or the speculative sciences. We cannot base this distinction, he says, on the statement that the objects known by the logician are propositions, and those known by the physicist are things; for propositions are known by the physicist in the same sense that they are known by the logician. In this sense, all knowledge is of propositions. It is not in this way that "rational science" is distinguished from "real science," but rather by the fact that the propositions of logic are composed of terms that signify or stand for terms, while the propositions of a real science are composed of terms that signify, and stand for, things outside the mind.

> To the second principal argument, I say that a real science is not always of things as of that which is immediately known, but of others which however stand for the things. To understand this, and because of many things already said and to be said, for the benefit of those untrained in logic, it is to be known that any science whatever, whether it be a real or rational science, is only of propositions as that which is known, because it is only propositions which are known.[27]

This last sentence, above quoted, has sometimes been presented as an indication that Ockham acknowledged no objects of knowledge except words. Perhaps those against whom the 1340 statute was directed, did hold this view. But the rest of the discussion from which this quotation is taken, clearly shows that Ockham did not share this opinion.

> To the form of the argument I say, that for a science to be of things, can be understood in three ways. Either because the thing itself is what is known, and in this manner no science is of substantial things,

chiefly because only what is a complex is known, but a complex is not something outside the soul, except perhaps as in the spoken word or in some similar sign. In another sense, that things are parts of that which is known, and in this sense it is not necessary that a real science be of things outside. In the third way, that the things are what the parts of that which is known *stand for*, and in this sense a real science is of things. . . .[28]

As this passage indicates, Ockham's reason for denying that knowledge is of things, as immediate object, is the fact that he uses the term *knowledge* in the precise sense of that cognitive act by which we assent to the *true*. Since it is propositions, rather than things or simple terms, which are properly said to be true or false, it follows that it is propositions which are known, in this precise sense of the word "know." But that *by* which we know a proposition to be true, is the thing or the things signified by its terms, and for which the terms stand, in the proposition. As the authors of the 1340 statute say, knowledge is *mediately* of things, even if immediately of propositions, because the terms stand for things, and because we use terms for things which, as they say, "we cannot carry with us to the disputations." The conclusion of Ockham's discussion makes this same point a second time.

Briefly therefore, according to the intention of the Philosopher, it should be noted that a real science is not distinguished from a rational science by this—that a real science is of things in such manner that the things themselves are the propositions known, or parts of the propositions known, and that a rational science is not of things in this manner; but by this fact, that the parts, i.e., the terms, of the propositions known by a real science, *stand for things*, whereas it is not thus with the terms of the propositions known by a rational science.[29]

Ockham's position on this matter is very explicitly characterized by Robert Holkot, who did not agree with him. In Holkot's *Commentary on the Sentences* we find the following:

Concerning the act of belief, whether it is the complex itself, or the thing signified by the complex. There is among some people a doubt about this, and Ockham holds that universally, the object of science and of opinion and of faith, and of any such assent, is the thing signified by the complex, and not the complex itself.[30]

It seems clear enough, from the passages quoted, together with Holkot's testimony, that the sense in which the authors of the 1340 statute insist that knowledge is of things, is just that sense in which Ockham understands it to be of things—in the sense that the terms composing the proposition known, *stand for things.* If Nicholas of Autrecourt was the man who contended that there is no object of knowledge other than the proposition itself, it is possible that it was Holkot's position that he was defending. But the theory that knowledge is of things by mediation of the supposition of the terms, whatever be the merits or demerits of this theory, was acknowledged in common by Ockham and by the authors of the statute of 1340, as the quotations indicate.

Our examination of the content of this statute reveals, then, that the views expressed by its authors are substantially those expressed by Ockham, and that the practice of interpreting texts in their literal sense only, rather than according to the intentions of the author, is condemned as vigorously by Ockham as by the statute itself. As Michalski has shown, Buridan's remarks on this subject in his *Summulae logicae,* show that he too is in essential agreement with the viewpoint of the statute of 1340.[31] But we may now draw the conclusion, which is the opposite to that drawn by Michalski, that Buridan's readiness to sign the statute of 1340 put no strain on his Ockhamist sympathies, since the viewpoint embodied in the statute was very much the viewpoint of Ockham himself.

We are thus left with one definite indication of the person or group against whom this statute was directed—for we know that Nicholas of Autrecourt was the man indicted on the sixth count of that document. Was it then Nicholas, and his followers or partisans, who practiced the method of purely literal and grammatical textual interpretation? Of this we might have definite evidence, if a manuscript had survived of an exposition of Aristotle's *Politics,* which he gave at some time prior to the enactment of this statute of 1340. The terms in which he announced this series of lectures are preserved in the *cedula* of revocation prepared at Avignon, in which document he was reproved for his flippant manner of advertising his lectures, and for proving, by sophistical arguments from the aristotelian text, that robbery is a just act.[32]

Did Nicholas, in his exposition of the text of Aristotle's *Politics*, draw his sophistical and immoral conclusions from Aristotle's statements, by the method of purely verbal interpretation which the statute of 1340 so severely condemned? It seems very plausible that this was the case, especially since we know that Nicholas was envisaged by the sixth count of the statute. To admit into a disputation no statements other than in their precise literal sense, would seem to be an appropriate counterpart to Nicholas' more famous refusal to concede any proposition not deducible from the principle of contradiction. Both of these practices might well be stigmatized in the words of the 1340 statute, as "pernicious subtleties sowing unhealthy seeds from which intolerable errors can arise in philosophy and theology," characteristic of people who "seek to be wiser than they ought to be."

It is certainly more reasonable to attribute these sophistical traits of argument to Nicholas, than to Bernard of Arezzo or to the Egidius who came to Bernard's support in the controversy with Nicholas. The arguments which Nicholas restates, as those of Bernard, as well as the arguments against Nicholas advanced by Egidius, are of a traditional sort, and rest on the assumption of a natural causal order whereby substances can be known through the perceptible effects in which they are involved as causes.[33]

The evidence so far examined seems, then, to be against the assumption that the statute of 1340 was anti-Ockhamist in its intent, and against the assumption that Nicholas of Autrecourt was condemned for teaching Ockham's doctrine. On the contrary, it would seem that the statute of 1340, aimed against the party of Nicholas of Autrecourt, amounted to something of a victory for the Ockhamist faction of whom Bernard of Arezzo was a member, if not a leader. If Nicholas had interpreted the disciplinary statute of 1339 as a victory for him, and as a defeat for Bernard, his day of triumph was not a long one; for the statute of 1340, inculpating

Nicholas himself directly, and turning his victory to defeat, was by the same token a belated triumph for Bernard of Arezzo.

IV. Buridan and Nicholas of Autrecourt

We have yet to consider the views of John Buridan, as bearing on the controversy between Nicholas of Autrecourt and Bernard of Arezzo. In attempting to estimate Buridan's position in the Ockhamist controversies of 1339 and 1340, we can presume, from the fact that he signed the 1340 statute as Rector, and from the fact that his own doctrines have close affinity with those of Ockham, that his sympathies in the controversy were on the side of the defenders of Ockham, such as Bernard of Arezzo, and opposed to the position of Nicholas of Autrecourt. This opposition to Nicholas, at least, is clearly confirmed by certain passages in Buridan's own writings.

In Buridan's philosophical works we find two definite places in which he takes account of the doctrines of Nicholas of Autrecourt—one of them is in his *Questions on the Physics*, where he undertakes a very lengthy and detailed refutation of Nicholas' argument against the possibility of knowing causes, or substances, by their effects; and the other is in his *Questions on the Metaphysics*, where he deals briefly with Nicholas' position, but adds a highly significant observation concerning the root error underlying Nicholas' scepticism.

The reference in the *Questions on the Physics* occurs in Question 4 of the first book, where one of the initial arguments is taken, almost *verbatim*, from Nicholas' first letter to Bernard of Arezzo. Buridan's restatement of the argument is in these words:

Again, I revert to arguing that one thing cannot be made known from another, because there is not an evident consequence from one thing to another, on account of the fact that a consequence is not evident except through reduction to the first principle, and such a consequence cannot be reduced to the first principle, because the first principle is founded in contradiction, and a contradiction must be of the same thing with respect to the same, according to the thing as well as according to the name, whence if A and B are diverse things, it would be no contradiction for A to exist and for B not to exist;

therefore it is not an evident consequence to say, 'A exists, therefore B exists,' and thus it is for any other things you please, regardless of how close a relationship they may have between them.[34]

This argument is easily identified in Nicholas of Autrecourt's letter to Bernard, where it is given in these words:

In connection with these statements I laid down one conclusion, among others, which was this: From the fact that some thing is known to exist, it cannot be inferred evidently, by evidence reduced to the first principle or to the certitude of the first principle, that another thing exists.

In such a consequence, in which one thing is inferred from another, the consequent would not be really identical with the antecedent, nor with a part of what is signified by the antecedent; therefore it follows that such a consequence would not be evidently known, by evidence of the first principle, as described. The antecedent is conceded and posited by the adversary; the consequence is clear from the definition of contradiction, which is an affirmation and negation of one thing with respect to the same thing, etc. Since then the consequent is not really identical with the antecedent or with a part of the antecedent, it is manifest that the opposite of the consequent and the antecedent might be true at the same time, but this would not be affirmation and denial of one thing with respect to the same thing, etc.[35]

Buridan's refutation of this argument is extremely lengthy, and cannot be given here. He rejects, in the first place, Nicholas' initial assumption that all concepts (or incomplex cognitions) arise from immediate sense perceptions by way of *inference*; it is not by inference that our concepts of substance arise in us, but by a natural abstractive act of the intellect, of a nondiscursive character. Even against the argument as formulated by Nicholas, Buridan seeks to develop a refutation, and to prove that the existence of one thing can be demonstrated through the existence of another thing. Throughout his discussion he constantly refers to those whose views he is refuting, as contemporaries for whom he has no great respect, calling them "aliqui opinantes," "isti," "illi decepti," and so forth.[36]

It is in his *Questions on the Metaphysics* that Buridan touches on the fundamental issue involved in Nicholas of Autrecourt's scepticism, in a manner that casts considerable light on the background of the fourteenth century formulation of the problem of knowledge, which was intimately associated with that of the metaphysical foundation of the principle of causality. The argument drawn from Nicholas, in this first question on the second book of the *Metaphysics*, is substantially the same as the one already treated in the *Physics*, to the effect that knowledge of causes through effects, or of effects through causes, is impossible, since there is no evident inference from the existence of one thing to the existence of another. Against this Buridan argues briefly as follows:

> To the other, I say that effects are known through the cause *propter quid*, because the cause is better known even to us, than *why* the effect is. Likewise the cause is known through the effect, with respect to its existence (*quantum ad quia est*), because the effect bears a certain likeness to the cause, and can therefore represent the cause, in conjunction with the natural inclination of the intellect toward truth. When it is further said that one thing cannot be known inferentially through another, I deny it, and I say that there are almost an infinite number of principles known *per se*, either through sense or through experience or through inclusion of terms, without it being required that they be demonstrated through the first principle; now in the *Posterior Analytics* Aristotle proves that the indemonstrable principles are almost as many as are the demonstrable conclusions.[37]

In actual fact, Nicholas' arguments, taken in their precise form, and under the exact conditions in which they are presented, are by no means refuted by Buridan's arguments, either here or in the *Physics*. It is improbable that Buridan considered his refutations to be conclusive, on this basis. For if, as Nicholas contended, no proposition is to be admitted as evident unless its contradictory is *absolutely* impossible, then it would follow that most, if not all the principles of natural philosophy, which assume causes of observable occurrences, and account for accidents in terms of substances, would not be necessary or evident by this rigid criterion.

The root difficulty in all these discussions, which deserves more serious study than it has received in modern interpretations of fourteenth century thought, arises from the necessity of admitting the separability of accidents from substances, in the case of the Sacrament of the Altar. Though this be a supernatural case, it has definite metaphysical consequences which cannot be eliminated by merely overlooking them; for if, as Aristotle seems to have held, an accident is not any other *thing* than a substance, but is rather a way in which a substance exists, like the grin of the Cheshire cat which is nothing other than the cat grinning, then the traditional formulation of the Eucharistic doctrine involves a simple or metaphysical impossibility. To avoid this, it was necessary to modify Aristotle's analysis, and to admit some kind of separability and proper subsistence, for accidents, distinct from that of their substantial subjects, as the condition of the *possibility* of the supernatural case. There is a Question in Buridan's *Metaphysics* which presents this dilemma with great clarity, and with full consciousness of its far reaching consequences in the foundations of metaphysics.[38]

This "real" distinction of accidents from substances, required as ground of the possibility of a separable existence of accidents, made in one way or another by all the major scholastic theologians and philosophers, including St. Thomas, Duns Scotus, Ockham, Buridan, and Nicholas of Autrecourt himself. The obvious question, generated by this distinction, was not overlooked by any of these men. If the qualities and other accidents which are our only means of apprehending sensible things, can terminate our apprehension by their own proper being, without their having to be accidents or appearances *of* substances, in the supernatural case, how can we be certain that this is not so in all cases? Why posit substances, if it is accidents, and not substances, that terminate our perceptions as the *things perceived*?

Nicholas of Autrecourt earned for himself the title of "the mediaeval Hume," by drawing the conclusion that substances are useless fictions, since we can neither perceive them by our senses, nor infer their existence from the existence of the sensible accidents that we do not perceive. In abandoning substances, he quite

logically dispensed with causality; and in abandoning causality
he dispensed with causal explanations, and consequently with all
the natural sciences which demonstrate through causes. He was
left, like Hume, with only two types of cognition: the tautological
certainties of the principles of identity and of contradiction, and
the subjective certainty of awareness of his own acts of thinking,
and of perception of the qualities apprehended by his five senses.[39]

The alternative to Nicholas' drastic solution of the problem was
to admit an order of conditional or hypothetical necessity and
certainty, according to which the causal principles of natural
explanation, and the dependence of sensible accidents on substantial subjects, were conceived to be necessary *secundum quid*,
or "on the supposition of nature" (*ex suppositione naturae*).
This was the solution adopted by St. Thomas Aquinas as well as
by most other scholastics unwilling to abandon Aristotle's empiri-
cism in favor of a Platonist epistemology of separated forms.
We have seen how Ockham, and likewise Bernard of Arezzo,
applied this "supposition of nature" to the problem of intuitive
cognition, by arguing that such cognition cannot be had *naturally*
without its object being present and existing as cause, even though
it might be had *supernaturally* without the presence of an object,
through the power of God. This is of course only a particular
case of the general problem, since the intuitive cognition is related
to its object in the manner of an accident to a substantial cause.

Now Buridan's refutations of Nicholas' arguments hold only
insofar as he makes the basic hypothesis of the natural order,
which Nicholas himself, by reason of the supernatural case, will
not concede to be an evident hypothesis. Buridan is not unaware of
this gulf which separates him from Nicholas, and which, we
might suggest, separates the tradition of mediaeval Aristotelianism
from the tradition of Descartes or of Hume. For at the end of
his main discussion of this Question in his *Metaphysics*, he refers
to Nicholas' position in these pointed and reproving terms:

It is therefore concluded, as a corollary, that certain people speak
very evilly, seeking to destroy the natural and the moral sciences on
the ground that their principles and conclusions do not for the most

part possess absolute evidence, but can become false through possible supernatural instances; for evidence in the unqualified sense is not required for such sciences, but the above mentioned types of evidence *secundum quid*, or *ex suppositione*, are sufficient. Whence it is well said by Aristotle that the accuracy of mathematics is not to be looked for in every science.[40]

As Gilson has well recognized, the world did not have to wait until the sixteenth and seventeenth centuries to become aware of the problem of the metaphysical foundations of the physical sciences.[41] That Aristotle's philosophy made no provision for supernatural exceptions to the natural order, so that it could not be taken over without profound modifications of the concepts of substance, causality, and natural necessity, was no news to the philosophers and theologians of the Middle Ages. Even in the time of St. Thomas Aquinas, the lines of the battle were drawn; for those who argued, in the thirteenth century, against the distinction between a natural and a supernatural order, were already eliminating causes and substances from the created world and reducing physics to theology. But to preserve an order of nature, subject to God, as a free creative cause of all being who is able to produce natural effects without mediation of natural causes, required recognition of a radical distinction between science and metaphysics—the unqualified certainty and necessity of the latter, as expressed in the principle of contradiction and in the concept of the "logically possible," could not be ascribed to the proper principles, and "laws of nature," on which the scientist founds his explanations. Because the laws of nature are metaphysically contingent, they are scientifically necessary only by a hypothetical necessity—*ex suppositione naturae*. Thus an ineradicable element of *hypothesis* is introduced into the science of nature, and, as its counterpart, the principle that all scientific hypotheses require empirical verification, and retain an element of probability which cannot be completely eliminated.

While Thomas Aquinas was certainly aware of the modifications required in Aristotle's theory of scientific evidence and necessity, it remained for the fourteenth century to develop the full implications of these modifications in their scientific consequences, both theoretical and methodological. The reformulation of traditional logic, and of the basic concepts and principles of physical explanation, provided by William of Ockham, was undertaken as a consequence of these necessary modifications in the metaphysical foundations of natural knowledge, and as an attempt to reconstitute the sciences on a basis consistent with these metaphysical conditions. It was on the foundation thus provided, that John Buridan and the so-called "nominalists of Paris" developed the fertile scientific tradition which, as Pierre Duhem has indicated, was the starting point of what we call modern physical science.[42]

The controversy between Nicholas of Autrecourt and Berndar of Arezzo, understood in the light of Buridan's discussions of the basic metaphysical issues involved, brings to a focus a problem, and a dilemma, which has remained at the very heart of philosophy ever since. The scepticism of Nicholas of Autrecourt is clearly the consequence of his uncompromising requirement that scientific principles be of an absolute evidence and necessity such that God himself must conform to them, a demand which reduces science to the tautologies of formal logic, or to those of pure mathematics. The alternative, chosen by Ockham and Buridan and Bernard of Arezzo, is to accept conditional evidence and hypothetical necessity as sufficient for natural knowledge, the power of logic and mathematics being that of instruments for the analysis of a natural order to be found only through observation and experiment. From the standpoint of Nicholas of Autrecourt, such a compromise with contingency is the greater scepticism. Such was the dilemma of fourteenth century philosophy. But the problem itself was not invented by Ockham any more than by Nicholas of Autrecourt—it was common to all, entailed by the fact that the eternal, necessary, and predictable natural world of Aristotle had been replaced by the created, contingent, and only conditionally predictable natural order compatible with the Christian Faith.

V. The Meaning of the Statute of 1340
There remains only one piece to be fitted into our historical picture, to complete the solution of our puzzle. This is the question

of the significance of the final sentence of the statute of 1340, which called attention to the previous year's prohibition of the "dogmatizing" of Ockham's doctrine, stating that it was still in force. It is the presence of this sentence in the statute of 1340 which caused the editors of the *Chartularium* to describe it as an anti-Ockhamist measure, and which was the basis of the assumption that Nicholas of Autrecourt, against whom this statute was known to have been directed, was an Ockhamist. This assumption, in turn, so stretched the meaning of the label "Ockhamist" as to make it difficult to reconcile the Ockhamism of Nicholas with the Ockhamism of John Buridan, to say nothing of the Ockhamism of Ockham.

Our examination of the content of the statute of 1340, in comparison with the statements of William of Ockham, exhibited the point of view of the statute as one which accorded rather closely with the expressed views of Ockham himself, thus rendering it unlikely that it was issued as a condemnation of his doctrine. Our study of the controversy between Nicholas of Autrecourt and Bernard of Arezzo, revealing Bernard as the defender of Ockham's doctrine, and Nicholas as the critic of this doctrine, revealed a further reason for doubting that the statute of 1340 was directed against the partisans of Ockham. The part played by John Buridan, finally, both as signatory of the statute and as critic of Nicholas of Autrecourt's doctrine, confirms the results of our inquiry. Why, if this be the case, did the statute of 1340 call attention to the 1339 prohibition of the dogmatizing of Ockham's doctrine?

There is one very simple explanation of this fact, which accords fully with the other facts we have investigated. In condemning the teachings and practices of Nicholas of Autrecourt, leader of the anti-Ockhamist faction, this statute might well have been construed as a vindication and even an endorsement of the position of Bernard of Arezzo and the doctrine of Ockham. Aware of this fact, the authors of the statute of 1340 thought it wise to insert a sentence at the end of that document, stating that the statute of 1339 was still in force, lest it be thought that the new statute was a revocation of the earlier one. The wording of this final clause seems to accord very well with this interpretation of its meaning:

salvis in omnibus que de doctrina Guillelmi dicti Okam alias statuimus, que in omnibus et per omnia volumus roboris habere firmitatem.

If the statute of 1340 had been directed against the Ockhamist faction, it would of itself have been understood as a confirmation and reinforcement of the earlier, and milder, prohibition, so that special mention of the latter would have been superfluous. But if it was directed against those who, like Nicholas of Autrecourt, had been in opposition to the Ockhamist group, it might easily have been taken as a revocation of the earlier statute, unless an explicit warning was inserted to guard against taking it as such. In the light of the general circumstances of the controversy, revealed by our inquiry, this interpretation of the meaning of the 1340 statute seems much more plausible than the opposite.

There is one more question which might be raised. If the 1340 statute was, in its practical effect and in its point of view, a vindication of the Ockhamist position, why did its authors not wish to acknowledge it to be such? Why, if they had accepted the *doctrine* of Ockham, did they take care to dissociate it from the *name* of Ockham? The answer to this question lies in the circumstance that Ockham's bitter opposition to Pope John XXII and his immediate successors, involving his excommunication and flight to Munich, made it inadvisable for anyone to call himself a follower of Ockham. It was necessary to distinguish Ockham's philosophical doctrines, from his personal and political misfortunes, in order to preserve them and to defend them. Thus we find, in Buridan's writings, no acknowledgement of Ockham as the source of the Ockhamist doctrines which he took over and defended; since the name was *tabu*, the doctrine could be defended only on condition of its being dissociated from the name. It was not until the later part of the 14th century, when the echoes of Ockham's political controversies had died down, that Ockham's name was cited in connection with his doctrines, in scholastic writings and disputations, or that those who had been defending his doctrines were explicitly labelled as disciples of Ockham.[43]

What general conclusion can be drawn, concerning the historical meaning and influence of Ockham's teachings in the later 14th century, from our study? It has been customary among historians of mediaeval philosophy to transfer to the later fourteenth century an alignment of philosophic schools which existed at the beginning of the century. Thus, in the years when Ockham was at Oxford, his doctrine appeared radical as contrasted with the older teachings of Aquinas, Henry of Ghent, and Duns Scotus. But within less than a generation the situation was profoundly altered, if not reversed. The defenders of Thomism were few and inarticulate, and the Scotist school had changed rapidly into a varied group of loosely associated doctrines which had in many cases pushed partial aspects of Dun's teachings to unbalanced extremes. The determinism of Bradwardine, the extreme voluntarism of the theology of Holkot, reflected or paralleled by John of Mirecourt at Paris—these and many other extremist doctrines were prevalent between 1324, when Ockham's teaching career terminated, and the period between 1340 and 1350. In this newer atmosphere, the philosophy of Ockham was a conservative doctrine, powerful enough in its principles and methods to serve as an instrument of stabilization and reconstruction in the new environment. The moderate temperament discernible in John Buridan, or in his pupil Albert of Saxony, is not out of harmony with his adherence to Ockhamist doctrines which, in the context of the extreme positions prevalent at the time, stood for much that was traditional. As Hochstetter has so well shown, Ockham's philosophy based itself squarely on the principle of natural causation, and for all its emphasis on the omnipotence of God, it held fast to the scholastic conception of a natural order and of real secondary causes.[44] Since it was precisely this conception of natural causation which was impugned by the epistemological criticism of Nicholas of Autrecourt, and by the voluntaristic determinism of Bradwardine, John of Mirecourt, and other prominent teachers of the generation after Ockham, it is not surprising that Ockham's doctrines, in this later context, became a rallying point for the defenders of natural knowledge and the causal order.

One may, if he wishes, employ the term "Ockhamism" as a blanket designation for all the varied teachings and tendencies of the late mediaeval period, and one may, if he pleases, argue that these later doctrines, however opposed to each other or to the teachings of Ockham himself, are "logical consequences" of the position of the Venerable Inceptor. But such usage is unprofitable, and introduces obscurity and confusion into the history of ideas. If, as historians, we are concerned to reconstruct the intellectual environment of past ages, we must place ourselves in the perspective of the times we are studying, letting those ages judge themselves by what they actually did and said. If, in seeking to understand the significance of the Parisian statutes of 1339 and 1340, we permit Buridan, Ockham, and Nicholas of Autrecourt to speak for themselves, the picture of the times which emerges from such a study is less simple, but in many respects more interesting and suggestive, than that which has been traditional in our history books.

POSTSCRIPT

Two corrections should be made to statements in the foregoing study. First, it should not have been said that Nicholas of Autrecourt's contention, "clear intuitive cognition is that by which we judge a thing to exist, whether it exists or does not exist," is a thesis of Ockham. For although Ockham conceded that God could cause us to have an intuitive cognition of a non-existent object, he said that in virtue of such an intuitive cognition we would only judge that the thing did *not* exist. The second correction applies to the passage quoted from Robert Holkot's *Commentary on the Sentences*, ascribing to Ockham the view that the object of science and opinion and of faith "is the thing signified by the complex, and not the complex itself." Although the printed edition of Holkot's work reads this way, I have found evidence, in studying Holkot's writings in manuscript, indicating that it was not Ockham, but Chatton, to whom Holkot ascribed this view. For this evidence, cf. my article "A Quodlibetal Question of Robert Holkot, o.p., on the Problem of the Objects of Knowledge and Belief," *Speculum*, Vol. XXXIX, No. 1, (Jan. 1964), pp. 53–74.

NOTES

1. *Chartularium universitatis Parisiensis*, ed. by Denifle-Chatelain, Vol. II, Paris 1891, No. 1042, pp. 505–7: "Si quis autem contra premissa vel aliquod premissarum attemptare presumpserit, a nostro consortio ex nunc prout ex tunc resecamus et privamus, resecatum et privatum haberi volumus, salvis in omnibus que de doctrina Guillelmi dicti Ockam alias statuimus, que in omnibus et per omnia volumus roboris habere firmitatem."

2. Cf. J. Lappe, "Nicolaus von Autrecourt," in *Beiträge zur Geschichte der Philosophie des Mittelalters*, ed. Clemens Baeumker, vol. VI, fasc. 2, Münster 1908, pp. 1–3. Also B. Geyer, in *Ueberwegs Grundriss der Geschichte der Philosophie*, vol. II, Berlin 1928, pp. 589–90, who links together the statues of 1339–40 with the condemnations of Nicholas of Autrecourt and John of Mirecourt, as follows: "Paris und seine Universität bildeten einen Hauptherd für die ockhamistischen Neuerungen. Dies lassen schon die oben erwähnten Verurteilungen der Jahre 1339 and 1340 erkennen. . . . Ein noch grelleres Licht auf den mächtigen Einfluss Ockhams, seiner Lehren und insbesondere seiner kritischen Tendenzen in Paris werfen die 1346 und 1347 verurteilten Sätze, die Nicolaus von Autrecourt und Johannes von Mirecourt zu Urhebern haben." A similar view is given by M. De Wulf, *History of Mediaeval Philosophy*, transl. from 5th French ed., N. Y. 1926, vol. 2, pp. 190–1.

3. For such a criticism cf. Anton C. Pegis, "Concerning William of Ockham," in *Traditio* II (1944), pp. 465–480. Also Etienne Gilson, "The Unity of Philosophical Experience," N. Y. 1937, ch. 3, pp. 61–91.

4. C. Michalski, "Les courants philosophiques à Oxford et à Paris pendant le XIVe siècle," in *Bulletin international de l'académie polonaise des sciences et des lettres, Classe d'histoire et de philosophie, Année 1919–20*. Cracovie 1922, pp. 76–77: "Buridan était entièrement d'accord avec les théologiens de Paris, quand il rejetait la manière d'interpréter les Saintes Ecritures et le dogme, établie, depuis Ockham, sur la distinction entre la *suppositio propria* et *impropria, personalis* et *materialis*. La doctrine du philosophe de Béthune ne pouvait donc l'empêcher d'occuper sa haute situation à l'université de Paris." Cf. also E. Gilson, *La Philosophie au Moyen-Age*, 2nd ed., Paris 1945, p. 675, who goes so far as to state without qualification that the statute of 1340 was "un decret interdisant d'enseigner plusieurs des thèses d'Ockham."

5. E. Gilson, *La philosophie au Moyen-Age*, 2nd ed., Paris 1945, p. 673: "Nicolas d'Autrecourt a soutenu des thèses qu'on chercherait en vain dans

les écrits du *venerabilis inceptor*, et dont rien ne permet de croire qu'il les eût reconnues pour dérivant des siennes. Il n'est même pas certain qu'elles en dérivent, car rien ne prouve que l'oeuvre de Nicolas d'Autrecourt ne serait pas née, à bien peu de chose près telle qu'elle est, si celle d'Ockham n'avait pas existé."

6. Cf. F. Ehrle, *Der Sentenzenkommentar Peters von Candia*, Münster-in-Westf., 1925, p. 124, note 2, quoting Aventinus, *Annales ducum Boiariae*, II, lib. 7, c. 21 (ed. S. Rietzler, Munich 1884, p. 474): "Marsilius Bathavus, Joannes Buridanus, discipuli Vilelmii Ocumensis. . . ."

7. *Chartularium univ. Paris.*, II, No. 1023, pp. 485–6: "Cum igitur a predecessoribus nostris non irrationabiliter motis circa libros apud nos legendos publice vel occulte certa precesserit ordinatio per nos jurata observari, et quod aliquos libros per ipsos non admissos vel alias consuetos legere non debemus, et istis temporibus nonnulli doctrinam Guillermi dicti Okam (quamvis per ipsos ordinantes admissa non fuerit vel alias consueta, neque per nos seu alios ad quos pertineat examinata, propter quod non videtur suspicione carere), dogmatizare presumpserint publice et occulte super hoc in locis privatis conventicula faciendo: hinc est quod nos nostrae salutis memores, considerantes juramentum quod fecimus de dicta ordinatione observanda, statuimus quod nullus de cetero predictam doctrinam dogmatizare presumat audiendo vel legendo publice vel occulte, necnon concenticula super dicta doctrina disputanda faciendo vel ipsum in lectura vel disputationibus allegando. . . .

Insuper cum nobis liqueat manifeste quod in disputationibus que fiunt in vico Straminum talis abusus inolevit quod bachellarii at alii in disputationibus dictis existentes propria auctoritate arguere presumunt minus reverenter se habentes ad magistros, qui disputant, tumultum faciendo adeo ut in tantum quod haberi non potest conclusionis disputande veritas, nec dicte disputationes in aliquo sunt scolaribus audientibus fructuose: statuimus quod nullus magister, bachellarius aut scolaris, sine permissue et licentia magistri disputationes tenentis arguat. . . ."

8. J. Lappe, *loc. cit.;* and J. R. O'Donnell, "Nicholas of Autrecourt," in *Mediaeval Studies*, Vol. I, 1939. In *Mediaeval Studies*, Vol. IV (1942), Father O'Donnell published a critical study entitled "The Philosophy of Nicholas of Autrecourt."

9. J. Lappe, *loc. cit.*, p. 2*: "Legi enim in quadam scriptura, quam in schola Fratrum Minorum legistis et pro vera omni volenti habere concessistis, propositiones que secuntur: Prima, que ponitur a vobis I. Sentent. dist. 3, qu. 4 est ista: Notitia intuitiva clara est, per quam iudicamus rem esse, sive sit sive non sit. Secunda propositio vestra, que ponitur ubi supra, est talis: Obiectum non est, igitur non videtur; non valet consequentia, nec ista: Hoc videtur, ergo hoc est. . . . Tertia propositio ibidem posita est ista: Notitia intuitiva non requirit necessario rem existentem."

10. A. Pelzer, "Les 51 articles de Guillaume Occam censurés, en Avignon,

en 1326," in *Revue d'histoire ecclésiastique*, 1922, pp. 240–70; Article 10: "Item ponit quod notitia intuitiva secundum se et necessario non plus est existentis quam non existentis nec plus respicit existentiam quam non existentiam. Omnis res absoluta distincta loco et subiecto ab alia re absoluta potest per divinam potentiam existere alia re absoluta destructa. Sed visio intuitiva tam sensitiva quam intellectiva est res absoluta distincta loco et subiecto ab obiecto viso, sicut si videam intuitive stellam existentem in celo, ista visio intuitiva, sive sit sensitiva sive intellectiva, distinguitur loco et subiecto ab obiecto viso. Ergo ista visio potest manere stella destructa." A critical edition of the text of Qu. 15 of Ockham's commentary on the second book of the Sentences, containing the relevant discussion of this doctrine, was published by Philotheus Boehner, O.F.M., in an article "The Notitia Intuitiva of Non-existents according to William Ockham," in *Traditio* I (1943), pp. 223–275.

11. Cf. A. C. Pegis, "Concerning William of Ockham," in *Traditio* II (1944), pp. 465–480. This article was written in criticism of the article of Philotheus Boehner, in *Traditio* I (1943), pp. 223–275. A reply to this criticism was published by Father Boehner in *Franciscan Studies*, 1945, pp. 37–54, under the title "In Propria Causa."

12. J. Lappe, *op. cit.*, p. 3*: "Sed forsan dicetis, prout mihi videtur, volebatis innuere in quadam disputatione apud Predicatores, quod, licet ex visione non possit inferri obiectum visum esse, quando visio ponitur in esse a causa supernaturali vel conservatur ab ipsa, tamen quando posita est in esse a causis naturalibus precise, concurrente influentia generali primi agentis, tunc potest inferri. Contra. Quando ex aliquo antecedente, si esset positum in esse ab aliquo agente, non poterit inferri consequentia formali et evidenti aliquod consequens: nec ex illo antecedente poterit inferri illud consequens, a quocunque fuerit positum in esse.''

13. Philotheus Boehner, O.F.M., "The Notitia Intuitiva of Non-existents According to William Ockham," in *Traditio* (1943), pp. 248–9 (text of Ockham's *Sentent.* II, Qu. 15, E): "Sic igitur patet, quod per cognitionem intuitivam iudicamus rem esse quando est, et hoc generaliter, sive intuitiva cognito naturaliter causetur sive supernaturaliter a solo Deo. Nam si naturaliter causetur, tunc non potest esse, nisi obiectum existat praesens in determinata approximatione. . . . Si autem sit supernaturalis, puta si Deus causaret in me cognitionem intuitivam de aliquo obiecto existente Romae, statim habita cognitione eius intuitiva possum iudicar᷑., quod illud quod intueor et video est ita bene, sicut si illa cognitio haberetur naturaliter. Si dicis, quod obiectum non est hic praesens nec debito modo approximatum—Respondeo: Licet cognitio intuitiva non possit naturaliter causari nisi quando obiectum est praesens in determinata distantia, tamen supernaturaliter posset."

14. *Chartularium univ. Paris.*, II, No. 1042, p. 505: "Erroribus obviare, quantum potest, unusquisque tenetur, et viam omnimode ad eos precludere, maxime cum ex hiis possit agnitio veritatis occultari. Verum quia ad nostram

noviter pervenerit notitiam, quod nonnulli in nostra artium facultate quorundam astutiis perniciosis adherentes, fundati non supra firmam petram, cupientes plus sapere quam oporteat, quadam minus sana nituntur seminare, ex quibus errores intolerabiles nedum circa philosophiam, sed et circa divinam Scripturam, possent contingere in futurum; hinc est, quod huic morbo tam pestifero remediare cupientes eorum fundamenta prophana et errores, prout potuimus, colligemus, statuentes circa illa per hunc modum. . . ."

15. *Chartularium, ibid.:* "Item, quod nullus asserat absque distinctione vel expositione, quod Socrates et Plato, vel Deus et creatura nihil sunt, quoniam illa verba prima facie male sonant, et quia talis propositio sensum unum habet falsum, videlicet si negatio in hac dictione nihil implicita intelligeretur cadere non solum super ens singulariter, sed et supra entia pluraliter."

16. *Chartularium univ. Paris.*, II, No. 1124 (also reprinted in J. Lappe, *op. cit.*, p. 34*): "Item dixi in quadam disputatione quod Deus et creatura non sunt aliquid.—Falsam et scandalosam prout verba sonant."

17. An important exception is Fr. Philotheus Boehner, in his article in *Franciscan Studies* VI, 3 (Sept. 1946), entitled "Ockham's Theory of Supposition and the Notion of Truth." In this article, on pp. 275–279, Fr. Boehner gives an accurate and well documented exposition of Ockham's principles and methods of textual interpretation, in connection with the term *de virtute sermonis*, and with explicit reference to the Statute of 1340. Fr. Boehner takes into account the statements of Michalski, referring to this question, which appeared in his article in *Studia Philosophica* II (1937) entitled "Le problème de la volonté à Oxford et à Paris au XIVe siècle," and which I had not been able to consult. The findings of Fr. Boehner seem to accord fully with the results of my own study of Ockham's ideas on textual interpretation, and supply pertinent additional documentation. Only after completing the present study did I see this excellent article by Fr. Boehner.

18. *Chartularium univ. Paris.*, II, No. 1042: "quod nulli magistri, baccalarii, vel scolares in artium facultate legentes Parisius audeant aliquam propositionem famosam illius actoris cujus librum legunt, dicere simpliciter esse falsam, vel esse falsam de virtute sermonis, si crediderint quod actor ponendo illam habuerit verum intellectum; sed vel concedant eam, vel sensum verum dividant a sensu falso, quia pari ratione propositiones Biblie absoluto sermone essent negande, quod est periculosum. Et quia sermo non habet virtutem, nisi ex impositione et usu communi actorum vel aliorum, ideo talis est virtus sermonis, qualiter eo actores communiter utuntur et qualem exigit materia, cum sermones sint recipiendi penes materiam subiectam."

19. Gul. Ockham, *Expositio super Predicabilia*, Proem.: "Tertia utilitas logicae est facilitas virtutem sermonis et proprium modum loquendi percipiendi. Nam per istam artem faciliter scitur quid ab auctoribus de virtute sermonis profertur, et quid non de virtute sermonis sed secundum usitatum modum loquendi; vel secundum intentionem dicentis quid dicitur proprie, quid metaphorice; quod est maxime necessarium omnibus studentibus in

dictis aliorum, quia qui semper omnia dicta auctorum de virtute sermonis et proprie accipiunt, incidunt in multos errores et inexplicabiles difficultates." This text is established from five manuscripts: Firenze Bibl. Naz. B. 4. 1618 (dated A.D. 1331); Firenze Bibl. Naz. G. 3. 803; Los Angeles Univ. 6; Oxford Bodl. Misc. 558; and Bruges 499. The edition of the *Expositio aurea*, Bologna 1496, gives substantially the same content for this passage.

For further extensive statements by Ockham, concerning the necessity of interpreting texts according to the manner of speech used by the author, and in the light of the author's intentions, cf. "The *De Sacramento altaris* of William of Ockham," ed. by T. B. Birch, Burlington, Iowa, 1930, p. 40, pp. 42–44, and p. 54.

20. *Chartularium univ. Paris.*, II, No. 1042: "Item, quod nullus dicat simpliciter vel de virtute sermonis omnem propositionem esse falsum, que esset falsa secundum suppositionem personalem terminorum, eo quod iste error ducit ad priorem errorem, actores enim sepe utuntur aliis suppositionibus."

21. Gul. Ockham, *Expositio super Predicamenta*. Proem. (Ed. 1496, checked by manuscripts enumerated in Note 18): "Et ignorantia intentionis Aristotelis in hoc libro facit multos modernos errare, credentes multa hic dicta pro rebus quae tamen pro solis vocibus et proportionabiliter pro intentionibus seu conceptibus in anima vult intélligi."

22. *Chartularium* II, No. 1042: "Item, quod nullus dicat quod nulla propositio sit distinguenda, quoniam hoc ducit ad predictos errores, quia si discipulus unum propositionis sensum recipit, et doctor alium intellexerit, discipulus falso informabitur, donec propositio distinguetur. Similiter si opponens unum sensum recipiat, et respondens alterum sensum intelligat, disputatio erit ad nomen tantum, si non fiat distinctio."

23. Gul. Ockham, *De sacramento altaris*, ed. T. B. Birch, p. 124: "Nec est inconveniens exponere dicta eorum, cum multa dicta etiam sacrae paginae indigeant etiam expositione; quia multa non sunt vera secundum proprietatem sermonis, sed secundum sensum quem debemus habere, sunt verissima."

24. *Chartularium* II, No. 1042: "Item, quod nullus dicat propositionem nullam esse concedendam, si non sit vera in ejus sensu proprio, quia hoc dicere ducit ad predictos errores, quia Biblia et actores non semper sermonibus utuntur secundum proprios sensus eorum. Magis igitur oportet in affirmando vel negando sermones ad materiam subiectam attendere, quam ad proprietatem sermonis, disputatio namque ad proprietatem sermonis attendens nullam recipiens propositionem, preterquam in sensu proprio, non est nisi sophistica disputatio. Disputationes dyalectice et doctrinales, que ad inquisitionem veritatis intendunt, modicam habent de nominibus sollicitudinem."

25. G. Ockham, *De sacremento altaris*, ed. Birch, p. 62: "Et ideo Aristoteles minus de modo loquendi curabat; ex quo res fuit nota sicut patet Primo Physicorum, quod *modicam solicitudinem habebat de nominibus*. Et ideo multi propter hoc, quod recipiunt auctoritates antiquorum sicut sonant ad

litteram et secundum proprietatem sermonis, quod tamen intentum non habuerunt antiqui, in errores varios incidunt." The quotation is not from Aristotle's text, but from Averroes' commentary, as far as I can determine.

26. *Chartularium* II, No. 1042: "Item, quod nullus dicat scientiam nullam esse de rebus non sunt signa, id est, que non sunt termini vel orationes, quoniam in scientiis utimur terminis pro rebus, quas portare non possumus ad disputationes. Ideo scientiam habemus de rebus, licet mediantibus terminis vel orationibus."

27. *Guilhelmi de Ockham anglici super quattuor libros sententiarum subtilissimae quaestiones earumdemque decisiones.* Joh. Trechsel, Lyons 1495; Lib. I, dist. 2, qu. 4, M: "Ad secundum principale dico, quod scientia realis non est semper de rebus tamquam de illis que immediate sciuntur, sed de aliis pro rebus tamen supponentibus. Ad cuius intellectum et propter multa prius dicta et dicenda propter aliquos inexercitatos in logica, sciendum quod scientia quelibet, sive sit realis sive rationalis, est tantum de propositionibus tamquam de illis que sciuntur, quia solo propositiones sciuntur."

28. Ockham, *ibid.*, O: "Per hoc ad formam argumenti dico, quod scientiam esse de rebus potest intelligi tripliciter. Vel quia ipsa res est scita, et sic nulla scientia est de rebus substantialibus, maxime quia nihil scitur nisi complexum, complexum autem non est res extra animam, nisi forte in voce vel in consimili signe. Aliter, quod res sint partes illius quod scitur, et sic non oportet scientiam realem esse de rebus extra. Tertio modo, quod res sint illa pro quibus partes sciti supponunt, et sic scientia realis est de rebus. . . ."

29. Ockham, *ibid.:* "Breviter ergo ad intentionem philosophi est sciendum quod scientia realis non per hoc distinguitur a rationali, quia scientia realis est de rebus ita quod ipsae res sint propositiones scite vel partes illarum propositionum scitarum, et rationalis non est sic de rebus; sed per hoc quod partes scilicet termini propositionum scitarum scientia reali stant et supponunt pro rebus; non sic autem termini propositionum scitarum scientia rationali." Cf. also *Expositio aurea*, ed. 1496, fol. 1 *verso*, where Ockham says that logic is called *scientia rationalis* "quia determinat de hiis que sine ratione esse non possunt, aliae autem scientiae de rebus extra animam existentibus determinant."

30. Robert Holkot: *Quaestiones super libros Sententiarum*, ed. Joh. Trechsel, Lyons 1497. Lib. I, qu. 2: "De obiecto actus credendi utrum sit ipsum complexum vel res significata per complexum. Est apud quosdam dubium, et tenet Ockham quod universaliter scientie et opinionis et fidei et cuiuslibet talis assensus obiectum est res significata per complexum et non ipsum complexum."

31. C. Michalski, "Les courants etc.," *loc. cit. N. 4 supra*, p. 77.

32. J. Lappe, *op. cit.*, p. 40*, reprints the reference to these lectures from the second Avignon schedule of revocation. This states that Nicholas posted the following notice of his lectures: "Quicunque voluerit audire librum Pollitice Aristotelis una cum quibusdam questionibus, in quibus disceptatur

de iusto et iniusto, per quas . . . poterat novas leges condere, conditas, si que sint corrigenda, corrigere, veniat at talem locum, et inveniat magistrum Nicholaum de Ultricuria qui docebit omnia ista in lectura hac predicta."

33. J. Lappe, *op. cit.* p. 11*: "Sed contra propositam regulam instat Bernardus, quia sequitur evidenter, evidentia reducta ad certitudinem primi principii: Albedo est, ergo alia res est, quia albedo non posset esse, nisi aliquid teneret ipsam in esse. Item sequitur: Albedo est non primo, ergo alia res est. Item: Ignis est approximatus stuppe et non est impedimentum, ergo calor erit." Egidius' letter to Nicholas (Lappe, pp. 14*-24*) also uses such arguments to justify the traditional doctrine of causality.

34. *Acutissimi philosophi reverendi Magistri Johannis buridam subtilissime questiones super octo phisicorum libros Aristotelis diligenter recognite et revise a magistro Joanne dullaert de gandavo*, Paris, 1509, Lib. I, Qu. 4 fols. 4 *verso* B—5 *recto* A. "Item revertor ad arguendum quod non posset fieri notum unum ex alio, quia de uno ad aliud non est consequentia evidens, propter hoc quod consequentia non est evidens nisi secundum reductionem ad primum principium, et talis consequentia non potest reduci ad primum principium, quia primum principium fundatur in contradictione, et contradictio debet esse eiusdem de eodem et secundum rem et secundum nomen, unde si A et B sunt alia ab invicem, nunquam esset contradictio 'A esse' et 'B non esse'; igitur non est evidens consequentia dicere 'A est, ergo B est,' et sic de quibuscumque aliis quantumcumque propinquani habentibus habitudinem ad invicem."

35. J. Lappe, *op. cit.*, p. 9*: "Iuxta ista dicta posui alibi inter ceteras conclusiones unam, que fuit ista: Ex eo, quod aliqua res est cognita esse, non potest evidenter evidentia reducta in primum principium vel in certitudinem primi principii inferri, quod alia res sit. In tali consequentia, in qua ex una re infertur alia, consequens non esset idem realiter cum antecedente vel cum parte significati per antecedens; igitur sequitur, quod talis consequentia non esset evidenter nota evidentia primi principii descripta. Antecedens est ab adversario concessum et positum; consequentia apparet ex descriptione contradictionis, que est affirmatio et negatio unius et eiusdem, etc. Cum igitur nunc consequens non sit idem realiter cum antecedente vel cum parte antecedentis, manifestum est, quod, esto, quod oppositum consequentis et antecedens forent simul vera, at hoc non esset affirmatio et negatio unius et eiusdem etc."

36. Buridan, *Qu. in Phys.*, ed. *cit.*, fol. 5 *verso*. The conclusions which Buridan seeks to establish are these: "Prima est quod de aliquo subiecto potest demonstrari hoc verbum 'est' secundum adiacens. . . . Secunda conclusio contra illos est, quod non oportet omnem premissam demonstrationis fieri notam et evidentem per reductionem ad primum principium. Multa enim principia demonstrationum fiunt nota nobis per sensum vel per memoriam vel per experientiam absque hoc quod oporteat ea aliter demonstrari, sicut habetur secundo Posteriorum. . . . Tertia conclusio est quod non oportet omnis sillogismi demonstrativi consequentiam fieri evidentem per reductionem

ad primum principium. . . . Quarta conclusio est, quod in quibusdam per istam propositionem 'A est,' non solitarie sed cum alia premissa, ego possum demonstrative scire istam conclusionem 'B est,' licet A sit aliud quam B et B aliud quam A . . . et ex hoc etiam quod apparet nobis motum esse, concludimus motorem esse in virtute illius alterius premisse, quod non potest esse motus sine motore; et sic de multis aliis. Et ex dicta apparet quomodo rationes quas illi adducebant ad suam opinionem nichil valebant contra conclusiones positas, omnes enim procedunt secundum prius determinata."

37. *In metaphysicen Aristotelis Quaestiones argutissimae Magistri Ioannis Buridani* . . . et. Iodocus Badius Ascensius, Paris 1518, Lib. II, Qu. I, fol. IX *recto* B: "Ad aliam dico quod effectus sciuntur per causam propter quid, quia causa est notior etiam nobis quam propter quid effectus est. Similiter causa scitur per effectum quantum ad quia est, quia effectus gerit quandam similitudinem cause, ideo potest causam representare una cum naturali inclinatione intellectus ad veritatem. Quando etiam dicitur quod aluid per aliud non potest sciri conclusive, nego, et dico quod quasi sunt infinita principia per se nota, aut per sensum aut per experientiam aut per inclusionem terminorum, absque hoc quod indigeant demonstrari per principium primum; modo in libro Posteriorum demonstrat Aristoteles quod principia indemonstrabilia sunt fere tot sicut sunt conclusiones demonstrabiles." For Ockham's views on this subject, as agreeing with those of Buridan, cf. his *Summa logice, Pars 3a, Tractatus de demonstratione.*

38. Joh. Buridani, *Quaestiones in Metaphysicam Arist., ed. cit.,* Lib. IV, Qu. 6, fols. XVI *verso*—XVII *verso:* "Utrum hoc nomen ens significat substantias et accidentia secundum unam rationem sive secundum unum conceptum."

39. J. Lappe, *op. cit.,* p. 6*: "Et ideo ad evitandum tales absurditates sustinui in aula Sorbone in disputationibus, quod sum certus evidenter de obiectis quinque sensuum et de actibus meis."

40. Joh. Buridani, *Quaestiones in Metaph.,* Lib., II, Qu. 1, *ed. cit.,* fol. IX *recto:* "Ideo conclusum est correlarie quod aliqui valde mali dicunt, volentes interimere scientias naturales et morales, eo quod in pluribus earum principiis et conclusionibus non est evidentia simplex sed possunt falsificari per casus supernaturaliter possibiles, quia non requiritur ad tales scientias evidentia simpliciter, sed sufficiunt predicte evidentie secundum quid sive ex suppositione; ideo bene dicit Aristoteles quod non in omnibus scientiis mathematica acribologia est expetenda."

41. Et. Gilson, *La Philosophie au Moyen-Age,* 2nd ed., Paris 1945, p. 672: "Ces doctrines prouvent également que les penseurs du moyen âge n'ont pas eu besoin de secours extérieurs pour se libérer d'Aristote; toutes les raisons par lesquelles on explique que le fait se soit produit au XVIe siècle, échouent devant cet autre fait dès le XIVe siècle l'aristotélisme était déjà jugé et condamné."

42. Pierre Duhem, *Etudes sur Leonard de Vinci, 3me Série; Les Précurseurs Parisiens de Galilée;* Paris, 1913.

43. Thus Peter of Candia, in his Commentary on the Sentences written around 1378–80, cites Ockham frequently on the various questions discussed. Cf. Fr. Ehrle, *Der Sentenzenkommentar Peters von Candia*, Muenster, 1925, pp. 56–73. On p. 322 ff., Ehrle reprints the appeal made by the Parisian nominalists to Louis XI, in 1474, which refers to the Parisian statute of 1339 as having been issued as a result of pressure brought on the University by John XXII: "Propter has causas idem Johannes XXII multa privilegia dedit Universitati Parisiensi, ut ipsam doctrinam Guillelmi Okam condemnaret. Dicta tamen Universitas noluit eam condemnare. Sed facultas artium, importunitate victa, fecit statuum, in quo cavetur, dictam doctrinam non esse dogmatizandam, quia nondum erat approbata et examinata." While this document is untrustworthy as a source of information, because of its late date and its obvious bias, it seems likely enough that John XXII did exert some pressure on the University in this connection.

44. E. Hochstetter, *Studien zur Metaphysik und Erkenntnislehre Wilhelms von Ockham*, Berlin 1927, especially pp. 139–179. Cf. also N. Abbagnano, *Guglielmo di Ockham*, Lanciano 1931, pp. 170–3.

14

THE FIFTH LETTER OF NICHOLAS OF AUTRECOURT TO BERNARD OF AREZZO*

Julius R. Weinberg

NICHOLAS of Autrecourt wrote nine letters to Bernard of Arezzo and one to a certain Egidius in a controversy concerning our alleged knowledge of causes and substances. The first two of these letters are extant in their complete form, and the letter to Egidius exists in an almost complete form. The remaining letters to Bernard are known only by the fragmentary excerpts found in the proceedings of condemnation of Nicholas's doctrines. For reasons which I cannot indicate here, I believe that the entire correspondence took place in Paris between 1329 and 1336, and probably closer to the earlier date than to the later. Since some of the most important details of his thought are to be found in the fragments, it is desirable to attempt a reconstruction of the lost letters. The only one of these letters for which there is any considerable number of fragments is the fifth.

First I shall make a few observations about Nicholas's thought which will aid in an understanding of my attempted reconstruction. In the first and second letters to Bernard of Arezzo, Nicholas laid it down that the sole sources of certitude are the immediate

* This work was done with the aid of a grant from the American Council of Learned Societies.

315

data of consciousness and the law of non-contradiction. Every logically necessitated inference must be guaranteed by the law of non-contradiction, and every certain conclusion must be deduced from principles firmly and exclusively based on evidence which only the immediate data of consciousness can supply. Since the conclusion of a logically necessitated inference must be identical with its premises or with part of what its premises signify (otherwise such an inference would not be formally certifiable by the law of non-contradiction), it is impossible to obtain existential knowledge in a conclusion which has not already been asserted in the premises. From this the following fundamental proposition is obtained: from the fact that one thing is known to exist or known not to exist it cannot be logically inferred that something else exists or does not exist. This being so, inference is powerless to provide any existential knowledge of causes or substances. Nor is this all. Not only are experience and logical inference unable to provide the knowledge that there are or are not causes or substances, but also not even the possibility of such connections or entities can be discerned in experience or obtained by logical inference.

The logical foundation of Nicholas's critique of Scholastic epistemology is simply his formulation of a strict conception of certitude. Historically, however, this critique appears to have arisen from theological discussions concerning the power of God. The fact that God was held to be absolutely omnipotent led to an important distinction between the *absolute* and the *ordinated* power of God. In virtue of His absolute power, God can do anything that does not involve a contradiction. Thus He can cause human beings to have experiences of objects which do not exist outside the mind. He can interrupt the general course of nature and so change ordinary causal routines. He can produce or conserve sensible accidents without their proper substrata, and all other things of this sort. If the existence of sensible data implied the existence of external objects, or if the existence of something alleged to be a cause necessarily entailed the existence of other things alleged to be its effects, it would be logically impossible for omnipotence to produce an intuition without its external cause or any so-called cause without its effect. But since it is plainly not a contradiction that one thing exists and that another and different thing does not exist, it is within God's absolute power to produce the one without the other. The *ordinated* power of God is subject to further restriction. Since God has made certain decisions about the construction of the universe and the general course of history, it would be a contradiction to say that He will not act in accordance with His own decisions. Our knowledge of such decisions, however, comes principally from revelation.

So far as natural knowledge is concerned, we are unable to know for certain either the general order of the world or the particular facts of a given occasion. It is useless to argue that, assuming that no miracle is taking place, the existence of one thing logically implies that of another. Thus we cannot logically infer that the object of our cognition implies the existence of something external to the mind if no miracle is taking place. Such an inference is open to two objections, either of which is fatal: we cannot *know* whether a miracle is taking place on a given occasion, and we do not *know* (aside from the consideration of miracles) that there is any connection between the object of cognition and anything else whatever. Such knowledge would be vouchsafed to us only if the law of non-contradiction manifestly guaranteed an inference from one thing to another, and no inference of this kind can be guaranteed in this way.

Nicholas seems to have employed two kinds of argument in his critique of the alleged knowledge of causes and substances. With regard to causes he argued 1) that they are not experientially discernible, and 2) that they are not apodictically demonstrable. 1) Experience and logical deduction are the sole sources of certitude. Therefore, if we had knowledge that a cause exists it would come from experience or from logical deduction. But it cannot come from experience, because experience of an object is either (a) exclusively of that object or (b) of that object with another object. If (a), it is impossible that the simple experience of one object could reveal more than precisely that object, so that whether that object is a cause or an effect of something else cannot be determined by the experience in question. If (b), we have the experience of at least two objects, but, since nothing but their conjunction is given, nothing in the nature of causal efficacy can be discerned. 2) It follows that if causes are knowable, they must be deducible from experience rather than immediately discerned. But as the premises of a certain conclusion must themselves be certain, the premises of a causal inference must be either propositions exclusively about experience or principles known *ex terminis*. We have already seen that experiential propositions cannot provide indubitable information about causes. Therefore, principles known *ex terminis* remain as the sole possibility. The question now arises whether the terms of such propositions have been defined nominally or whether they have a real definition. For example, if we define an agent as anything which acts on something else when it is brought into appropriate relation with that something else, it will follow from the premises "x is an agent and is brought into appropriate relations with y" that "y is affected." But whether x *is* an agent or is merely *called* an agent is not decided by such an inference. The fact that experience is noncommittal with regard to causes makes it impossible for logical inference to yield any causal information.

His argument against the alleged knowledge of substances is similar to the argument against causal knowledge. We cannot intuit substances because that which partially or wholly transcends the content of experience cannot be grasped in and through experience. We cannot deduce their existence from experience unless we apply to the items of experience nominal definitions whose appropriateness to those items must always remain an open question. If probable inference is based solely on experience, there is not even a probability that substances exist. For, if the premises of a probable inference are confined to the conjunctions observed in experience, no substance can be said probably to exist because no substance can be a member of a conjunction manifested in experience.

No one who has read these arguments can fail to notice that they anticipate Hume's negative critique even to the details of

Hume's dialectic. There are also noticeable affinities between the philosophy of Nicholas and those of Leibniz and Kant. Yet, however interesting these parallels may be, I have found no conclusive evidence of any direct connection between Nicholas and the immediate predecessors or contemporaries of Leibniz and Hume. And since there are many differences between fourteenth century thought and the intellectual climate of modern opinion, it is best not to repose too much confidence in any analogies of this sort. This much will suffice for an introduction.

Lappe,[1] Gilson,[2] and Vignaux[3] have attempted to reconstruct the Fifth Letter of Nicholas to Bernard but without much success. As more fragments of this lost letter remain than of any of the other lost letters, the chances of its reconstruction are correspondingly greater, but the nature of the fragments makes any simple scheme of interpretation seemingly impossible.

As given in the so-called Articles of Cardinal Curty,[4] the fragments of Letter Five are as follows (the numbering and grouping are my own. Their purpose will be presently explained):

I, 1 . . . haec con [sequentia non est evidens evi]dentia deducta ex primo principio:[5] 'ignis est approx[imatus stupae et nullum e]st impedimentum: ergo stupa comburetur.

I, 2 . . . nescimus evidenter, quod ali[a a deo possint] esse causa alicuius effectus.

I, 3 . . . nescimus evidenter, quod aliqua causa causet efficienter quae non sit deus.

I, 4 . . . nescimus evidenter, quod aliqua causa efficiens naturalis sit vel esse possit.

I, 5 . . . nescimus evidenter, utrum aliquis effectus sit vel esse possit naturaliter productus.

I, 6 . . . quibuscumque acceptis, quae possunt esse causa alicuius effectus, nescimus evidenter quod ad positionem eorum sequatur effectus positio.

II, 1 . . . nescimus evidenter, quod in aliqua productione concurrat subjectum.

III, 1 . . . nulla potest esse simpliciter demonstratio, qua existentia causarum demonstretur existentia effectus.

III, 2 . . . non est nobis evidenter notum, quod possit esse aliqua demonstratio a priori differenti realiter.

IV, 1 . . . non potest evidenter ostendi nobilitas unius rei super aliam.

IV, 2 . . . quacunque re demonstrata nullus scit evidenter qui[n excedat no]bilitate omnes alias.

IV, 3 . . . [quacun]que re demonstrata nullus scit evidenter, quin ipsa sit d[eus, si per deum in]telligamus ens nobilissimum.

IV, 4 . . . aliquis nescit evidenter, quod una res sit finis a[lterius].

IV, 5 . . . [nu]llus scit evidenter qualibet re ostensa, quin sibi debea[t impendere maximum ho]norem.

IV, 6 . . . aliquis nescit evidenter, quin ista possit rationabiliter conce[di: si ali]qua res est producta, deus est productus.

The notice of John of Mirecourt[6] on Nicholas's philosophy makes it plain that a theological principle is presupposed in fragments I, 1–6. God being the omnipotent Father, He can accomplish anything which does not involve a manifest contradiction.[7] Hence, whatever God does with the cooperation of second causes He can accomplish without that cooperation. Because neither deductive inference nor direct experience can afford evident knowledge of the action of second causes, natural reason can find no impossibility in the supposition that God is the sole and immediate cause of everything. Moreover, reason and experience cannot discern causes or causal connections. This satisfactorily explains the import of I, 1–6.

Since God preserves the species of bread and wine after the consecration of the Host has deprived these species of their proper and natural substrata, it follows that He can always separate accidents from substances and preserve the accidents supernaturally. The existence of a substratum cannot therefore be logically inferred from the perceived generation of accidents. It is possible that Nicholas at this point of the letter also repeated the argument that substances cannot be directly perceived. This explains the import of II, 1.[8]

III, 1 and 2 may be easily understood in terms of the second letter to Bernard[9] in which it is explained that because, in every logically necessary implication, the consequent must be identical with part or all of the antecedent, no logical inference is possible from the existence of one thing to the existence of another. Hence, causes cannot be inferred from effects nor effects from causes. This argument is intended to discredit both *demonstratio quia* and *demonstratio propter quid*, and so in a sense constitutes a criticism of any alleged cognition of the existence or nature of formal causes. Thus I, II, and III are criticisms respectively of our alleged knowledge of efficient, material, and formal causes.

It will be observed that thus far the argument of this letter has two aspects. The logic of the argument, it is true, does not require the theological context in which it is stated. The rhetorical advantage of such a context is plain, and it would be impossible to reconstruct this letter without keeping that context constantly in mind. Moreover, while there is reason to believe that Nicholas doubted that natural reason could have any knowledge even of divine causality, it was natural for him to put his philosophical argument in theological terms.

The IVth part of the letter, however, is difficult to reconstruct for several reasons: 1) The theological premise of the argument ought to be the same as that of the earlier parts. It is not plain that this is the case. 2) It is difficult to see how IV, 2–5 prove or elucidate IV, 1. Why is it the case that anything you may point out may be the noblest being? No reason is suggested in the fragments themselves, nor in the logic of the argument, nor even in the theological context as given thus far. 3) Fragment IV, 6 seems almost meaningless in the context, and Vignaux remarks "nous préférons abandonner la proposition au jeu des conjectures."[10] Any tenable interpretation, however, must take account of this fragment.

I suggest that the fourth part of the letter can be given perfectly good sense in the light of a theological question which was much agitated in Nicholas's time. The advantage of my interpretation is that it not only takes account of all the fragments, but also allows that the theological principle underlying this part is, just as in the case of the earlier parts of the letter, the absolute power of God.

In the thirteenth and fourteenth centuries the problem of the

Incarnation was much discussed. One of the questions, to put it briefly, was how Christ could be both God and man. In discussions of this question by Ockham,[11] Mirecourt,[12] and others it was pointed out that, in virtue of His absolute power, God *could* have united Himself with any finite being whatsoever had He chosen to do so. Hence, He could have assumed the form of a stone or of any animate creature. The fact that He elected to become man is known to us by revelation, but for natural reason there is nothing absurd in the proposition that God becomes a stone, a plant, or an animal.

In my judgment, this theological problem figured in Nicholas's argument that the nobility or perfection of one thing over another cannot be demonstrated by natural reason. Since, that is to say, it is logically and metaphysically possible for God by His absolute power to assume the form of anything that anyone might point out, it is impossible to prove by natural reason that that indicated thing is not God. Anything of the humblest appearance could, for all that natural reason can prove to the contrary, be God. Hence, natural reason cannot demonstrate that anything perceived by man is really nobler or more perfect than anything else so perceived. The doctrine of final causes is thus open to question because, by a similar argument, any attempted proof that one thing is the final cause of another can be successfully refuted.[13] It is reasonable to suppose that at this point Nicholas used some other arguments of a non-theological character against the alleged knowledge of final causes and degrees of perfection. Although the theological argument was probably dominant, the other arguments would have been appropriate. For example, he may have also argued that the final cause of anything can neither be discerned in, nor deduced from, any of the early stages of its history, since this would be to deduce the existence of one thing from something different. He may also have argued that degrees of perfection could be proved only if causal efficacy could be proved. Since the latter is never evident, neither is the former.

If God and the creature with which He might elect to unite Himself truly constitute one individual with a dual nature, and if that creature begins to exist, it will be true to say that that creature is produced. Therefore, in the sense in which God is unified with that creature it will be true to say that God is produced.[14] This explains what is meant by the statement "si aliqua res est producta deus est productus." It must be noted that a doubt is raised here whether anything is produced. Things might be eternal for all that natural reason can prove to the contrary. Nicholas is suggesting that if anything is produced and if God has united Himself with that thing, then in a sense God is produced. The argument that because a thing comes into being it is less noble than the thing which has produced it, therefore, turns out to be invalid, since in this particular case God would be both creator and creature. Hence, it is still true that the nobility of one thing over another is not evident to natural reason.

In an age in which Aristotelian philosophy and Christian theology were the principal contexts of learned discussion, it was not unusual that all the four causes should be discussed in succession, when our knowledge of causation was the question at issue. It will be noted then, that this letter successively discusses our alleged knowledge (1) of efficient causes, (2) of the material cause, (3) of the formal cause, and (4) of final causes. This interpretation is consistent with all of the extant fragments of the Fifth Letter.[15]

NOTES

1. Lappe, J. *Nicholaus von Autrecourt, Beiträge zur Geschichte der Philosophie des Mittelalters*, Band VI, Heft 2.

2. Gilson, E. *La Philosophie au Moyen Age*, II, pp. 114–115.

3. Vignaux, P. *Dictionnaire de Théologie Catholique*, Tome XI, art. "Nicola d'Autrecourt."

4. See Lappe, *op. cit.*, pp. 31–48.

5. The law of non-contradiction.

6. Bibl. Nat. Paris, ms. latin. 16408 (16409): quod nulla demonstratio seu inquisitio de effectibus quibuscumque, unde proveniunt, vel causis naturalibus, quos vel qualis effectus producent vel producent, est aliquo modo evidens sive certa: hoc satis deducti Autricort, et oppositum dicere divinae libertati contradicere.

7. Epistola secunda ad Bernardum, Lappe, *op. cit.*, 7* 34–35: ". . . nec aliqua potentia facere potest, quod contradictoria sint simul vera."

8. See also the fragment from the Sixth Letter, Lappe, *op. cit.*, 33* 35–37: . . . pane demonstrato non potest evidenter ostendi, quod ibi sit aliqua res quae non sit accidens.

9. Lappe, *op. cit.*, 9* 16–19: Ex eo, quod aliqua res est cognita esse, non potest evidenter . . . inferri, quod alia res sit.

10. Vignaux, *op. cit.*, p. 567.

11. Ockham, *Centiloquium Theologicum*: 6a conclusio est ista, quod deus potest assumere omnem creaturam sive omne aliud a deo in unitate suppositi. Item non concludit contradictionem deum assumere naturam asinum, ergo deus potest facere; . . . pari ratione potest assumere lapidem et lignum etc. 7a conclusio: deus assumpsit et potuit assumere quamlibet creaturam . . . igitur omnis propositio talis est possibilis . . . et quod ista consequentia sit bona, patet ex hoc, quia facta assumptione alicuius creaturae in unitate suppositi divini, statim fit communicatio idiomatum sive dictionum, sc. dei et creaturae illius assumptae, sicut quando fuit facta assumptio naturae humanae in unitate suppositi divini statim fuit communicatio idiomatum facta, et statim fuerunt tales propositiones verae: deus est homo, homo est deus, deus est mortalis, homo est eternus, deus est genitus, . . . deus incepit esse homo, etc. . . . per consequens omnes tales propositiones sunt possibiles: deus est asinus, deus est lapis, etc.

12. Mirecourt, *Lectura sup Sent.*, Univ. Bibl. Erlangen, ms. 370, f. 151r (quoted by Ernest Borchert, *Der Einfluss des Nominalismus auf die Chritologie der Spaetscholastik*, B.G.P.M., Band 35, Heft 4–5, p. 66, n. 89): 4° sic, quia deus de sua potentia absoluta creare posset unam animam in puris naturalibus sine omni actu vel habitu creato in ipsa anima, et posset tunc illam animam in tali dispositione unire sibi vel cum humano corpore; probo antecedens, quia deus de sua potentia absoluta posset assumere lapidem sicut tenet expresse sanctus Thomas 3 sent., d. 2a, qu. 1, art 1 et doctor, subtilis 3 sent., d. 3, qu. 1, art 2.

13. Cf. Nicholas's *Exigit ordo executionis* (edition of O'Donnell, *Medieval Studies*, vol. I, New York, 1939, p. [190], (10)–(33)).

14. See quotation from Ockham in note 11. That this is heretical can be seen from the creed "Quicumque vult": "Unus autem, non conversione divinitatis in carnem, sed assumptione humanitatis in Deum."

15. I have just learned from the article of P. Boehner, O.F.M. ("The CENTILOQUIUM attributed to Ockham," *Franciscan Studies*, vol. 22, New Series, vol. 1, No. 1 March, 1941) that the Centiloquium may have been erroneously attributed to Ockham. Since the earliest ms. of this work goes back to about 1380 (*Amploniana Q*. 104, Erfurt), and since quotations similar in content to the one I have taken from the Centiloquium can be found in several authentically attributed mss. of contemporaries of Nicholas, the possibly spurious character of the Centiloquium does not affect my argument.

BIOGRAPHICAL
NOTES
🔲🔲🔲🔲🔲🔲🔲

BIOGRAPHICAL NOTES

I. M. BOCHENSKI is Professor of Philosophy at the University of Fribourg. He was formerly Privatdocent at the University of Cracow; Professor at St. Thomas University, Rome; Visiting Professor at the Universities of Notre Dame, California at Los Angeles, Kansas, and Pittsburgh; and President (Rector) at the University of Fribourg. His books comprise *La logique de Théophraste; Ancient Formal Logic; Formale Logik; Die Zeitgenössischen Denkmethoden;* and *The Logic of Religion.*

PETER T. GEACH is Professor of Logic at the University of Leeds, England, Adjunct Professor of Philosophy at the University of Pennsylvania, and Chairman of the *Analysis* Editorial Committee. He is a Fellow of the British Academy. He was formerly Reader in Logic at the University of Birmingham. He is author of *Mental Acts, Reference and Generality,* and *God and the Soul.*

DESMOND PAUL HENRY is Reader in Philosophy at the University of Manchester, England, and a Member of the Société Internationale pour l'Etude de la Philosophie Médiévale. His publications include *The "De Grammatico" of Saint Anselm, The Logic of St. Anselm,* and numerous articles on logic and its history in *Mind, Philosophical Quarterly, Ratio,* and other journals. He specializes in the fields of medieval philosophy and logic.

GARETH B. MATTHEWS is Professor of Philosophy at the University of Massachusetts. He was formerly Associate Professor at the University of Minnesota and Assistant Professor at the University of Virginia. He was a George Santayana Fellow in Philosophy at Harvard University (1967–1968).

RALPH M. McINERNY is Professor of Philosophy at the University of Notre Dame. His publications include *The Logic of Analogy; History of Western Philosophy:* Volume 1, *From Beginnings to Plotinus* and Volume 2, *From Augustine to Ockham; Thomism in an Age of Renewal;* and *Studies in Analogy.* He was the associate editor of *The New Scholasticism* and the editor of *New Themes in Christian Philosophy.*

ERNEST A. MOODY is Emeritus Professor of Philosophy at the University of California at Los Angeles and Fellow of the Mediaeval Academy of America. He was Chairman of the Department of Philosophy at the University of California at Los Angeles (1961–1964), and President of the American Philosophical Association, Pacific Division (1963). He is the author of *The Logic of William Ockham* and *Truth and Consequence in Mediaeval Logic* and co-author with Marshall Clagett of *The Medieval Science of Weights.* He also edited *Joannis Buridani Quaestiones Super Libris De Caelo et Mundo,* and *Gulielmi Ockham Expositio in Librum Porphyrii De Praedicabilibus.*

JOHN A. MOURANT is Professor of Philosophy at Central Michigan University and was Professor of Philosophy at Pennsylvania State University. He is the author of *Formal Logic, Augustine on Immortality,* and numerous articles and reviews. He edited *Readings in the Philosophy of Religion* and *Introduction to the Philosophy of St. Augustine,* and was co-editor with E. H. Freund of *Problems of Philosophy.*

JOSEPH OWENS is Professor of Philosophy at the Pontifical Institute of Mediaeval Studies, Toronto, and is a member of the editorial boards of *The Monist, The New Scholasticism,* and *Mediaeval Studies.* He is also Secretary of the Humanities Section of the Royal Society of Canada. He was visiting Professor at Purdue University in 1968. His books comprise *The Doctrine of Being in the Aristotelian Metaphysics, A History of Ancient Western Philosophy, St. Thomas and the Future of Metaphysics, An Elementary Christian Metaphysics,* and *An Interpretation of Existence.*

TIMOTHY C. POTTS is Lecturer in Philosophy at the University of Leeds, England. In 1960 he was a John Locke Scholar at the University of Oxford, and in 1963 he was Visiting Lecturer at the University of Michigan.

A. N. PRIOR is Fellow and Tutor in Philosophy at Balliol College, Oxford, England, and is a Fellow of the British Academy. He took his degrees at the Universities of New Zealand, Manchester, and Oxford. He was formerly Professor of Philosophy at the University of Canterbury, New Zealand, and at the University of Manchester, England. He was a John Locke Lecturer at Oxford University in 1956, and Visiting Professor at the University of Chicago in 1962, at the University of California at Los Angeles in 1965, and at the University of Oslo in 1969. He is the author of *Logic and the Basis of Ethics*, *Formal Logic*, *Time and Modality*, *Past, Present and Future*, and *Papers on Time and Tense*.

JAMES F. ROSS is Professor of Philosophy at the University of Pennsylvania. He was Assistant and Associate Professor of Philosophy at the University of Pennsylvania and Instructor and Assistant Professor at the University of Michigan. He has written *Philosophical Theology* and *Introduction to the Philosophy of Religion*, and translated *Disputation VI: On Formal and Universal Unity* by Francis Suarez.

JULIUS R. WEINBERG is Professor at the Institute for Research in the Humanities at the University of Wisconsin. He was formerly Assistant and Associate Professor at the University of Wisconsin and Instructor and Assistant Professor at the University of Cincinnati. He is the author of *An Examination of Logical Positivism; Nicolaus of Autrecourt; Abstraction, Relation and Induction; A Short History of Medieval Philosophy;* and numerous articles.

HARRY A. WOLFSON is Nathan Littauer Professor Emeritus of Hebrew Literature and Philosophy at Harvard University. He is the author of *Crescas' Critique of Aristotle*, *The Philosophy of Spinoza*, *Philo*, *The Philosophy of the Church Fathers*, and *Religious Philosophy*.

ALLAN B. WOLTER is Ordinary Professor of Philosophy at the Catholic University of America and Editor of Quincy College Publications. He taught at Our Lady of Angels Seminary and the Franciscan Institute. He was Visiting Lecturer at Princeton University in 1965 and Visiting Professor at the University of Michigan in 1967 and at New York University in 1969. He has been the editor of *Franciscan Studies*, *Franciscan Institute Publications*, Philosophy Series, and Associate Editor of *New Scholasticism*. His publications include *The Transcendentals and Their Function in the Metaphysics of Duns Scotus, Summula Metaphysicae, Duns Scotus; Philosophical Writings, John Duns Scotus; A Treatise on God as First Principle;* and he was co-author with J. F. Wippel of *Medieval Philosophy from St. Augustine to Nicholas of Cusa.*

Inquiries into Medieval Philosophy was composed in Times Roman with Monotype 258 display by W & G Baird Ltd., Belfast, Northern Ireland. The entire book was printed by offset lithography by Litho Crafters, Inc., Ann Arbor, Michigan.